ORGANIC GARDENING 5 BOOKS IN 1

How to Get Started with Your Own Organic Vegetable Garden, Master Hydroponics & Aquaponics, Organic Farming, Learn to Grow Vegetables the Easy Way and Achieve Your Dream Greenhouse

RACHEL MARTIN

TABLE OF CONTENTS

ORGANIC GARDENING FOR BEGINNERS
Learn How to Easily Start and Run Your Own Organic Garden, and How to Grow Your Own Organic Fruits, Vegetables, and Herbs!

Introduction 3
Chapter 1 *Why Practice Organic Gardening* 4
Chapter 2 *The Basics Of The Organic Method* 12
Chapter 3 *Healthy And Rich Soil* 20
Chapter 4 *Controlling The Weeds* 35
Chapter 5 *Growing From Seeds, Clippings, And Seedlings* 41
Chapter 6 *Easy Plants For Everyone* 49
Chapter 7 *Container Gardening And Gardening By The Foot* 59
Chapter 8 *Keeping Plants Healthy* 69
Chapter 9 *Organic Gardening Tips And Tricks* 74
Chapter 10 *Problem-Solving* 79
Conclusion 82
Description 83

Organic Vegetable Gardening
Beginner's Guide To Quickly Learn And Master How To Grow Your Own Vegetables And How To Start A Healthy Garden At Home

Introduction 87
Chapter 1 *The Basics Of Why & How: Organic 101* 88
Chapter 2 *Soil And Seeds: Getting Started* 95
Chapter 3 *Vegetable Victory: Choosing The Best Plants For Your Garden* 104
Chapter 4 *Preparing For Pests: Embrace The Inevitable* 114
Chapter 5 *Healthy Harvest: Weeding, Pruning, Using* 119
Chapter 6 *Preserving Your Produce: Strategies For Zero Waste Gardening* 135
Chapter 7 *Sustaining The Seasons: Making The Best Of Your Garden Year Round* ... 143
Chapter 8 *Imagining Your Impact: The Final Payoff* 147
Conclusion 151
Description 152

Hydroponics
Beginner's Guide To Quickly Start Growing Your Own Vegetables, Fruits, & Herbs And Learn How To Build Your Own Hydroponics Home Gardening System

Introduction 156
Chapter 1 *What Is Hydroponics?* 157
Chapter 2 *Must Have Tools* 166

Chapter 3 *Types Of Hydroponic Systems* 176
Chapter 4 *Advantages And Disadvantages Of Hydroponics* 189
Chapter 5 *Getting Your Feet Wet* 200
Chapter 6 *Common Mistakes Hydroponics Beginners Make* 212
Chapter 7 *Useful Tips For Hydroponic Farming* 222
Chapter 8 *New Developments In Hydroponics Gardening* 232
Conclusion 242
Description 243

Aquaponics
Beginner's Guide To Building Your Own Aquaponics Garden System That Will Grow Organic Vegetables, Fruits, Herbs And Raising Fish With Your Own Aquaponics Home Gardening System

Introduction 247
Chapter 1 *What Is Aquaponics?* 248
Chapter 2 *Why Aquaponics?* 250
Chapter 3 *The Master Plan Basics* 257
Chapter 4 *How To Create A Proper Aquaponics Environment* 287
Chapter 5 *Nutrient Cycle & Bacteria* 303
Chapter 6 *How To Do It Yourself* 307
Conclusion 324
Description 325

Greenhouse Gardening
Beginner's Guide To Growing Your Own Vegetables, Fruits And Herbs All Year-Round And Learn How To Quickly Build Your Own Greenhouse Garden

Introduction 329
Chapter One *Why Should I Build A Greenhouse?* 331
Chapter Two *Types Of Greenhouses* 335
Chapter Three *Planning Your Greenhouse* 339
Chapter Four *Greenhouse Essentials* 345
Chapter Five *Maximizing Your Greenhouse Space* 350
Chapter Six *Seasonal Preparation And Care* 353
Chapter Seven *What To Plant In Your Greenhouse* 356
Chapter Eight *Starting Seeds* 363
Chapter Nine *Caring For Your Plants* 368
Chapter Ten *Year-Round Growing* 376
Chapter Eleven *Common Greenhouse Problems* 381
Conclusion 387
Description 388

ORGANIC GARDENING FOR BEGINNERS

Learn How to Easily Start and Run Your Own Organic Garden, and How to Grow Your Own Organic Fruits, Vegetables, and Herbs!

**BY
RACHEL MARTIN**

© Copyright 2019 by Rachel Martin - All rights reserved.

This book is provided with the sole purpose of providing relevant information on a specific topic for which every reasonable effort has been made to ensure that it is both accurate and reasonable. Nevertheless, by purchasing this book you consent to the fact that the author, as well as the publisher, are in no way experts on the topics contained herein, regardless of any claims as such that may be made within. As such, any suggestions or recommendations that are made within are done so purely for entertainment value. It is recommended that you always consult a professional prior to undertaking any of the advice or techniques discussed within.

This is a legally binding declaration that is considered both valid and fair by both the Committee of Publishers Association and the American Bar Association and should be considered as legally binding within the United States.

The reproduction, transmission, and duplication of any of the content found herein, including any specific or extended information will be done as an illegal act regardless of the end form the information ultimately takes. This includes copied versions of the work both physical, digital and audio unless express consent of the Publisher is provided beforehand. Any additional rights reserved.

Furthermore, the information that can be found within the pages described forthwith shall be considered both accurate and truthful when it comes to the recounting of facts. As such, any use, correct or incorrect, of the provided information will render the Publisher free of responsibility as to the actions taken outside of their direct purview. Regardless, there are zero scenarios where the original author or the Publisher can be deemed liable in any fashion for any damages or hardships that may result from any of the information discussed herein.

Additionally, the information in the following pages is intended only for informational purposes and should thus be thought of as universal. As befitting its nature, it is presented without assurance regarding its prolonged validity or interim quality. Trademarks that are mentioned are done without written consent and can in no way be considered an endorsement from the trademark holder.

INTRODUCTION

There are many benefits to incorporating more organic choices into your life, which is why more people around the world are choosing to go organic. At first, going organic may seem to be more expensive. And yes, it is true that many organic options in your local grocery store are pricier. However, over time you can find that living an organic lifestyle can save you money! By choosing organic, you can benefit the health of your family, your home and yard, and even the planet. Many studies have found that by going organic people experience a wealth of physical benefits and a reduced risk of disease, saving you money on medical bills in the future.

One way you can begin your organic life is with growing your own organic garden. By doing this, not only will you be provided with organic, fresh, local, in-season produce, but it will also be available at a fraction of the price.

When you practice organic gardening, you learn that the earth has many natural and organic options to feed into a cycle of sustainability. The earth is fully equipped to allow plants to flourish without the need for harmful chemicals or pesticides. If you use the knowledge of the earth you can learn to start organic gardening literally from the ground up. You begin with the soil you are planting into the water and fertilizer that you feed the plants with. Over time, as you use these techniques you will find that both your yard and your garden flourish, providing you with a wealth of ingredients that only have to travel from your backyard to your kitchen table.

By reading this book, you can learn to live a healthier and happier life through the power of organic gardening. Providing your body and mind with the foods it craves you will soon find that you feel better than ever and have the satisfaction of knowing that you know exactly what you are eating.

Get ready to change your life!

CHAPTER 1

Why Practice Organic Gardening

Most people who practice organic gardening hope to live a more sustainable, clean, healthy, and earth-friendly way of life. However, there are many reasons that a person may choose the organic gardening method. In this chapter, we will go over the many reasons why you may choose organic. Whether you are a beginner or a pro at gardening it is never too late to begin the organic transition!

The Effects of Pesticides

Chemical pesticides are known to have many problems in the environment, health, and more. However, the information of these effects is often hidden by large corporations who make their money off of these pesticides. This leaves the public largely confused on the effects, despite being eager to make the best choices from themselves and their families. Thankfully, while large corporations may try to hide this information, they are unable to get rid of it altogether. In this portion, let's examine what is known about these chemical-based pesticides and their risks.

While you may think that the use of chemical-based pesticides doesn't cause long-lasting effects, the truth is that they linger for long periods of time. In truth, long after these chemical pesticides have been used they remain in the soil, atmosphere, and even waterways. As these have been used throughout the world for nearly a hundred years, there is quite a bit of chemical pollution lingering in the atmosphere due to their use. By continuing to use chemical-based pesticides, the problems they cause are only compounded upon.

Why do chemical pesticides cause such far-reaching damaging effects? The Agricultural MU Guide for Pesticides and the Environment explains the problem. In order for chemical pesticides to be effective, they must have the ability to travel within the soil. However, by having this ability the pesticides move too far within the soil, contaminating a larger area than intended. This not only contaminates more soil than intended, but it also contaminates water, the atmosphere, animals, and humans. These pesticides always travel and contaminate outside of their intended area of use.

The United States government has released reports proving that with the use of chemical-based pesticides the nutritional value of fruits and vegetables has declined. Between the years 1940 and 1991, the trace minerals within produce dropped by a shocking seventy-six percent, directly related to the use of pesticides.

Research has routinely found that many foods have a depleted nutritional value and that these foods contain residual presides from being grown with non-organic methods. Some foods contain an especially high number of residual chemical-based pesticides after being grown, including strawberries, tomatoes, spinach, potatoes, apples, grapes, celery, pears, kale, peaches, nectarines, and cherries.

These chemicals may help to fight off insects, but in the same way that they kill and harm insects, they cause harm to the environment, animals, and even humans. These chemical-based pesticides are simply not meant to be ingested by humans, as they are designed to kill and harm living organisms.

It is plain to see how chemical-based pesticides can cause a myriad of problems when ingested by humans. Because of this, there have been many studies examining the matter. One of the biggest literature reviews, a series of multi-university studies in Toronto, concluded that people should limit their ingestion and exposure to chemical pesticides as much as possible, due to them being linked to causing serious long-term illnesses.

There are many illnesses that these pesticides have been linked to. To name a few they have been found to cause nervous system diseases, infertility, asthma, depression, birth defects, Parkinson's disease, miscarriages, and even cancers such as lymphoma and leukemia. The more a person is exposed to these pesticides the larger their risk of developing one or more of these diseases. Studies have found that people with certain types of cancer are more likely to have pesticides within their bloodstreams.

You don't even have to eat these pesticides in order to be contaminated by them. As they travel within the soil, water, and atmosphere they can easily affect anyone. In fact, they can be brought indoors when pets and children play outdoors and they come inside. The pesticides stick to clothing, fur, or skin to come inside, where it can then be absorbed by the skin and get into the bloodstream or also breathed in. This is most often the result of chemical pesticides being used for lawn care.

The United States Environmental Protection Agency (EPA) conducted a study and found that indoor pollutants can be two to five times greater than that outdoors. In fact, indoor air pollution has been rated as one of the top four environmental health risks in America. As pesticides, gases, and microscopic particles build up indoors families suffer the effects.

Thankfully, you can greatly decrease this by making a change and going organic. You don't have to risk your health or that of your family. Even if you don't go organic in all areas of life, by making a change and beginning organic gardening you can greatly decrease the pesticides your family is affected by.

Benefits to the Going Organic

Now that we've explored the dangers of pesticides, let's examine the benefits of going organic. You now know the repercussions of not going organic, but the benefits of an organic lifestyle are more than you would imagine.

Organic farming greatly benefits the environment and helps it heal from the damage caused by chemical-based pesticides. This is because organic farmers know that if they take care of the environment it will, in turn, take care of them by providing them with nutrient-dense fruits and vegetables. Not only that, but it also decreases water pollution, topsoil loss, soil poisoning, toxic runoff, and the death of environmentally beneficial bugs and animals.

To this end, organic farmers greatly focus on the health of the soil that they plant their seeds in. Rather than using pesticides, fungicides, and herbicides, these organic farmers are able to use environmentally beneficial and natural methods to keep the soil healthy and also promote the health of the food grown in it.

Due to the care that organic farmers put into their soil, the vitamins and minerals found within the foods grown this way are much higher than those found in non-organic methods. This is due to the organic soil itself containing more minerals and nutrients that humans require. A systematic review by The Soil Association found that organically grown foods on average contain a higher amount of vitamin C, iron, magnesium, calcium, chromium, and other nutrients than non-organic produce. In fact, the independent review found that organic produce contains higher levels of all analyzed twenty-one nutrients. The study found that organic potatoes, cabbage, spinach, and lettuce contain an especially elevated number of minerals.

Along with elevated nutrition and decreased risk of disease by going organic, it may also benefit your mental health. Not only will the decrease in pesticide consumption likely reduce depression, but spending time in the garden is known as horticultural therapy. This is because spending time outdoors while working with plants and in the soil is peaceful and meditative. Horticultural therapy has been used in many ways, including to help people with psychological, educational, social, and physical adjustments while improving their mind and body.

This type of therapy was made official in 1973 when the American Horticultural Therapy Association (AHTA) was established. This organization works to train medical personnel and therapists on how to treat mental illness, substance abuse, and physical illnesses with gardening. Yet, even if you are perfectly healthy in mind and body, horticultural therapy may still benefit you! Studies have found that adults have much higher levels of daily stress and anxiety than in past generations. But, by utilizing gardening and horticultural therapy you can decrease your daily stress, improve your mood, and therefore improve your long-term health.

Everyone can improve their mood and mental health by feeling personal rewards from accomplishments. Imagine when you were a child, how satisfied you felt whenever you successfully hit a baseball, got praise for drawing a picture, or got a good grade. Whether a person struggles with their mental health or not, these feelings of accomplishment are an important part of staying happy and satisfied in life.

Gardening can increase a person's sense of accomplishment and reward, as they can directly see the beneficial outcomes gained from their efforts. As a person sees their sees beginning to grow, flowers bloom or bring in the harvest they can feel proud of themselves and enjoy the fruits of their labor. This process can also increase feelings of peace, patience, compassion, and gratefulness, which have been shown to increase a person's overall mood, improve their intersections with others, and decrease stress levels.

If you have children, then gardening may also help to bring your family together. The National Gardening Association claims that gardening has the ability to teach children valuable life lessons. If you bring your family into the garden, then it is a wonderful way to teach children the importance of hard work, completing chores, and helping the family. Children can also learn patience as they wait for the seeds to grow into plants, how to handle disappointment when a plant dies at the end of the growing season, and responsibility as they must properly and consistently water and care for the garden.

With a largely damaged economy and many Americans unable to afford basic healthcare, owning their own homes, or new vehicles people look for a way to save money. Thankfully, while organic living may at first appear to be expensive, you would be surprised by how much money it can save you. Even if you live in an apartment, as long as you have a balcony you can practice these methods with container gardening, as detailed later on in this book.

Yes, synthetic chemicals and pesticides are less expensive than purchasing organic supplies. However, there are many ways in which you can save money with organic gardening, making it less expensive in the long-run.

While chemical-based gardening supplies focus on feeding the plants, organic gardening focuses on feeding the soil. Not only does this increase the nutritional value of food grown in the soil, but it keeps the soil healthier for years to come. This means that rather than buying supplies to feed your garden time and again, the soil stays healthy with just a little work. Over time, you will find that you are spending much less money on sustaining your garden while maximizing its health and efficiency. This method is known as "feeding the soil, not the plant" as it is more sustainable and will continue to keep an entire garden healthy for years to come, rather than only feeding a plant for a single season.

One of the best approaches to both saving money and keeping your garden soil healthy is composting. By allowing organic materials, such as fruit and vegetable peels, to healthfully and naturally decompose it creates a nutrient-dense fertilizer for your garden. This saves you money so that you don't have to buy fertilizer and is also better for the planet

America is the worst country when it comes to having large landfills. While other countries have virtually eliminated landfills and replaced them with innovative recycling methods, America is behind the times in this aspect. These landfills are harming the environment. Not only that, but these landfills are filling up and finding new spaces for landfills is not easy. But, by practicing organic gardening paired with composting you can help make a dent in these landfills. Studies have shown that one-third of America's landfills are full of organic waste from peoples' kitchens and yards. You can recycle your kitchen waste, leaves, and grass in a compost bin, which will benefit the environment, your garden, and your budget.

A study by the National Gardening Association (NGA) found that a small garden with an average-sized plot can produce approximately three-hundred pounds of fresh produce, retailing at a six-hundred-dollar value. This data is based on the average gardener investing seventy dollars into their garden, giving them a return of five-hundred and thirty dollars! This is pretty impressive and can be easily achieved whether you use gardening beds or container gardening.

In order to save the most money, look at produce you already regularly eat or those which you most enjoy. For instance, if you like to cook with fresh herbs these would be a wonderful investment to grow yourself. While buying fresh herbs in the grocery store is expensive, they are easy to grow both outdoors and indoors. Similarly, if you know that you enjoy tomatoes, cucumbers, kale, and green beans then you may choose to focus on growing these items. By growing what you most purchase and enjoy you can save money and decrease your grocery budget.

If you have the time and space, rather than buying plants at the gardening center you can begin with seeds. These cost a great deal less, and if you start sprouting them in seed starters at the beginning of the season you can have a plant at a fraction of the cost. If you purchase heirloom seeds online, you can even reuse the seeds that you gain from your vegetables the following year if you save them properly.

If you find yourself with a harvest larger than you can eat, this is even more beneficial! You can learn to freeze and can excess fruits and vegetables, which you can then eat when they are out of seasoning and no longer growing. This effort will save you money in the future and provide you with delicious home-grown vegetables when they could not otherwise be grown. Because of this, you may even decide to purposefully grow more than you can eat in a season so that you can enjoy them in the offseason.

Many people who garden use chemical-based pesticides, fungicides, herbicides, and fertilizers. These people simply don't feel like there is another choice. Even if they have heard about organic farming they may have a misconception that it's difficult. Yet, these people have not stopped and asked themselves a simple question about gardening. This question is so simple that it is easy to forget, it's unnoticeable. But, the question is why do we need to use these chemical-based products in a garden if they are not needed in nature? Plants can thrive in nature without these products, without dying due to disease and insects. Why is it that these chemical-based products only seem to be needed in domestic gardens?

The answer is that they are not needed. Many people simply don't have the knowledge of how to garden without these products, largely due to marketing by the chemical-based product companies. Thankfully, learning this knowledge is easy and can be used by any beginner.

A large part of the problem is that with domestic gardening many people focus on growing single types of plants in a row together. Yet, in nature, you see many types of plants growing nearby and intermingling. The way domestic gardens do this is problematic because disease and bugs can easily spread from one to the next. For instance, if you have a row of roses aphids can easily cross from one rose bush to the next. The same is true when you are growing fruits and vegetables of the same type or similar types in a row together.

But, with organic gardening, you can learn the value of inter-species planting with companion planting, which allows one plant to offer protection to another. This makes use of nature's system of planting in your own backyard to decrease disease and insect infestations.

If organic gardening is so great, you may be wondering why it isn't further promoted. It's simple, companies make more money by ignoring nature and producing easy to manufacture chemicals to sell. When people grow their own gardens, collect seeds, and share them with their friends then the big companies such as Monsanto don't make money from selling patented genetically-modified seeds.

While composting and companion planting is best for your garden, health, and the environment, this doesn't allow large oil companies to make a profit of sacrificing your health. Oil companies produce petroleum-based fertilizers, herbicides, and pesticides. But, these products that they create overtime decrease the health of the soil and create pests that are increasingly resistant to interference.

You can make a beneficial impact on your health, your family, the environment, and your community by choosing organic. Along with growing your own organic garden, you can also choose to buy local and organic produce from your community. You might even consider selling some of your excess produce at a local farmers' market to make a little money and to help provide others with organic options.

Don't listen to the big companies who are only out for their own profit, even at the expense of the environment and millions of people. Organic gardening is possible, easy, sustainable, and beneficial. You can make a change for improved health and a better life.

Yes, organic gardening is a change, but within this book, you will find all the answers you need to have a successful and productive organic garden, whether you live on a farm, in the suburbs, or in the middle of a city with nothing but a balcony and windowsill.

CHAPTER 2

The Basics of The Organic Method

When you plant and care for a garden you experience something that is truly gratifying and fulfilling. As you watch flowers bloom, herbs grow, and both fruits and vegetables ripen you are satisfied with and proud of your accomplishments. Not only are the flowers beautiful and calming, but you are able to use the produce and herbs you grow to make more delicious meals, sustain your family, save money, and benefit the environment. By gardening you get to experience something that along with being helpful and fulfilling is also peaceful and fun. This is only compounded upon when you choose the organic method.

By choosing organic and natural options to garden with, rather than the synthetic chemical-based fungicides, herbicides, pesticides, and fertilizers, you can benefit the earth and environment. It may seem like a small change, but as people continue to make the change to organic the beneficial effects will grow and the earth will gradually heal from the chemicals we have poisoned it with. By choosing organic gardening you can naturally fertilize the earth with options that will refuel it with the minerals and vitamins it requires in order to grow healthy plants that will nourish those who eat them.

It doesn't matter if you have a green thumb and years of experience with gardening or if you are a complete beginner. Maybe you tried to grow some plants in the past and they always died, that's okay! With the right approach and knowledge, anyone can grow a successful garden yielding fruits, vegetables, herbs, and flowers. All you need are the right tools of knowledge, which are provided within these pages. Let's explore some of the basics of the organic method to get you on your way to success!

Plan Your Garden

Before you focus on the ever important soil, watering, and planting of your garden you first must plan. When gardening, it is important to know the size of your garden, the hours of sun access, wind, and more. All of these factors will greatly affect what you can plant and how well your crops grow. Thankfully, with a little knowledge, you can plan the perfect garden.

1. **Garden Size**

If you live in an apartment then you really only have one option for a garden, which is to practice container gardening. Thankfully, there are many options for container gardening and you would be surprised by the crop size you can yield.

If you live in the suburbs or city with an average-sized yard then you should find that your garden is easily accessible from your house. Even if your backyard is on the smaller side, you should be able to plant a decently large garden if you practice gardening by the foot. With this gardening method, you can maximize your gardening space and crop yield with a little extra planning.

Lastly, if you live on a large property you can have an especially large garden. You will likely be able to not only provide enough crop yield for your family, but even excess to sell at the local farmers' market or to gift to neighbors if you desire. However, if you do live on a larger property try to not place the garden too far away from your home or a place where you regularly walk past. You want to be able to easily view and examine the garden on a daily basis so that you know when it needs to be watered, weeded, or harvested.

2. **Sun Exposure**

There are some plants that need shade. Although, most crops require ample sun exposure. Unless you are planning on growing shade-hardy plants you need to ensure that the gardening location you choose received a minimum of six hours of full sunlight on a daily basis.

3. **Wind Exposure**

Heavy winds can greatly damage a garden by breaking the plants and carrying away the precious and nutritious topsoil of a garden bed. Therefore, try to find a gardening location that is not overly windy. If you are unable to avoid planting in a wind-resistant location or live in an area that gets high winds, then you may need to build a windbreak for your garden. There are many types of windbreaks, which we will detail further on in this book.

4. **Find Your Hardiness Zone**

When planting, it is best to choose plants native to your area. These plants are non-invasive species which are designed to grow well where you live. You can easily find these plants by looking up the United States Department of Agriculture's (USDA) local hardiness zone map. This map is organized by ten different numbered zones. Once you know the number for your zone you can easily find which plants grow well in your local area based off of temperatures and other factors.

5. **Create a Garden Wish-List**

   After you know your hardiness zone, create a list of all the plants within your zone that you hope to grow. This includes vegetables, fruits, herbs, and flowers. Some plants are annuals (grow year after year) while others are perennials (die off at the end of each season). You may want to organize your list between these two categories so that you can more easily decide where to plant everything.

6. **Create a Garden Map**

   Measure out the exact garden space you will be using and then create a to-scale map on graph paper. When creating this map, you want to create a layout of where you will plant everything, keeping in mind to arrange it in a symbiotic manner. While doing this, you will need to know exactly how much space each plant will require, which you can usually find in organic seed catalogs and seed packets.

7. **Schedule Your Planting**

   The seed catalog you purchase from should have details on when your seeds should be sprouted and transplanted. This will be impacted by your local frost-free date. You must ensure that you plant after this date, otherwise, the seedlings will die. In order to find your frost-free date, you can easily search online or call your local extension office. DavesGarden.com has a handy frost-free date page where you simply have to type in your zip code to find when your standard frost-free date occurs.

Soil

The most important thing when practicing organic gardening is to start with your soil. In chemical-based gardening, people rarely pay attention to their soil, they just cover it up in chemical-based fertilizers and pesticides. This leaches the nutrients out of the soil and causes it damage for years down the road. But, organic gardening literally starts from the ground up. If the soil is healthy and nutrient-dense then you are more likely to have healthy and thriving plants.

Because the soil is the most important factor, you need to spend some time analyzing your soil to optimize it for gardening. This will be more difficult if you have previously used chemicals in your gardening bed. But, this does not mean that you are unable to switch to organic gardening. This simply means that you will need to put more effort into healing the soil and rejuvenating it with organic options. Optimizing your soil will be easiest if you are starting from scratch in a garden bed that has never been used or by planting in containers.

Check out this list to determine the health of your soil and how you should proceed:

1. **Ensure You Have Enough Soil**

    Many people are surprised to find that the soil in their yards is not ideal for gardening. Many of these yards, especially those built within the previous fifty years, do not have enough topsoil to grow plants well. This is because construction companies will often build the house and then only add a thin layer of topsoil afterward in order for grass to grow. To make it worse, this small amount of topsoil is often highly compacted. You want to test your gardening area to ensure you have enough of this vital topsoil. In order to do this, pierce the ground with a shovel and see how easy it is to pull up the soil. You want six to eight inches of easily penetrable soil, known as topsoil. If you do not have this six to eight inches, then you will need to build up your topsoil before gardening.

    To create a layer of topsoil simply combine ten percent peat moss, thirty percent topsoil, and sixty percent compost. Some people may confuse compost with manure, but they are different products and not interchangeable. You can combine this topsoil mixture in the ground, in a container garden, or in a raised garden bed.

2. **Find Your Soil Type**

    There are multiple types of spoil, including sandy, loam, and clay. To determine which type of soil you have, pick up a small handful of soil that is moist but not wet. Firmly squeeze the soil in the palm of your hand before examining it. If the soil falls apart as soon as you open your palm, then it is sandy. If the soil holds its shape but crumbles upon being poked, then it is loam. Lastly, if the soil holds its shape both when you open your hand and when poked then it is clay.

3. **Learn the Soil's pH and Nutrients**

It is important to know your soil pH, as if your soil is overly acidic or alkaline then crops will have trouble growing. The pH scale runs between zero and fourteen with a reading below seven being acidic, seven being neutral, and above seven being alkaline. This level is important, as it affects the availability of many nutrients within the soil. Most crops grow well in the range between six and seven and a half.

Along with knowing your soil's pH you need to ensure that the soil is well-balanced with the essential nutrients it requires. Without these nutrients, plants will be unable to flourish and the produce grown will be less nutritious.

In order to test both the soil's pH and nutrients, you need to take a sample of the soil and send it off to a lab. There are many labs that will test the soil. In order to find the right lab for you simply search "soil testing [state you live in]" in your preferred search engine. In some states, you may even get your soil tested at a local university.

4. **Nourish Your Soil**

After you get the test results of your soil back then you can use the information to improve your soil. To do this, read Chapter 3: Healthy and Rich Soil to best know how to adjust the nutrient and pH level of your soil.

5. **Enhance Your Soil**

After you fully nourish your soil with nutrients and balance its pH to an optimal level, then you want to enhance the soil to further improve growth. You can do this by adding in compost and manure. When adding these to your garden bed you want to mix it well into the top eight to ten inches of soil.

Compost is full of nutrients, but also has a neutral pH level of seven, making it optimal for all gardens. You can either produce your own compost or purchase organic compost. Any compost you use should be a rich dark brown.

Manure is also full of many nutrients. However, the type of manure you use has to be taken into account based off of your soil's pH level. This is because depending on the type of animal that produced the manure the pH can vary. Sheep and chicken manure tend to be highly concentrated while cow and horse manure are milder. If you live on a farm and hope to use the manure from your own animals you must let it compost for at least ninety days before using, as it contains many seeds from weeds that you don't want sprouting in your garden.

Watering

While watering your garden isn't difficult, there are certainly some tricks you have to keep in mind in order to keep your plants healthy. For instance, it is not only how much you water your plants that matter, but the time of day, as well.

1. **Water Requirements**

    Not all plants have the same water requirements, some require a more moist soil while others need to stay drier. Although, most plants require to be watered regularly, especially during the summer and hot days.

    Rather than watering a small amount every day, it is better to give your plants a deeper watering more infrequently, as this simulates the way plants are often watered by rain in nature. Allow the soil to slightly dry between watering, which encourages the roots to grow deeper and stronger.

    On average, plants should receive an estimated one to two inches of water every week between intentional watering and rainfall.

2. **Watering Times**

    You want to avoid watering during the hot portion of the day, as the water will evaporate, giving your plants less water to absorb. Not only that, but if you water earlier in the day it will help fortify your plants for the heat ahead. Therefore, early mornings are the best time of day to water your plants. If you are unable to water in the morning, then water in the late afternoon after the hottest portion of the day has passed but before the evening has arrived.

3. **How to Water**

    You often see people pouring water over the entire plant, but this is not advised. When you pour water on top of the plant then the flowers and leaves can begin to rot, leading to disease. Instead, try to target the bottom of the plant's stem and its roots when watering.

4. **Drip Irrigation**

    While you can certainly water your plants with a watering hose, especially if you are using container gardening, you may want to invest in a drip irrigation system if you are using garden beds. While this system does require a bit more upfront cost, it is well worth the investment for people who are serious about practicing organic gardening. This watering system helps to target the roots while watering to prevent disease and is also much less labor intensive. If you are someone who is tight on time then you don't have to worry about going outside and watering the garden before work. Instead, you can simply have a drip irrigation system on a timer to ensure that your garden is always perfectly watered.

Disease and Weed Prevention

Rather than using chemical-based weed killers, you can easily reduce the number of weeds that grow by using mulch. There are multiple types of mulch, including wood, straw, and plastic. This mulch will prevent most weed growth. But, if some weeds do appear then you can easily pull them by hand while wearing gardening gloves. You may also prevent weeds by rotating the crops planted yearly.

If you notice a portion of one of your pants begins to come down with a disease then you trim it until the entire diseased section is cut off. Once you have trimmed the plant transplant it to a container away from your other plants so that it will not contaminate others with the disease. Keep an eye on the plant and continue to care for it to see if it becomes healthy again. If you notice an entire plant is diseases and unable to be salvaged remove it from your garden completely.

Pest Prevention

Many people believe that you must use chemical-based pesticides in order to grow a healthy garden. But, this is simply not true. There are many natural and organic methods of controlling these pests, some of which are creatures in the wild. Animals and insects such as birds, toads, spiders, lizards, ladybugs, and beetles can all prevent pests from infesting your garden. If you work to attract these creatures, then they can greatly benefit your garden.

When you do spot pests, your goal will be to keep their population as low as you can. For instance, if you see aphids you can try spraying them with water or removing them from the plant with gardening gloves. This is an easy method to start with, but, if it isn't effective you can always try more extreme organic measures. Remember, pests such as these are a natural and normal part of gardening, whether or not you use chemical-based pesticides. But, there are organic methods you can use to protect your plants and remove these pests once they arrive.

Let's look at some of the options for dealing with these pests:

1. **Manual Removal**

   As previously stated, you can manually remove pests from your garden by hitting them with a stream of water from the hose or with a hand covered in a gardening glove. For instance, along with aphids, you may also remove Japanese beetles, hornworms, red spider mites, caterpillars, and grubs.

   However, it is important to know which insects are pests and which are beneficial in preventing pests. For instance, ladybugs, green lacewings, braconid wasps, damsel bugs, ground beetles, minute pirate bugs, and aphid midges are all beneficial insects which keep the damaging insects at bay. Be careful to never remove beneficial insects from your garden.

2. **Organic Pesticides**

   If you continue to have problems with pests, you may try making a homemade pesticide or even purchasing a certified organic pesticide from the gardening center. While chemical-based pesticides are certainly more common, organic options are becoming more widely available. However, you may prefer to make your own rather than purchasing it as it will save you money and will likely be equally as effective.

3. **Create Barriers**

   If you live out in the country or near a patch of woods you may experience trouble with not only insects but also from animals. If this is the case, you may have to create various barriers in order to prevent squirrels, groundhogs, rabbits, deer, and birds from stealing your harvest or tearing up your garden. The type of barrier you need will vary depending upon which animal you are struggling with.

There are many important aspects of gardening, especially when you are trying to have a successful harvest and yield. But, as long as you have the basic knowledge and tools you will soon find that gardening is an enjoyable and peaceful process. There is a lot to learn about the practice of organic gardening. But, if you start at the basics you can slowly take your time and build up your knowledge until you have the garden of your dreams.

CHAPTER 3

Healthy and Rich Soil

The rare gardener may have the blessing of their garden naturally containing the perfect soil for growing crops. However, this is now the case for most people. Sure, you could dig a hole and stick your plant in it, but this is not a recipe for success. Even if the plant stays alive, it will be unable to thrive or offer you a decent crop. This is because most soil has either too much sand or clay in, is too acidic or alkaline, contains too many stones, or not enough minerals. Whatever the case is for your garden, don't worry. Sure, your garden may have poor soil at the moment, but with a little knowledge and work you can elevate your soil to fitting under the optimal conditions.

What is soil composed of? No matter the garden, your soil is composed of organic matter such as leaves and grass that have broken down over time, weathered rock, air, and water. But, that is not all. Healthy soil is also home to many minerals, microbes, worms, and insects that allow the plants grown within the soil to flourish. In this chapter, we will explore how to optimize your soil to best care for your plants and receive a large harvest in return.

Weathered Rock

Approximately half of the soil within your garden is made up of tiny granular pieces of weathered rock. Over time, this rock has been broken down by rain, wind, temperature changes, and other natural biological processes. As this weathered rock is broken down it becomes one of three types of soil: sand, silt, or clay. Each of these particles is made up of different consistencies and sizes, with sand being the largest and clay being the smallest. It's important to have a good balance of these three soil types, as it affects the nutrient content and drainage ability. If the consistency is off then the roots will be either get too much water or not enough, along with not having enough nutrients.

Along with testing the soil type by squeezing some in the palm of your hand, as we discussed in the previous chapter, you can also better understand the composition of your soil with a water test. The steps are quite simple!

1. Begin by filling a quart-sized glass jar one-third of the way with the topsoil from your garden. Fill the remainder of the jar with

water until it is mostly full. Screw the lid on top of the jar and then shake it vigorously until no soil clumps remain.
2. Place the glass jar in a windowsill and keep an eye on it as the largest components begin to sink to the bottom of the jar. After a minute or two the entirety of the sand portion should have sunk to the bottom. Using a marker mark where the level of sand is on the side of the jar.
3. Allow the jar to continue to sit for several hours so that the silt portion may sink to settle on top of the sand layer. You should notice that there are slight color variations in the layers, showing that the particles are of two different types. Mark the silt layer.
4. Continue to allow the jar to sit in the windowsill overnight. The next morning you will notice there is a layer of clay, which you also want to mark the position of. But, not only will there be a layer of clay, but on top of the clay will be a layer of organic matter. Although, there will likely still be a little organic matter floating in the water leaving it murky. If the water is not murky with the organic matter, then this means your topsoil is deficient in this vital element.
5. After you have marked the three layers on the jar, use a measuring tape to determine the thickness of each layer. For instance, the sand layer might be two inches with the silt layer being a quarter of an inch and the clay layer being half of an inch.
6. After you measure out the thickness of the three layers to determine how much of a percentage of the soil each layer makes up. In the case above it would be approximately seventy percent sand, ten percent silt, and twenty percent clay.
7. Lastly, use the soil texture calculator from the <u>United States Department of Agriculture's (USDA) website</u> to determine your soil type. This calculator will use the percentage value of all three soil components to calculate your soil type. You will be provided with a triangular graph of all possible soil types with your soil type marked in red. In the illustrated case the USDA categorizes it as "sandy clay loam".

Once you know what type of soil you have, you can easily customize it to make it ideal for any plant type. Different plants require different soil types, for instance, more tropical plants wouldn't grow well in a garden bed customized for growing vegetables.

Sandy Soil
The largest of particles, sand, are irregular pieces of rock. Due to the larger and irregular shaped particle, it allows for air space to travel between the particles and for water to drain quickly and effortlessly. However, this also means that nutrients wash away with the water without giving the plants within the soil an opportunity to absorb them. This leads to most sand-based soils being nutrient deficient. Sandy soils are low in organic matter and clay, meaning that they don't stick together when wet and simply crumble apart.

Improve sandy soil with these few steps:
1. Combine three to four inches of organic matter of both compost and manure to your topsoil.
2. Combine at least two inches' worth of organic matter into the topsoil every year.
3. Grow cover crops (also known as green manure) in the garden bed to add nutrients to the soil. Some good cover crops include buckwheat, crimson clover, cowpeas, annual rye, wheat, Austrian peas, hairy vetch, sorghum, alfalfa, soybeans, velvet beans, sweet clover, oats, and buckwheat.
4. Mulch around the plants with straw, hay, leaves, or wood chips in order to retain moisture and reduce soil temperature.

Silty Soil
Unlike sandy soil, the particles in silty soil are much denser with small pores. This means that silty soil has poor drainage. But, it also tends to have more nutrients than either sandy or clay soils, making it more fertile.

Improving silty soil is quite easy and requires fewer steps than other soil types.
1. Avoid compressing the soil as much as possible by walking on the garden or tilling.
2. Focus most of your attention on the top few inches of topsoil to prevent silt from crusting and becoming a dense tough layer.
3. Consider possibly using raised garden beds.
4. Each year add one inch of organic matter.

Clay Soil
The particles of clay are flat and small, making them easily pack together in a tight mound. Due to this, there are hardly any pores, leaving it unable to drain during the wet months and becoming hard and unworkable

during the dry months. This can lead plants to become waterlogged in the spring and deficient in water during the summer.

The lack of pores in clay also means that it usually is low in microbial activity and organic matter, leaving the plants nutrient deficient. Not only that, but due to the hard compact nature of clay, the roots of plants become stunted, as they are unable to push through the clay to get a deep hold into the ground. The hard compact nature of clay only becomes worse if the ground is tilled or walked on.

Thankfully, the one thing going for clay soils is that they are generally rich in minerals, which the plants will be able to absorb once you improve the soil. Follow these few steps to make the most of your clay soil:

1. Minimize the use of garden tools such as spades and tills.
2. Create raised beds to reduce foot traffic and improve water drainage.
3. Combine three inches of organic matter such as compost and manure into the topsoil. Afterward, continue to add one inch of organic matter to the topsoil every year.
4. When adding organic matter to your garden bed it is best to add it during the autumn months.

Organic Matter

There are two types of organic matter that you can add to your garden, which includes manure and decomposed plant life. The main type of organic matter that you find in nature includes decomposed grasses, leaves, mosses, lichens, trees, and other vegetative matter. This organic matter makes up an average of five to ten percent of soil, which may seem small, but it is absolutely essential. This portion of the soil is full of microorganisms that feed plants, minerals, retains moisture to keep plants hydrated and increases air availability.

As plants and manure breakdown to form organic matter, it consists of these components in various stages of decay, which allows helpful enzymes to be released, beneficial fungi and bacteria to grow, and minerals to be released. Once the plant matter is highly decomposed it is known as humus.

In order to increase organic matter within your garden beds, you can grow cover crops which will decompose over time, making a natural compost simulating the growth and decomposition process found in nature. You may also add in compost, humus, peat moss, mulch, worm castings, or aged animal manure.

Just like all living organisms, plants require a variety of nutrients to grow well. There are seventeen essential nutrients for plants, some of these are required in large quantities while others in only small amounts. The nutrients that are needed in large numbers are known as macronutrients and include calcium, carbon, nitrogen, hydrogen, oxygen, magnesium, sulfur, potassium, and phosphorus.

The nutrients required in smaller numbers, known as micronutrients, include manganese, iron, zinc, copper, chlorine, molybdenum, and boron. Your soil is most likely deficient in at least one of these vital nutrients, therefore, if possible you should have your soil tested in a lab to let you know which nutrients you need to add.

There are many ways you can add nutrients to your garden along with the previously recommended organic matter. Some of these options include:

- ☐ Potassium: wood ash and cotton gin trash
- ☐ Phosphorus: ash, bone meal, cotton gin trash, cottonseed meal, fish meal, leaf mold, and poultry manure
- ☐ Nitrogen: fish meal, fish powder, feather meal, dried blood meal, fur, hair, horn meal, food, cotton gin trash, soybean meal, alfalfa meal, and corn gluten meal. When adding high-carbon components to your gardens such as leaves, straw, wood chips, and sawdust you should be careful. While these are great in moderation, the microorganisms within the soil have to consume a lot of nitrogen in order to breakdown and digest these components. This will cause your garden bed to become deficient in nitrogen.

You may also add nutrients to your garden bed by using coffee grounds. Recycling coffee grounds and adding them to compost piles has been popular with gardeners for years. Many experienced gardeners will even improve upon this by adding the coffee grounds to their red worm bins. However, the acidity of coffee grounds must be kept in mind, as well. Thankfully, by composting this acidity can be lessened, which can be further reduced if you compost them in a worm bin. Research by Chalker-Scott found that the grounds were only minimally acidic, and sometimes their acidity was completely removed during the composting process. Although, this doesn't mean you can add an endless amount of used coffee grounds to your garden. It is recommended that no more than twenty percent of your compost bin contain coffee grounds, as it was found that levels of thirty percent could be detrimental.

Some people may get recycled coffee grounds from coffee shops and cafes in order to use as mulch. But, this is recommended against as they are a fine texture that will easily become compact. Once the coffee grounds are compacted it prevents the free movement of air and moisture.

Coffee grounds are wonderful to add in moderation to your composting bin as they reduce the risk of disease, discourage fungal rot, increase mineral content, and improve the structure of the soil.

Soil Organisms

There are many organisms within the soil that work together to help your plants grow. Some of these include earthworms, mites, fungi, bacteria, springtails, protozoa, nematodes, and other tiny creatures and microorganisms. These are essential for the growth of plant life as they work together in order to convert matter and minerals into hormones, compounds, vitamins, and nutrients that plants require for growth. These organisms also have excretions that nourish and help bind soil particles in a way that makes it loose and crumbly, allowing water and air to freely move throughout the garden bed.

A gardener's job is to ensure that these soil organisms are healthy and have the ideal conditions in order to do their task to help plants grow. In order to do this, a gardener provides oxygen through well-aerated soil, a balanced proportion of water, and food from organic matter.

Air

You may not think about there being air underground, because certainly there is not enough to support human life, but it is important that the ground remains well-aerated in order to support soil organisms. A healthy and well-balanced soil should contain an estimated twenty-five percent air, which then supports earthworms and insect microbes. The air also helps to feel the plants, as it is a source of atmospheric nitrogen. When the soil is well-aerated there are pores between the soil particles that allow free movement. This is most seen in sandy soils which are a large and irregular particle. On the other hand, finer soils such as clay and silt have very small pores that often don't allow air circulation. But, this doesn't mean you can simply use sandy soil, as too much air causes the decomposition of organic matter at an accelerated pace. It's important that in order to keep your garden bed well-aerated that you don't allow its compaction with heavy-weight garden equipment or by walking in the bed. Similarly, avoid working with the soil when it's especially wet and add in plenty of organic matter to keep the soil healthy and loose.

Water

Along with containing twenty-five percent air, healthy soil also must contain an approximate twenty-five percent water. Just as air travels between the soil particles through the pores, so too does the water. Sandy soil allows water to quickly move through the pores and travel downward, causing it to drain and dry out quickly.

Finer soils such as clay and silt allow water to move back upwards due to capillary action. They become easily waterlogged, and instead of allowing the water to drain naturally it fills all of the pores and prevents air access. This causes the suffocation of plant roots and soil organisms.

For healthy soil and balanced watering, you need both small and large pores within the soil. For instance, you are unable to grow your plants in just clay or solely sand. You need a mixture of sand, clay, silt, and organic matter. The key ingredient in this mixture is the organic matter which helps the soil to have a healthier and balanced consistency. This matter also helps to absorb and retain water, which can then be used to water the roots of plants as needed.

Soil pH

We discussed the importance of soil pH in passing earlier, but it is important to have a full understanding of the matter if you want to get the most out of your garden. If your soil pH is off then you can do everything else right and still have trouble keeping your plants alive and bearing a harvest. Thankfully, soil pH is easy to track and easy to balance. The soil pH allows you to know how acidic or alkaline your soil is. You can have this professionally tracked when you first begin your garden, and if you like once a year or every couple of years. By having it professionally tracked by a lab you can trust in its accuracy and also get results back on the nutrient density of your soil. This is especially important, as it will allow you to know if you need to increase specific nutrients within your garden bed. But, if you want to be able to quickly and easily check your garden's pH occasionally then you can get a pH meter for an average of ten dollars USD at most gardening stores.

These pH tests will measure the negative and positive ions, also known as hydroxyl and hydrogen, within the water of the soil. When these two ions are found in equal number then you have a neutral pH of seven. When the hydroxyl ions are higher than you have an alkaline pH of any number above seven to fourteen. If the hydrogen ions are higher than you have an acid soil with a pH with a number below seven.

While some plants may prefer more acidic soil, most prefer an almost neutral pH balance with a slight bit of acidity, as the nutrients are more soluble at this range. The ideal range is often between six and a half and six and three-quarters. It doesn't take much of alteration from this range for the nutrients to become unusable by the plants grown in the soil. Soon thereafter the plant will begin to suffer and slowly wilt away as the roots are unable to absorb their required nutrients.

You can improve the health of your soil and its overall fertility by balancing the pH. However, it is important to know that you shouldn't try to change the pH balance overnight. This process takes time and it may be one or two full growing seasons until the pH of your garden bed is fully balanced. Even after you balance the pH in your garden, you will have to continue to maintain it every year to ensure it doesn't get out of sync again. One way in which you can do this is something you should already be doing: adding in ample organic matter. Organic matter tends to have a balanced neutral pH, allowing you to improve both acidic and alkaline soil with one ingredient.

While some plants, such as blueberry and azalea bushes, require more acidic soil (with a pH below six and a half) this is too acidic for most garden plants. Although, if you live in the eastern United States then plants may require a slightly acidic soil rather than neutral or alkaline.

If your soil is overly acidic you can raise the pH level by adding powdered limestone or dolomitic limestone which also contains manganese. When adding limestone into your garden you must add it into the bed during the autumn months, as it takes multiple months for it to alter the pH balance.

When adding limestone follow these simple procedures:
- ☐ When adding to clay use eight to ten pounds for every one-hundred square feet
- ☐ When adding to sandy soil add three to four pounds for every one-hundred square feet
- ☐ When adding to loam (balanced gardening soil) add seven to eight pounds for every one-hundred square feet

You may also raise the pH balance by adding in wood ash. This is beneficial as it contains potassium and other trace elements while also taking effect much more quickly than limestone. However, you have to be extremely careful with wood ash, as it can quickly and drastically alter the pH and cause nutrient imbalances if you add too much. If you choose to use wood ash apply it to the garden bed during the winter months and never apply more than two pounds for every one-hundred square feet. You can apply wood ash once every two to three years.

If you have a soil pH of higher than six and three-quarters (6.8) then you will need to decrease the alkalinity and increase the acidity. The soil in the western United States is more likely to be alkaline. This can be rectified with the addition of ground sulfur along with acidic plant matter such as oak leaves, conifer needles, peat moss, and sawdust.

To increase the acidity of soil by approximately one point follow the proceeding procedures:

- ☐ When adding sulfur to clay add two pounds for every one-hundred square feet
- ☐ When adding to sandy soil add one pound for every one-hundred square feet
- ☐ When adding to loam (balanced gardening soil) add one and a half to two pounds for every one-hundred square feet

Composting

While you can certainly buy compost, it is more expensive and you won't know exactly what all is in it. But, by making your own you get to control everything that is within it to optimize your garden. Not only that but, you can also recycle uneaten food and supplies from your yards such as leaves and lawn clippings by making your own compost. This is better for the environment because it lessens the impact on landfills, and will decrease the amount of trash you throw out every week.

While composting has many benefits, many people are unaware of how to start their own composting bin or pile. Worse yet, people may add the wrong foods to their composting bin, causing it to rot in a damaging manner and causing harm to the garden if it is used. Thankfully, with a little knowledge, you can be a composting pro in no time!

1. **Bin or Heap**

    When beginning there are many people who choose to simply keep their composting in a heap or pile in a back corner of their yard. This is a cheaper method and certainly works well. However, many people prefer to purchase a simple composting bin so that it doesn't affect the visual atmosphere of their yard. Using a bin is also needed if you want to add some red worms.

2. **Location**

    You can't place your composting heap or bin just anywhere. Where you place your composting needs to be on a level surface that drains well to prevent water from pooling. This is especially necessary if you choose to go with a heap rather than a bin, as it will allow worms to easily access and break down the compost.

3. **Using Worms**
Most people may not give worms a second thought, but they are very important to the gardener. These worms can provide amazing help when they are in your compost bin or heap, as they eat through the compost and then excrete it into compost and liquid food for your plants.

4. **Adding to the Compost**
There are many things you can add to your compost to provide nutrients and food for worms to break down. Some great options include fruit remains, vegetable peelings, coffee grounds, tea bags, grass clippings, and plant prunings. These will all break down quickly to provide compost before long, and in the process increase moisture and nitrogen. You may also want to add in some slower compost ingredients such as fallen leaves, used paper, and cardboard which increase carbon and fiber content as well as increasing air flow within the compost pile. Lastly, you can throw in eggshells to increase the mineral content.

5. **Avoid Adding...**
You can't add anything and everything to your compost, otherwise you could be in for a mess. For instance, you never ever want to add dairy products, meat, and oil, which will rot and cause disease rather than breaking down in a healthy and beneficial manner. Similarly, you never want to add feces from cats or dogs, diseased plants, weeds such as thistles or dandelions, or non-organic material.

6. **Finding Balance**
In order to have a good outcome with your composting, you need to have a good mixture. For instance, earlier we mentioned that you never want your composting pile to consist of more than twenty percent coffee grounds. But, you also want to make sure that your mixture of recycled fruits and vegetables is balanced with cardboard, paper, and leaves. This is because if you have too many fruits and vegetables your composting pile can become overly wet. On the other hand, if you have too many leaves, paper, and cardboard then it may become too dry. You need an even balance of both mixtures to ensure that your composting heap or bin has optimal air flow.

If you notice that your compost is looking too dry decrease the number of dry ingredients you are adding, and if it is looking overly wet decrease the number of fruits and vegetables. Over time, you will learn to know the right ratio.

7. **Increase Airflow**

   You can simply pile your compost into a heap or bin and then ignore it, as it required regular attendance. Thankfully, this does not take much effort or time. Using a shovel or compost aeration tool with a long handle you need to turn your compost around and allow it to mix up every few days. This will allow for proper airflow and combine all of the ingredients together, speeding up the composting process.

8. **Compost Activator**

   You can help your pile compost more quickly and encourage the proper enzyme growth if you choose to use an organic compost starter or activator. There are various types of activators, but they are always a mixture high in nitrogen. By adding this nitrogen-rich ingredient you allow the leaves, grass, and recycled matter to compost into a dark and rich mixture half the time. To use compost starters, you usually combine the powder with water, stir it into your compost heap, and ten weeks later your compost fully decomposed and full of nutrients to feed your plants.

9. **Compost Leaves**

   During the autumn months, if you have more than one tree in your yard then you are likely to have more leaves than you can add to your composting heap or bin. But, you can still save all of these leaves for composting! You can find biodegradable leaf and lawn bags at gardening stores and online, which you can then fill with excess leaves and grass trimmings. Once these bags are full simply place them in a dry and level area to naturally decompose. Over time, both the leaves and grass inside the bag along with the bag itself will decompose until you are left with a large pile of compost. This can then be added to your topsoil or used in place of peat moss.

10. **Get the Most Out of Compost**

    You will know that your compost is ready when it is a rich dark brown that is so dark it's nearly black. The texture of the compost at the bottom of the bin or heap should be similar to that of soil and spongy. The time it takes to reach this stage varies greatly depending on the size of your compost pile and how well you care for it. Ultimately, compost can be ready in as little as three months or as long as two years. Once ready, spread this mixture into your garden to reduce weeds, retain moisture, increase airflow, and add nutrients.

Red worms

If you have spent much time in gardening stores you have most likely noticed them selling worm castings, otherwise known as worm manure or worm excrement. This may sound disgusting, but it is one of the best additions found in nature that you can add to your gardening bed. Not only that but unlike manure from farm animals, worm castings do not smell.

But, why are worm castings superior? The worm has a superior ability to refine the organic materials it consumes and digests. The result is that the worm castings are organic and contain nutrients, minerals, trace elements, and microbes in their easiest to process form with a neutral pH of seven. This allows plants to reach their full potential, grow well, and ward off disease. They also increase the absorbance of soil, preventing plants from drying out and becoming dehydrated.

Along with smelling like the forest rather than a farm, a cow and other manures, worm castings also don't pose the risk of burning plants due to high levels of nitrogen. While they do contain four or five percent more nitrogen than most gardening soil, it is slowly released rather than all at once. This is due to the mucus secreted by worms during the digestion process.

The digestion process from worms introduced innumerable beneficial bacteria and microbes into the worm castings, along with humic acid which increases nutrient absorption. Not only can they add stuff to your compost and soil, but they can also remove components you don't want. Studies have found that worms naturally are able to remove harmful heavy metals and toxins from soil. In short, this makes worm castings are the best addition to your garden. Studies have even found that seed germination and growth is improved by the addition.

If you are already planning on composting, why not add worms to the addition? It is quite simple to add red worms (the most popular type) to your compost heap with little extra effort. This will both add worm castings to the finished product and increase the composting rate so that you have the finished product sooner.

When adding worms to your composting bin you will want at least one-thousand worms or one pound of worms for every pound of organic compost. Depending on the size of your compost bin, you should be able to add worm castings and compost to your garden bed or potted plants every couple of months.

To keep your worms happy and healthy you will need to ensure you feed them plenty. They will eat a lot of vegetable peelings, discarded fruit, grains, cereals, bread, coffee grounds, tea bags, and unbleached coffee filters. Along with this food, they will need bedding such as cardboard, newspaper, used paper from around the house, leaves, straw, coconut fiber, or wood chips.

Cover Crops/Green Manure

Cover crops are frequently used in order to protect unused soil. Up north, gardeners will frequently use cover crops during the winter months so that the soil is not bare over the season. This is known as overwintering, in which cold-hardy crops are used. Once winter is over the gardener will then till the soil in order to plant the next harvest.

Known as green manure, the same process is used in order to increase nutrients found within the soil. A year before planting a new garden a gardener will remove weeds from the new bed and plant legumes to increase nitrogen and organic matter in the soil. Grains which grow quickly, such as alfalfa and buckwheat, may also be used as they smother out the growth of potential weeds.

Whether you are using this method for cover crops or green manure, you will need to till the garden bed at least three weeks prior to planting your harvest for the coming season. This will allow the planted cover or manure to breakdown and partially decompose into organic matter.

There are many plants you can use for cover crops and green manure, but the most popular tend to be legumes, grasses, and cereals. Although, brassicas such as forage radish, mustard, and rapeseed are increasingly being used, as well.

Following is a list of a few of the more popular cover crop and green manure options:

1. **Oats**

    This cereal is a reliable and cost-effective option which grows well in cool, well-drained, and well-watered conditions. This option is beneficial as it is a natural weed suppressant, increases the nutrients within the soil, and can produce a large amount of organic matter to feed the soil with.

2. **Cereal Rye**
   The most popular choice in Iowa, cereal rye is known as being a great option for beginners. While this plant can grow in nearly every climate, it does best in cooler temperature zones. Rye acts as a natural weed and pest suppressant, reduces topsoil loss during the winter months, and creates a large amount of organic matter.
3. **Turnips**
   This plant grows well during the winter months and is easy for newbies to grow. Farmers may prefer this option, as their cattle can graze the plants after harvest. This plant also naturally suppresses weeds and increases nutrients within the soil.
4. **White Clover**
   Clover is a wonderful option to reduce weeds by acting as a mulch with its shallow roots and tough stems that easily cover the entire ground. In turn, this successfully reduces the loss of topsoil during the offseason. Clover is edible, making it an option to feed to cattle on a farm and increases nutrients in the soil.
5. **Tillage Radish**
   This is one powerful option for gardeners and farmers who don't till. While they do require a smooth bed which is well-drained with plenty of moisture, they have many benefits when grown. For instance, this plant has a large taproot, which pulls in nutrients to prevent them from being washed or leached away before again releasing the nutrients back into the soil as the plant decomposes and turns into organic matter. This plant can also prevent soil from becoming compacted and suppress weed growth.
6. **Ryegrass**
   This simple plant has the ability to grow nearly anywhere, allowing it to increase soil health in the process. The benefits of ryegrass include weed suppression, increased nutrient density, and can quickly transition soil properties to a no-till method for farmers cutting the time significantly.

Seaweed

If you want to increase the nutrients within your soil then seaweed is one of the best organic options. This simple plant contains over sixty micronutrients, including manganese, iron, zinc, copper, boron, and much more. Seaweed, while underrated, can even increase the growth of your plants. This is because seaweed naturally contains growth hormones, which increase root growth, aid in frost resistance, reduce shock from transplanting, promote fruit growth, and increase the storage life of plants. As if all of that weren't powerful enough on its own, seaweed also contains antitoxins, which aid in plants fighting off pests, viruses, and harmful bacteria.

You can increase the health of your soil by simply adding in powdered seaweed, sometimes known as kelp meal or liquid seaweed. It's important to know that this can't act as a fertilizer on its own, as it does not contain enough phosphorus and nitrogen for garden plants, but in addition to compost and worm castings, it is a wonderful option.

As you can see, a lot goes into building the right soil for your garden. But, if you get the soil rich and healthy then the rest will follow suit. Believe me, it is well worth the time and effort you put into it, as it will allow you to have a much larger harvest and healthier plants.

CHAPTER 4

Controlling the Weeds

When starting a garden everyone tells themselves that they won't let weeds build up and overtake their garden. They are sure that they will prevent or pull up any dandelions, thistles, bittercress, or chickweed that happens to pop up. But, then the weeds grow faster than the gardener expects and their life gets busy. Before they know it their garden is equally as full of weeds as it is their crops. This happens both with complete beginners and those who have gardened for several years. Yet, there is no need to fear. You don't have to make the same mistake as gardeners who've come before you or that you might have made in the past. By using organic weeding methods, you can keep your garden weed-free and thriving.

When many people begin their gardening journey they invest in chemical-based herbicides to keep the weeds at bay. These brand-name products seem like a quick-fix to a problem that nobody wants. But, over time you will come to regret using these chemical-based products, which come to live in the soil and deprive it of nutrients, infect nearby water, kill important organisms that live in the soil, and overtime affects both animals and humans who live in the area. You don't even have to eat the food grown in the garden to be affected by the herbicides, as they get on your skin when you go outdoors and then absorb into your skin and bloodstream. Thankfully, there are organic options that work just as well in keeping weeds away without the nasty side effects.

However, you don't want to use just any organic option, as is organic doesn't necessarily mean that it is good for your garden. For instance, many organic options will use vinegar, salt, or soap, which can cause serious damage to the health of your soil gradually. Sure, it won't cause negative effects to humans like the chemical-based herbicides, but it will cause the quality of your garden to deteriorate slowly. Yes, they are able to keep the weeds at bay (despite often not killing them completely), but it is not worth damaging your soil for, especially as there are better options. In this chapter, we will explore safe and effective organic herbicide and weeding options, that won't damage your garden.

Mulching

One of the most effective weed prevention techniques is mulching your garden. Not only does this keep weeds at bay, but it can also improve overall garden health. Mulching works by both smothering growing weeds and preventing future weed seeds from germinating. There are many options when you mulch, with some of the more popular options being compost, grass clippings, straw, wood chips, and newspaper. Although, you want to avoid using hay, as this is full of seeds that can cause more weeds to grow.

While mulching is a simple process, there is some important information to know and rules to follow. Firstly, you never want to put down mulch in a garden bed full of weeds. Before putting it down you must first remove all of the weeds.

When you lay down the mulch you must make sure you lay down enough to smother out potential weed seeds, but not so much that you overcrowd your crops. The ideal amount of mulch is often two to three inches in shaded gardens and four to six inches in regular full-sun gardens. If you know that your garden is full of weed seeds that crop up every year then you can take an extra precaution by first laying down newspaper and then topping it with your preferred mulch.

When adding mulch, it is vital that you keep in mind that it retains moisture and increases the time it takes for the soil to warm from the afternoon sun. Because of this, you can't have the mulch too close to the base of your crop. Keep a mulch-free two-inch circle around the stems of your plants. Otherwise, the stems of your plants can become rotted from the moisture in the mulch. You may also want to pull the mulch away from bulbs and perennial flowers during the spring so that they can grow more quickly.

You not only need to be careful of keeping mulch away from the stems in your garden but also away from the trunks and woody stems of trees and shrubs in your yard. Similarly, the mulch can cause even the woodier stems and trunks to rot. Not only that, but it can attract rodents such as rats, mice, and voles. Keep a mulch-free circle of six to twelve inches around these stems and trunks.

When mulching there are two basic options to choose from: organic and inorganic. The organic options naturally decompose and often offer nutrients to your garden, as they were previously plants themselves. This includes options such as chopped leaves, grass clippings, compost, straw, wood chips, pine needles, sawdust, and paper.

The inorganic options usually include plastic and landscaping fabric. In general, organic options are superior. However, as the black plastic mulch retains heat some vegetables, such as tomatoes and eggplants, may prefer the warmth they provide throughout the night.

You must also keep in mind that if you use compost as mulch it needs to remain moist. While compost is an incredibly beneficial mulch to your garden, as it contains many nutrients, it is damaging to plants if it becomes dry in the sun. Therefore, if you choose to use compost as a mulch use it in a thin layer with another mulching option (such as straw or wood chips) on top to protect the moisture level and increase the benefits to your plants and garden.

When choosing which type of mulch to use, there are many aspects that you must keep in mind. Many people will be hoping for a less expensive option, which is thankfully easily available. You can easily recycle chopped leaves, grass clippings, compost, straw, wood chips, sawdust, and newspaper for your vegetable garden. You may collect these from your own yard, leaves from local forests, contact farmers to see if they have the straw that has gotten wet and they can no longer use, or contact local tree care companies and see if you can take any sawdust or wood chips off their hands. However, if you recycle these ingredients for mulch you must first ensure they have not been treated with chemicals. For instance, many kinds of grass are treated with herbicides, which you want to avoid.

While you may be able to recycle these options for your vegetable garden, you will likely want more visually appealing options for your flower gardens. This is especially true if you live somewhere with a homeowners' association. In this case, you might have to purchase bark chips for your mulch.

There are a few potential drawbacks to organic mulch, but these will not cause a problem for some gardeners. Ultimately, you have to try a mulch and hope that it works. If the mulch you end up using causes problems you may have to replace it with another option down the road, but it is impossible to know this ahead of time as all mulch options contain some drawbacks. For instance, grass clippings may attract voles, mold, fungi, and slugs. However, this can also often be avoided. Along with attracting slugs, mulch may also attract natural slug predators, such as beetles, therefore keeping the slugs at bay. You may also prevent the growth of mold and fungi by not over-watering and occasionally stirring or raking the mulch.

Ultimately, there are pros and cons to every mulching choice. But, it is usually best to choose organic options that improve the soil over time rather than risk leaching toxins from inorganic materials. Some of the best options are compost, leaves, and straw. These will add nutrients to the soil over the growing season and don't have to be removed after the harvest. However, while these are generally superior options, whatever you choose will greatly depend upon what you have available, your budget, and your preferences.

Hand-Pull Weeds

Yes, hand-pulling weeds aren't fun. But, if you hand pull a few weeds that pop up here and there, combined with other methods of weed control, such as mulching, then you will find it easy to manage the weeds in your garden. After all, if you use the mulching method you shouldn't get many or any weeds, so you simply need to pluck a few from around your plants when they crop up.

When pulling weeds you want a few tools. Firstly, you will want a good pair of gardening gloves to keep your hands safe. Using tools such as a hori-hori or a small trowel may also help with small weed work. However, this is backbreaking work if you are trying to pull up more than a few weeds.

Thankfully, there are other options that you can use on a larger project. There are a variety of stand-up weeding tools, one of the best is by Fiskars. This tool has a serrated stainless-steel claw in the bottom of the base attached to a long pole and a handle. You can easily place the tool on top of the weed, step on the base, twist the claw into the soil, and pull it back up. You can quickly pull many weeds in quick succession this way. Then, once you are done simply pick up and throw out the weeds and cover the garden bed with mulch to prevent future weeds.

Flame Weeding

Flame weeding is a great option, not only for your garden but also if you want to keep your entire lawn organic! Rather than using herbicides to remove weeds between the cracks in the concrete, along the fence, or next to your driveway you can use a propane torch or flame weeder. You can even adjust the flame so that it only affects a narrow range so that you can easily get weeds out of your vegetables and garden beds. But, you have to be careful when using them in the garden.

When using a flame weeder it works best if you catch the weeds early before their roots have time to spread or they go to seed. There is no need to burn the weeds to a crisp, but you do want to burn them well enough to damage the cell structure. This will cause the weeds to slowly die. Flame weeding can kill the roots of some weeds, but not all. While they do a great job on annual weeds, it may not completely kill the roots of perennial weeds. These weeds may need a second burning if they crop back up. Thankfully, they do a good job at preventing perennial weeds from seeding and spreading.

Boil Weeds

One of the cheapest and easiest weeding methods is to boil water and then pour it over the plants. This method will kill any plant it is poured over, as they are unable to withstand the extreme heat. Not only that, but it will also kill soil life such as worms. You can easily use this method to kill weeds in a sidewalk, along your driveway, or next to a fence. Boiling water can also be used in the garden, but you must be careful. You don't want to accidentally boil your crops or kill the soil in your garden beds. Use a kettle when boiling your weeds and ensure it is at a full rolling boil before taking it off the heat. The kettle you use should have a small spout so that you can easily control the amount of water you pour. Similarly, you should pour the water very slowly so that you can ensure you don't pour too much and kill soil life or other plants.

This method is extremely successful and non-toxic. While it will kill any plant, it is worth noting that perennial weeds, such as dandelions, which have a long taproot might come back if you don't kill the entire root system. With these weeds, you may want to dig a small hole with a trowel at the base of the plant. You can then pour the water in order to kill the entire taproot. Once done immediately refill the hole with soil in order to prevent airborne weeds from sprouting.

Manage Your Compost Pile

There are many amazing benefits to using homemade compost in your garden beds. But, it is important that you are careful what you add to your compost bin, otherwise, it could cause problems once added to the bed. For instance, if you add a giant pile of plant matter from your yard to the compost bin without stopping to pay attention to what all plants are in the pile, then you could be adding a large variety of weeds. Yes, you can add leaves and grass clippings to your compost, but if you add in weeds then you will only be promoting the growth of weeds in your garden, as the seeds will get mixed into the soil and eventually sprout.

Just in case the odd weed happens to make its way into your compost pile by mistake, you should turn the pile around and aerate it at least once a week to introduce oxygen and help kill the rare weed seed.

Be Careful when Transplanting

Believe it or not, many weeds may be introduced into your garden accidentally, especially when transplanting. If you have friends who know your garden, be careful of using plants that they have dug up from their own gardens. While you can certainly accept their generous offer, you don't want to transplant it directly into your garden bed, but rather into a container. This is because many times when people dig up plants from their garden beds they accidentally remove the roots from weeds, as well. As the weed's roots get stuck into the roots of the other plant you and your friend are ignorant of the disaster waiting to happen. Before you know it you could have mugwort, crabgrass, thistle, or stinging nettle infestation in your garden bed.

If you first allow the plant to grow in a container garden for a few weeks you can ensure that no weed roots got mixed in. After a three to four-week quarantine, you can then transplant the plant to your garden bed or allow it to stay in the container garden.

Commercial Organic Herbicide

While synthetic chemical-based herbicides are certainly more widely used, there are more organic herbicides coming onto the market. While each brand is different and you should read the ingredients label, most contain a blend of citrus oil, clove oil, acetic acid, and citric acid. This blend can quickly kill grasses and annual weeds, but like many weeding methods, persistent perennial weeds might require a second application. It's important to keep in mind with these products that they are non-discriminatory and will, therefore, kill weeds and your garden plants alike. Any plant these herbicides come into contact with will die. Therefore, follow the instructions for the brand you are using and be extra vigilant that it does not come into contact with your plants.

As you can see, there are many weeding options for organic gardeners. In general, if you practice hand-weeding with mulching you should not have many problems. But, if the occasional weed problem does sprout up, there are many ways in which you can rid them from your garden bed.

CHAPTER 5

Growing from Seeds, Clippings, And Seedlings

There are many benefits to starting your own plants from seed and then transplanting them to your garden after they have sprouted. Firstly, there are many more options when you grow from seeds rather than buying already started plants at the garden center. There are many online seed catalogs that offer a wide variety of options, including heirloom seeds. Some of these options include Burpee, The Living Seed Company, and Seed Savers Exchange.

You can also save money by beginning from seeds! Simply filling a medium-sized garden bed with plants from the garden center can cost you fifty dollars USD. While you will definitely see a return in the harvest the plants' yield, you can make a better turnaround if you begin from seeds. This is because a single packet of fifty seeds costs an average of only two or three dollars.

Lastly, when you start from seeds you know the quality of the plants you have. Often times when you go to gardening centers, you have no idea if the plant has a weak root system or has been infected with a disease. On the other hand, if you begin the seeds yourself you will know that you protected them from disease and that they can survive transplantation to your garden bed.

What to Sow

Before you can purchase your seeds you need to decide what you can grow. This will depend on multiple factors, but the main ones being your local temperature zone as taught by the USDA and the season. For instance, if it is summer you can grow tomatoes but not asparagus. If you live somewhere with a short growing season, such as up north, you will also need to take this into account. In this case, you may have to start your seeds indoors prior to the beginning of the season and then transplanting them outdoors after the last frost. Although, not all crops can be started inside, as peas, beans, and root vegetables do not handle transplantation well.

Choosing Your Seeds

When purchasing seeds, you don't want to use anything lying around. Instead, choose to purchase from reputable suppliers. These companies should run germination tests, and some may even run a variety of trials to ensure the highest quality. This greatly affects seeds, as higher quality seeds are more likely to sprout, sprout more quickly and produce stronger seedlings which can hold up to transplantation and slight weather shifts.

While you can buy seeds online, another and often better option is to find seeds that you know are well-adapted to your local region. You can do this by going to local seed swaps where you may offer to buy seeds if you have none to trade or from regional suppliers.

When possible, it is best to purchase heirloom seeds rather than hybrids. These have many benefits, but many people choose them simply because their flavor is superior to that of hybrids, as while developing hybrid seeds manufacturers often sacrifice both nutrition and flavor. Another benefit of heirloom seeds is that they are open-pollinated, which means that you are able to save seeds to plant for years down the road. This is a wonderful ability as if you plant a hybrid vegetable you are unable to remove the seeds from the harvest to use again in the future.

Timing

When beginners are starting their gardens they don't want to wait. But, this leads to many people who are starting their plants from seeds starting too early. While it is a good idea to start your seeds outdoors, if you do it too long before you are able to transplant the seedlings outdoors then they can become weak and root-bound. This is a problem as the seedling will then have difficulties once outdoors. On the other hand, if you start your seeds too late then you will miss the best time of the season for growth. Therefore, follow the directions for your specific seed and temperature zone. There is no one rule for this, as it varies based on your location and plant type.

Soil

Just as the soil in your garden bed is important to be well-balanced, it is of equal importance to have proper soil to start your seeds in. You want soil that can drain well to prevent roots from rotting. Using a soil blend with peat or coconut fiber (coir). While peat is a more traditional option, it is being used less now as it has an extremely slow growth rate and is difficult to harvest. However, coconut fiber has the same texture as peat moss but stays hydrated better. Coconut fiber is also much easier to produce and harvest.

When planting your seeds, you can use a high-quality soil from the garden center, or you can make your own with one part each of high-quality soil, coconut fiber, and compost. When starting your seeds in these you can place the prepared soil mixture in either recycled egg cartons or plastic seed starters supplied at gardening and hardware stores.

Food and Water

Three to four hours before you begin planting your seeds pour the prepared soil mixture into a large bucket or bowl. Add just barely enough water to moisten the soil mixture and then stir it together until uniform. Add the moist soil to your seed starting containers. You don't want to water the seeds as soon as you plant them, as the water may dislodge them. By first watering the soil you are able to give the seeds a chance to take hold before risking watering them.

After the three to four hours have passed, add two to three seeds to each of the prepared seed containers. You will need to follow the directions for the individual seeds regarding the depth they must be planted at. As soon as the seeds are covered in the recommended amount of soil cover the containers with either a plastic dome or plastic wrap. This will allow the seeds to have enough moisture to germinate.

As soon as sprouts begin to emerge in the following days, remove the plastic from the top of the container. Whenever the soil in the containers is dry to the touch gently water with a mister or spray bottle. You will also want to use organic fertilizer such as fish emulsion once the first leaves appear on the seedlings.

Prevent Disease

If you give your seedlings too much humidity and moisture they can develop a fungal disease, known as damping off. You can aid in preventing this condition by adding in a half-inch of light-colored sphagnum moss to the top of your prepared soil mixture. This moss can absorb up to twenty times its weight in water, acts as an aeration source for young seedlings, and contains beneficial bacteria that prevent fungus and disease. One study conducted at the University of California concluded that by using sphagnum moss in planting seeds you can prevent an average of eighty to ninety percent of damping off diseases.

Keeping Warm

In order for seeds to germinate and sprout, they need a temperature of between seventy and ninety degrees Fahrenheit. Yet, most homes are unable to provide this type of warm constantly throughout the winter. Therefore, if you are trying to start your seeds indoors before spring begins you may want to purchase an electric germination mat. These an average cost forty dollars USD and are placed beneath the container of soil and seeds to provide the ideal temperature.

Light Exposure

Just as plants outdoors need sun exposure, you need to ensure that your seedlings get plenty of light, as well. However, seedlings require more light than most homes can provide during the late winter months. Thankfully, you don't have to go out and buy expensive grow lights, as regular fluorescent lights will do the right. Simply use lamps with fluorescent bulbs and suspend them no more than an inch above the seedlings. You will need to adjust the position of the light bulbs as the seeds grow so that it remains one inch away. The seedlings will require fourteen to eighteen hours of solid light daily, which you can easily provide by buying a simple timer for your electrical outlet.

Encourage Strong Growth

You don't want your seedlings to suffer from a lack of root space, water, or nutrients. Therefore, after the sprouts are established and growing well, you will want to pinch and pluck away the weakest of the seedlings in each container. As each small container has two to three seeds this means you will need to remove one to two sprouts in each container. By doing this, you are ensuring that the strongest of the seedlings have the opportunity to grow strong and flourish. As the seedlings grow lightly brush your hand over the tops daily. You want to do this gently as to not overly disturb the seedlings, but enough to lightly jostle the stems. This practice stimulates the effects that wind provides and promotes stems to grow more sturdy and strong. If your seedlings begin to outgrow their containers before you can transplant them outside then immediately move them into larger containers.

Transplanting

Seedlings should be ready to be transplanted into your garden bed or outdoor container after four to six weeks. You can help the seedlings by making this transition as easy and painless as possible. In order to do this, you can keep the seedlings in a covered outdoor location (such as a porch or open garage) during the daytime before bringing them inside in the evening. After the first day begins slowly moving the seedlings to a more brightly lit area to prevent sunburn. This process should take about a week. Once the seedlings are fully adjusted to being outdoors during the day, known as hardening off, then you can transplant them to your prepared soil.

In order to give your seedlings, the best chance of success, you will want to ideally transplant them on a moderately cool and overcast day. If it simply won't stay cool outside, perhaps you live in the south, then you will want to wait and transplant the seedlings in the evening after the heat of the day has passed.

Before you begin transplanting the seedlings, give them a light watering one to two hours before you get to work. Once you are ready to transplant your seedlings, you want to gently tap the flat bottom of the containers on the ground, this will help the soil loosen. Then, use a trowel and gently remove the seedling and a little of the soil surrounding it form the container and place it in a prepared hole in the garden. Pat some soil over any remaining holes, leaving the plant level with the ground.

Propagating Cuttings

While you will likely be purchasing partially-grown plants or seeds, not all plants can be grown from seeds. Actually, there are many perennial plants which are best grown when propagated from cuttings. This is especially beneficial if you particularly like the mother plant, as the new plant grown from the cutting will be genetically identical. This means that it will share the same qualities, such as color.

Plants that grow well from cuttings include:
- ☐ Lilac
- ☐ Hydrangea
- ☐ Dogwood
- ☐ Bergonia
- ☐ Sage
- ☐ Birch
- ☐ Verbena
- ☐ Elm
- ☐ Maple
- ☐ Ginkgo
- ☐ Fuchsia
- ☐ Cotoneaster
- ☐ Basil
- ☐ Redbud
- ☐ Fuchsia
- ☐ Broadleaf evergreen trees

- ☐ Oak
- ☐ Rosemary
- ☐ Boxwood
- ☐ Clematis
- ☐ Cedar
- ☐ Lavender
- ☐ Honeysuckle
- ☐ Oregano
- ☐ Citrus
- ☐ Wallflower
- ☐ Holly
- ☐ Dianthus
- ☐ Penstemon
- ☐ Hyssop
- ☐ Thyme
- ☐ Willow
- ☐ Fig
- ☐ Pomegranate
- ☐ Kiwi
- ☐ Mint
- ☐ Fir
- ☐ Sycamore
- ☐ Locust
- ☐ Poplar
- ☐ Forsythia
- ☐ Jasmine

The season in which you need to take cuttings, the area you need to cut, and the length of cutting all vary based off of the type of plant you are using. Therefore, if you are looking to learn how to use cuttings for a specific plant you will need to research how to best care for that plant as it varies from plant to plant and there is no single rule or process.

However, there are a few tips that may help you no matter the plant type. These include:

1. Use clean cutting shears.
2. Do not cut a portion of the plant that has flower buds or flowers, as the nutrients within the plant needs to go to the root.

3. When you take your cutting do so in the early morning while it is fully hydrated.
4. Keep cuttings in a cool and moist place until you plant them.
5. Use a rooting medium that provides good drainage and aeration with low fertility. You can combine your own with equal parts of coconut fiber (coir) and perlite.
6. After cutting, dip a piece of the plant into an organic rooting hormone, which will promote the growth of roots.
7. After you have dipped the cuttings in rooting hormone, place them one-third to one-half of an inch into the prepared rooting medium with the tips point upward into the air.
8. Water the cuttings and then place the container in indirect sunlight. You want to avoid full sunlight.
9. Keep the cuttings in humid conditions with a clear plastic dome or a plastic bag placed over the container.

While there are different cutting recommendations based on the source plant, one of the most common types of cuttings you can take are stem cuttings. When you propagate stem cuttings, they are taken from woody ornamental plants, shrubs, and houseplants. Oftentimes the easiest of these to propagate are houseplants.

When taking a stem cutting you want to find a plant free of disease and insects, plus the stem you cut from needs to be free of flowers and buds. Using a sanitized pair of gardening shears cut a three to a six-inch portion at a forty-five-degree angle. Cutting at this angle increases the rooting area. You want your cutting to include at least two or three leaves and the tip of the stem.

Remove any leaves that are growing from the bottom where you cut the stem and then dip it into the organic rooting hormone. Place the cutting into the rooting medium and follow the remaining instructions as written above. You can test the roots on the stem by lightly pulling on it. If the stem easily pulls out then it is not ready, but if there is a little resistance then the roots are ready for it to be transplanted.

It is important to know that this is often not a quick process. While it's possible for roots to grow in a matter of days, sometimes it may take up to a few months. During this process, if any leaves fall or if you notice any stems looking sickly remove them immediately to prevent the spread of disease or fungus.

As you can see, growing from stems, starting seeds, and caring for seedlings can take time. Yet, this time is well worth it and greatly affects the health of your plants. If you follow the simple steps in this chapter, then you will likely experience success and before long will be able to enjoy the fruits of your labor.

CHAPTER 6

Easy Plants for Everyone

One of the best ways to maximize your gardening space is to plant crops in succession. While many gardeners will prepare their garden bed and plant all of their crops in a single day in early spring, this is not the best option to make the most out of your garden. Sure, this isn't a problem if you want to casually garden, but if you want to get the most out of your garden and provide your family with an abundance of flavorful and nutrient-rich ingredients then there are better options.

Not only that but when you try to fit all of your gardening work into a single weekend it is much more difficult than gradually picking away at the work. With planting your crops in succession, you plan ahead to plant new vegetables every few weeks of the season. For instance, you may plant peas and greens during the colder beginning of spring, and then once summer approaches you can prepare to plant tomatoes and zucchini. By planting throughout the seasons rather than only having a spring or summer garden, you will be able to offer your family not only a larger quantity of vegetables but a larger variety, as well.

As harvest approaches the end of its season, you can clear those plants out of the bed. You may still have other plants in the bed with a longer growing season, but you can still go ahead and plant the next vegetable on the schedule for the season. You want to always have your garden full and producing rather than waiting for the following season to start over from scratch.

While there are certainly innumerable plants that you can grow, in this chapter we will be focusing on some of the easiest and most productive choices for beginners: herbs and fruits, and vegetables. But, before we look at herbs, let's have a look at fruits and vegetables according to the seasons that they are most often planted during.

Spring

The spring and autumn seasons have many crossover vegetables, which is good news for people who love dark leafy greens, peas, and root vegetables!

- **Spinach**
  Fresh baby spinach is quite delicious in a variety of foods, both raw and cooked. Many people will be happy to know that this

spinach is also quick and easy to grow, and incredibly resistant to frost which is helpful when planting early in the season. You can further improve its frost resistance when growing it under a cover. Of course, you can allow the spinach to fully mature, but if you plant to harvest it as baby spinach then you can place the plants close together and then harvest the leaves while they are still small. By doing it this way, you can have baby spinach in three to four weeks from the time of planting.

- ☐ **Lettuce**
The colder months are perfect for growing lettuce, and you can get many more varieties than the grocery store offers! Not only that, but you have more control over how the lettuce grows. Either you can allow it to grow to large full-sized heads, or you can cut it off as baby greens for a quick and easy near-constant harvest. Just keep in mind that if you plan to grow the lettuce into full heads, you will need to leave more room between the plants, but if you harvest them as baby greens you want to plant them more closely together to save space. Try to mix things up by planting lettuce with different textures, colors, and flavor profiles.

- ☐ **Chard**
While eaten less frequently than lettuce and spinach, chard deserved to be more widely loved. Firstly, you can enjoy this vegetable raw, cooked, or even in your morning smoothie. Secondly, like lettuce, you can find numerous types of chard to enjoy and mix things up. Chard is another vegetable that you can allow to grow until full-size, or some varieties can be harvested as baby greens in three to four weeks.

- ☐ **Peas**
There are many different peas that are the perfect option for spring. These are easy to plant and even children might try eating them, as they can first experience the fun of picking the peas off the bush. Snow peas and pod peas can grow quite quickly, whereas snap peas and shelling peas take a bit more time. However, children can also enjoy preparing the snap and shelling peas in the kitchen. As there are many types of peas there are types that grow as vines and others grow as bushes, so be sure to look into the exact variety you plan on buying. Either way, peas tend to take between fifty and sixty-five days to ready for harvest. If growing peas from seed, it is best to allow the seeds to soak in

water overnight before planting for increased chances of successful germination.

- **Potatoes**

A fun crop to grow during the spring, especially for children, are potatoes. You begin by placing seeding potatoes in a large bag, known as a potato bag, with a small amount of compost around them. Once shoots appear above the soil, you add more on top and you continue repeating this process until the bag is eventually full. After the leaves start poking out of the top of the bag start to turn yellow and die down, ten to twenty weeks later, you can dump the contents of the bag and harvest all of the potatoes from inside!

- **Green Onions**

These onions, also known as spring onions, are really quick to grow, making them a great option when you want a tangy crunch added to your meals or are running low on white or yellow onions. These green onions can be added to a variety of dishes, both cooked and raw.

- **Onions and Garlic**

Two of the easiest crops to grow are onions and garlic, which require almost no maintenance. To plant these simply bury individual garlic cloves and onion bulbs during the spring or autumn, and allow them to sit until late summer. You will know that they are ready once the leaves die back and turn yellow. Before storing them, lift them out of the ground and allow the bulbs to dry in the sun.

- **Beets**

Beets, like many root vegetables, are incredibly easy to grow. They are planted between March and July and then harvested between May and September. If you are someone who has never cared for beets, then you may want to try growing golden or orange beets, which have a much sweeter and often pleasant flavor.

- **Runner Beans**

These beans are climbers, which means that they require a support frame to grow up onto. You plant them in the spring, keep them well-watered, and once summer arrived you will have a large supply of beans! Just remember that they will go bad on the bush quickly, so you must pick them as soon as they are ripe.

- ☐ **Strawberries**

    Strawberries are easy to grow and in exchange, you get plenty of freshly-picked berries! These plants grow annually, and the bushes only need to be replaced every three to five years. One benefit of this berry is that they don't only grow in the spring, as there are many varieties for various seasons. If you invest in two or three different varieties then you can have fresh berries all through the spring and until the end of autumn.

- ☐ **Figs**

    While figs grow on a tree, which does take up space, there are varieties of smaller fig trees you can grow. Just because figs grow in trees don't mean you have to plant them in the ground either, as many varieties grow well in containers. This plant typically doesn't require very much pruning, and there are few pests you have to worry about.

Summer

The vegetables grown in the summer are the very definition of fresh-tasting, including tomatoes, cucumbers, bell peppers, and more! These only grow during the warmest months of the year, so enjoy them while you can.

- ☐ **Tomatoes**

    The most popular choice, no matter a gardener's experience or their garden size, are tomatoes. These are wonderful because they can grow in pots, garden beds, or even hanging baskets! But, be sure that wherever you choose to grow your tomatoes that they have full sun access and a stake holding up and supporting their stalk against the weight of their fruit. Beginners are best starting with small tomato varieties, such as grape and cherry tomatoes. While you can certainly practice growing larger varieties as well, it is best if most of your harvest consists of smaller tomatoes until you have more experience. This is due to larger tomatoes having a habit of splitting and then rotting and developing blossom end rot.

    Consider planting basil directly next to your tomato plants. Not only is this useful for when you want to make an Italian dish, but it will also keep pests away from the tomatoes.

- ☐ **Cucumbers**

    Cucumbers, like many types of beans, require support to be able to climb. However, this doesn't have to be anything elaborate, as they can easily climb up a string that is suspended by nails. Of course, you can always choose to use a trellis. Cucumbers are easy to grow but do prefer warm temperatures, bright sunlight, and regular watering. Although, if you provide cucumbers with these few basic needs you will likely have more than you can ever eat fresh! If this happens, you can always give them away, but you may also give pickling a try.

- [ ] **Zucchini**

Summer squash is easy to grow and is famous for having a high yielding harvest. If you plant a couple of vines, before you know it, you will have more squash than you know what to do with! But, there are plenty of ways you can serve these vegetables, whether in a stir-fry, as low-carb noodles, pickled, roasted, in a casserole, in zucchini bread, and much more. One of the most popular summer squash options is zucchini, which has a mild and pleasant flavor that can be used in a variety of ways.

- [ ] **Carrots**

Root vegetables are notoriously easy to grow, and one of the easiest options is carrots! While you may typically think of carrots growing in a large field, they are also a great option for container gardening. By planting in a container you can ensure that the soil is loose enough to optimize the growing and that the carrots do not become overcrowded.

- [ ] **Bell Peppers**

Bell peppers are easy to grow as long as you provide them with full sun, plenty of heat, and compost! These vegetables are full of nutrients, and even contain three times the vitamin C as an orange. Bell peppers are versatile and can complement almost any savory dish.

- [ ] **Melons**

A great option when you don't want to grow a shrub or tree is melons. There is a large variety with various flavors to offer, and they can be grown both in a garden bed and in a container. While melons are easy to grow, they do need a lot of space as the vines grow out far, along with a lot of sun and heat. Larger melons, such as watermelon, are more difficult to grow as they become heavy and may break the vine, but smaller melons such as cantaloupe (muskmelon) are quite easy to grow.

Autumn

Many of the spring crops you may also grow in the autumn months, which is good news for many people as there are quite a few nutrient-dense dark greens, peas, and other vegetables full of flavor.

- ☐ **Broccoli and Cauliflower**

  Some of the more nutritious and vitamin-rich vegetables you can choose to grow are broccoli and cauliflower. While you may be used to seeing the typical green and white varieties in stores, there are many other types which boast even more vitamin options! For instance, you can find these vegetables in purple, yellow, and more. This can even be a great way to trick picky children into eating vegetables if they don't like anything green.

- ☐ **Bok Choy**

  This Chinese cabbage is a quick growing vegetable which can be ready to harvest in only thirty days. You can enjoy this by making stir-fries, salads, soups, and even kimchi.

- ☐ **Mustard Greens**

  This gar green has a tangy and peppery flavor which pairs well in mixed green salads, but which can also be cooked down with bacon or used as a low-carb option for lunch wraps. You can enjoy a milder flavor by harvesting mustard green as baby leaves after thirty days, or allow them to fully grow for sixty days.

- ☐ **Kale**

  People either love kale or hate kale, however you feel about it, there is no denying that this vegetable is versatile. Even if you don't love kale, you can always grow some to mix into your smoothies where you will get all of the nutrients but without the flavor. While you are most likely familiar with a single type of kale, there are many types, some of the most popular being curly, Russian, redbor, and lacinato. If you don't enjoy the more bitter flavor of kale, then you might try harvesting it while it is still a baby green for a gentler and sweet flavor.

- ☐ **Radishes**

  One of the most quickly growing options to enjoy from your garden are radishes, which can be harvested in as few as three weeks. While most people are only familiar with small red and white radishes, there are many other varieties with other sizes, colors, and shapes to be enjoyed. Some of these varieties are sweeter while others are spicier. While you can certainly enjoy radishes on a salad, you can also roast them for a low-carb potato substitution.

Winter

Winter may be cold, but there are still crops you can enjoy during these months! There is no need to wait until spring to begin your garden. In fact, by continuing to garden throughout the winter you can add more nutrients to your garden's soil and prevent topsoil loss from the wind. However, the crops you can grow in winter will vary greatly. In northern areas where there are harsh winters, there may be few options, whereas areas with mild winters may be able to grow more autumn and spring varieties of fruits and vegetables. Look at your local temperature zone to know what you can and can't plant during the winter.

- ☐ **Perpetual Spinach**

    Perpetual spinach belongs to the same plant family as beets and chard. But, it tastes more like true spinach than chard. This crop is great to grow, as you can easily cut leaves off of it as it grows and more will grow back in their place. If you plant perpetual spinach during the autumn, then you can be supplied with fresh greens throughout the entire winter and until summer. However, be careful to ensure you remove the flowers as they pop up or it will go to seed.

- ☐ **Arugula**

    Many people grow this lettuce during the autumn and spring, but it can also be grown during the winter months for many people if you choose the right varieties. A more cold-tolerant type of arugula is wild, but garden arugula can also grow in the winter.

- ☐ **Leeks**

    This mild and sweet vegetable, leeks are a wonderful option to replace sharp onion in dishes. Similar to green onions but larger, leeks can be used in vegetable roasts, soups, or anywhere else that you would use onions. Leeks may cost a lot at the store, but they are incredibly frost-tolerant and can be grown over winter in temperate zones seven and warmer.

- ☐ **Fennel**

    A great multi-use vegetable, you can use the leaves and seeds to season food and the bulbs sliced to roast or add to salads and side dishes. Many people love fennel as it has a sweet licorice-like flavor complementing meat, fish, tomatoes, and potatoes. This vegetable is sensitive to cold, but it will grow over the winter in warmer temperature zones.

Herbs

Spices and herbs are an incredible part of cooking, as they offer food a range of flavors. However, fresh herbs can cost a fortune when purchases in the store. Thankfully, they are easy to grow, and some people even grow them in containers in their kitchen windowsill!

- ☐ **Mint**

    One of the most incredibly versatile herbs is mint. There are many types of mint, including peppermint, spearmint, wintergreen, apple mint, and even chocolate mint! These mints, especially the classic peppermint, can be used in both sweet and savory dishes. Whether you want to add mint to ice cream, mojitos, or spring roll wraps, the choice is up to you. Many people will also be happy to know that mint is an ideal container plant, as the container helps prevent it from taking over your entire garden bed.

- ☐ **Chives**

    With their bright green stems and flavor chives are a wonderful addition to add to soups, salads, potatoes, fish, and many other dishes. Bees are especially drawn to the flowers on the chive plant, bringing the important pollinators to your garden. If you don't get much sun, that's okay, as chives do well with only four to five hours of sun and damp soil.

- ☐ **Parsley**

    If growing from seeds, parsley is a little slow to get going, but once it is well established you will find that it will give you plenty of leaves to use in all your dishes for nearly two years. If you are someone who really loves using parsley in Italian and other dishes, then you may want to grow multiple plants to ensure you can get your fill.

- ☐ **Cilantro**

    This plant is known as both cilantro and coriander. Typically, when talking of cilantro, people are referring to the leaves of the plant, and when saying coriander, they are referring to the seeds. The cilantro plant doesn't live long, but you can keep it longer if you are careful to delay its blooming flowers and going to seeds. In order to delay this process, you want to keep it in a more shaded area, water and feed it with compost, and regularly trim the leaves. Once the plant does flower it will attract hoverflies, which are a great bug that eats damaging aphids, and you will then be able to harvest the coriander seeds, as well.

The coriander plant is less likely to go into bloom if you plant it in August or September, and then it is able to survive the cold of most winters. If the plant does survive winter, then it will come back with increased growth in the spring.

- [ ] **Basil**

This versatile herb thrives when it is given a bright and warm location with plenty of compost, meaning it loves the summer months. However, basil does not like having wet roots, so be sure that it is in well-draining soil and that it is watered in the morning rather than in the evening.

- [ ] **Dill**

People love this herb when used in pickles, dairy-based sauces, chicken salad, rice dishes, and more. Along with using the leaves of dill, you can also use the seeds and flowers to season your food. Dill does the best when grown in full sun. Be aware, that if you allow the seeds to ripen while remaining on the plant it will seed into the nearby soil where they will pop up the following year.

- [ ] **Lavender**

There are many types of lavender, but the most loved variety is English lavender. This variety grows well as a perennial in full sun and well-draining soil, but there are other hardier types that grow well in harsh regions. This herb grows beautiful flowers and the smell is amazing. You can use this herb to freshen clothes in the dryer or sock drawer, added to the bath, in calming tea before bed, added to ice cream, and it pairs amazingly with honey in a cake.

- [ ] **Oregano**

Used widely in Italian foods such as pasta and pizzas, oregano has many other uses as well as meats, stews, bread, and even for improved health. There are many types of oregano, with the Greek variety having the most intense flavor. Like most herbs, oregano grows well in container gardens. This herb also does best in full sun with well-draining soil.

- [ ] **Rosemary**

This herb is incredibly hardy and tolerant, and it can grow as either a shrub or be trained to grow in upright in a tree-like manner. Although there are varieties that grow in a trailing manner and ground cover. If you live in colder climates you can grow rosemary in a container and then bring it inside during the winter months. While hardy, rosemary does best in full-sun and an environment that is hot and dry.

- [ ] **Sage**

This herb has a strong flavor, meaning that a little goes a long way. When a few leaves are added, sage is the perfect addition to poultry, beef, and pasta. You will find that sage is especially delicious when it is added to browned butter. There are over nine-hundred varieties of sage, but typically it does best with full sun and well-draining soil.

- [ ] **Thyme**

This herb has a habit of trailing and acting as ground cover, which is used for cooking, medical treatment, and landscaping. The most common type of thyme grows an average of a foot tall, covers the ground around it well, does best in full sun, and blooms small pink or lavender flowers during the summer. If growing in a container garden thyme looms beautifully as it grows and drapes over the sides of the pot.

- [ ] **Bay Leaf**

The bay plant can be used both dried and fresh, but it is best when the leaves are used in moderation. Oftentimes, people will add just one or two whole bay leaves to a pot of soup, stew, or stock, which they will then remove after cooking. The bay leaf plant does not do well with too much water and instead prefers to have the soil slightly dry out between watering.

CHAPTER 7

Container Gardening and Gardening by The Foot

Having pots, barrels, and tubs full of flowers, herbs, vegetables, and fruits can add appeal to any garden, lawn, or balcony. But, container gardening is about much more than appearance. Sure, having visual appeal is a great benefit for many people. But, more importantly, container gardening makes growing your own food accessible to people with little to no garden space. If you live in an apartment, it's okay, you can easily plant some pots on a balcony or even a few small herbs in a windowsill. Some people may even keep their containers in their driveway during the day and off to the side in the evening when they need to park their vehicle. Some other benefits of container gardens include:

1. **Save Water**
   Gardens require frequent watering, which adds up in both the amount of water and price over time. Whether you are hoping to be more environmentally friendly, live somewhere that you need to preserve water, or hope to spend less on your monthly water bill, container gardening is a great way to do all of the above.

2. **Healthy Plants**
   Using container gardens, you are able to customize the soil variety, sunlight requirements, given water, and more to each individual plant. Because of this, you are able to more easily and successfully grow healthier plants.

3. **Fewer Pests**
   When gardens are in a single isolated location, it makes it easier for pests to invade. However, if you can move your containers around, you can more easily isolate invested or infected plants from others, and you can also confuse the pests as they will be unable to easily find the plants.

4. **Perfect Sunlight**
   It may be difficult for people with high levels of shade in their yards to grow a traditional garden bed. But, with a container garden, you are able to move the containers around throughout the day so that they are able to get the optimal amount of sunlight.

5. **Convenience**

   You will find that container gardening is extremely convenient. It is quicker and more easily to water, weed, keep pests away, and more. If you have never tried growing a garden before then you can start with one or two containers of food, and then always add later as your confidence increases.

Now that you understand the convenience and practicality of container gardening, let's look at some of the basics which can allow you to have success with most plants.

Container Size

When growing container gardens, there are benefits to both larger and smaller containers. However, in general, it is easier to keep plants healthy in large containers. This is because these containers have more room for the roots and soil, which enables the plants to get dried out less frequently. The size of the containers also allows them to be more resilient to daily temperature fluctuations. While small hanging baskets may have visual appeal, these are especially prone to drying out during the summer and the plants in them can quickly die.

There are many factors that go into deciding how large a container you need for your mini garden. You need to know the details of what you are planting, for instance, is it a perennial or annual? What is the size and shape of the plant's root system? How quickly does the plant grow? This is incredibly important because if a plant's root system fills up the entire pot, known as being root bound, it will have less soil available, not enough nutrients, dry out more quickly, and will be unable to grow well. Therefore, if you are growing multiple plants in a single pot or a type of plant with a large root system you will require a larger container. When purchasing your container, it is often better to choose lightly-colored options, as they won't absorb heat as much as the darkly-colored containers. Of course, if you live in a more moderate climate and are growing heat-loving vegetables such as bell peppers then you may prefer a dark container. When deciding on the size of the container, you also must determine how much room you have to store a full container and if you will be moving it. Keep in mind, once a container is full of soil and plants it will be much heavier. If your container is too big then you will be unable to easily move it unless you store it in a wagon.

Drainage
Whether you are using a traditional pot, a large tub, or a wagon, it is vital that the container has some sort of drainage holes. If your container doesn't have these holes, then it will become unable to drain and waterlogged, leading to the death of the plants within. These holes don't have to be large, but there needs to be enough so that any extra water in the container is able to drain away. It is often easy to add your own drainage holes if a container is without by the simple use of a drill. If you have a pot that you are unable to drill into, such as a large ceramic pot, then you can use it as a cachepot to place slightly smaller plastic pots inside of. This will allow the plastic pot to have drainage holes, but it will look nice due to the outer ceramic pot.

Materials
There are several types of container materials you can choose from. Each of these has benefits and drawbacks. You will have to decide for yourself which of these options will work best for you and your circumstances. Terracotta and clay containers often look beautiful and attractive, but they are more prone to being damaged and broken. Simple changes in temperature over the seasons can cause these containers to crack in half. This is especially important to consider in colder more northern areas, where a single frost could damage the container. If you are up north and using a terracotta or clay pot it should be brought inside during the winter.

Plastic and fiberglass containers are inexpensive options that weigh much less than most of the competition. These containers also come in many sizes, shapes, and are somewhat flexible which aid in helping them to remain in one piece during fluctuating temperatures. Some of these pots are thinner and made of more stiff material, but these should be avoided as they are poorer in quality and will more easily break. Wood containers look natural and complement the plants within them, as well as having the ability to protect the roots of the plants from drastic temperature shifts. You can buy these pre-made, or save some money by assembling some yourself. You want to avoid treated wood (which is not organic) and those that are prone to rot, but non-treated cedar and locust are both great options. If you want a cheaper wood option, then molded wood-fiber pots are less expensive than solid wood containers.

Some people may like the appearance of metal containers to sow their garden in, and these are sturdy, strong option, but they are not the best option. Metal containers conduct heat quickly and expose the root system of a plant to rapidly changing temperatures.

Polyurethane foam containers weigh ninety percent less than concrete and terracotta containers, but they look shockingly similar. These containers also protect the roots from extreme temperatures and resist cracking or breaking. But, these containers are made with a variety of inorganic materials, and therefore the organic gardener will want to avoid them.

Containers made out of concrete come in a variety of sizes and styles, which tend to be much longer-lasting than most other containers. Due to the durable nature of these containers, they won't break when left out in extreme shifts in temperature. However, these containers are very heavy and not easily moved. You will want to place them where you plan to leave them before filling them with soil and plants.

Preparing your Containers

The larger the container, the heavier it will be upon being filled with soil and plants, this is especially true for terracotta and concrete containers. Therefore, if you have an especially large container or heavy container then you will want to decide where it will stay located and move it there before filling it. If you are unable to reliably water your plants in the morning, then you may need to find somewhere that offers partial shade during the afternoon. Remember, container gardens dry out more quickly than garden beds, so it's important that you keep an eye on the soil.

Sometimes people add gravel to the bottom of the container before adding in the soil. This is not necessary, as you have drainage holes and the gravel will not improve the drainage into these holes. In fact, gravel can block the holes and black drainage occasionally. Although, if your pot is much deeper than you require you can add some gravel to reduce the amount of soil you have to use. Instead of gravel, you might add a layer of newspaper into the bottom of the pot, which will help prevent the soil from washing out.

Regular garden soil is too dense for container gardening. Therefore, you will want to mix organic houseplant soil and compost for your container garden. Don't fill the soil to the brim, as you will need enough space not only to add the plant but also to water it as needed. Before you add your plant to the container, moisten the soil mixture and stir it together so that it is all uniformly moist. After you add your plants into the container, pat the soil over the roots and the base of the stem until it is level with the soil level and then settle the plant into the pot with a good watering.

Caring for a Container Garden

How frequently you water container gardens depends greatly upon the size of the container, plant size, and the weather. But, when you do water them, you want to do so thoroughly. Similarly, don't allow the containers to completely dry out as it will be difficult to get the soil back to optimal hydration and it could damage the roots due to the nature of being in a container rather than the ground. You can increase nutrition for the plants, boost visual appeal, and retain moisture if you spread mulch over the top of the soil. However, just as you would in the garden bed, keep the mulch approximately one inch away from the stem of the plants so that it doesn't cause rot.

The container garden must be fed well. In order to do this mix compost into the soil and fertilize it with seaweed extract or fish emulsions diluted in water. You will want to feed your plant on average once every two weeks, but you may adjust this time depending on how your plants respond.

Selecting Plants for Containers

Most herbs, vegetables, fruits, shrubs, and even small trees can be grown well in a container. There are even dwarf tree varieties which are especially suited to container gardening. You can get a variety of dwarf fruit trees, such as citrus and fig trees if you don't have space for a full-grown average tree. You will want to select plants for your container that best fit the sun, shade, and temperature requirements that you can provide.

Keep in mind that some plants that are less hardy and could otherwise not survive the winter weather can be brought indoors if in a container garden. But, if this is the case, you will need to plant them in a container that is light and small enough to move without too much difficulty.

When growing vegetables in containers you must keep in mind that you have limited space, and therefore you should choose options that you most enjoy or know that your family will eat the most. It is also better to forgo single-harvest vegetables such as onions and instead choose those that give you a continuous harvest. This is because onions and other vegetables that have long growing seasons with a single harvest can require three to four months to grow for a single bulb. This is simply not worth it when using a container garden, as onions are cheap and you could make better use of the space with other vegetables.

Vegetables such as dark leafy vegetables, eggplants, peppers, zucchini, tomatoes, and cucumbers offer you a new constant harvest, making them ideal options for container gardens. Fast-growing root vegetables such as radishes, turnips, and beets are also good choices.

Potatoes are especially ideal for container gardening, as you don't even need a traditional container. Instead of using plastic, terracotta, wooden, or another container you can simply use a lightweight potato bag and continuously add soil over a period of a few months until the bag is full of potatoes. If you are someone who really loves potatoes you might consider having multiple bags of regular potatoes growing, or have different bags for different varieties. You don't only have to grow regular potatoes, you can also enjoy golden, red, fingerling, purple, and sweet potatoes.

Following is a list of some of the more popular vegetable and fruit container gardening options:

- ☐ Peas
- ☐ Green Beans
- ☐ Eggplant
- ☐ Lettuce
- ☐ Kale
- ☐ Broccoli
- ☐ Beets
- ☐ Small Cabbages
- ☐ Asian Greens
- ☐ Tomatoes
- ☐ Carrots
- ☐ Cucumbers
- ☐ Spinach
- ☐ Radishes
- ☐ Turnips
- ☐ Swiss Chard
- ☐ Zucchini
- ☐ Summer Squash
- ☐ Peppers
- ☐ Beans
- ☐ Chilies

- ☐ Winter Squash
- ☐ Strawberries
- ☐ Small-Medium Melons
- ☐ Dwarf Fruit Trees
- ☐ Blueberries

Gardening by the Foot

If you have a yard but are still tight on gardening space, then you may want to give square foot gardening a try. This method was created by a garden expert, engineer, and efficiency expert Mel Bartholomew in order to produce a highly productive garden that can produce large crops in a limited space.

With square foot gardening, you create a garden grid full of one-foot squares, common sizes are four feet by four feet or a larger bed of four feet by eight feet. Each of the one-foot squares within these grids is managed individually with densely planted vegetables of a single variety within a foot of space. The number of vegetables you plant inside of each square depends upon the individual requirements for the plant, for instance, you only plant one tomato plant per square, but you can plant up to sixteen radish plants in one, as well. These beds are designed to have no wasted space and loose soil which is never trampled upon as it is in a raised bed.

The benefits of square foot gardening include:

- ☐ **High Yield Crops**

    By planning out your garden in detail, you can fit more plants in less space, allowing you to have a large harvest even if you only have a small backyard.

- ☐ **Less Daily Maintenance**

    You will also have less work to do as it is a smaller garden bed than most, helping you to save time with regular maintenance. You will simply have to keep an eye on watering and harvesting on most days.

- ☐ **Fewer Weeds**

    Square foot gardening often uses raised beds without soil, which leads to fewer weeds. If you are someone who hates weeding or simply looks to save time, then you will be happy with this method. However, slowly weeds might become slightly more common as weed seeds blow in the wind and land in your garden.

Thankfully, if you take care of these as soon as they pop up then you will be able to keep the weed level low.

- ☐ **Quick Setup**

    While square foot gardening does take more planning, the setup phase is often quicker. This is because you can set up raised beds wherever you like, whether it is on grass or pavement, fill it with your soil-less compost mixture, add in the plants, and water. As you already have a plan, don't have to remove grass, perfect soil that is pre existing, or setup paths through the garden you will find that it takes less work and time.

While square foot gardening does have many benefits, it also has a couple of drawbacks that are important to be aware of.

Firstly, there are two methods of gardening by foot. You can either have traditional raised beds, which were the first method used in square foot gardening, or you can use Bartholomew's newer method. With this updated method he created garden beds that had only six inches of compost mixture. While this can certainly work in some cases, in others, this depth is not deep enough for roots to firmly take hold. However, there is an easy solution to this: make it deeper. Instead of having your garden bed only six inches' deep try making it twelve inches deep, which will allow the roots twice the space.

Secondly, as raised beds are similar to container gardening (only larger) the compost mixture in them can dry out more quickly than ground-based beds. If you allow your compost to become completely dry then it can become more difficult to get to the correct hydration level, potentially leaving you watering on a daily basis during the heat of summer. However, you can avoid this by using soaker hoses or a drip irrigation system. You can also further reduce moisture loss by topping the garden with mulch.

When using square foot gardening, you begin by building your raised garden bed frame. You will want to use non-pressure-treated lumber, as when lumber is treated chemicals are used, which can leach into your compost mixture. Treated lumber may better withstand the elements, but it is not worth it contaminating your food. You want the depth of your bed frame to be between six and twelve inches deep. You can create single or multiple four-foot square beds, or a larger four foot by eight-foot bed. You want to ensure that your garden bed is no wider than four feet, as you need to be able to easily access everything growing within the bed without pushing on or trampling the soil.

You can make your garden beds as simple or elaborate as you like. You can use simple pieces of cheap untreated lumber, or use more expensive lumber and add decorations onto it, such as with wood burning designs. Once done building your frame you will need to place it in a location that gets at least six hours of full sunlight a day.

Under your garden bed, you will want to add a weed barrier. There are two main options when doing this, you can either use weed cloth or cardboard. By placing one of these options down you will be able to smother the grass and weeds underneath your garden bed and prevent their seeds from getting into your compost mixture. This will drastically reduce the number of weeds that grow in your garden. The weed cloth will withstand time well and keep your compost mixture separate from the ground or pavement beneath. On the other hand, if you place cardboard down it will decompose and become a part of the compost over time. This will allow the roots of your plants to go deeper and into the soil later on if they wish, while still smothering and killing the weeds and grass below.

Using a pencil and measuring tape go around your garden bed and mark off every one square foot. After you have the bed firmly and accurately measured out, you can section it off with rope or wood to create square foot boarders. Many people use thin slats of wood. But, you can also use a string tied to nails. This option is easy, inexpensive, and quick to assemble. This option is less permanent than wooden slats, but as the string wears down gradually you can always replace it with fresh string.

Next, you will need to add a compost mixture to your garden. Bartholomew recommends using this instead of soil as it is full of nutrients, drains well, and is less likely to grow weeds. In order to assemble your mixture, combine one part each of organic compost, peat moss, and coarse vermiculite. Some garden centers will sell square foot gardening compost mixture, but if you assemble it yourself you can save money and even use your own homemade compost if you have any.

However, if you do choose to purchase some from the garden center first ensure that it is organic. You will also want to read the ingredient label and make sure that it has a variety of ingredients in it, such as compost, manure, worm castings, and mushroom compost. By having a varied blend, your plants will have access to all of the nutrients they require.

When adding seeds or plants to your garden you can easily determine how many can go into a single square with the following method:

- ☐ Small Spacing – Plants must be planted an average of three inches apart, add sixteen seeds for each one-foot square.
- ☐ Medium Spacing – Plants must be planted an average of four inches apart, add nine seeds for each one-foot square.
- ☐ Large Spacing – Plants must be planted an average of six inches apart, add four seeds for each one-foot square.
- ☐ Extra Large Spacing – Plants must be planted an average of twelve inches apart, add one seed for each one-foot square.

You care for your plants the same as usual, keep an eye on watering, sunlight, weeds, and add extra compost each time you harvest a plant and add a new crop of seeds. Before long, you will find that square foot gardening has many benefits, saves time, money, energy, and increases your harvest an average of twenty percent!

CHAPTER 8

Keeping Plants Healthy

There are many ways to keep your plants healthy, from good watering practices to creating windbreaks. In this chapter, we will explore some of the best ways to easily increase the health of your plants and garden for a better harvest.

Windbreaks

When wind tears through your garden, it causes damage in multiple ways. Firstly, the wind causes damage to the stems and roots of the plant by pushing it too hard in any direction. Secondly, the wind can cause damage to the soil by causing moisture to evaporate and by blowing away precious topsoil. This can affect plants negatively no matter their size or age, but it is especially damaging to young seedlings and plants with weak stems and root systems. After all, winds can blow down even the tallest and strongest of trees, it can do much more to a small seedling.

You may not have a problem with the wind where you live. However, there are places that get strong and damaging winds. Harsh summer winds full of drying heat, and brittle winter winds full of sleet that can freeze the plants. No matter the season, these strong winds will take a toll on your garden. During the colder months of the year, you especially have to take wind chill into account. While it may only be fifty degrees outside, the wind chill could be thirty degrees directly blowing on your crops.

What can you do to protect plants from this wind? Firstly, you may want to add mulch to the garden to protect the topsoil and root system. This will protect some of the most vital and vulnerable portions of your crops. Secondly, one of the most successful ways you can protect your crops from wind damage is with a windbreak. These are walls you can make out of a variety of materials. When the wind blows into the walls it is directly blocked from hitting your crops. These can be used anywhere, but are most often used in rural and open areas with large plains that are easily overcome with gusts of wind. But, even small suburban yards can be affected by gusts of wind if you are in the right or wrong location. Only you will know if where you live has strong winds. Keep an eye on your garden area, along with local weather details, so that you can learn whether or not your garden will be affected with seasonal winds. If you find that you do need a windbreak there are many options. Some people will build a medium-sized wood slat fence. But, you can also use hay or straw bales (be careful to use ones without seeds to prevent weeds), shrubs, densely planted trees, screens, or fabrics.

If you want to build a fabric windshield, you simply place some wooden stakes around your garden, about two to three feet apart each, and wrap burlap or canvas around these steaks. You can keep the fabric in place with the help of a nail gun. Although, you don't have to use fabric, even! Some people have chosen to use thick plastic wrapped around steaks.

Whatever you choose for a windbreak, keep in mind to pick something that fits your space, budget, and time requirements. There are many options and none are right or wrong, you simply need to find what works best for you and your garden.

Drip Irrigation Watering

When trying to keep your plants consistently watered a drip irrigation system can be incredibly helpful. This system allows your plants to be watered precisely and without direct input from you. This system is often placed on a timer, so once you know how frequently and how much water your garden needs you can easily have the timer set to water your plants in the morning while you are asleep or at work or school.

There are other benefits of a drip irrigation system, as well. Which include:

- ☐ **Save Water**

    If you are attempting to save water for the environment, due to a shortage, or to save money then you will be happy to know that studies have found using a drip irrigation system uses between thirty and fifty percent less water than more traditional watering methods, such as sprinklers.

- ☐ **Save Time**

    When you are having to set up and move sprinklers around or stand at a garden bed with a watering hose in hand you are wasting a lot of time that could be used elsewhere. But, with the drip watering system, you will be able to use your time how you like while also keeping your garden well-watered.

- ☐ **Improved Growth**

    Rather than applying a large amount of water in a short period of time, as people often do when watering plants with a hose one by one, drip irrigation systems apply a small amount of water over an extended period of time. This better mimics natural rain conditions and leads to the ideal growth of plants. When you use a drip irrigation system you can prevent nutrient runoff, soil erosion, and over-watering. This system also allows water to slowly penetrate the soil more deeply, allowing the roots to better absorb their needed hydration.

- **Fewer Weeds**
  When water is spread over an entire garden bed it is not only watering your plants, but also the weeds. With this method you are able to target your crops directly, therefore starving the weeds of water.
- **Fewer Fungal Diseases**
  Fungal diseases grow best when they have plenty of moisture. This is often caused by wet leaves and flowers on their crops, which is usually caused when people use more traditional watering methods. But, drip irrigation systems only water the soil around plants, nut their foliage.
- **Adaptable**
  If the requirements of your plants and garden change over the seasons that's okay, as you can easily adapt the drip irrigation system to your needs.

While there are different types of water irrigation systems you can use for your garden, the most popular type are soaker hoses. These hoses have either tiny holes along the length of the hose, or they are made out of a porous material that allows water to slowly leak through. You can place these hoses either on the top of the soil or underneath a layer of mulch where it won't be seen but can still water your plants.

In order to get the best results from your water irrigation system start with these steps and tips:

1. Use Level Ground

Be sure that when you set up the soaker hose that you use the level ground, as these hoses are based on a system that requires a uniform distribution of the water inside of the hose. If there are any dips or slopes on the ground where you have the hose places, then it will force the water to be stronger on one end of the hose. This interferes with the basic principle of the hose, causing one area of the ground to remain mostly dry while another area is over watered. When setting up your soaker hose level out the ground and remove any rocks or sticks that may interfere with the hose staying level.

2. Completely Fill the Hose

For a soaker hose to work it must have the ability to force water through small porous holes in the tubing. But, if there isn't enough water pressure pushing against the hose then it simply will be unable to seep out properly. Therefore, when starting your soaker hose, first let the entire hose's length fill with water. You will know that it is full when the entire hose is cylindrical and does not have any deflated or flat sections. Keep an eye on the hose for a minute and ensure that water begins seeping throughout the entire system.

3. Limit Your Water Source

While soaker hoses have many benefits, there is a limit to what they are able to do. You can connect multiple hose lines to water a large garden. But, you shouldn't connect hoses longer than one-hundred and fifty feet. After this point, you should begin connecting hoses to an additional water source. If you try to have more than one-hundred and fifty feet of soaker hose connected to a single water source, then there will be too little water pressure to properly soak the area as it is supposed to. Therefore, carefully choose your soaker hose layout, especially when you are planning to water a larger garden.

4. Avoid High Water Pressure

Due to the previous tip, some people may simply try to increase the water pressure so that they can have more than one-hundred and fifty feet connected to a single water source. But, it is a bad idea to try to force more water into the soaker hose with a higher pressure. This is because these hoses work much like a balloon. These hoses are made with approximately seventy percent recycled rubber, so like a balloon, they expand which then allows the water to escape. But, if you force higher pressure water through the hose it will expand too much and in turn, cause the porous holes to expand more. More water than is needed will escape, flooding your garden bed and damaging both the roots of your plants and the hose. Over time, the porous holes will be overly large, unable to go back to their original size. You will be stuck with a hose with holes too big and that possibly cracks or breaks completely.

5. Keep a High Water Source

Some water sources may be placed low on the ground, which then causes the water to be pushed uphill. Due to simple physics and gravity then causes the water to fight harder to go where it is required, as it naturally will want to flow downward instead of upward. This decreases pressure and the amount of water going to your garden bed. Therefore, ensure that whatever water source you use that it is higher than the location of your hose. Ideally, the water source will be in a high spigot off the side of a pole or your house, where it easily travels downward and through the hose, which itself should be on level ground.

6. The Right Timing

Soaker hoses work slowly, giving the roots of your garden the best type of hydration. Although, the time you need to water your garden can be deceptive. Most gardens and lawns require an average of two inches of water each week, more during periods of intense heat which causes the water to evaporate. For a standard soaker hose, which is a five-eighths of an inch, you will need four-hundred minutes for these two inches of water. Keep an eye on your garden to see how it is doing, and if possible try to watch your property's water gauge use so that you can adjust the time to what is best suited for your garden.

7. Testing... Testing... One, Two Three...

Before you bury your soaker hose in mulch or soil, be sure to test it out and see how it works. Watch the water run through it to ensure it has even dispersal, soaks the plants well, and doesn't have any problems. You may want to coil the hose around larger plants or bushes to ensure that they have enough water access for their roots. Once you are sure the hose is finalized, then you can top it with soil or mulch if desired.

Setting up a soaker hose can seem like a lot of work, but slowly it will save you a great deal amount of time and energy. If you don't feel comfortable setting up this system completely on your own, that's okay! There are plenty of soaker hose and water irrigation system kits available on the market that have all the supplies and instructions you need.
Lastly, be careful if you have a latex allergy. Soaker hoses are made of seventy percent recycled latex rubber, and should, therefore, be avoided by anyone with these allergies.

CHAPTER 9
Organic Gardening Tips and Tricks

There are many tips and tricks that can help the organic gardener improve their garden, increase their harvest, and more. In this chapter, we will go over some of the more helpful tips that you may find beneficial in your daily life.

1. Recycle when Sowing Seeds

You can certainly go to the local garden center and buy seed starters to help you sprout your small seeds. But, these are pricier than you have to pay, especially considering that many people have objects around their house that they could recycle. Why pay for more plastic to end up in landfills when you could instead repurpose something you already own but don't need? There are everyday items such as egg cartons, eggshells, citrus peels, empty K-cup containers, bathroom cups, and more.

2. Become Familiar with Organic Fertilizers

There are certainly organic fertilizers on the market. But, rather than using pre-made organic fertilizers, you can make your own. By mixing up your own fertilizer, you can save money and customize it to your garden's needs. There are many options such as compost, tea, Epsom salt, seaweed, and fish emulsions.

3. Recycle Eggshells

There are many nutrients inside an egg. While you are unable to compost eggs themselves for your garden, there are many benefits to adding eggshells. After you use the egg from within the shell, clean and dry the shells before grinding them up. You can then add them to your compost pile or directly to your garden for an increase in calcium.

4. Using Epsom Salt

If you are someone who is interested in living naturally and organically, you probably already love Epsom salt. But, if you are unfamiliar with this amazing product you may want to try using it more. This salt, while great for human use, is also helpful in the garden. By adding this salt to your soil, you can feed your plants nutrients and decrease the shock produced from transplantation. Better yet, this salt can keep pests such as slugs away!

5. Use Essential Oils

Essential oils don't only have to be used on humans! While you shouldn't typically use these oils on animals, there are many beneficial ways you can use them in your garden bed. After all, these oils are derived from plant life and can, in turn, feed more plant life to grow stronger in the future. Why not try using rosemary or peppermint oil to rid your garden of pests? Tea tree oil is powerful against fighting off fungal diseases. Pine will ward off slugs. Peppermint will keep mice and other animals away. And, neroli and lavender will attract bees!

6. Fight Insects with Insects

Pest control is a big concern for many people when gardening, for a good reason. These small bugs and insects can quickly kill a crop. But, it doesn't have to be this way. There are many safe and effective ways in which you can fight off damaging insects such as slugs, aphids, and caterpillars. While there are many options, one of the best and easiest ways to fight off these damaging insects is to introduce their natural predators, helpful insects. You can learn what to plant in order to directly fight off specific insects you are having problems with. For instance, if you plant basil next to tomatoes it can help ward off tomato hornworms. Learn more about using cohort plants that will draw to your garden helpful insects while repelling harmful insects.

7. Rid Your Garden of Aphids

While there are many insects that can destroy crops, one of the worst out there are aphids. These tiny little insects come in the thousands to eat and destroy your harvest and flowers. While you may try to use organic pesticides, these tiny insects have a hard waxy coating on their bodies which protects them from most of these pesticides. Worse yet, they reproduce shockingly fast, making them even harder to rid yourself of. Thankfully, you don't have to let aphids kill your garden.

First, you can add some neem essential oil to water and spray it onto any plants that aphids are attacking. However, avoid spraying plants not affected by aphids, as the neem oil may also cause beneficial insects to keep away.

The larvae of green lacewings eat aphids and are one of the best ways to rid your garden of these pests. To draw lacewings to your garden try planting dill, caraway, cilantro, and fennel. Ladybugs are another helpful insect to keep away the aphids. To draw this cute little bug to your garden plant dill, butterfly weed, cilantro, Queen Anne's lace, and fennel. Lastly, you will want to attract hoverflies to eat the aphids. In order to attract these insects plant dill, caraway, cilantro, fennel, English lavender, lemon balm, spearmint, parsley, and wild bergamot.

8. Keep the Bites at Bay

Gardening is peaceful and relaxing… that is until you begin to get mosquito bites and bugs swarming around you. To save yourself during this season try using natural bug repellents and bug sprays rather than the strongly scented chemical sprays sold at stores.

In order to create a natural bug repellent, combine two ounces of grapeseed or coconut oil in a container with five drops of peppermint, three drops of lavender, three drops of tea tree, two drops of citronella, and lastly four drops of vetiver essential oil. After the mixture is combined you can rub the oil onto your limbs and neck to keep the bugs at bay while you work on your gardening.

9. Feed the Microbes

There are billions of microbes within the soil, which is just as important as the nutrients within the soil. You need to feed these microbes, which include algae, fungi, bacteria, protozoa, and actinomycetes. In order to feed these microbes, combine a gallon of water with a quarter cup of molasses and four cups of compost. Pour this mixture over the garden bed before fully watering the soil. This will allow the mixture to fully be absorbed deeply by the soil, and the molasses will feed the beneficial microbes.

10. Aerate Your Compost

We've talked a lot about how aerating your compost is important. But, a simple trick to improve the air within a new compost heap is to start your pile on top of a bed of sticks and branches. In the center of the pile, place a PVC pipe with holes drilled in its sides, sticking it partially in the ground so it sticks straight up in the air. Place your compost ingredients around the pipe and on top of the sticks and branches, which will increase air flow and therefore helps reduce the time it takes for the ingredients to become fully composted.

11. Invite Toads Over

Toads are wonderful at controlling pests in your garden. They eat plenty of bad bugs and keep the harmful slugs and snails away. Try to attract toads to your garden by adding a little "pond" and a house for them. This pond can be a simple dish that you fill with water and place in a hole in the ground. While toads may not live in the water, they still need a wet environment. This pan of water will give them just what they need. Toads also need cover from the sun and predators, therefore making them a simple house. You can easily build this house by placing an upside-down broken pot on the ground. The pot will need to have a hole in it that is big enough for toads to use as an entrance and exit.

12. Grow Marigolds

Both American and French marigolds are wonderful at killing harmful pests known as nematodes. These are pests that are microscopic, but live in the soil and causes damage to potatoes, tomatoes, and many other crops. Thankfully, the roots of marigolds and their decaying leaves and flowers release chemicals within the soil that kill nematodes. If you plant these flowers around plants that are susceptible to nematodes you can protect them.

13. Rotate Crops

Plants that are in the same family and closely related are often affected by the same diseases. If you continue to grow plants from the same family in the same location year after year, they can develop diseases and reduce nutrients within the soil. This is especially true for nightshades such as tomatoes, peppers, potatoes, eggplants and squash family which contains summer and winter squash, cucumber, and watermelon. Therefore, to increase nutrients and prevent disease it is best to rotate crops from year to year. For instance, don't plant nightshades in the same location each year, move them to another portion of your garden and plant another type of vegetable where they had previously grown.

14. Prioritize Cleanliness

When leaves and flowers fall off of the plants in your garden, they can quickly become diseases and infect your other plants with fungi or bacteria. Therefore, walk through your garden daily and pick up any fallen foliage you see to prevent this disease.

CHAPTER 10

Problem-Solving

Organic gardening is a wonderful experience which greatly benefits your mental and physical health. Not only will this gardening provide you and your family with a wealth of food and nutrients, but it will also provide you with physical exercise and peaceful relaxation. But, there are always hurdles to overcome no matter what your hobby is, and the same is true for gardening. Thankfully, in this chapter, we will go over some common problems and their solutions so that you can have the best chance for success.

1. Black Rings at the Base of Tomatoes

When you discover there are black rings on the bottom of your tomatoes, it is caused by blossom end rot. This condition is due to a lack of needed calcium within the blossom of the tomato fruit while blooming. The lack of calcium is often a result of irregular watering. While a difficult condition for tomatoes, thankfully, it is not a disease and will not spread to other vegetables or fruits.

Don't allow your tomato plants to dry out, they need about an inch or two of water weekly. When watering, stick to a regular schedule so that the calcium becomes easily dispersed throughout the soil. You may also increase the calcium content in your soil by adding powdered limestone and ground up eggshells.

2. Squash Plants Dying

If your squash plants are dying for no known reason, then it may be due to an insect known as the squash vine borer. This is the worm of a moth that burrows into the stem of squash plants and then hollows them out. You will find that this is one of the most difficult problems to treat, as by the time you can diagnose what is wrong it has already killed your plant. The squash vine borer is also difficult to prevent. Therefore, you may want to try to grow pest-resistant varieties of squash.

It may also help to plant your squash as early in the season as possible, as well as planting nasturtiums and radishes near them which will further deter pests. While it may not prevent all cases of these insects, by wrapping the stems of the squash plants in foil you may be able to deter some of them.

3. Plants Aren't Growing

When your plants simply aren't growing, it is usually due to inhospitable soil which hasn't been fully prepared. You will need to till the soil and break up any red clay that may be blocking the roots from growing and add plenty of nutrients with compost. It can further help if you add a couple of pounds of red worms, which will help keep the soil loose.

4. Rabbit Invasion

Even if you live in an urban or city environment, you aren't immune to having rabbits in your garden. If you don't have raised beds or a fence around your garden, then rabbits can invade and eat young and tender plants before they have a chance to mature. If you are having problems with rabbits, then you can place some chicken wire around your beds. If you are having animals dig into the garden bed, then try digging a foot-deep perimeter around the garden bed and burying a foot of chicken wire to prevent voles and moles from digging in. You may also try placing more delicate crops, such as berries and lettuce, in container gardens to keep natural predators away.

5. Soggy Soil

If you live somewhere that has a rainy season during the prime growing months then you may want to try raised garden beds. These beds will allow for the soil to dry out more quickly due to increased air circulation and better soil drainage. You may also avoid using mulch during these months, as mulch increases moisture.

You may also begin your seeds indoors instead of outdoors, to prevent seeds from being washed away or rotting. Once the seedlings are strong, you can transplant them outside.

6. Short Summers

If you live somewhere with a short growing season, it is vital that you begin your seeds indoors. These locations, whether it is due to high elevation or northern temperatures, have short seasons that simply won't allow for seeds to fully grow outdoors and then produce a full harvest. But, if you start the seeds inside and then move them outside after the last frost you will be able to enjoy the full fruits of your labor.

7. Fleeing Soil Nutrients

If you find your plants aren't growing well, it may be due to the soil's nutrients being washed away. This is because when a location experiences fifty inches or more of rain, the nutrients get washed to lower lying soil. But, if you frequently add organic matter, compost, seaweed, limestone, and fish emulsions then you will be able to greatly increase the number of nutrients within the soil.

To prepare your garden space you will want to get to work two months prior to planting your crop. At this point, add nutrients to your soil and mix it together well. This will give it time to be fully prepared for your crop. Once you plant your crop, add in further nutrients and continue to add every couple of months.

8. Grow Season After Season

There are many areas in the world where you can work to garden year-long if you take the time to plan ahead and study your calendar. You can enjoy many of the cool season crops not only in spring but also in autumn and winter if you live somewhere with a more temperate climate. If you live somewhere with harsher summers, such as in Texas, you can experience a summer almost double its usual length, giving you plenty of time to harvest tomatoes, melons, peppers, and cucumbers. These warmer climates also make growing throughout the winter easier, as they often have a later first frost and early last frost.

9. Cloudy and Cool Environments

Many areas, such as Washington and Oregon have gray cloudy and cool days. This may make growing tomatoes and peppers more difficult, but don't let this make you believe that your area isn't suited to gardening. In fact, there are many cool crops such as dark greens, cabbage, artichokes, asparagus, and raspberries that grow wonderfully well in these areas. Furthermore, blueberries and potatoes do great with the acidic soil in these regions.

10. Winter Crops

There are some crops that simply do terribly in the heat. But, if you live somewhere with a hot climate then you can make use of your mild winters and autumns in order to continue growing throughout the entirety of the cold seasons. While lettuces, broccoli, and cabbages usually only grow during the autumn and spring, you will be able to fully enjoy them throughout the winter, as well.

CONCLUSION

You now have all of the tools you need to begin your journey with organic gardening. There is a lot that can go into making your garden the best it can possibly be. But, with the knowledge you now have, you can make a garden that thrives much more than the typical crop. By choosing an organic lifestyle, you can benefit the environment and improve your health, well-being, and your finances and your family as well. You may have to spend a little money upfront to purchase the seeds and other items needed for your garden, but before long you will find that you can experience financial savings up to tenfold with the produce you will harvest. As if that weren't beneficial enough, you won't believe how much better fresh organic food tastes straight from the garden! Even children who are usually picky will find themselves enjoy new fruits and vegetables.

It takes time to grow a healthy garden, but if you focus on the soil and water health, you will find the rest comes along much more easily. Be sure to use plenty of compost, fish emulsions, mulch, and water each plant regularly according to its individual care instructions. Even if you are too busy to regularly water your plants, that's okay. You can always try using a drip irrigation system which will water them for you and take the work off of your shoulders.

What are you waiting for? You have all of the tools you need to begin your road to success and health. Before long you will know first-hand the benefits of organic gardening and never want to go back. Thank you for reading *Organic Gardening for Beginners*, I hope that your organic gardening journey is full of peace and enjoyment.

DESCRIPTION

Whether you are new to being organic or an old pro, there are many benefits to adding an organic garden to your backyard, patio, windowsill, or even driveway. You don't have to have a large backyard or a large wallet for that matter to benefit from this method. You don't even have to spend that much time for daily maintenance if you know the right tricks. At first, going organic may seem like a handful, but you will soon learn that this process can be much simpler and fulfilling than you might think. By taking up organic gardening, you can find therapeutic peace while tending your gardening, increased physical exercise, recycle waste to turn into compost rather than allowing it to build up in landfills, lower the number of chemical-based pesticides and herbicides in the environment, and find increased health for both you and your loved ones as you are provided with nutritious and flavorful harvest season after season.

Whether you choose to use a traditional garden bed, raised beds, container gardening, or square foot gardening, you will learn in this book all the tricks you need to have a healthy and thriving crop and harvest. No longer will you have to rely on the chemical-laden and taste-deficient vegetables and fruits from the grocery store. By choosing organic gardening, you will be able to grow fresh produce free of nasty chemicals, full of nutrients, and bursting with flavor. Traveling no further than your backyard to your dining room table, this produce will be the freshest food you've ever enjoyed.

With the easy to understand and helpful knowledge presented in this book, there is no reason to not practice organic gardening. If you choose to take up this practice, you will thank yourself later. Are you ready for a better and healthier life?

In This Book You Will Find:
- ☐ The benefits of going organic
- ☐ The disastrous effects of man-made chemical pesticides
- ☐ The basic approach to the organic gardening method
- ☐ The importance of creating a rich and healthy soil, and how to make a healthy garden bed no matter your soil conditions
- ☐ How to recycle to begin composting
- ☐ Easily and effectively controlling weeds
- ☐ Growing plants from seeds, seedlings, and clippings
- ☐ How to effectively grow in a container

- ☐ Square foot gardening and how you can a large harvest with little space
- ☐ Easy fruits, vegetables, and herbs for beginners to start with
- ☐ How to keep your plants healthy and thriving
- ☐ Organic tips and tricks
- ☐ Solutions to common garden problems
- ☐ *And more...*

ORGANIC VEGETABLE GARDENING

Beginner's Guide to Quickly Learn and Master How to Grow Your Own Vegetables and How to Start a Healthy Garden at Home

By
Rachel Martin

© Copyright 2019 by Rachel Martin - All rights reserved.

This content is provided with the sole purpose of providing relevant information on a specific topic for which every reasonable effort has been made to ensure that it is both accurate and reasonable. Nevertheless, by purchasing this content you consent to the fact that the author, as well as the publisher, are in no way experts on the topics contained herein, regardless of any claims as such that may be made within. As such, any suggestions or recommendations that are made within are done so purely for entertainment value. It is recommended that you always consult a professional prior to undertaking any of the advice or techniques discussed within.

This is a legally binding declaration that is considered both valid and fair by both the Committee of Publishers Association and the American Bar Association and should be considered as legally binding within the United States.

The reproduction, transmission, and duplication of any of the content found herein, including any specific or extended information will be done as an illegal act regardless of the end form the information ultimately takes. This includes copied versions of the work both physical, digital and audio unless express consent of the Publisher is provided beforehand. Any additional rights reserved.

Furthermore, the information that can be found within the pages described forthwith shall be considered both accurate and truthful when it comes to the recounting of facts. As such, any use, correct or incorrect, of the provided information will render the Publisher free of responsibility as to the actions taken outside of their direct purview. Regardless, there are zero scenarios where the original author or the Publisher can be deemed liable in any fashion for any damages or hardships that may result from any of the information discussed herein.

Additionally, the information in the following pages is intended only for informational purposes and should thus be thought of as universal. As befitting its nature, it is presented without assurance regarding its prolonged validity or interim quality. Trademarks that are mentioned are done without written consent and can in no way be considered an endorsement from the trademark holder.

INTRODUCTION

Never has the time been riper to embark upon the joyful challenge of growing your own vegetables—organically, healthfully—at home. This book will guide you through the process, from the basics of why and how to the fruitful activities of harvesting and preserving.

First, we will begin with a quick overview of *what* it means to garden organically, *why* it is important, and *how* to do it simply and skillfully. From there, we will tackle some basics: preparing the soil and sourcing the seeds get the garden off the ground, literally. Next, determining what vegetables and herbs to grow is obviously fundamental and, certainly, a big part of the fun of gardening; customizing your garden is one of the pleasures of having one. Once the basics are in place, planning for the inevitable—if you build it, the pests will come—becomes a necessary task, albeit one more welcome than it might at first seem. As you start to garden, you will find that combating garden nuisances brings out the innovative best in many of us.

Next, we will examine the best ways to keep the garden healthy throughout the growing season and, more importantly, how to harvest and utilize your bounty. This includes some ideas for simple recipes and longer term preservation: unearthing a bag of vine-ripened roasted tomatoes from your freezer in the middle of February is akin to harnessing the summer sunshine. And, of course, sustaining a garden throughout all four seasons is the ideal.

Last, a look back on what has been accomplished and the impact it creates in our lives and for our world: From the back yard to the table, growing your own vegetable garden is a wonderful way to sustain yourself and all those you love.

CHAPTER 1

The Basics of Why & How: Organic 101

What Is Organic Gardening?

The U.S. Department of Agriculture, under the auspices of the National Organic Program (NOP), determines the definition and regulation of how the term organic is used and labeled in our food supply. To put it simply, the term organic indicates foods that have been grown or raised without the use of genetically modified organisms (GMOs), sewer sludge—many industrial farms water their crops with treated sewage runoff—and, in the case of meat products, irradiation.

The NOP also requires organic crops to be grown without the use of petroleum-based or otherwise synthesized fertilizers and pesticides, though these rules are subject to modification every five years, and the NOP has come under criticism for allowing small amounts of synthetic materials to be used even under the label "organic." The NOP also oversees the nationwide certification program by which a farm attains the "certified organic" label. Be aware, however, that the certification process is lengthy and costly, so many smaller farms—such as those who sell at local farmers' markets—may in practice follow the regulations for growing organic crops but do not actually hold a certification. If you buy at local farmers' markets, which I urge you to do as most home gardeners cannot grow everything they might want for their table, simply ask your farmer what kind of chemicals and methods he or she uses at their farm. If a local farmer sprays a typical pesticide once a year, it is still far healthier than buying an industrially farmed product that is constantly sprayed.

For the home gardener, this all becomes pretty simple: in order to garden organically, you simply need to avoid synthetic fertilizers in favor of natural ones, such as compost (which will be discussed in the next chapter), and synthetic pesticides. The home gardener need not worry about sewer sludge, one assumes, though locating your garden away from neighborhood ponds or parks is always a good idea, as areas that are kept up by communities or government-run entities often use synthetic materials; avoiding runoff ensures that your garden maximizes its healthy, organic potential.

Why Garden Organically?

As most of us are very much aware, the ills of industrial agriculture are well documented. The use of petroleum-based fertilizers and pesticides are destructive to the environment—the soil, the air, groundwater—as well as being a non-renewable resource fraught with the political implications of how and where oil is obtained. In addition, most of us are aware that the health costs of eating produce laden with chemicals are certainly significant, especially so for children. As a pediatrician, I once knew put it bluntly: "I would not feed my children a non-organic apple." There are other factors involved in the industrial production of our food supply that are also worth mentioning and should give us reason to rethink our food choices. Some prime examples include the simple matter of taste, the imprint of our carbon footprint, the danger of monocultures, the unknown threats levied by GMOs, and the unseen costs of human rights abuses.

- **Taste**: While many might argue that taste is subjective, a matter of personal opinion, when it comes to a homegrown, vine-ripened tomato, I defy anyone to compare it to a supermarket tomato and give an unfavorable review to the backyard version. Supermarket tomatoes have been bred for hardiness, so they can be harvested easily and shipped for long distances, not taste. They are most often picked off the vine while green—this allows for the use of machine harvesters which essentially knock the unripe tomatoes to the ground; ripe tomatoes would splat—and ship them in trucks that spray them with manufactured ethylene gas to artificially make them appear "ripe." What you are buying at the grocery store is an unripe, sour, bland tomato that has been mechanically coaxed into blushing slightly. While here the tomato provides the example, it can easily be extrapolated to include any number of vegetables and fruits that are grown for convenient consumption rather than satisfying flavor.
- **Carbon Footprint**: As the above example acknowledges, with industrial agriculture, shipping becomes of primary concern. Most of our produce is grown elsewhere unless you happen to live in parts of California or Florida. Thus, our fruits and vegetables are grown for hardiness not only with regard to disease or pests but also for their ability to withstand the rigors of shipping. So, the carbon footprint left behind by the average American table is quite concerning: fertilizers and pesticides used notwithstanding, the oil used in transport is staggering. In fact, industrial agriculture is considered to be the second largest contributor to greenhouse gases, second only to the energy industry.
- **Monocultures**: Another danger involved in the intensive farming that is the hallmark of industrial agriculture is the creation of monocultures. This is when a particular crop, usually one particular strain, is grown extensively over a large area of land. The traditional American farm consisted of many different crops, as well as livestock, working together in harmony: the fertilizer created by the livestock nurtured the variety of produce grown which, in turn, fed both the animals and the family. On

contemporary industrial farms, one product is grown exclusively—think of the wheat fields of Kansas (now mostly soybean fields, actually), stretching as far as the eye can see. This is true not only of grain crops but also of tomatoes, apples, citrus, and many other varieties of produce. The danger in monocultures is that, when one kind of crop is grown intensively in one area, it depletes the soil of nutrients and becomes increasingly vulnerable to disease. For example, in recent years, we have seen banana crops—grown intensively in tropical regions—virtually wiped out in places because of disease: when one strain of banana, the Cavendish, supplanted most other strains, the crops became vulnerable to a quick-spreading fungal invasion. Monocultures are always at risk, on the verge of extinction.

- **Genetically Modified Organisms**: While the effects of the widespread use of genetically modified organisms (GMOs) are still largely unknown, the dangers that are present in the practice of monoculture farming are similar to that created by GMO farming, the susceptibility to disease and the depletion of the soil. In addition, the use of GMOs also brings with it a host of other potential threats, not least of them the invasiveness of some of these crops. For one example, Monsanto created a genetically modified corn crop that was so successful, its seeds invaded other fields in many areas, choking out the more traditional breeds. It should be noted that this particular strain of corn was bred to resist the weed killer, Roundup (called "Roundup ready," there are several crops that were genetically modified in this manner); this allowed farmers to spray their fields with weed killer throughout the growing season without harming the corn (or canola, or soybean, etc.). As well, Monsanto patents these products which means that farmers cannot use their seeds without paying for them—and must buy new seeds every year, as the plant is also bred to be sterile—and at least one farmer has been sued by the corporation because Roundup ready plants were found in his field, his seeds being contaminated by the GMO version. Thus, the increasingly widespread use of GMOs represents the continuing intensification of corporate control over our farms and crops, as well as posing potential threats to our health. The FDA does not require testing on humans before GMO crops are approved, and furthermore, does not require products containing GMOs to be labeled.
- **Labor Issues**: The last problematic symptom of the ills of industrial agriculture is one of the least talked about and largely unseen concerns, that of human rights abuses. While many of us are aware that a great deal of agricultural labor which has not been mechanized is done by migrants, few of us know of the

conditions under which many of these laborers must endure. Many of the migrant laborers who work in the field could actually be considered indentured servants. These vulnerable men and women are lured onto farms with promises of decent pay for hard work, yet they find themselves trapped into paying exorbitant rents for shacks without running water or electricity while making just a few dollars a day. Bosses often give them "advances" on their meager pay so the laborers can purchase food or liquor, which leaves them in debt. There are also reports of physical abuse if workers do not move fast enough or work hard enough. A full account of what goes on at some farms is exposed in detail in Barry Estabrook's thorough account of the tomato-farming industry, *Tomatoland*.

All of that said, the advantages of home gardening organically seem clear: you can avoid the potential health risks of exposure to petrochemicals and the ethical conundrums involved in the practices of industrial agriculture all the while growing much tastier, more beautiful, and most satisfying food. The benefit to yourself, your family, and your environment cannot be overstated, and even the smallest of gardens have an outsized impact. So, let us tackle the logistics and get started today!

How to Garden Organically?

Even if you have never gardened, doing so organically is not terribly complicated, though knowing a few ground rules certainly eases the process. And, if you have gardened in the past but wish to do so a little more healthfully now, then the transition will be particularly easy. In the next chapter, we will start to look more specifically into the basics of *organic* gardening, but to begin, let us take a look at what we might need to think about to get a garden of any kind growing.

First, any good gardener worth his or her salt should invest in **quality tools**. Visit your local gardening emporium or, if necessary, for convenience and cost-effectiveness, a big box mart for advice and products. A handy list of some basic tools you will want to acquire follows.

- **Small Shed:** This may not be a necessary item for the lucky gardener with plenty of convenient, non-used garage space, but for many of us it will become a crucial item. If you garden in your backyard, as quite a lot of us do, with a garage in the front of the house, then a storage shed on the back porch can be a huge timesaver. Not only will everything be readily at hand, but this setup also allows for ease of organization. Sturdy plastic sheds can be purchased relatively inexpensively at any number of garden centers. I went without for my first two seasons of gardening and was amazed at the increase in my efficiency (along with a decrease in my irritation) by getting one and keeping it well organized.

- **GLOVES!:** This comes in at the top of my list because their importance cannot be overstated. It is difficult to garden with a missing fingernail or cuts all over your hands (though getting some dirt under the nails can make one feel accomplished). I'd recommend more than one kind of glove: a thin pair of washable gloves that allow for dexterity when planting seeds and fine weeding; some latex gloves for wet jobs or weeding amongst thorny plants; and a pair of heavy leather gloves for tough jobs like digging large holes, moving soil, or raking. If you have sensitive skin—cucumber and tomato vines are quite prickly—you might also want to invest in some elasticized arm protectors (or an old long-sleeved shirt and some sturdy rubber bands).
- **Shovels:** Round-headed shovels are best for all-purpose work, like digging holes and moving soil or compost. Make sure to get a sturdy one and keep it clean after use, to prolong its life. Steelheads are typically sturdier than aluminum.
- **Rakes:** There are two types of long-handled rakes useful for gardening in general: a lightweight leaf rake for raking leaves and grass clippings and a bow rake for leveling soil and spreading compost and mulch. For the vegetable gardener, a hand rake also comes in handy for close work, such as removing debris from around the base of a plant without damaging stalks or roots.
- **Hand Trowel:** This is used for digging small, precise holes for planting and close weeding. A hori-hori knife of Japanese origin can be used in the same way as a hand trowel, with the added advantage of having a saw blade when needed to divide young plants.
- **Shears and Scissors:** a good pair of shears is especially useful at the end of the gardening season, to cut down any dead or dying vines; it is also great for pruning should you have larger items in your garden, such as hedges, to tackle. Designating a sturdy pair of scissors for garden work is indispensable for clipping tender herbs and pruning back delicate plants.
- **Pruners:** while a solid set of shears and scissors works for most vegetable gardening, a sturdy pruner is sometimes necessary when growing larger plants and bushes. It can be used to cut thicker branches, and if you get a long-handled one, to prune trees.
- **Transplant Spade:** this tool is like a larger, longer handled trowel and saves the back when transplanting a lot of young plants at one time. Recommended if you intend your garden to be large.
- **Digging Fork:** this is used to move loose soil and turn it over. There are short handled forks and long-handled forks. I tend to

use a short handled one for close work while a bow rake suits most other tasks.
- **Watering Solutions:** The most basic watering tool for the casual backyard gardener is the garden hose; and this, certainly, will work for any gardener with the time to spend watering thoroughly. It served me well, along with a handheld watering can and a water breaker attachment (which provides a gentle even flow of water to avoid damaging plants), for a few years. But, when I finally invested in a soaker system—or, drip irrigation—I was pleased and relieved: just turning on the hose for 30 minutes in the morning (and another 30 in the early evening during hot weather) did the trick while I could do other things. This is a more expensive option, but it is well worth it for the serious home gardener, especially if you live in drought-prone areas.
- **Composting Solutions:** If you truly want to garden organically, you absolutely must invest in some sort of composter. There are numerous models on the market with prices varying from the modest to the expensive, from the small indoor to the large outdoor. However, while most of these models are fuss-free and efficient, it is also possible to make your own composter with a few simple items. In the next chapter, the basics of composting are discussed in detail.

Second, it helps for the home gardener to have some reliable resources on hand—such as this book!—to consult for advice and troubleshooting. Besides this book, below is a list of some other resources available to most home gardeners.
- **Local Stores:** In the age of online shopping, which admittedly cannot be paralleled in terms of ease and convenience, it is still important to remember that your local store can give specific and useful advice. Typically, the proprietor knows the area and what works best in said area. As well, frequenting a particular business with regularity forms a lasting relationship, wherein a past purchase leads to a present conversation which prevents a future problem.
- **Farmers' Markets:** If you have the pleasure to enjoy a farmers' market in your area, it behooves you to frequent it and become friendly with your local farmers. Most farmers at the market are huge proponents of backyard gardens, seeing them not as competition but as bedfellows in a project to create a healthier and more environmentally friendly world. As well, they are purveyors of much wisdom and will often happily pass said advice along. In addition, many farmers welcome visitors to the farm and, if your market boasts any organic farm stands, I urge you to visit and to ask many questions. They can assist you in almost every aspect of farming, from what and when to plant, to how

much and when to water, to combating disease and pests, to harvesting and preparing what you grow. And, you can procure many lovely vegetables and fruits (or humanely produced meat, eggs, milk, cheese, honey) that you don't happen to have in your backyard.

- **Co-op Research and Extension Services:** The USDA sponsors a nationwide network of agricultural resources through their co-op and extension services. Essentially, it assists local cooperatives—farms, educational institutions, markets, and other cooperative businesses—in research and development related to agriculture and human health. If you live near a Land-Grant institution, you more than likely live near an extension service, which houses local cooperative members in order to assist with disseminating knowledge throughout the community on such topics as sustainable agriculture and food safety and quality. These resources can help you by testing your soil's pH, for example, or providing seminars on organic gardening, or bringing together local gardeners to create a network of support. If you don't have an extension service near you, there are resources online. Check out https://www.usda.gov/topics/rural/cooperative-research-and-extension-services for links.

Third, you must challenge yourself to put words into action: now that you have the tools and resources ready at hand to get started, the next two chapters will guide you through the process of setting up your garden, from preparing the soil and handling seeds to choosing what plants work well together. The great outdoors is calling: let us answer!

CHAPTER 2

Soil And Seeds: Getting Started

The first step to beginning a garden is setting one up in a satisfactory location with a solid foundation; depending on where you live, there are many ways this can be achieved. Then, focus on the soil; this is one of the keys to successful organic gardening, maximizing compost and other organic fertilizers to create a rich and bountiful bed for your vegetables. Once you have your location set up and your soil in place, then you can turn to procuring seeds, nurturing seedlings, and handling transplants.

Foundation: Setting Up Strong

How you set up your garden is most often dictated by where you live. For many of us, the backyard is the best place to set up a garden—though there is a growing movement among some environmentalists to turn all lawn areas into gardens—but you can also successfully garden on a balcony or terrace, even indoors. Light exposure should be one of your first considerations, as most vegetable plants require a certain amount of direct sun during the growing season. With indoor gardening, that can be achieved via a sunny windowsill or, less alluring but workable, with grow lights.

If you plan to set up a garden in the backyard, you must first decide how big your plot will be. I started with a small 8' by 4' plot, just for herbs, chiles, and a couple of tomato plants then expanded with an additional 12' by 4' plot for lettuces, peas, beans, and a variety of other vegetable plants. The size is completely up to you, depending on your yard and your ambition for how much you'd like to grow in the garden. Also remember that, while you can certainly follow some tips for how to maximize space (addressed throughout this book), you also need to be aware not to overcrowd. Staggered planting is the best way to achieve maximum harvest for a small plot: for example, direct seed young lettuces in your garden while you tend to tomato and chile seedlings indoors; once your lettuces are harvested—they will not withstand the heat of summer—transplant your seedlings. Other plants are good for overwintering, such as garlic, when the garden has exhausted its summer heights of production.

Another consideration for setting up your garden is understanding your area's climate or **USDA Plant Hardiness Zone**. There are roughly 11 zones in the United States, which essentially tracks average temperatures throughout the country, with Zone 1 having the coldest average temperatures and Zone 11 having the warmest (click here for a link to the most current USDA map). The zone map does not necessarily track weather patterns other than temperature, however, or note the effects that altitude can have on a growing season. Still, it gives you a rough idea of what plants are most suitable for your area, as well as what times of year one might plant various crops. This is where a resource such as a local garden shop or extension service (see the previous chapter) will come in handy. I have mostly gardened in Zone 7 and have long followed the local wisdom to not plant delicate seedlings before tax day; there's always a chance for an unexpected freeze around Easter Time.

Another issue of note is the quality and kind of soil in your area (obviously, we will discuss how to enhance this below, but nonetheless it is important to note what you're starting with), as well as rainfall averages. This can determine whether you can simply till up a plot of your backyard, add some compost and organic fertilizer, and garden as is. For many if not most places, however, it makes more sense to make a raised bed garden. The raised bed garden has the advantage of allowing water to drain more effectively through the soil—especially if you live in areas where the soil is clay-based—and demarcates a specific area for your garden, not necessarily the backyard. It also means that you more effectively control the quality of soil in which you are cultivating your vegetables; this may be of concern in heavily suburban areas where contamination of the soil by lawn care and other factors—public parks, ponds, golf courses—are of concern. A raised bed also allows for greater distribution of even sunlight.

There are many raised bed options for purchase on the market, some of them raised so far up that the need to bend over is eliminated (though these are for very small-scale operations, for the most part). You can also create your own with a bit of ingenuity and a little extra effort. I like to get untreated, rot-resistant wood planks from a good local source and shingle these together until the bed, once filled with compost and soil, will be about 12" from the subsoil. A quality drill and some rebar can anchor this bed to the ground, with the added benefit that the rebar above the surface allows you to put up some kind of fencing to keep small animals out. Keep the raised bed narrow so that you don't have to walk into the garden, for the most part, and if you put up fencing, cut in a small gate so that you have easy access to the interior when necessary.

Two other concerns for setting up a garden, raised bed or not, are how to get rid of grass, should you be planting in a yarded area, and how to water effectively. To get rid of grass, it is certainly possible to cut out sod and roll it away, though not very practical for the home gardener. What is easier, though not foolproof, is to line your garden bed with cardboard or landscaping fabric before you add your topsoil—though if your concerns are to remain truly organic, be sure to check what these products are made from or treated with. The other effective deterrent to grass is mulch; after planting, keeping a nice layer of organic mulch throughout the garden not only prevents excessive grass growth but also helps to retain moisture and maintain temperature.

When setting up your garden, think carefully about how you intend to water. Installing a drip irrigation system at the beginning of the growing season is highly recommended, though not absolutely necessary. The advantages of drip irrigation, soaker hoses and spot watering emitters, are that it more effectively conserves water than spraying a garden with your hose and that it saves a lot of time throughout the growing season. Another consideration for a watering system is whether or not to use a rain barrel. This collects rainwater, which you can hook up to your hose or irrigation system, for use in watering your garden. It is ecologically sound and efficient, though impractical for areas that get little in the way of rainfall.

Last, consider the pot: if you don't have the space to dig a plot or install a raised bed, you can always garden using pots made of natural or recycled materials. Even if you do have a garden plot in the backyard, pots are an excellent way to grow vegetables and herbs that are sensitive to too much light and heat or have a tendency to take over spaces where they are planted. For example, tender herbs like parsley and chives are sensitive to heat in the height of summer, if they are in pots, they can be moved to shadier areas during the day. And remember that mint—wonderful to use when freshly grown and occurring in a mind-boggling array of varieties (chocolate, lemon, lime, pineapple, to name a few)—will dominate any area in which it is grown. It is always a safer bet to set any mint varietal aside in a pot.

Soil: Food for Plants

Now that you have your garden location set up, the focus turns to the soil, the key to creating a strong and vibrant garden. When gardening organically, the importance of composting cannot be overstated. Not only is it the most successful way to improve and enrich your soil, but it is also environmentally friendly and cost-effective.

Obviously, in your first year of gardening, you must first provide some topsoil, whether from your own backyard or via a garden sourcing outlet. Over time, you may produce enough compost to replenish your soil each year, while adding some organic fertilizers when and if necessary, but at first build a strong foundation. Source your topsoil from a reputable local source or from a garden center that carries organic potting soil. Then, add your compost and get started.

Basically, **composting** is the method by which you break down organic matter—grass, leaves, food waste—into a kind of fertilizer. The goal is to achieve a balance of particular elements that encourage plant growth and, in some cases, discourage pests and disease. Essentially, compositing takes time, some management, and a conscientious view of reusing materials.

Again, there are many varieties of composters on the market, and many are reasonably priced. The advantage to some of these models for purchase is that they can shorten the amount of time it takes to create usable compost. For compost to be useful to your soil, it must have a suitable time and enough internal heat to break down; thus, for first time gardeners who wish to compost in do-it-yourself mode, you must either start composting about a year before you plan to garden (or less with some composting models: check into manufacturer's claims carefully) or buy your compost from a reputable source.

Truly, composting can be virtually cost-free and simple for the do-it-yourself gardener. It simply requires an out of the way space—naturally, composting does give off some odor as it is working and can attract bugs—some basic materials, and patience. I have made my own composting set up using rebar, chicken wire, and dark plastic sheeting: plant the rebar sturdily into the ground in a wide circle (about the size of a backyard garbage can), then wrap it in chicken wire and cover the wire in dark material (recycled plastic works well). The dark covering traps in heat and encourages the aerobic breakdown of the material you put in the composter, while the chicken wire allows for adequate oxygen and moisture levels to penetrate. While not absolutely necessary, a nice covering—I used an untreated round of cedar wood, with a loop of rope for a handle—can speed up the process slightly and keep odor down.

What to put in your composter is simple, but it does require some balance. Lawn cuttings can be put in a composter but beware of overwhelming your compost with cuttings from each mowing throughout the year. Also note whether the grass you are putting in the compost has been treated with petrochemicals, such as fertilizer or herbicides. Leaves raked from the yard near the end of the growing season is an excellent source of compost, but again consider what kind of chemicals the trees in your area may have been treated with. And, of course, food scraps are imperative to creating compost rich in nitrogen: vegetable scraps, fruit peels, coffee grounds (and filters, if organically produced), egg shells, and so on. Avoid meat and dairy products, as these take much longer to break down and can attract a host of unwanted pests.

The ideal is to create a ratio between "green" compost—food scraps, grass clippings, and the like—and "brown" compost—leaves, newspaper, untreated cardboard. Typically, a ratio of 1:3 is ideal (one part green compost to three parts brown compost), but it isn't crucial to be exacting. Basically, green compost heats things up, creating nitrogen and protein, while brown compost adds bulk and carbon to your compost while keeping down the odor. I highly recommend having a kitchen top composter to throw in your scraps while cooking that you can then transfer once or twice a week to your outdoor unit: this convenient setup ensures you keep your composter full and your trash can relatively empty. These units are moderately priced and are available at many garden stores and online.

How does one know when compost is ready? Essentially, it should be broken down by about half, should look like topsoil with few if any individual particles are recognizable, and should have lost any odor other than an earthy soil smell. When mixing in your compost at the beginning of the growing season, take from the bottom up, and leave behind whatever top layer has accumulated in the few months prior. Again, some commercial composters will not require that you take this step.

While compost is the key ingredient to your topsoil, you can also consider other **organic fertilizers**, such as manure and certain meals, to accelerate the health and growth potential of your garden. Manure is the most common addition to gardens, considered a complete fertilizer with lots of organic matter. Never use fresh manure in your garden during the growing season, as this can contaminate plants and lead to illness for anyone consuming them.

Organic bone meal and blood meal can also be used to assist your soil's potential: bone meal contains calcium and phosphate and promotes strong root health, while blood meal is high in nitrogen and stimulates leaf growth (though too much can burn plant roots, so apply judiciously). There are also fish and seaweed-based meals and emulsions for the garden. I can attest personally to the efficacy of fish skeletons: after a particularly successful fishing season, I will keep my fish scraps, frozen, until the end of growing season then simply till them into the soil before overwintering (even throwing in some past-their-prime whole carcasses). This technique has led to some of my lushest gardens.

Last, one option to consider when starting an organic garden is to get your **soil tested**. Finding out the pH of your soil can help you determine what kinds of organic fertilizers and how much compost to add. This can be done at an extension center (see Chapter 1) or at some local gardening centers; home testing kits are also increasingly available. What this test will tell you is how acidic or alkaline your soil is: most plants prefer a soil that is very slightly acidic with a pH of about 6.5 (7 is considered neutral). This is the level at which the most important nutrients, including nitrogen and potassium, are most available to plants. Usually, lime is used to treat acidic soils, while sulfur is used to treat alkaline soils. This is where an extension center becomes very useful, as their testing can pinpoint exactly what nutrients your soil lacks and/or what nutrients are too prominent. Thus, you can amend your soil with more or less of whatever specific nutrient you may need, different plants requiring different amounts, an issue that will be discussed in the next chapter.

Seeds: Nurturing Success

There are many venues from which to procure seeds, such as via seed catalogs, local farms, and seed saving. Remember that, when attempting to garden organically, the seeds themselves must come from an organic source; this does not mean that hybrids cannot be used, but it does bar the use of genetically modified seeds. Thankfully, GMO seeds are not much of a problem for the home gardener, as they are typically relegated to large industrial crops, such as corn and canola, but it does not hurt to check. Some tomato varieties—the Flavr Savr, for example—are indeed GMO products, and the FDA has recently approved GMO potatoes for market.

But, for the home gardener, the biggest decision will be whether to use heirloom varieties—which are older varieties passed down through generations—or hybridized seeds. Heirloom varieties are wonderful and can expand our experience of what certain vegetables taste like, though they can be hard to grow if they are not originally local to your area. Hybridized varieties are typically hardier but can be less impressive than heirlooms. For the first time gardener, I would recommend sourcing some of both, to ensure maximum harvest while providing a valuable learning experience.

To clarify, the difference between GMO seeds and hybridized seeds is that one is a high-tech, relatively new innovation in creating almost entirely new plants while the other is a centuries-old tradition of selective cross-breeding of similar plants to produce a heartier version.

Hybridized seeds cross different strains of the same plant to maximize the best qualities of each strain. Thus, a hybridized plant may come from two strains, one that proved to be particularly abundant and one that proved particularly disease-resistant; the hybridized plant created from this mix thrives well and survives well. Hybrids have been nurtured to match human desires for centuries: the corn that we recognize today is the result of thousands of years of hybridization, selecting for the plant that produced the largest ears; corn is a grass plant, and early corn produced tiny, tough, inedible-without-processing kernels. Through crossing strains over time, we now have large ears of corn with juicy, ready-to-eat kernels. The disadvantage to using hybridized seeds is that they do not necessarily reproduce in exactly the same manner each season; that is, if you save seeds from a hybridized plant to use the following season, these may or may not produce the desired qualities initially derived from the hybrid plant. So, buying seeds each year, while not necessary, is recommended to achieve the same results in a hybridized strain.

GMO seeds have been genetically engineered in a laboratory, produced quickly by technological means and not subject to years of selective breeding. Since these kinds of seeds have only been widely used since the early 90s, there is still little known about the environmental consequence of adding these seeds and plants to the biome. GMO seeds are not limited to cross-breeding within their plant family, and thus, science has produced seeds that are genetically engineered to contain bacteria and, in some cases, viruses, along with the original plant matter. While advocates of GMO products point to their success in creating a more stable food supply enabling food security for more people, critics are quick to point out that the unintended consequences of such genetic engineering have yet to be measured, in terms of environmental stability and human health. Stories abound of third world countries rejecting genetically modified products (research "Golden Rice" for an example) as an extension of colonial domination, relegating local populations to the status of unwitting guinea pigs. While the European Union has more closely monitored the use of GMOs in its food supply than the United States, the National Organic Program has designated the use of GMOs in organically labeled food unacceptable.

The other type of seed to consider when raising an organic garden at home is the **heirloom seed**: these are traditional seed varieties that have passed down throughout generations with little to no manipulation. Most heirloom plants are raised from seeds that have been around for 50 years or longer. Considered the pinnacle of organic gardening, heirloom seeds are excitingly refreshing, diverse, and somewhat challenging to grow. When choosing heirloom seeds, be sure to look for varietals that have been commonly cultivated in your area; this means they will be prepared for the climate of said area and have some natural defenses against the local pests and diseases, usually. For example, Cherokee Purple tomatoes grow well in my area, though I've heard that they are difficult to grow farther north. These open-pollinators are the best plants to use if you are considering saving seeds for the next garden season.

*Some popular **seed catalogs** to pursue include Seed Savers Exchange, Eden Brothers Heirloom Seeds, Johnny's Selected Seeds, Southern Exposure Seed Exchange, and the ubiquitous Burpee Seeds (which includes a section on heirlooms).*

Once you start your garden, **seed saving** is an incredibly cost-effective and environmentally sound practice to replenish your garden for the following year. There are many places where you can order seed saving kits, but it is a practice that's simple enough to follow at home with a handful of old, empty spice jars, or paper envelopes. Make sure your seeds are dry and free of debris before tucking them away for next season in a cool, dry place. The Seed Savers Exchange site contains lots of useful information on how to save seeds, as well as advice on which seeds are most practical for the typical home gardener to save (some plants require more effort than others to grow from saved seeds; reliable ones to save include bean and tomato seeds).

Now that you have your seeds, the decision as to how best to use them—direct seeding or seeding and transplanting—depends on what you are growing and where. For the home gardener, it is often most practical to utilize a mix of direct seeding and transplanting, either via purchasing seedlings or fostering them at home. It takes a dedicated gardener to put in the time and effort required to start seedlings from scratch and transplant later in the season, so be aware of how much time you are willing to spend. Many seeds can and should be sown directly into the garden and, while technically speaking, one can grow any plant from a seed in the soil, in many cases using seedlings makes better sense for the home gardener.

Direct seeding is when you sow the seeds directly into your prepared garden soil. This technique is great for delicate plants that don't take well to transplanting, like lettuces and greens. Usually, seed packets will have instructions on how deep to plant and how far apart to place seeds and certainly follow those. But don't worry too terribly much about spacing when it comes to the tiny lettuce seeds; it is inevitable that you'll accidentally drop more than one seed right next to each other in your shallow row. Simply start separating plants, thinning your lettuce patch, once they've grown to height large enough to harvest some bay leaves. Be sure to pull the plant up by its roots to leave its neighbor enough room to grow. Enjoy the baby lettuces immediately and compost the roots. With many lettuce and greens varietals (kale, collards, swiss chard), you can cut leaves to use, leaving roots in ground so leaves grow back, at least two or three times before the lettuce will start to taste too strong or bitter. At that point, simply pull up the roots and compost or, if you have the room, leave them to go to seed should you have the patience to try to harvest the minute seeds.

Direct seeding is also appropriate for plants with climbing vines, such as sugar snap peas and pole beans. Seed these next to your fence and encourage vines to grow into the mesh or wires. Beware of vines snaking into other parts of your garden, however; you might create an internal barrier, as well, to keep the vines in their place.

Tomatoes, of course, are technically vines, though most have sturdier "trunks" and grow like haphazard bushes. The best way to tame a tomato plant is to put a circular tomato cage around it when the plant gets a foot or so off the ground. Otherwise, you'll end up with tomato vines lying on the ground, which causes the fruit to rot or leaves it unripe without direct sunlight.

The other factor when determining whether to direct seed or use **transplants** is the climate. Some plants will survive a hard freeze—indeed, many need it to grow successfully—but many will not. Thus, seedlings that are nurtured in greenhouses or indoors are excellent shortcuts to getting a jump on the growing season, particularly if you live in colder climes, and a convenient way to plan your garden space with a clear visual representation of what will be sprouting up where.

Experience has led me to direct seed lettuces, greens, and beans and to use transplanted seedlings for tomatoes, chiles, and herbs, just as a few examples. Root vegetables, of course, are difficult to transplant without disturbing or destroying the edible root itself. In the next chapter, some specific vegetables and herbs well-suited for the organic home garden are discussed in detail, with some advice on how to treat each.

CHAPTER 3

Vegetable Victory: Choosing the Best Plants for Your Garden

In addition to determining which plants you'll grow, this chapter should help you with how to maximize the space in your garden and how to utilize companion planting. This is the time-honored idea that certain plants grown together nurture each other by attracting beneficial insects and repelling pests while also providing each other with nutrients and/or other kinds of support.

Before jumping into the following list (and to fend off endless arguments around the dinner table), I am indeed characterizing some plants that are technically fruits—tomatoes, cucumbers, chiles—as suitable for a vegetable garden, as well as including herbs. I think even the most hidebound gardening expert will agree that any home garden worth its salt will include some, if not all, of these interlopers.

Last, this list provides a very general overview of each plant. When and how to plant will depend on what zone you live in and what kind of garden you have decided to cultivate. Some basic tips are provided; consult with local sources for details about how to get each and every plant you choose to thrive in your organic garden. See Chapter 5 for ideas on how to use your plants in the kitchen.

Herbs:

Among the easiest and arguably some of the most useful plants to cultivate in your garden, herbs are nearly as indispensable to the home cook as salt and pepper. Additionally, herbs can be readily grown in pots, leaving the bulk of your raised bed to other plants (if using a drip irrigation system, pots are fairly easy to integrate with spot watering emitters). It is undeniably satisfying to simply pop outside and scissor off a small handful of herbs to enhance any meal during the growing season. And many herbs will return each year—again, depending on your location—and be some of the first pleasures to be harvested at the start of the next spring.

Herbs can be either direct seeded or grown from seed and transplanted into your garden if you like, though herb seeds are typically so tiny that they are difficult to handle. I prefer to procure seedlings from a reliable local source who uses organic methods. With annual herbs, plant seedlings after the last frost.

Parsley
Truly, one of the invaluable workhorses of the garden—and the kitchen—parsley is more than just a garnish; it can be a major player in salads and fresh sauces. Italian flat-leaf parsley is my go-to; it is more robust in flavor than curly parsley and its broad, flat leaves are more appealing in many applications. Parsley can stand the full sun, though it isn't as hearty as basil. If you live in a hot climate, plant in a pot that can be moved to shaded areas when the weather gets really warm. Takes about two to three months to mature. If your area does not get terribly cold winters, parsley may come back, but only for another year.

Basil
Another garden wonder, Genovese basil is a marvelously hearty, generous plant that reaches about two feet in height at full maturity. I have also grown globe basil and purple (Thai) basil; all are good, though Genovese is the most "all-purpose" varietal. Plant in the garden bed for best results. There are many other heirloom varieties of basil, though Genovese is one of the strongest and most productive kinds you can grow. It takes about three months to reach its full potential but can be carefully clipped throughout the season. Basil likes full sun—and does NOT like cold at all, so don't clip and store in the refrigerator, as it will wilt and turn black quickly—and trim back the flowers that appear during the season to keep your plant from bolting. A lot of instructions will say "pinch" off flowers, but the rough action of pinching can allow for greater disease penetration into the plant. Cutting is always healthier.

Chives
One of the earliest harbingers of spring, chives will keep cropping up for several years before they need replanting. As such, I keep chives in pots so that when I am ready to till my garden plot for the new spring season, I don't worry about digging up the chives. Don't limit yourself only to delicate "onion-y" chives; the stronger flavor of garlic chives is marvelous in a lot of Asian cooking and otherwise. Chives thrive in most zones and require very little attention to do well. When they flower, don't make the mistake of getting rid of the chive blossoms; they are a delicious garnish, or, if you end up with a lot of them, soak them in vinegar for a few days to make a flavored vinegar for salad dressings.

Mint
Virtually indestructible, I have grown numerous varieties of mint over the years—spearmint, peppermint, lime mint, chocolate mint, Corsican mint—and have only managed to sabotage a plant one time by attempting to plant it in a frustratingly wet part of the yard. Even mint couldn't withstand the onslaught of water. As cautioned before, mint will quite easily take over a garden, so segregate your mint plants in pots. Along with chives, mint will be one of the first plants to pop up in early spring.

It will return for several years, as well, and like basil, mint does not enjoy being put in the 'fridge. If you clip a little more than you wanted, put the rest in a water glass with a bit of water and leave on the countertop for a day or two.

Tarragon
An underutilized herb in American cooking, tarragon has a lovely and delicate anise-like flavor. It is wonderful to stuff a chicken with, along with lemon and garlic, as well as to roast, and making tarragon vinegar is an end of season treat around my house. Tarragon likes full sun, as well, making it a good choice for planting in the garden. It grows close to the ground and likes to spread out, so give it some room to do so. This is an herb that takes well to drying, unlike basil and chives, so be sure to rescue it before winter sets in.

Oregano
Absolutely essentially for Italian and Mexican cooking, I always have oregano on hand. It is impossible to buy fresh or dried oregano that is equal to what you can grow in your own garden (though, arguably, that could be said of most herbs). This is another low growing plant and, while it does not need as much room as tarragon, give it a good 10" of space to flourish in. Along with basil and tarragon, plant this one in your bed. Because it hugs the ground, it can be susceptible to overwatering.

Other Herbs
There are many other herbs that I have grown organically with great success; the above are merely the ones I prefer to always have on hand. If you like dill, it is a natural pest repellent, so it is a great fit for your garden bed. Don't forget cilantro (which I don't plant but love: there's only so much space in the garden, and cilantro is cheap at my local market), of course. Sage, rosemary, and thyme are all great candidates for drying at the end of the season. There are also less common herbs, such as lemon verbena (delicious though aggressive in the garden like mint), lavender (as pretty as it is fragrant), and lovage (a celery-flavored herb).

Vegetables:
The crowning achievement of any home garden, and the envy of every neighbor, will certainly be the beautiful crop of multicolored, delicious, and nutritious vegetables that you coax out of your lovingly tended soil. The following are merely a handful of suggestions, included because they thrive well in organic gardens and are, for the most part, relatively easy to tend. I also tried to include representative vegetables for each season, so that you can practice succession planting, if you like, ensuring a continuous crop of homegrown, organic produce throughout the year. See Chapter 7 for more on the practice of succession planting.

Lettuces

Direct seed in early spring for lovely tender greens throughout spring and early summer. Most lettuces do not like intense heat, so give your garden space to other plants for summer. At the onset of fall, as your summer crops start to fade, replant lettuces for a later harvest. As mentioned in the previous chapter, don't worry too much about placing a single seed in a single hole with lettuce; simply carve out a shallow trough and sprinkle seeds down the length of it. Thin your crop as necessary once they start leafing out; use the baby lettuces in early spring salads. Crisphead types of lettuce tend to be the heartiest and less vulnerable to pests, so these are good for the first-time gardener. But do be adventurous and try looseleaf, butterhead, and romaine varietals, too. Most lettuces will produce at least two nice heads, sometimes three: cut the leaves near the base of the plant instead of pulling up by the roots to get a second or third harvest.

Greens

Other green plants that love the springtime are spinach, arugula, swiss chard, and various Asian greens (mizuna, gai lan, bok choy). Direct seed in early spring and, like lettuce, these greens will continue to produce until the heat of summer sets in. These plants can also be cultivated in early fall, though I like to switch to hearty kale and collard greens at that time of year, along with savoyed spinach which can produce through much of the winter, as well. All of these greens produce well in cooler weather, but need direct sunlight and adequate water. Be advised: insects enjoy munching on lettuce and leafy greens as much as we do. Just expect to lose a bit to the bugs. See Chapter 4 for more on combating pests.

Sugar Snap Peas

I gardened for many years before I took a chance on sugar snap peas (and pole beans), thinking that these would be too much trouble, with their vine-y needs. Turns out, they're easy to grow (especially if you've had experience with the wily ways of tomato plants) and find their way onto whatever trellis you set up for them. Direct seed in early spring in the corner of your garden, where you've cordoned off a portion (say, about 2' in from your garden's border) with some chicken wire or recycled plastic fencing. The pea tendrils need something to grab onto, and this keeps them from latching on to other plants. These are among the first vegetables to mature in the spring. Other peas, such as English peas or snow peas, can also be grown this way; I simply like the ease—no shelling!—and taste of the sugar snap. Once sugar snaps are done, pole beans start producing.

Radishes

Another early spring crop, radishes are quick growing, taking only about a month to mature. Direct seed in the garden (as with root vegetables, transplanting does not work well). Depending on your climate, you can produce two or three rounds of radishes before the weather gets too warm. Radishes thrive in weather that does not get much above 70 degrees. Keep soil moist for best results. French breakfast radishes are a favorite of mine, tender and mild, and Easter egg radishes produce lovely pink, purple, and red bouquets.

Cruciferous Vegetables

Cabbage, broccoli, cauliflower, and Brussel sprouts are the most common cruciferous vegetables seen in markets and gardens. Of these, broccoli and cabbage are easier to grow, while cauliflower is the most temperamental. As with lettuces and greens, these are early spring and fall crops (Brussel sprouts are the last to harvest at the end of the fall). To make a harvest worth your while, you must have enough room in your garden plot to grow a nice row or two. These are also best when direct seeded.

Pole Beans

These are the easiest kind of beans to grow, akin to peas (see above for more details on where to plant). They need a trellis and some time, and you'll have a satisfying harvest. Since these harvest later in the season, you can—if pressed for space—direct sow these after your sugar snaps are done for the season in early summer; your trellis will already be in place and ready for climbing. If your climate gets terribly hot early in summer, the beans may not produce much, however. I like Provider beans, in particular; they are a prolific producer. Harvest often to encourage more growth. Note: growing beans to dry is a different matter entirely, and one that is beyond the spatial confines of most home gardeners.

Okra

This plant is extremely prolific and does very well in hot, humid climates, though it can be grown almost anywhere that it can get direct sunlight. Transplant in late spring and grow only as many plants as you think you will use; in my area, gardeners are hard-pressed to give it away at the height of summer, so much okra is growing. Also, be sure to monitor the plants well once they start producing. Okra is at its tastiest when it is about the length of a pinky finger, and within the space of a day, it can nearly double in size.

Tomatoes

These guys are the reason I started gardening in the first place: compare a homegrown tomato to a supermarket tomato and you will instantly see why. While all produce tastes better coming out of the ground, fresh and organically grown, tomatoes in particular showcase the glories of home gardening (and the horrors of what industrial agriculture has done to this beloved fruit). There are so many varieties of tomatoes out there that a type of tomato that can be grown in virtually any location. These plants can be direct seeded indoors in late winter/early spring for transplanting after the last frost. Typically, I don't risk planting seedlings until after tax day in my Zone 7 area. Caring for seedlings indoors is time-consuming, but cost effective if you plan on growing lots of tomato plants. I like to get my seedlings locally from an organic producer, as I only grow about six or seven plants each season.

Tomatoes need direct sun and adequate water throughout the growing season. In my garden, tomatoes start producing in earnest in July (I usually get lucky with a couple at the end of June) and continue through October, excepting drought years with 100+ degree temperatures. Once seedlings are planted and start thriving, put up a tomato cage around each plant. Give your tomato plants plenty of room to flourish, and check on them regularly once they start growing fast and producing, gently taming the vines through the cage. Tomato vines will always start to look a bit wild at the height of the growing season, so don't worry too much about that, as long as they are healthy. Also, beware of the avian risks from above: the first year I planted tomato seedlings, I left them alone for a couple of hours to make dinner. When I went to check on them that evening, the birds had stripped all the leaves off every single plant! Most survived, but since then, I've strung a makeshift net over the perimeter of the garden—make sure netting is suspended so as not to smother the plants—to prevent such an apocalypse. Just about everyone, birds and bugs and marauding neighborhood children, love tomatoes: see Chapter 4 for some help with all but the neighborhood kids.

I like to grow cherry or grape tomatoes (Black Cherry and Yellow Pear are favorites) in a large pot near the garden, as these smaller plants don't need as much room and often don't require cages. They also mature faster and are ready to pluck off the vine and throw into a salad in mid-summer. For other varieties, I tend to rely on heirloom tomatoes that are local to my area, such as Arkansas Travelers, Cherokee Purples, and Royal Hillbilly tomatoes (a rarer heirloom most definitely worth seeking out); check with your local farmers' market or gardening store for what varietals might be common for your location. Other famous heirlooms include Brandywine and Green Zebra (this one remains green when ripe). If you are interested in canning, paste tomatoes work best for this, the San Marzano being the standard-bearer. Be sure to visit Chapters 5 and 6 for many suggestions on how to use and preserve these beauties.

Cucumbers

Another prolific, vine-y plant, cucumbers thrive in most warm climates. Since they are so prolific, and since their vines tend to grow willy-nilly, I recommend setting up another small bed for them (which can also be used for larger squash varieties and/or melons) or, at the least, cordoning off a section of the garden to limit the vine expansion within the rest of your bed. There are numerous varieties of cucumbers you can grow, from traditional slicing and pickling cucumbers to Asian types that have fewer seeds. I did not bother with cucumbers for a long time—they are cheap and plentiful in the supermarket, albeit grown industrially and most often coated with wax—until I discovered the Armenian cucumber: these pale varietals produce large, long fruit with small seed pods and a clean, crisp taste that reminds you that cucumbers are closely related to melons. They produce so well (and don't turn bitter even when large) that I supplied a local restaurant for a couple of years from my small patch. One decent sized Armenian cucumber can provide a side dish for a table of six or eight people. Direct seed in the garden in spring in a plot that gets lots of direct sunshine; most cucumber varieties thrive throughout the hot summer into early fall.

A quick tip: if you grow cucumbers (or tomatoes or melons) and you have any issues with sensitive skin, I'd recommend wearing long sleeves or long gloves when weeding and harvesting among these vines. Cucumber vines will make me itch for two days if I don't cover my skin when rooting through them.

Melons

Another low-growing vine, melons can be prolific given enough space and by choosing the right varietal for your climate. For most backyard gardeners, the familiar melon crops of watermelon, honeydew, and cantaloupe are not practical to grow because of space issues. If you would like to grow some—and growing melons organically produces beautiful, pure-tasting fruit (essentially, a melon is a water filtration system)—investigate some lesser known, smaller varieties such as Chanterais melons. When mature, they fit in the palm of your hand and have the flavor of a sweeter cantaloupe. They aren't as easy to grow everywhere—too much or too little water will hamper their development—but with some nurturing, these are tasty treats to harvest throughout the summer. Treat like cucumbers (above) when planting.

Chile & Other Peppers

Chile and bell peppers are colorful and tasty additions to your garden. They are also, for the most part, quite hearty and produce well in warm regions. The larger the pepper, the more room it will need, of course; otherwise, most pepper varieties can be planted in spring for a harvest throughout the summer and into early fall. I have had success with typical peppers like jalapenos, serranos, Anaheims, and poblanos. I've also grown padrons, lovely Spanish peppers that can be sautéed in olive oil and eaten whole (the fun is in the surprise: most are sweet and mild, but one or two will pack a spicy punch); shishitos, a Japanese pepper treated similarly to padrons; habaneros, the super spicy brilliant orange pepper; Bolivian rainbow peppers, more of an ornamental plant with its purple, red, and orange bouquets of small peppers; and huge bushes of cayennes, which I use to make pretty *ristras* (the pepper wreaths you find in the Southwest) for drying. Grinding your own cayenne powder will ruin you for the dusty supermarket stuff forever. Most peppers are easy to grow—IF you have a decently long summer.

Squash & the Like

Squash, like okra, can be an over-performer in warm climates, though their easygoing presence ensures likely garden success. Again, squash varieties need space to spread out and flourish, so make sure you have adequate room. Direct seed in spring for a late summer abundance. Try zucchini, yellow crook-necked squash, and patty pan varietals which do well in most regions with a stretch of summer.

Other squash varieties, such as acorn and butternut, mature later and grow larger. Thus they are good for fall harvesting. However, they need more space and time accordingly. Also, eggplant, which is technically a nightshade plant, is similar in its growing capacity and timing as squash.

Alliums (Garlic & Onions & Leeks)

Garlic and onions are excellent crops to grow in a small garden if you follow succession planting: these are typically overwintered; thus, you plant in late fall for a harvest the next spring or early summer, clearing out that space for later plantings at the height of the growing season. There are many places to source garlic and onion bulbs, and you will be surprised at the amazing variety that is available: Filaree Garlic Farms has an outstanding collection of organic, heirloom bulb varieties from which to choose, and I've successfully grown more than a dozen different kinds of garlic and shallots (Filaree Farms also has a selection of potato seeds and other plants). If you aren't interested in exotic varietals, you can literally just buy a head of garlic in the store and plant the bulbs in your garden, root end down. Thrifty, if not guaranteed heirloom. In my area, I plant in mid- to late October and harvest in early June. Usually, I plant 50 or 60 bulbs because garlic—like onions and shallots—will keep if stored properly until your next growing season.

Leeks grow in both spring and fall, so you can plant seeds in late summer (after you've harvested your garlic and shallots, say) to mature over fall and winter. Pluck them in spring to be replaced by your spring seedlings. The allium family is an excellent source for creating a year-round garden experience.

Potatoes

This is another crop that needs a lot of room to make it worth your while, but if you have it, the sheer variety of potatoes available along with their long shelf life creates an exciting crop. Potatoes do best in cool soil, so be sure to time your planting so that harvesting can be done before the heat of summer settles in. Some varieties take well to overwintering, while others can be planted in the early spring to harvest at the beginning of summer. My grandparents grew potatoes by cutting out the eyes of older, withered potatoes and planting them; for more certain results, source some seed potatoes from a reputable grower (Filaree Garlic Farms or Seed Savers Exchange are reliable online sources).

Some Less Common Considerations

All of the above-mentioned crops are good candidates for organic gardening and allow you to stagger your planting throughout the year in order to make the best use of your garden space. There are many, many other vegetables and fruits out there for consideration, as well. The above are crops with which I have familiarity growing and, for the most part, are relatively easy to grow. Some other crops I adore, like asparagus and berries of all kinds, I seek out at farmers' markets rather than grow myself, simply because they are either temperamental or so delicious to pests that I can't keep up with them. Another crop I have tried and failed to grow—it is just too warm where I am—is artichokes; there are some excellent heirloom varieties out there just waiting for you to discover.

In addition, the world of gardening is whatever you make of it. You are limited only by location, and even then, you can sometimes exercise some control over nature via a greenhouse or hoop house planting. I have indulged in the rather more time consuming practice some seasons of moving plants from outdoors to indoors to outdoors: a small kumquat tree that thrived for several years by protecting it from winter; a bay leaf tree that produces a continuous supply of leaves (fresh bay leaves are astoundingly fragrant); and many ornamental plants, some I've had for more than a decade. Gardening in any form is a kind of rare pleasure in our technologically saturated age. Take a chance and get your hands dirty—in a good way!

Companion Planting:

This is the practice of planting certain groups of plants together in order to gain from their mutually beneficial characteristics. These characteristics include complimentary nutrient needs, abilities to repel pests, and/or habits of growth. Companion planting has long been used in many cultures, the received wisdom of hundreds of generations of farmers who have learned, through trial and error, what works well together.

Before the onslaught of industrial agriculture, companion planting was a reliable way in which farmers could ensure decent harvests. For one example, think of Native American cultures, where the planting of maize (corn), beans, and squash is ubiquitous: the tall maize plants shade the low-growing squash while providing a natural trellis for the climbing beans; in turn, the prickly vines of the squash discourage pests, and the nitrogen-rich beans provide soil nutrients. Some version of this ancient wisdom can be employed in any backyard plot.

- **Herbs** are excellent natural pest repellants: for example, strong scented herbs such as basil and dill are fine companions for tomatoes, warding off hornworms. Rosemary, sage, and mint can keep moths that munch on greens at bay. Other herbs attract beneficial insects, such as ladybugs that eat leaf-destroying aphids (parsley is good for this). Many gardeners swear by marigolds which act to protect roots, fending off harmful worms. Earthworms are great garden companions, but there a host of nematodes out there that will thrive on your plant roots rather than your soil.

- **Shade** is crucial to certain plants: leafy greens like a bit of shade if you want them to last into late spring or early summer, so taller plants can act as a shield against the sun.
- **Space** can also be a common sense product of companion planting wisdom: planting lower growing herbs such as tarragon, oregano, and rosemary in between tomato plants give vines room to spread while also providing pest protection. Also, sequential planting is another sub-category of companion planting—planting continuously throughout the year (see above for examples)—has the added benefit of discouraging weed growth.
- **Nutrient** swapping benefits various companion plants while also boosting the quality of your soil. For example, nitrogen-rich plants such as peas or beans (or cover crops: see Chapter 7) replenish your soil of the nitrogen that is much needed by tomatoes.
- **Seasonality** is a basic rule of thumb when considering companion planting: for example, radishes and greens grow well together, as they both like cool temperatures and well-drained soil; tomatoes and squash grow well together, as they both like lots of sun and do well in heat, while peppers also thrive at this time of year and provide some natural pest repellent.

These are merely a handful of examples of the vast reserve of material concerning the benefits and techniques of companion planting. Farmers Almanacs, farmers' markets, cooperative extension services are all excellent places to get further advice on how to set up your garden for maximum success.

CHAPTER 4

Preparing for Pests: Embrace the Inevitable

The first rule of organic gardening that I learned after going to a seminar at the local cooperative extension service was simple: "one for me, one for the pests." It can be frustrating when you start gardening organically, especially if heretofore you have used traditional petrochemical fertilizers (MiracleGro) and pesticides (Sevin Dust) as quick fixes. Indeed, it can be heartbreaking to find a gnawed leaf or a wormy tomato after all the time and effort invested in creating your lovely garden.

However, I would strongly argue that the quick fix benefits of petrochemical fertilizers and pesticides are absolutely not worth it in the long term: the effects on the health of your soil, the potential contamination of groundwater, the ethical conundrum of sourcing petroleum-based products, not to mention the proven health risks posed to humans, far outweigh the perceived benefit of producing more unblemished produce.

Besides, organic gardening also attracts welcome critters, such as ladybugs and earthworms, while the use of petrochemicals indiscriminately lays waste to your microbiome. Accepting the inevitable does not mean that you accept defeat; in fact, it means that you embrace the thriving biological community that you have worked diligently to foster and nurture. That said, we'd all still like to put more of our produce on our own plates rather than leave them to the pests. See below for some ideas on how to manage your potential pest population.

Note: I don't bother to address herbicides as they really should have no place in a backyard garden. Fertilizer is dealt with in <ins>Chapter 2</ins>.

Organic Pesticides

There are many quality organic pesticides on the market currently, as demand for purer products has continued to gain prominence in the last twenty years. If you decide to invest in buying these products commercially, look for the OMRI seal: this indicates that the product has been vetted by the Organic Materials Review Institute, a non-profit organization that works under the auspices of the NOP (USDA's National Organic Program). This seal should give you confidence that the product meets the highest standards as designated by the government.

If, however, you wish to circumvent the use of commercial products, then there are any number of pesticides that you can make at home, with some easy-to-source ingredients. Stock up on some spray bottles for ease of use.

- **Neem oil** has been used for centuries by native farmers for its overall effectiveness at keeping pests away. The juice from the neem plant has been shown to contain fifty or more natural pesticides. Organic neem oil can be found at many garden stores and online. Mix half an ounce into two quarts of warm water with about a teaspoon of organic liquid soap. It loses effectiveness as it sits so use within a day or two.

- **Mineral oil** is also an effective pesticide, in that it dehydrates insect eggs. Mix about twenty milliliters of quality mineral oil into a liter of warm water.
- **Citrus oil** mixed with cayenne pepper is particularly effective on ants. Essential citrus oil can be found in many natural food stores and online. Mix a few drops of essential oil (about ten) into a cup of warm water, then stir in a teaspoon of cayenne. Use immediately. Another use for citrus oil is to mix a full ounce of orange essential oil along with three tablespoons of organic liquid soap into a gallon of water. This seems to work well on slugs.
- **Eucalyptus oil** wards off wasps and flies (though it also deters bees, which you might want around). Simply sprinkle a few drops around where you've seen the wasps or flies, and the strong scent will keep them away.
- **Salt spray** is an incredibly simple and effective way to get rid of spider mites. Mix a couple of tablespoons of coarse salt (some recommend Himalayan salt in particular) into a gallon of water, then spray directly onto affected plants.
- **Garlic and onion spray** is a longer lasting solution that will keep for a couple of weeks, refrigerated. Chop a clove or two of organic garlic and a medium-sized organic onion and add to a quart of warm water. Let sit for an hour or two, then add a teaspoon of cayenne and a tablespoon of organic liquid soap. Strain out solids before putting into a spray bottle, but keep solids in any solution that you store.
- **Some other suggestions** are to make a tea from chrysanthemum flowers, dropping in some neem oil to enhance effectiveness; or to make a tobacco spray by steeping loose tobacco in warm water overnight; or to mix chile powder with diatomaceous earth and water. These are mentioned with reservations as the first two can actually be harmful to certain plants and the latter can weigh down delicate plants.

Other Home Remedies

Organic gardeners learn quickly how to get creative in the battle against pests. The above organic recipes for pesticides are a surefire start, but there are other tricks and tips that gardeners pass along, word of mouth, to help with certain problems. (Remember: insects aren't the only creatures who might find your garden attractive.) The efficacy of the following methods has not been put to rigorous scientific testing;

nevertheless, many of them are simple, common sense ideas that are easily employed and arguably effective.

- **Coffee grounds and eggshells** sprinkled around the base of a tomato plant will keep hornworms from crawling across that prickly barrier and up to your vines and fruits. Other gardeners swear by planting an old coffee can with the bottom cut out to encircle your seedling; this does work but can impede root growth.
- **Beer** can also be used to attract certain critters like slugs. Bury a container of beer in the ground near your plants (alternatively, place a low saucer next to them); the bugs will crawl in but not emerge.
- **Diatomaceous earth** is a natural substance composed of finely ground fossilized material and works much like eggshells and coffee grounds. As with the aforementioned, this should be sprinkled only around affected plants so as not to disturb your soil's balance.
- **Hand picking** slugs, snails, and hornworms off your plants is a low-tech, non-intrusive way to get rid of these pests, should they make it to your plants. Drop the intruders into a bucket of brine to kill them. Do this in the early morning when the slugs are active for best results.
- **Vinegar** can be easily used to keep away small pests, especially fruit flies (which actually should more appropriately be called "vinegar" flies, as they are attracted to the gases that fruits release—which is mimicked by vinegar—not the fruit itself). For outdoor use, spray lightly on pest areas; this can also be used on weeds, but be careful not to harm your own plants. For indoor use, put vinegar in a small bowl next to your problem area—produce that isn't refrigerated or next to an indoor composter—and cover with plastic wrap punctured with toothpick-sized holes.
- **Netting** is almost indispensable if you live in an area that attracts any number of critters, from rabbits and possums to birds and neighborhood cats. Netting can sometimes be a nuisance—and can ensnare butterflies—but usually it is worth saving the garden from the raiding hordes. Even **cheesecloth** can be used, draped over plants; it allows for light and water to penetrate, but its fine holes will keep out small pests and insects. It isn't as durable as garden netting.
- **Foil strips** can also be used, scarecrow-like, to keep birds away. Change locations regularly to ensure you keep them on their toes.
- **Fake snakes** have been an effective deterrent to rabbits and birds for me in the past. Again, change their location regularly.

- **Mulch** is an effective way to keep your soil moist and regulate temperature. Cedar and eucalyptus mulch are also reported to be good at keeping pests away, as the strong scents repel many insects. Mulch also works to keep weeds down during the growing season. You can use a mulch to protect your soil over the winter if you aren't succession planting or using cover crops.

Combating Disease

I have found that disease has been more destructive to my gardens than pests and that many diseases come down to soil health and simple maintenance techniques. The best way to combat disease is to prevent it, and there are several simple things that you can do to avoid common garden problems.

- **Soil health** is perhaps the most important step to preventing disease. See Chapter 2 for more details on how to prepare your soil, but as a reminder, one of the best things you can do before the main gardening season begins (or, indeed, at the end, so you can get a jump on next year's plans) is to have your soil tested. Be sure that the pH is at the right level (for most edible plants, that pH is around 6.5), and that your soil nutrients are at sufficient levels. Too little nitrogen in your soil prohibits or stunts growth, while too little calcium can cause the dreaded bottom end rot in tomatoes. Regular testing and correcting of your soil can head off a multitude of problems.
- **Proper maintenance** is also simple but key. Over-fertilizing a garden can foster disease so use a judicious hand. Keep your equipment clean and get rid of old rusty tools, especially pruners, and do use tools rather than pinching or tearing for pruning work. The more ragged you leave the stem when pruning or bobbing flowering shoots, the more vulnerable the plant is to disease. Perhaps most important, **water in the morning** so that plants have time to dry before nightfall; this prevents fungal diseases, among the most prominent problems for home gardens. In the event of an exceptionally wet spring, do keep a careful eye out for fungal diseases like tomato blight. If not tackled immediately, this will stunt and eventually kill your tomato plant.
- **Natural fungicides** such as bicarbonates can be used preventatively to avoid blight, rot, and mildew. Baking soda can be used though it isn't nearly as effective as bicarbonates containing ammonium or potassium. These are considered non-toxic to humans. GreenCure is a well-regarded fungicide readily available on the market.
- **Biological fungicides** such as Bacillus subtilis are effective in combating many common diseases in the garden with no harmful effects to humans or animals. While prevention is still better, the

biological fungicides can be helpful in combating disease once it has already spread.
- **Copper and sulfur-based products** can be used for prevention, as well, though they can sometimes be harmful to certain plants and animals. So, these should be used with caution.
- **Soil bacteria-based products** are used to protect roots and seeds while causing no harm to earthworms and other beneficial insects. If you have ever had problems with seeds rotting in the ground or roots failing to take hold, treat your garden with one of these products, such as Mycostop or Root Shield, before planting.

CHAPTER 5

Healthy Harvest: Weeding, Pruning, Using

While many preparation and maintenance issues have already been mentioned throughout the book, here the focus is on what to do once your seedlings have sprouted and your garden has sprung. Following that are suggestions for what to do with the produce that you have on hand, with some quick and easy recipe ideas for making the most of your healthy harvest.

General Tips for Weeding

As with many great endeavors in life, preparation and prevention are almost as important as execution. That is, the best tip for keeping weeds in your garden under control: prevent them from growing rampant in the first place. The best way to do this is to, first, use a raised bed of some kind; this discourages weed growth by placing a healthy layer of topsoil over your subsoil. Second, block the weeds that will inevitably sprout from the subsoil by placing a barrier between your garden's subsoil and topsoil (good soil, compost, manure if using). The barriers can be made of anything that isn't chemically treated (which would be harmful to soil, groundwater, and plants, as well as subtracting from your proudly organic brand): old cardboard, a thick layer of newspapers, and biodegradable fabric will all work to varying degrees.

In addition, using a drip irrigation system is helpful: since the irrigation system is more pointedly directed at the plants you want to grow, it does not encourage grass seeds to grow willy-nilly. Smart planting will also help to impede weed growth: while you should avoid crowding your plants, of course, the close planting of desired crops leaves little room for the undesirable weeds.

Be aware, however, that no amount of preparation can prevent ALL weed growth. If you have a garden, weeds will inevitably grow. Your focus should be one keeping weed growth to a minimum, thus providing more room and more nutrients for your desired plants to grow.

So, when the inevitable weeds crop up, there are other ways to bring and keep them under control. Mulching your garden is always an effective barrier for weeds; plus, it provides temperature control for your topsoil, keeping it warm in cooler weather and shielding it from the direct heat of summer. Keep your mulch to a depth of about two inches, and beware: some commercial mulches may contain chemicals and/or be contaminated with weed seeds. Choose wisely.

Pulling weeds by hand will become a necessary effort at some point during the growing season. Some easy advice on how to manually weed effectively: weed in the dewy mornings or after a light rain, as wet soil releases the weed root more easily. Be sure to pull the weed up, root and all, or it will quickly grow back. Use a small garden trowel if your weeds get tough or aggressive, to help pull up grassroots without damaging nearby plant roots. Weed often! The longer the weed has to settle into your soil, the harder it will be to yank up.

Last, while it isn't clearly understood as to why this may be, most horticulturists will acknowledge that organic gardens with lots of good compost simply don't sprout as many weeds. Healthy soil makes for a healthy garden.

General Tips for Pruning

While pruning is not really the most important concern for a vegetable garden—it is more about the harvesting—there are some simple tips that you can use for your entire backyard to keep it looking good and growing well.

If you have perennials planted in your garden—things like mint or chives—then be sure to prune them back at the end of the growing season, so the dead material does not over mulch the soil and prevent new growth from cropping up next season. Also prune any dead growth that you may see during the season (although be aware that if you appear to have "dead" growth on one of your plants during the season, it is often indicative of disease). Last, do be sure to top any flowering plants, such as basil and lettuces, during the growing season, to keep them producing and avoid going to seed.

What not to do in terms of pruning in a vegetable garden may be even more important: no matter how tempting it may be to prune back vine-growing plants (tomatoes, cucumbers, squash, beans, peas), *do not do it*. While very occasionally helpful, most often this kind of pruning stunts growth of fruits or vegetables and can introduce disease.

How to Use Your Harvest

Finally! After all the work, the hours, the days, the months, you are able to enjoy the fruits of your labors, quite literally. This is the most satisfying and rewarding—nay, delicious—part of gardening. Below you will find some basic tips of harvesting your plants and how to use them once you have them happily lined up on your kitchen countertops. The following suggestions are not "recipes," per se, with an exact list of ingredients and measurements, but merely methods of preparing certain dishes focusing on what you've harvested. These methods are ripe for improvisation and substitution, so channel your creative energies!

Herbs:

When harvesting herbs, the general rule of thumb is to harvest only as much as you need at the time (that's the point of having them in the backyard, no?). If you do happen to gather a little too enthusiastically, avoid the refrigerator; instead, put the extra cut herbs in a glass of water and place in a windowsill (or, alternately, use an herb arrangement as a centerpiece for your dinner table: lovely and practical). Be sure, when gathering herbs, that you snip or cut them; don't pinch or pull them, which can introduce disease.

Dishes with Herbal Starring Roles

The first preparation that inevitably springs to mind when thinking of fresh garden herbs is **pesto**. While not really a stand-alone dish, it can be a star of dinner in its own right, adding layers of bright flavor not only when tossed with pasta but also when spooned over grilled steak or chop, swirled into soup, or stirred into a grain salad. A basic ratio of about 2 cups of herbs, with a ½ cup of nuts, a couple of garlic cloves, some acidity (lemon, lime, orange, light vinegar) to taste, and about a ¾ cup of quality olive oil. Cheese can be added, depending on what you're serving it with, usually about ½ cup hard cheeses, such as parmesan or pecorino. Whirl this together in a food processor or blender, or if you're lucky enough to have a good mortar and pestle, take the time to grind together slowly by hand. This latter, old-fashioned method produces a superlatively creamy pesto.

While most people automatically think first of the classic basil and pine nuts pairing when considering pesto, many other herb-nut combinations are wonderful in this kind of preparation, as well: think mint and walnuts, especially well-suited for spooning over lamb chops; parsley and pecans, great with steak; or chives/garlic chives and peanuts, to add an Asian flair. Also consider arugula, that spicy green, for pesto; it makes for a robust accompaniment to grilled meats or fish.

You can also make a great **salad** using your herbal bounty. A mix of tender young herb leaves tossed with a light vinaigrette and topped with some delicate shavings of cheese, or grated nuts is a lovely starter for any occasion. I love a mix of parsley and mint (3 to 1) with a lemon-based vinaigrette of 1 part lemon to 2 parts oil, with a splash of Dijon mustard and honey for emulsification and balance. A little smoked Spanish paprika (pimentón) adds a touch of sweet heat if you have it on hand, and salt to taste. Shave some hard cheese over with a vegetable peeler, letting it curl nicely, and/or grate some toasted pecans or walnuts over with a rasp. Beautiful, healthy, and delicious!

Another famously herb-forward dish in the salad category is **tabouli**. While many Americanized versions contain a lot of other ingredients—and there is nothing wrong with this, but still—the traditional version contains copious amounts of herbs with just a bit of bulgur wheat, lots of lemon and oil, some onion and maybe some tomato. Really, for a truly traditional Middle Eastern tabouli, you need only about ¼ cup of bulgur wheat, soaked or steamed until tender (a tip, if you have the time: soak the bulgur in lemon and olive oil along with a chopped tomato, if using, for several hours rather than steaming or boiling; it softens the bulgur while allowing it to absorb more flavor). To that amount of bulgur, add 2 cups herbs—chopped by hand! no processing!—and douse with equal parts of lemon juice and quality olive oil (1/3-1/2 cup of each). I like to use 1 cup parsley, ½ cup mint, and ½ cup cilantro. Add a small onion, chopped, or sliced scallions (about a ½ cup) and a tomato, chopped if you like. There is no better tabouli on earth than one made with herbs fresh from the garden.

Herbal **teas or tisanes** are yet another excellent way to make use of your herbs. I can tell you from firsthand experience, that fresh mint tea with lots of sugar is as good an afternoon pick-me-up as any other. Simply pour lightly boiling water over a handful of fresh leaves, add sugar to taste, and if you're squeamish, sieve out the leaves after steeping for a few minutes. You can also add some green tea leaves or bags to this to amp up flavor and caffeine content. Another wonderful herb for tea is lemon verbena, a rarer herb that is quite strong when raw but fragrant and tasty when used for tea.

Lastly, you can use your herbal bounty to make **flavored syrups**—a fine way to save your herbs for use after the season is over. Make a sugar syrup by lightly boiling equal amounts of sugar and water (add a touch more water if using a coarser raw sugar), then add a handful of fresh herbs to that and steep until cool room temperature. Strained and refrigerated in a sterilized jar, this will keep for several months. Again, lemon verbena is lovely in this preparation, as is lavender, mint, and basil. You can riff on this method by steeping citrus peels along with your herbs (lime loves mint, while basil enjoys lemon). If you're feeling fancy, add half a vanilla bean to any of these for the extraordinary depth of flavor. Use these syrups to flavor tea and cocktails, drizzle over dessert, or make sorbet.

Of course, herbs are the crowning touch of many a dish, adding a distinct freshness of flavor to nearly anything, and you'll find countless uses for the ones you have in your backyard. Roast chicken stuffed with tarragon; rolled omelet with chives; bread stuffing laced with lots of oregano and sage are just a few ideas for more ways to highlight your herbs.

Vegetables:

Lettuces

Obviously, the first thing that comes to mind when thinking about lettuce is a salad. A simple green salad with freshly picked lettuce is a true glory of spring and early fall. One caveat for using homegrown lettuces: *wash well!* Your lettuce will have dirt in it, undoubtedly (sometimes a critter or two), and while in an organic garden that dirt isn't perhaps too hazardous to your health, it is certainly unpleasantly gritty and not very tasty. The best way to wash lettuces (and greens) is to fill a clean sink full of cold water and add your lettuce; swish around for a minute, then let everything settle (the loose dirt will sink to the bottom of the sink). Carefully scoop out the lettuce with your hands, taking care not to disturb the dirt at the bottom, and let drain on clean dish towels. If you harvest after a rain, I'd recommend doing that two or three times. Then, rinse lettuce again, just to be sure you've dislodged all grit and spin in a salad spinner. You can store lettuce in the fridge for an afternoon or overnight—the cold can make lettuce exceptionally crisp—rolled up in a clean flour sack towel; spread the lettuce over the entire towel, leaving some border, then carefully roll up. The towel absorbs excess moisture while providing a protective layer against other fridge odors.

To dress your lettuce, you need nothing more than a bit of acid, some oil and a pinch of salt. Two tips on **vinaigrettes** that I've picked up via my travels: first, make a vinaigrette directly in your—very large!—salad bowl. Rub the bowl with a cut clove of garlic, add some Dijon mustard, and one part acid (lemon, white or red wine vinegar, sherry or balsamic vinegar) to two parts oil (extra virgin olive oil or walnut oil). Second, a lot of older recipes call for one part acid to three parts oil; for contemporary cooks, and especially on light and fresh lettuce, that feels heavy. Keep it 1:2 for best results.

Another important **dressing** to have in your repertoire is homemade ranch: trust me, you will never buy the bottled stuff again (and, if you ask me, it is nearly criminal to use chemically laden bottled dressing on fresh, organic lettuce). Basically, mix equal parts mayonnaise and buttermilk (let us say a ½ cup of each) to a clean jar, add a couple of tablespoons each of freshly minced parsley and chives, and about half a teaspoon each of garlic salt and onion salt. Shake well to mix. Add more mayo if too thin, more buttermilk if too thick, and more seasoning if you desire. Add some blue cheese to this for your cobb salad or buffalo wing dip; or, puree with some tarragon and avocado for green goddess-style dressing. This will keep in the fridge for a couple of weeks, though I doubt it will last that long.

Greens

Perhaps my favorite early spring and late fall harvest, greens can be light and crunchy, rich and velvety, star and side, depending on how you wish to prepare them. Again, as with lettuce, the first step in creating good food from garden greens is to *wash well!* See the above section on lettuces for some simple instructions on how to ensure that your greens are clean. I'd say that erring on the side of excess washing with greens, especially when consuming raw, is better than erring on the side of the deficit. Little worms love to live in the greens; if you see their tell-tale holes in any leaves, check your leaves well.

One of the first treats I make during the spring season is a **classic spinach salad** with warm bacon dressing. This method works well with arugula, too, or with a mix of spinach and arugula. Have ready a big bowl of cleaned spinach and to this add 4 or 5 thinly sliced mushrooms. Sauté 4 or 5 slices of bacon, chopped, in a skillet. When bacon is crisp and fat is rendered, whisk in 2 tablespoons of cider vinegar and a couple of teaspoons of brown sugar. Correct seasoning, if necessary (more vinegar and/or sugar, salt). Pour warm dressing over salad and toss well. Top with 2 or 3 sliced hard-boiled eggs. This is a full meal for two or a filling starter for four.

For a fall harvest of greens, one of my favorite things to do (besides traditional stewed collard greens: a Thanksgiving must) is to make a big pot of **Mediterranean style chard or kale**. Fill a large skillet—one that has a matching lid—to overflowing with cleaned chard and/or kale (you can mix them, but I find that using one or the other makes for a purer flavor). Don't bother to spin dry, as the water clinging to the leaves helps in cooking. To that add 1/3 cup of cilantro, one small bunch chopped scallions, a couple of minced garlic cloves, ¼ cup or more of quality olive oil, and a big tablespoon of smoked paprika. Let that wilt down over medium heat, stirring very carefully (as your pot should be literally overflowing with stuff), until the lid fits on top. Cover and turn to low heat; let cook for about 20-30 minutes for chard, 30-40 minutes for kale. You can turn this into a vegetarian main dish by throwing in a can of drained chickpeas.

There is also, of course, the Southern classic of **braised collard greens**. Though the methods for doing so are numerous, I happened upon a variation that I find even tastier than the traditional. Prepare your greens for stewing by stacking leaves then rolling them into a cigar shape and slicing; this a quick way to prep when you're using a bunch of greens. In a large pot, heat some olive oil and sauté the chopped onion and some chopped garlic (measurements depend on how many greens you're using and your own personal taste). Soften that a bit, then add collard greens by the handful and stir as each batch wilts slightly until all greens are incorporated and barely wilted. Throw in a smoked turkey wing—or, if you have access to some smoked duck, this is even better—and a cup or so of water. Cover and simmer for a couple of hours, then remove the wing and shred meat before returning to the pot. Add a few splashes of vinegar and some red pepper if you like a bit of spice. I used to do this when I had ducks from hunting trips. After smoking the duck, I'd reserve the wings and skin to add to collard greens. Rich and tasty while still being a bit lighter than the usual salt pork seasoning.

All greens lend themselves well to salads, though heartier greens such as mature Swiss chard, kale and collards must be treated a little differently. Thinly slice or finely chop these heartier greens and rub with a little coarse salt and lemon juice; let sit for an hour or so. The greens will soften a bit but remain crunchy. Toss with more juice, some oil, and salt to taste, and serve as is. Or add dried fruits, such as cranberries, and toasted nuts.

Sugar Snap Peas

As the name suggests, these little pods are sweet and neat, ready to eat out of hand. I always have a few right off the vine as a reward for my weeding efforts. You may want to "string" certain varieties by pinching the top off and pulling the fibrous string down the back of the pod, but it is only necessary if you find the fibrous string unpleasant.

I use sugar snap peas indiscriminately when they are in season, throwing them into salads or adding them to a quick sauté any time a few are at hand. They pair particularly well with radishes, and all you need to dress a salad of thinly sliced peas and radishes is some lemon and oil.

My favorite early spring dish with snaps is a **sautéed pea medley**: if you've grown garlic, pull up an early head or two; this immature garlic—green garlic it is called at the market—makes a wonderfully fragrant accompaniment. Cook your sliced green garlic or some spring onions in some good olive oil until softened, then toss in about a cup each of thinly sliced sugar snap peas and regular green peas (shelled or frozen). Cook until peas are tender yet still crisp. If your market has pea tendrils, fava beans, and/or green almonds, add them to the mix; the more, the merrier. Top with minced herbs of just about any kind: mint, parsley, and/or tarragon are fantastic.

I also love them with steak salad, such as **Thai beef salad**: if you have leftover grilled steak, slice thinly and toss with crisp lettuce and sliced sugar snap peas. Make a dressing with equal parts lime and soy sauce (or, better yet, half soy sauce, half fish sauce), and throw in some minced garlic and hot green chiles—the spicier, the better in my household. Whisk in a dash of sugar and pour over vegetables and steak. The green vegetal taste of the snaps really sings in this salty, funky, spicy dressing.

But they are also excellent when **sautéed or roasted** quickly in a hot oven. Simply coat with oil and sauté over high heat or blast-roast in a really hot oven. When lightly blistered, toss with a dash of toasted sesame oil and salt, then sprinkle with sesame seeds.

Radishes

Crunchy and lightly spicy, the radish is yet another lovely spring vegetable that livens up any number of salads. Like sugar snap peas, they can be eaten out of hand with little to no preparation (just, of course, some cleaning). As mentioned above they are great paired with sugar snap peas and these two can be substituted for each other in any number of recipes.

My go-to recipe for radishes is a **crunchy relish**, one that pairs so well with spring lamb or pork that I find myself making it several times throughout spring and fall. A food processor is best for this, but chopping by hand can certainly work if a little more time-consuming. Throw about 10 trimmed radishes in your processor, along with about ¼ cup mint and/or parsley and/or a mix. Add ¼ cup nuts and a couple of tablespoons of lemon juice and olive oil and pulse until coarsely chopped (adjust texture according to how you're serving it: coarse for a salad-like presentation, finer for a relish). I use local pecans for this, and sometimes add a seeded jalapeno and a minced clove or two of garlic for a stronger flavor. Not only lovely spooned alongside grilled lamb or pork chop but also tasty spooned into cooled, cooked rice with a dash of mayonnaise to combine (add some drained tuna for a non-vegetarian lunch).

Another extraordinary thing to do with radishes, particularly the **French breakfast radish**, is to simply wash and trim radishes that have been refrigerated until cold. Serve whole or halved alongside a pot of the best butter you can buy or make and a saucer of coarse sea salt. Dip radishes in butter then dab into salt. With some fresh baguette and charcuterie, a heavenly lunch.

For an **Asian riff on the radish side dish**, trim and halve radishes (quarter if large), then soak in equal parts red wine vinegar and soy sauce for about an hour, turning a couple of times. Salty, sour, crunchy counterpart to a stir-fry or a curry.

Cruciferous Vegetables

One of the last vegetables to mature in the spring or fall seasons, cabbages, broccoli and cauliflower, and Brussel sprouts are both sweeter and heartier when homegrown. Almost every cook has a recipe or two in their pocket for these common vegetables; hopefully, these few methods will give you some new ideas for how to use them.

Fresh, sweet cabbage from the garden just begs for some **coleslaw**, and most ambitious home cooks have a recipe they use already. I like to thinly slice the cabbage and salt it first, leaving it to stand and drain in a colander for an hour or two; this ensures that the final slaw isn't watered down. Some people add carrots or purple cabbage to their slaw, and this is fine—and pretty—but when I have fresh garden cabbage, I like to leave it the lone star. I just add a minimal amount of mayonnaise, some cider vinegar, and a bit of sugar; I like the slaw to taste of cabbage, not mayo and tart-sweet as opposed to sweet-tart. Toss in some chopped toasted pecans to deepen the flavor, and/or some fresh herbs to freshen.

Raw cabbage is also **exceptional on tacos**—better than delicate lettuce which gets overwhelmed by the spicier, meatier flavor of most tacos. Toss with lime and salt before topping your taco or tostada.

Cabbage can also be cooked—though many don't enjoy the sulfurous odor of cooked cabbage—and I adore **Southern-style smothered cabbage**. Simply chop an onion and a small head of cabbage and add to a big skillet, along with more butter than you think you should use (a good half stick). Sprinkle with salt and coarse pepper, cover, and cook it over low for 45 minutes or more. Take the lid off, raise heat and let it brown up a bit.

Broccoli, cauliflower, and Brussel sprouts all take exceptionally well to roasting; this creates a caramelized and even crunchy exterior while keeping the vegetable juicy and rendering it tender. As each takes different lengths of time to roast, I don't recommend cooking them as a medley; also, don't crowd the pan when roasting for best results. Use a sheet pan, if you have it, lined with aluminum foil. Toss broccoli or cauliflower heads or halve Brussel sprouts in enough quality olive oil to coat and roast at 425 degrees for 30-45 minutes, until browned. Any of these are great as a side dish, as is, but they also take well to some post-roasting additions: broccoli with pine nuts and pecorino cheese; cauliflower with capers and walnuts; Brussel sprouts with a splash of fish sauce and some Asian chile powder (shichimi togarashi, for example) sprinkled with toasted rice Krispies. I know the latter sounds odd, but it is truly delicious, inspired by David Chang of Momofuku.

I also like to make **a broccoli-cauliflower casserole**. Blanch equal parts broccoli and cauliflower in boiling salted water for a couple of minutes (don't overcook or your casserole will be mushy); drain well. Make a basic béchamel sauce with butter, flour, and milk. For about a cup of béchamel, mix equal parts butter and flour (2 tablespoons) and cook over medium heat until flour starts to color a bit, then whisk in a cup of milk slowly, stirring constantly to prevent lumps. Toss your vegetables with the béchamel, put in a greased baking pan—thinly spread out if you like the crunchy bits—and top with grated Gruyere cheese and a sprinkle of panko bread crumbs. You can use other cheeses, but the Gruyere really complements the flavor of the broccoli-cauliflower mixture.

Another great way to use broccoli and/or cauliflower is in **soup**: this is an especially handy way to make sure that excess produce does not go to waste, as soup freezes well. All you need is a head of broccoli or cauliflower, a small onion, and some good quality vegetable or chicken stock. You can leave chunky or puree (use an immersion blender for a quick coarse puree or whirl in a processor or blender). Whatever else you add is up to you: potatoes or rice for some starchy bulk; milk or cream for a silky-smooth puree; some diced tomatoes and/or a handful of fresh corn kernels for acidity and sweetness; or, as my mom couldn't resist, a hefty serving of cheese. She used Velveeta for which I will forgive her (I still love her version, despite my better instincts), but a good melting cheddar elevates the idea a bit.

Pole (Green) Beans

Sitting on a cool back porch snapping beans is certainly a revered summer pastime. It is a chance to reflect on the spring that has just passed while not worrying too terribly much about the summer heat and potential drought to come.

There are two basic ways I like to cook green beans: blanched and stewed. Blanching lends itself to endless variety, as you can toss quickly **blanched beans** with any number of vinaigrettes and add-ins. Simply blanch beans in boiling salted water to the desired doneness, 2 minutes for crisp and up to 5 minutes for near-tender. Plunge immediately into a bowl of ice water to stop cooking and preserve the color. These can be kept in the fridge for a day or two before using; or frozen for later in the year (more on that in the next chapter). Dress with a red wine vinaigrette and toss in a bunch of slivered basil and some minced garlic for an excellent side salad. Or, toss with a walnut-oil vinaigrette and a handful of chopped toasted walnuts.

Green bean and potato stew is one of the glories of Southern cooking, and it wouldn't be summer without making a couple of pots of this. Coarsely chop a 12-ounce package of bacon and add a pound of snapped green beans and a pound of new potatoes, halved if on the larger side. Throw in a cup of water, some salt and pepper, and simmer lightly for an hour or so. Dead simple cooking that requires only the increasingly rarest of treats: absolutely fresh vegetables.

Okra

Onto the height of summer, the almost invincible okra will pop up and proliferate in what seems like minutes. Of course, almost everyone knows that fried okra is the way to go, but there are a couple of possible variations on that theme, as well as some lovely stewed preparations that are wonderful with okra.

One of the not-so-secret characteristics of okra—its sliminess—can be either a boon or a bane, depending on what you're cooking. That gelatinous character can be an excellent thickener (think gumbo), but in quick, stand-alone preparations it can be off-putting. A secret: leave the top of the pod alone. **Traditional fried okra** calls for cutting okra into rounds and tossing with cornmeal, or a mix of cornmeal and flour, and pan-frying in vegetable oil. This is excellent, of course, but for virtually slime-free results, cut pods in half, leaving top trimmed but intact. For **Asian fried okra**, don't dredge in flour but pan fry, halved, over high heat. You want the okra to be nearly burned. Toss with minced garlic and hot chiles, some chopped fresh basil and/or cilantro and season with some fish sauce or salt. Prepared this way, okra can be served as an hors d'oeuvres.

Certainly, if you ever make gumbo, okra is a must-have ingredient (well, some people use file powder, but they certainly wouldn't if they had Cajun relatives). But **stewed okra and tomatoes** is another fine way to use some of your bountiful crop. Put whole okra pods in a pot—smaller is better for this dish—and add about half as many (by volume) chopped tomatoes; pour in a glug of olive oil and let simmer for about 30-40 minutes, until tomatoes have dissolved and created a kind of sauce for okra. The long cooking time, plus the whole pod preparation, eliminates the typical mucilaginous texture. Add some fresh herbs and a squeeze of lemon for brightness.

Tomatoes

The uses for garden ripe tomatoes are endless, and even when unripe (fried green tomatoes, anyone?), tomatoes have their uses. It would be easily possible to pen an entire book just on the use of tomatoes, but I'll limit myself to a few quick and simple preparations, alongside a couple of more involved but less typical ideas. See the following chapter for methods using tomatoes for preservation, such as sauce preparations.

By far the easiest and most anticipated way to eat tomatoes—after a long winter and spring, deprived of the joys of a perfectly ripe, just off-the-vine tomato—is to **slice and serve**. Friends of mine beg for sliced tomatoes arranged on a platter, drizzled with the best olive oil I can afford, a splash of sherry vinegar (most people use balsamic; that's fine, too), some slivered basil, and a sprinkle of blue cheese. The variations are virtually endless: intersperse sliced mozzarella (or, better yet, burrata) with tomato slices and shower with basil; scatter some capers (fried until crisp, if you're up to it) and olives over your platter of tomatoes; make a cheese cracker dough (equal parts flour, butter, and cheese), bake in a pie pan, and layer drained slice tomatoes on top. Just about any salty, savory, umami-laden ingredients, you can fish out of your pantry or fridge goes well with tomatoes.

Of course, you will usually have **cherry tomatoes** first, and these are great added to any salad or marinated in oil and vinegar (with garlic and herbs or not) and served as a side on their own. But if you end up with too many to eat out of hand, roasted cherry tomatoes are absolutely delicious with grilled meats, especially fish: in a baking dish large enough to hold a single layer, throw in your cherry tomatoes and enough good olive oil to coat; there's no need to halve them, but I do recommend you use a paring knife or skewer to poke a tiny hole in each, to prevent bursting and splattering. Splash with some sherry vinegar, tuck in some whole peeled garlic cloves, and top with several sprigs of oregano. Roast at 350 degrees for 30-40 minutes, until tomatoes have broken down and garlic is soft. Mash together or leave chunky, depending on how you serve it. Great smeared on toasted bread, as well.

Of course, you can't have fresh summer tomatoes without making a **salsa** or two: Mexican style with jalapenos, garlic, cilantro and lime; Italian style with olive oil, balsamic vinegar, garlic and basil; Middle Eastern style with olive oil, lots of lemon juice and tons of fresh parsley.

A world-famous preparation of tomatoes has to be **gazpacho**, and there are many variations on that theme, from the thin Andalusian-style cold soup to the thicker salmorejo style originating from Cordoba. There are also endless variations that have roots in the American Southwest. I am a purist when it comes to gazpacho, given that I have an ample supply of vine-ripened heirloom tomatoes. In its simplest form, tomatoes, excellent olive oil, and aged sherry vinegar are pureed and strained; poured around a cold seafood salad and some sliced avocado, this is truly shatteringly good, but dependent wholly on ingredients. Most Andalusian-style gazpacho recipes call for some water-soaked bread to act as a thickener, and perhaps some cucumber and bell pepper to boot. Salmorejo is simply a thicker version, with more bread to tomato ratio, and usually topped with crunchy croutons, chopped hard boiled egg, and crisped Serrano ham.

A cousin to gazpacho is a **Moroccan-inspired cold tomato soup** that incorporates some spicier elements. Heat a tablespoon of olive oil and gently cook a few minced garlic cloves and a couple of teaspoons each of smoked paprika and ground cumin until garlic softens and the mixture is fragrant. Grate a couple of pounds of tomatoes (or pass through a food mill, if you have one), then add the oil-spice mixture, some chopped cilantro, and a couple of stalks of diced celery. Add some lemon juice for brightens, salt to taste, and stir in a bit of water to thin, if you deem it necessary. Serve very cold.

Grated tomatoes also make an excellent marinade, with the addition of some acid and oil, perhaps some garlic and herbs. The tomatoes help tenderize the meat when marinated. I especially like to do this with chicken, to be grilled kebab style.

During the height of the season, I'm mostly indulging in raw preparations of tomatoes, but there are a couple of exceptions. If I have the grill going, some **stuffed tomatoes** are always a delicious side: put halved and seeded tomatoes into a baking pan that you don't mind putting on the grill, drizzle with olive oil and stuff with a mixture of equal parts bread crumbs and grated parmesan, streaked through with chopped herbs (basil and oregano good, but tarragon also works for a different flavor). Place on grill until tomatoes wilt and cheese begins to brown. This can also be done in an oven, of course.

Cucumbers

Cucumbers, like tomatoes, are one of the summer's delights and can be prepared with simplicity and ease for an excellent fresh crunch to any meal. Slice and serve is great, with only a splash of vinegar and some salt needed to make a side dish for just about any meal.

Quick pickles are also useful to have on hand, to have on the side, in a sandwich, or as a relish. I like to seed my cucumbers for most recipes, as the seeds can be hard to digest. Peel and seed a couple of cucumbers (leave the peel on if the early season and cucumbers are young and tender); toss in a bowl with enough vinegar to coat, and season with equal parts salt and sugar. Place into a baggie and tightly seal, squeezing all the air out. These can be eaten within a few hours and up to a couple of days after preparing, and obviously take well to other seasonings, if you like.

Cucumber salsa is also a refreshing break from the usual tomato-based salsas. Excellent with spicy grilled meats, one of my favorites goes well with jerk chicken or pork. Stir together 1 part cucumber to half mango; add enough oil to coat. Season with salt and toss in fresh herbs (thyme is really nice here), some minced scallion or onion, and some seeded chile peppers.

Melons

Melons, like the other summer fruits detailed above, are also quick and easy to eat: peel and cut or halve, seed, and eat with a spoon. Some classic preparations include cantaloupe-style melon cut into wedges and draped with prosciutto or serrano ham; pickled melon rind; and a reminder of old Americana, melon with cottage cheese. Melon can also be treated just like tomatoes and cucumbers and make good savory salads and salsas.

One other preparation popular in Latin American cultures is the **melon cooler**—one of many *agua frescas*—served in markets and restaurants. Fill a blender nearly full with cubed melon, add ¼ to a ½ cup of sugar (depending on how sweet your melon is), and a couple of tablespoons of lime juice. Puree until very smooth, then pour into a couple of pitchers and add a cup of ice water to each pitcher. Adjust with more sugar and/or lime to taste.

Chile & Other Peppers

Chiles and other peppers are usually relegated to supporting ingredients, and many renowned cuisines would not be the same without these hearty new world ingredients. Fresh chiles are crucial to salsas and add a punch to stir fry and curries.

Many dishes call for peppers to be **roasted**, then peeled and seeded before use: the roasting intensifies the flavor of the chile, and adds a subtle smokiness as well. There are a couple of ways to do this. If you are only roasting a couple of chiles for a dish and have a gas stove, simply take the ring off the stove and, using heat proof tongs, roast the chiles directly in the flame for a few seconds on each side until the skin blackens and the chiles smell fragrant. Alternatively, place an oven rack at the topmost part of your oven and heat oven to 450 degrees. Roast chiles directly on oven rack, turning once or twice until skins are charred. If you are roasting a lot of chiles—for a batch of stew or sauce or for freezing—use a large sheet pan lined with foil. In this case, you might want to halve and seed your chiles before roasting, placing them on a sheet in a single layer. This eliminates the need to turn chiles, as well as making de-seeding simpler. For ease of peeling, place roasted peppers in a paper bag to let steam for a few minutes after roasting.

Peppers can also be **stuffed**, as in the ubiquitous jalapeno poppers on menus of the recent past, or in more refined dishes such as chiles en nogada, the Mexican specialty served at the holidays. I like to make **chile rellenos** when I have decent-sized Anaheims or poblanos in the garden: after roasting and peeling, stuff peppers with cheese or ground beef cooked with garlic and cumin (or a mix), then carefully coat in a tempura batter and deep fry until batter puffs and cheese melts. I keep a quick tempura batter mix on hand: mix together three cups cake flour with a ¾ cup of cornstarch and leaven with a couple of teaspoons of baking soda; add a teaspoon or two of salt. When ready to use, mix with seltzer water to form a batter (usually, a ration of two parts batter to one part liquid). Serve chiles rellenos with a smooth enchilada style sauce or fresh salsa, if you have it.

Squash & the Like

Squash is another prolific crop, whether in summer (yellow crookneck, zucchini) or fall (acorn, butternut). Squash is virtually foolproof to grow and lends itself to any number of simple recipes.

Zucchini-corn sauté is one of my favorites; it makes an excellent vegetable side dish to put out on a table laden with enchiladas or tacos. Slice a couple of zucchinis into half-moons, then sauté in a large skillet for a couple of minutes; throw in a cup or so of corn kernels, preferably fresh off the cob, and increase heat, cooking until both zucchini and corn start to brown. Finish with a squeeze of lime juice and a shower of chopped cilantro.

Squash can also be hollowed out and **stuffed**, then baked, for an elegant side dish to a summer meal. Sauté the squash insides with garlic, onion, and herbs, then stir in cooked rice or crispy breadcrumbs and return to squash shells. Sprinkle with more breadcrumbs and/or grated hard cheese, and bake until shells are tender. Sometimes I add some black olives to the mix for some salty punch.

Acorn squash is a beautiful fall squash that works well for stuffing: simply cut in half and scoop out stringy flesh and seeds, then add a filling: a big pat of butter and some cinnamon mixed with brown sugar, or some crumbled Italian sausage spiked with maple syrup. Note that the squash is left unpeeled, but the skins aren't meant for eating; scoop out servings, or serve half a squash as a full entrée. Be sure to slice a piece off the underside of the squash, so it sits flat while baking.

Alliums (Garlic & Onions & Leeks)

Another group of supporting players, alliums show up just about everywhere in cooking. Here are a couple of recipe ideas that highlight each of these usually supporting players.

Chicken with 40 cloves of garlic is a famous French preparation and a delicious way to make your house smell warm and inviting. Basically, this is just a garlicky roast chicken. I like to spatchcock a whole chicken (this is the process by which you remove the backbone, then flip the chicken and break the breastbone, thus flattening it—makes for more even cooking) but you can cut a whole chicken into pieces if you'd rather. Pour a thin layer of olive oil into a roasting pan and add your chicken or chicken pieces, skin side up. Scatter peeled garlic cloves around and some sprigs of fresh chicken or tarragon, if you like. Cover with foil (or use an oven-safe pan with a lid) and cook at 350 degrees until done, about an hour. Make sure you have plenty of good crusty bread to spread the soft garlic cloves on.

Caramelized onions are one of those kitchen staples that are always wonderful to have around: make more than you think you'll need and freeze for later use. All you need is a nonstick pan, preferably, some butter and/or oil, lots of onions of any color, and some patience. Cook sliced onions in butter or oil (I use a mix) over relatively low heat, stirring occasionally until they get really dark brown, up to an hour and a half. Serve with grilled meats, atop burgers and sausages, or add to homemade pizza.

When leeks and potatoes come together during the season, I always think of **vichyssoise**, the cold pureed French soup. It is easy to make and light yet filling. Sauté equal parts leeks and potatoes in some butter (only use white and light green parts of leek and peel potatoes). Add chicken stock to cover and toss in a bay leaf and some herb sprigs, if you like. Simmer until leeks and potatoes are very tender. Puree in blender until smooth, then allow to cool and add a bit of cream or half and half. Chill, and serve with sliced chives on top. For about 4 servings use 5 leeks, 5 potatoes, and 5 cups of chicken stock.

Potatoes

This hearty vegetable, ubiquitous on the American table, lends itself to almost any preparation: baked, boiled, fried, roasted, scalloped, and pancaked, most home cooks have a handy set of potato recipes on call. I've already mentioned them as co-stars in such dishes as green bean and potato stew and potato-leek soup (vichyssoise). Some more out of the ordinary recipes for the humble spud follow.

While it is not often that we think of the potato as a suitable vegetable for stir-frying, there are many places in China that have adopted the potato; in the southern part of China, you'll find **Sichuan-style stir-fried potatoes**. Cooked quickly and left slightly crunchy, these potatoes are very different than your average roasted or baked potatoes. Peel and cut about a pound and a half of potatoes into slivers, like matchsticks. Soak them for a while in cold salted water to remove starch. Drain well. Heat oil in a wok or heavy skillet until very hot, then cook a half a dozen small dried red chiles (leave them whole) and a teaspoon or two Sichuan peppercorns for a couple of minutes until fragrant. Add matchstick potatoes and some salt and stir fry for about another 5 minutes. Drizzle with some toasted sesame oil and serve.

Another fun and different way to prepare potatoes hails from Spain. Best with small red or white potatoes—creamy not fluffy potatoes—**patatas bravas** (brave potatoes) are a ubiquitous part of a tapas-style spread. Boil potatoes whole until tender, then lightly smash and coat with oil. Spread in a single layer on a baking sheet and roast in a 450-degree oven for 35-45 minutes, until potatoes are very brown and crunchy. Meanwhile, make the brava sauce: sauté a small chopped onion, some chopped garlic, and a can of tomatoes (or use your own, roasted and peeled) until onion is very tender. Cool slightly then puree in blender or processor with a couple of teaspoons smoked paprika. Serve over potatoes, or on the side for dipping, along with homemade mayonnaise. (You don't know how to make homemade mayonnaise? It's easy and delicious: whirl one egg, one egg yolk, some lemon juice and a splash of Dijon mustard and some salt in blender or processor until just mixed. Slowly—*slowly*—drizzle in *very fresh* olive oil, about a ¾ cup, until mixture is emulsified.)

CHAPTER 6

Preserving Your Produce: Strategies for Zero Waste Gardening

After months of hard work—planning, planting, growing—the last thing a gardener wants is to let any of his or her harvest to go to waste. If, like me, you have a relatively small plot on which you're planting just a few items, then you may easily be able to use everything you grow as you pick it. However, if, like me, you turn out to be better than expected at the gardening endeavor—an unexpected pleasure—then you may have to come up with ways in which your crops aren't wasted. In addition, many people, again like me, simply wish to preserve something of spring and summer to hold them over the long winter months. February is perhaps the dreariest month of the year (unless you live in southern Arizona), and nothing lifts the spirits as much as cracking open a can of cucumber pickles or rescuing a freezer bag full of homemade tomato sauce. There are many methods by which you can successfully maintain a "zero waste" garden, from the complex to the simple.

Lest we forget: one of the simplest ways to ensure that not a single fruit, vegetable, stem, or vine goes to waste in your garden is to feed your compost pile. Any inedible or undesirable bits of skin or core or bird-picked fruit should be tossed in the pile (or, alas, the occasional neglected scrap at the bottom of the vegetable bin). When one season rolls into another and you are clearing away the last roots from your spring plants or vines from your summer plants, be sure to grind these up as best you can and add them to the pile, as well. Each year your garden is fed by the garden of yesteryear, a true cycle of life (to paraphrase a famous film).

Other ingenious ways to keep your crops throughout the year are as follows: canning, freezing, dehydrating (drying), fermenting, and smoking. See details on each method, plus some recipe suggestions, below.

Canning

A nearly foolproof way to preserve your harvest for months—even years—to come, canning is a lost art among most home cooks. Supermarkets have made it far too easy to obtain whatever produce you want at whatever time of year you desire it. While there is nothing inherently wrong with this, it is certainly economically and environmentally sound to grow your own food and to preserve it. Canning is a time-honored way to do just that.

For canning, you do need a little specialized equipment, such as a water bath canner and/or a pressure canner, canning jars (mason jars, such as Ball and Kerr) with lids, and a jar lifter. If you become very serious about canning, be aware that there are two types of canning deemed safe for long term preservation: water bath canning for high acid products and pressure canning for low acid products. Thus, if you want to can your vegetables straight from your garden, you'll need to invest in a pressure canner. If you intend to can sauces or pickles or jellies made with the produce from your garden, a water bath canner should work. For details on how to obtain canning equipment and how to can safely, the Ball© Kerr© company provides an excellent site; click <u>here</u> for more information.

I have done some canning in my time, but I found I don't produce quite enough to justify the investment of time. Should you acquire a large parcel of land upon which to grow numerous plants of each variety, I urge you to learn. For those of us in suburban or urban areas with small raised beds, a more practical way of keeping fruits and vegetables through the winter is freezing.

Freezing

If, like me, you don't have the time, space, or equipment to do much canning, and you don't have a garden big enough to need to save a harvest for longer than a few months, freezing is the way to go. The only equipment you need besides your produce is sturdy storage bags—quart size is the best for ease of storage and size of portion—and a black sharpie. While a lot of produce freezes well, some items are not as well suited. Freezing things like lettuce and radishes isn't recommended. A general rule to follow: if the produce can be blanched without altering its characteristics drastically, then it can be frozen. For example, green beans are excellent for freezing: simply blanch the green beans in boiling salted water for a couple of minutes; shock them quickly in ice water to halt cooking and preserve color; then dry and place on a sheet pan or cookie tray in a single layer; put into freezer until frozen; then pack into a freezer bag labeling the contents and—this is important—*the date on which it was frozen*. Most vegetables will keep well if stored properly for about six months, but after that, they start to lose flavor and can become frostbitten.

The **above blanching and freezing method** can also be used for sugar snap peas, broccoli, cauliflower, Brussel sprouts, and some low moisture squashes. Greens of various kinds take well to this, though the method is a little different: blanch hearty greens like kale and collards for about five minutes, while softer greens like spinach and chard only take a minute or two. When blanched, drain in a colander and rinse with cold water. Sometimes I throw a handful of ice cubes on top to speed the cooling process, but then you've got to pick bits of green off the cubes. I don't like using an ice bath on greens as I feel it tends to waterlog them a bit too much. When cool enough to handle, squeeze as much liquid as you can out of the greens, and coarsely chop before packing into a labeled freezer bag. Other vegetables, such as okra and cucumbers, are better served by pickling of some kind (see the fermenting section below for details on that).

Potatoes can also be frozen in this manner, for a french fry preparation. Blanch in hot oil until lightly cooked but not colored; drain well and pat dry before freezing in a single layer on a baking sheet. Put in your prepared freezer bags and, when ready to eat, cook them in hot oil (about 325 to 350 degrees) until browned and crunchy. No need to defrost.

Another method by which you can prepare certain crops for freezing is **roasting**. Roasted peppers are excellent candidates for freezing (see Chapter 5 for details on how to roast peppers), and I like to make a mixed bag of roasted peppers—jalapenos, poblanos, and anaheims—to pull out for making green chile stew during the winter. So, if you don't have enough of one kind for freezing, make a "house blend," as it were.

Tomatoes are also ideal for roasting, and I invariably put several freezer bags of both plain roasted tomatoes and tomato sauces away each season. For the best-roasted tomatoes, core each tomato and score an X in the bottom end; place tomatoes in a single layer on a foil-lined baking sheet, core side down. Roast near the top of the oven at 450 degrees for ten minutes or so (timing depends on the size and ripeness of tomatoes; use your best judgement, as there really isn't a way to fail at this), until the tomatoes emit juice and the X starts to curl the skin back. You want the skin to easily peel off but not for the tomatoes to fall to mush (though, if they do, no matter: still usable). When cool enough, peel and, if you like, squeeze the tomatoes to release most of the juice and seeds before packing into labeled freezer bags. This method most closely mimics what you would get in a supermarket can of whole tomatoes (though large heirloom varieties typically have a higher moisture content). Another tip: *don't throw away the juice from the roasted tomatoes!* Simply pass through a fine sieve to remove seeds and bits of the skin; add a bit of salt and lemon or lime juice to taste, and drink it for breakfast or in a glorious Bloody Mary.

I also like to make **sauces** from the roasted tomatoes. In a good harvest year, I put away three or four bags of plain roasted tomatoes and two or three bags each of three ready-made sauces I like to have on hand.

The first is a simple **Italian red sauce**, delicious on spaghetti with nothing more than a sprinkle of cheese or to add to baked pasta dishes or Italian-inspired roasts. Most years, just about every ingredient in this comes directly from my lovely little organic garden. Sauté a coarsely chopped yellow or white onion and garlic in some quality olive oil (be generous: it is Italian cooking, after all). When onion and garlic have softened a bit, add about 8 to 10 roasted, skinned, seeded tomatoes, crushing them lightly with your hands as you go. Throw in half a dozen large basil leaves, season with salt, and let lightly simmer for 20-30 minutes. You want flavors to meld and all the ingredients to be soft, but for some liquid to remain. Let everything cool, then whirl in the processor with another half dozen basil leaves. You could also use some oregano here, or a mix of basil and oregano. Since basil does not dry well, I use it in sauces and save oregano for drying. Put sauce in your labeled freezer bag: the above recipe should fit in your standard quart-sized bag.

The second is an even simpler **Mexican-inspired chipotle sauce** for enchiladas or fideo dishes. Simple puree 8 to 10 roasted, skinned, seeded tomatoes with 2 or 3 canned or homemade chipotle peppers (see below) and some salt. If you want a slightly more complex sauce, sauté some onion and garlic until soft and add to the above. Put into prepared freezer bags.

The third is a **Mediterranean-syle tomato sauce**, excellent with grilled meats and kebabs or as a sauce for meatballs or chickpeas. Sauté some chopped garlic in a generous amount of good olive oil in a small pan until softened, then add a couple of teaspoons each smoked paprika and cumin and a teaspoon of Aleppo pepper (a marvelous coarse flaked dried pepper with hints of tartness and mild heat: well worth seeking out). Let the mixture cook for a minute or two, until the spices "bloom," then pour over your roasted, skinned, seeded tomatoes (8 to 10) in a processor or blender. Give it some salt and pulse until combined. Add a squeeze of lemon if it needs some acid or a pinch of sugar if it needs some mellowing. Put into prepared freezer bags.

Again, all of these recipe suggestions can be canned in a pressure canner, should you have one.

Dehydrating (Drying)

Even if you don't own a specialized home dehydrator, there are a few simple ways to preserve certain items from your harvest for later. A dehydrator is a nice piece of equipment if you decide to embark on such things as fruit leathers or vegetable chips, but with just a little patience and care, you can stock your pantry through the winter.

The most obvious **candidates for dehydrating are herbs**, and drying your own herbs makes for a far superior product than the vast majority of commercially processed herbs on the market. Certain herbs take to drying more readily than others; basil and chives both lose too much flavor in the process (and basil tends to rot before it thoroughly dries), so I find those aren't worth the trouble. But tarragon, oregano, and mint take especially well to drying and the process couldn't be simpler: at the end of the growing season, pull up your plant if you don't wish to overwinter or cut it all back if you do (keep the mint, for sure) and wash well. It is nearly impossible to remove dust from dried leaves so don't skimp on the washing. Place the plants on a large sheet tray and stick it on top of your refrigerator (or another cool, dry place) for a couple of weeks. Once dry, strip the leaves off the plants in store in airtight containers away from sunlight. These should stay fresh and fragrant until next year's harvest.

Many people also utilize a microwave for quick drying. It is considerably faster—just microwave in short ten second bursts until herbs are dried—though I always fear I might "cook" the herbs instead of preserving their fresh flavor. **Oven drying** over the lowest heat is also another way in which to dry herbs and other small crops; this can take from two hours to ten hours depending on what you're drying. Again, this kind of heat-based drying will change the characteristics somewhat. That said, oven drying is excellent for making "sun-dried" tomatoes, with smaller paste tomatoes such as the Roma.

The **other prime candidates for drying are peppers**. Once you've made your own pure chile powders, you will inevitably be disappointed by most commercial brands. With cayenne peppers, I make a *ristra* (wreath) of peppers, threading them onto a string as they become ripe throughout the season. To thread peppers, simply push a needle threaded with a double layer of sturdy string that's been tied off at the end through the stem of the pepper, slide it down, then slide the next one. Hang this from your kitchen windowsill or other sunny spot where you will not forget it. As I said, just add as peppers turn a bright red and once growing season is over and all are nicely dried, grind in a clean coffee or spice grinder until the consistency is to your liking. Save some whole, if you like, to throw into soups, stews, stocks or stir-fries for a bit of a punch.

The above *ristra* method works well for small, skinny peppers but not as efficiently for thicker, juicier peppers such as jalapenos and poblanos. These peppers are more likely to rot before they dry—unless you have a dehydrator—because of their size and moisture content. In addition, these peppers are typically used in smoked form, transforming into chipotles and anchos, respectively. See below for quick ideas.

Smoking

If you have a backyard smoker, smoking is another effective way to preserve certain crops. It is essentially an intensive way of drying foods while adding the layer of smoke flavor. If you don't have a backyard smoker or wood-fired grill, a propane grill can be used, though it will burn through a good bit of fuel in the process.

Whenever you get prepared to do some smoking, remember your garden: prepare a *ristra* of jalapenos and/or poblanos. Typically, this is done when these peppers are very ripe and have turned red. When still green, they are used fresh or roasted. Make sure they are hanging quite close together so the string will not burn and cut a long slit in each pepper to encourage the juices to drip out more quickly. (In fact, it is best if you harvest the peppers a week or so in advance and let them dry out a bit before smoking; this speeds the time they'll spend in the pit.) When they have shriveled and hardened, take them off the smoker. Make sure they are devoid of moisture, or they can spoil (if they are still somewhat moist, throw them in prepared freezer bags; they'll still be great).

Dried chipotles can be used like commercial canned chipotles, though they will need to be rehydrated in soaking liquid first. They will not taste quite the same without the adobo sauce that coats them in the can, though you can make your own and store your dried chipotles in it for a couple of months in the fridge. It is usually a mix of tomatoes, onions, garlic, cumin, oregano and dried milder chiles or chile powder.

Other products take well to the smoker, too: tomatoes, particularly smaller paste varieties, such as Roma, can be halved and smoke-dried. Lightly smoking larger varieties of tomatoes will not necessarily help you preserve them in the pantry, but these can be stored and frozen like roasted tomatoes with a smoky kick: these make the most delicious tomato soup in the known universe.

Fermenting, Pickling, and Other Tricks

I am including a hodge-podge of ideas here that I have used throughout the years to preserve vegetables and fruits. Almost everything I mention here will need to be kept refrigerated or frozen at some point, though almost all here also takes well to canning, should you have the time and resources.

Fermented foods have made a comeback in recent years as the growing consensus suggests that the active cultures, or probiotics, in naturally fermented foods are remarkably good for our overall health, especially in maintaining a healthy digestive system. Pickles that you buy in the supermarket are typically heat-treated in some way or pickled using vinegar and not fermentation; both of these methods effectively kill any active microorganisms. Naturally fermented or "pickled" vegetables made at home contain a host of good probiotics if monitored carefully and taste superior to mass-produced items.

The fermented vegetables collectively known as **kimchi** are no longer an exotic food, thanks to the rapidly growing popularity of Korean food throughout the country. Jars of cabbage kimchi are found on most grocery store shelves but, again, that made at home with your own organic produce is tastier, fresher, and healthier. While some of us may be more familiar with sauerkraut, another traditional fermented cabbage dish, cabbage kimchi is spicier and livelier and fairly simple to make.

To make cabbage kimchi at home, start with brining your cabbage: put a chopped head of cabbage into a brine of 6 cups of water and 3 tablespoons of salt. Weigh the cabbage down with a plate topped by cans and let it sit overnight. The next day, drain cabbage, reserving brine, and mix with half a dozen sliced scallions, half a dozen minced cloves of garlic, a tablespoon or two of grated fresh ginger, and two or three tablespoons of chile powder (gochugaru is the traditional Korean chile powder, but you can, in a pinch, substitute cayenne or other spicy chile powders), and a couple teaspoons of sugar. Make sure the spices coat the cabbage leaves well and pack into sterilized quart jars (I used to use old mayonnaise jars when they were glass; alas, I'd avoid the new plastic ones) and pour over reserved brine just to cover. Put the rest of the reserved brine into sealable plastic baggies and push these into the mouth of the jar; these allow for fermentation bubbles to escape—if you screw a lid on top, the jar will potentially shatter—while preventing scum from forming on top. Place in a cool dark place (ideally no hotter than 70 degrees: I use the garage in winter) for three to seven days. It will get slightly fizzy and more sour with each day. When it is as sour as you want it—if you're doing this in hot weather, err on the side of sooner rather than later—remove baggies, pouring brine back into the jar, seal, and refrigerate. This will keep for six months or more.

This kimchi method will also work well for radishes, cucumbers, and members of the allium family (I like a mix of leeks, onions, and garlic), and of course, you can customize this basic recipe to suit your tastes. Some kimchi recipes call for the addition of dried shrimp or fish sauce to up the funky ante.

Other kinds of **pickling** calls for vinegar which, while not quite as rich in the probiotic lottery, is still a delicious and healthy way to preserve your harvest. Again, these recipes will need to be kept refrigerated, unless you have canning equipment.

A very basic pickling brine can be made with equal parts vinegar and water with enough salt to both flavor and promote preservation. Many recipes will call for pickling salt which is merely table salt without the iodine; because it is finer than kosher or sea salt, it dissolves in brines more quickly. I myself never bother with it to no detrimental effect. I usually use kosher salt, as it has no additives; you just need to increase the amount called for to compensate for the coarser grains and be sure that it dissolves completely.

So, for example, 2 cups of cider vinegar, 2 cups of water, and 1 tablespoon plus a pinch more of kosher salt makes a great basic pickling liquid for about 2 pints worth of vegetables. Bring brine to a boil, stirring to dissolve the salt, then pour over vegetables packed in sterilized jars. For variety and flavor, add aromatics, such as garlic cloves and dried peppers; add as much sugar as salt for sweet and sour versions; vary the kind of vinegar used. Many vegetables take well to this, including okra and green beans: don't use sugar and do add garlic and peppers. Make sure, if you aren't canning, to blanch these beforehand. For pickled garlic and cucumbers, use the lighter rice wine vinegar and add some sugar. For a lovely blush color and some natural sweetness, add a peeled and sliced beet to some radishes pickled in this manner.

Pickles made in this manner can also be frozen for longer storage.

Other tricks include such things as preserving in oil, vinegar, salt and sugar. All of these elements promote longer storage and/or bring out the flavors of certain suitable produce.

For example, you can make flavored oils. Warm the oil and then gently heat your chosen aromatic in it: herbs, fresh or dried; garlic cloves; chiles, fresh or dried; and/or dried tomatoes. Steep for a day or two, then strain and store in a cool dark place for a couple of months. Other things you can add are citrus peels and whole spices for flavor boosts.

This same method also works for vinegars, though no heating is required and straining isn't always necessary as the acidity in vinegar keeps the produce from spoiling. I particularly enjoy tarragon vinegar, and the delicate flavor of rice wine vinegar preserves the tarragon flavor the best, I think.

Salted vegetables can keep for long periods of time, refrigerated. Simply pack into crocks with layers of salt and fish out bits for use as seasoning. Rinse the salt off and use judiciously as anything kept this way will become intensely salty. Think of preserved lemons or salt-packed capers for examples of what this might entail: salted radishes pack a lovely salty-spicy punch, for one. This method can be used with miso, the fermented soybean paste common in Asian cooking, as well.

Sugar is used in the preservation of fruits that take well to jams and jellies, of course, and I like to make hot pepper jelly at the end of the season on occasion.

Last, a condiment-tonic that I like to keep around in the fridge is **pepper water**. In a sterilized jar, put 4 chopped hot peppers (serrano, jalapeno, Thai, cayenne, or a mix). Add a couple of tablespoons of cider vinegar, a teaspoon each of soy sauce and fish sauce, a bay leaf, and a couple of crushed garlic cloves to your peppers. Bring about 10 ounces of water to a boil then pour over the ingredients in a jar. Let it cool a bit before refrigerating where it will keep indefinitely. Sprinkle it on plain rice; use it to bring some tart heat to soups, stews, curries and the like; add a shot of it to plain tomato juice or a Bloody Mary. Or just have a sip or two of it after dinner.

CHAPTER 7

Sustaining the Seasons: Making the Best of Your Garden Year Round

While many of these tips and techniques have been briefly discussed in various other chapters, here you will find some specific advice on how to care for your organic garden during each season. Of course, the objective is to garner as much yield as you can throughout the year while also maintaining soil health and sustainability.

Overwintering

There are three things that you can do to provide a healthy winter season for your garden: one, continue to grow appropriate crops; two, plant a cover crop that will both re energize your soil with nutrients and provide warming ground cover; three, mulch the garden well to prevent degradation of topsoil. Or, of course, you can employ a mix of all three.

Crops for overwintering include garlic, onion, and leeks, as discussed in Chapter 3. You can also overwinter certain root vegetable crops such as potatoes, parsnips, and carrots. If you live in regions where winters don't stay too cold for too long—that is, the ground does not stay in a state of hard freeze for an extended period of time—you can also overwinter several varieties of greens such as collards, kale, and heartier varieties of spinach and arugula. Keep in mind, that if you leave crops in the ground for harvesting in the spring, you will need to protect your garden with mulch and be sure to visibly mark where plants are located in order to avoid accidentally digging them up when you turn your garden over for spring planting. Also, be aware that continuously planting can sometimes exhaust your soil: this can be avoided by continuously feeding your garden rich, organic compost or by giving it a winter break and planting an appropriate cover crop.

Cover crops are plants that you grow to promote soil health, not crops you grow to eat. These include field peas, alfalfa, vetch, and some cereal grains (oats, barley, rye, buckwheat). The best crops to choose depend on where you are, what your soil needs, and how long you intend to maintain the cover crop. For a short overwintering, field peas and buckwheat are ideal. Not only do cover crops return nutrients to the soil, but they keep weeds out of competition for garden space, attract beneficial insects, and act as an organic mulch. If your garden seems to produce less one growing season, or if you encounter diseases that are the result of poor soil health, giving your garden a rest with a couple of months of cover crops will rejuvenate. And, when you're ready to turn the garden and plant for spring, your cover crops provide excellent fodder for the compost pile.

If you don't have the time or the inclination to plant during the winter, do your garden the favor of **mulching** well. Mulch also works to keep weeds under control and keeps your soil warm and relatively moist. It also protects any crops that are dormant throughout the winter but will pop up again in spring. Be aware that different mulches will affect your soil in different ways, and seek out organic mulches, of course, from reputable sources. Many biodegradable mulches are readily available and provide the added benefit of being easily tilled back into the soil; these include lawn clippings, raked leaves, or straw. Just be sure that these come from non-chemically treated sources. Wood chip mulches are the most effective at providing winter warmth for your soil; cedar or eucalyptus mulch have the added benefit of being a natural insect repellant. Again, consult your local garden shop, farmers' market, or cooperative extension for specific advice about your region.

Last, be sure to tend to your compost in the winter, as well, adding organic materials to it and making sure it is well covered and continuing to break down.

Preparing for Spring

The first item on your to-do list before the onslaught of the prime growing season is to have your **soil tested**. Find out if your soil is in balance with the right pH (6.5 is ideal) and whether it lacks certain nutrients (or, occasionally, has too much of some). You can do this at home with a soil testing kit, though the information that home kits give you is limited and does not have the advantage of an expert to provide you with advice on how to correct your soil, if necessary. The best place to get your soil tested is at a cooperative extension service if there is one located in your area. If you don't have an extension service near you, there are resources online. Check out the following <u>USDA resources</u> for links. Barring that, consult with a local farmer from your market or a gardening expert in your area.

Next, you'll want to **turn your garden** well, making sure not to disturb any overwintered crops. Here's where you might want a tiller if you have a larger garden. Turning soil breaks up any unwanted roots that may be lurking there as well as aerates the soil and prepares it for planting. Add your compost and organic fertilizer at this time, and be sure that this material is tilled into your garden well before planting.

If the soil in your area isn't conducive for gardening—if it is made up largely of clay, for example—you'll want to **create your topsoil layer** with organically sourced soil. Depending on how large your plot is, you can purchase gardening soil at many large retail outlets—again, look for organic—and gardening shops. This can get expensive if you have a lot of ground to cover, so you can also look to local farmers and/or cooperative extension services to find out where you might purchase soil in bulk. You should only need to do this your first year of gardening, barring some disaster, as the compost you keep should provide you with plenty of healthy new soil to add each year.

This is the time of year that you will typically want to **map out your garden space**, organizing crops according to some basic rules of seasonality, succession planting, and companion planting, with an eye on the practical logistics of space, weed control, and ease of harvest. Herb plants that you will snip throughout the spring and summer should be easy to access, for example, a long, squat raised bed plot should promote ease of harvesting with all crops.

Certainly, spring is the time of year during which you will do much—if not most—of your **planting**. Again, timing is based on your region or agricultural zone (see Chapter 1), but typically, you'll want to direct seed lettuces, greens, radishes, and cruciferous vegetables sometime in early spring, while transplanting seedlings such as tomatoes, herbs, and chile peppers in mid-spring. See Chapter 3 for advice on how and when to plant a variety of vegetables well-suited to organic gardening.

Sustaining Through the Summer

Summer offers up its own challenges, depending on your region. For most of us, the summers will get hot and dry—to what extent is out of our humble control. This is also the season during which weeds and pests will be at their most prominent, typically speaking. It is also a wonderful time of year when your garden will be at its most productive, so prepare for **regular harvesting and preserving**, if necessary. See Chapter 5 and Chapter 6 for recipe and preservation methods.

Most issues that arise during the summer months are issues that are combated or controlled through preparations that have already been put in place: companion planting to provide shade for plants susceptible to heat, using drip irrigation to provide precise watering to the most important plants when it gets dry, and mulching with appropriate materials to control weeds and keep moisture in the soil.

Be prepared to **visit your garden every day**—once in the morning and once in the evening is ideal—in order to keep up with weeds, pests, and diseases. See Chapter 4 for some more specific advice on dealing with these. Also, be sure to harvest daily: not only do you avoid losing a fruit or vegetable to overgrowth or pest invasion but you also keep the plants healthy and productive.

Extending Into Fall

The concept of **succession planting** cannot be emphasized enough, and as detailed in Chapter 3, several crops that do well in spring can be replanted for an additional fall crop. The more actively you cultivate your garden, the healthier it will be, and while fall presages the cold nearly dormant time of winter, it can be a lovely time to garden. Pests are fewer, weeds die back, and diseases tend to dissipate.

Fall is the ideal time to **plant any crops that you intend to overwinter**, such as garlic, onions, leeks, and various root vegetables or hearty greens. While some of these you will not harvest until the following year (garlic, onions, some root vegetables), you can maximize your harvest by cultivating some fall spinach or other greens to eat through Thanksgiving in certain areas, then cutting the plants back before winter mulching; these will be among the first to poke their green heads up again in spring.

Also consider cruciferous vegetables, some lettuces and greens, and autumn squashes as potential fall crops. One important thing to consider when planting a fall garden is when to plant: it is difficult to germinate seeds in the hot dryness of summer, but your plants need enough time to mature before the first hard freeze of winter. While some plants will survive a frost—and some will even benefit from it in terms of flavor—many will not. If your summers are hot and your autumns are short, it is best to cultivate your seedlings inside for a month or two before transplanting to your garden outdoors.

CHAPTER 8

Imagining Your Impact: The Final Payoff

Now that you have achieved your goal of becoming a successful backyard gardener, take a moment to reflect upon the wide-ranging impact that your efforts have had. Not only are you providing yourself, your family and friends with healthy, nourishing food but you are also reducing your carbon footprint and participating in a movement that promotes sustainability and accountability.

The contemporary American relationship to food is tortured, to say the least. From the inevitability of our *Fast Food Nation* to our passive acceptance of *Dinner at the New Gene Café* to the agonizing deliberation over *The Omnivore's Dilemma* (to use compelling titles of recent books), the reasonably informed consumer might be well justified in throwing up his or her hands in dismay. The corporate takeover of our foodways is no longer limited to the economic dominance of the convenience industry—fast food, supermarket chains, big box marts—and its partners in industrial agriculture, but is also increasingly relegated to scientists and the global giants of genetic engineering. Behind these contentious matters lurks one central theme: the vexed issue of how to produce authentically nutritious and delicious food. Seasonal food, sustainable agriculture, locally grown, preferably organic, produce: these have become the rallying cries of the new resistance. In an age of globalization—asparagus from South America in the dead of winter, even at a Whole Foods market—and in a country where the public discourse continues to confuse even the most conscientious consumer, the problem of how to feed our families well becomes an imperative part of the campaign to restore an ethically compromised system of producing, distributing, and consuming food.

Organically grown food is healthier: there is no other simpler way to say it. It nourishes our bodies and our environment in ways that mass-produced agriculture cannot. Gardening organically means that you are able to grow tastier food with more nutrients within a short walk from your back door. In addition, as we are well aware, organic gardening enriches our soil, our water, and our air by avoiding the use of petrochemicals and instead relying on the creation of a natural microbiome that cycles and recycles its main ingredients in order to continue thriving.

Foremost, your impact hits home—literally. The food that you grow with your own conscientious labor is both more satisfying and more delicious. Most produce that comes out of the agricultural system is bred (or modified) for heartiness and convenience, rather than taste. A bland supermarket tomato or mushy apple have been treated to ship well and to appear attractive without much thought given to the quality of taste or nutritional benefit. It really goes without saying that harvesting your evening meal—even a small part of it—from your own backyard or terrace is immensely pleasurable, both sensually and psychologically.

This also clearly engenders a sense of accountability: if you depend on your soil and your environment for your own food, then you begin to actively support those things, even beyond your own plot of land. This breaks a cycle wherein the corporate control over our foodways feels like our only choice. We have other paths we can choose to take.

Also, consider that your garden is an inspiration. No matter how frustrating gardening may sometimes seem, in those dark moments when the weather is too hot, too cold, too wet, too dry, in the end, it is nothing short of miraculous to create life out of the soil. By engaging in the practice of gardening organically, you provide a role model for your children, your family, your friends, and your neighbors. Good habits have a way of proliferating, and I can tell you from personal experience that, after a couple of seasons gardening in my suburb, I had the pleasure of talking to neighbors from all across the area who would knock on my door to ask advice. I helped a handful of neighbors to set up their own gardens, and I'm certain they inspired more. In what was once a fairly drab neighborhood with clipped lawns, identical hedgerows, and carefully pruned trees became a veritable oasis of gardens—colorful, riotous, delicious, and healthy. Within a few years, a local farmers' market grew out of this. Impacts are powerful in that they create waves of inspiration.

Second, your participation in the relatively simple and enormously satisfying act of gardening organically reverberates beyond the local. It means that you are acknowledging, even if in only a small way, that industrial agriculture isn't necessarily the best thing for human health or the health of the planet. Your decision and desire to garden may not necessarily be an act of rebellion—maybe it is just a fun hobby or a nod to getting healthier—but it is still a small symbol of what might be wrong with a larger system that depends on petrochemicals and relies on science more than it considers the health and well-being of its consumers and its land.

It must be noted that industrial agriculture has brought with it some positives: that we are able to feed more people more consistently and with more convenience is undeniable. But it is also most certainly true that the industry has become politically entrenched and thus wields enormous amounts of power in determining what we eat and how we eat. As many people are aware, only five corporations control the vast majority of our food supply; this results in an increasingly vulnerable population that is held hostage to the decisions made in corporate boardrooms. One small garden plot may not change the world, but it is certainly a start, an acknowledgement of our desires to live in a kinder, gentler, more sustainable world.

Yet, gardening organically is not merely about abstract thinking, it is about getting one's hands dirty, literally, working with the earth and the weather in order to feed the body, the mind, and the soul. It is hard to overestimate the kind of respect one gains for where our food comes from until you've worked a farm or a garden. If your children's only experience of food comes from shrink-wrapped packages or orderly supermarket shelves, then it is unlikely that a strong respect for nature will inherently come out of that. Gardening and farming model the ethics of hard work— reveals the "fruits of our labors," quite literally speaking—and creates strong moral considerations regarding waste and carelessness. It is easy to ignore a shriveling head of lettuce in the fridge if you picked it up for a couple of dollars at a corporate run grocery store; it is nearly impossible to let that go when you planted it, nurtured it, and harvested it yourself. Not only do we gardeners begin to view waste as an opportunity— compost, anyone?—but we also start to react squeamishly to the sheer amount of plastic that is generated by one trip to the grocery store. Your organic vegetables never see plastic or the inside of a refrigerator truck: a carbon footprint of virtually zero.

On that note, I would like to make a quick aside. Clearly, when gardening on a small plot in the backyard, even when supplemented by trips to the farmers' market, it is unlikely that the grocery store can be completely avoided. Still, yet, we can make choices within that realm that continue to reverberate in some of the same ways as our own choice to garden has. Seek out local producers; avoid out of season produce; buy organic when feasible. Even the largest of grocery store chains—Wal-Mart, for one startling example—have started to carry locally grown or locally made products and have expanded their still somewhat meager organic offerings. If you don't live in a community with a good-sized farmers' market or have access to local, fresh producers, do not despair: you can vote, as they say, with your pocketbook, simply by choosing products that are good for yourself, your family, and your planet.

It is up to us to make small changes in our own lives that impact the larger community and world. As Margaret Mead, the famous anthropologist once said: "Never doubt that a small community of thoughtful, committed citizens can change the world; indeed, it is the only thing that ever has." Our power as consumers lies in not only in our pocketbooks but also in our values. We can do our small part and reach out to others to do theirs.

Though some of the calls to go organic can sometimes be unreasonable— extreme localism is untenable as a way to feed a nation, not to mention a world (remember: our ancestors were hungry much of the time)—there is still much to be gained by engaging in the struggle over the politics of the plate. In the end, there is no one idea or action that can change the history of industrial agriculture but to simply leave it at that is dangerous, a passive invitation to allow more and more genetically modified organisms, processed foods, and corporate control into our grocery stores and homes. It is to divorce ourselves from the communion of the table and to close ourselves off from our neighbors, new and old. To believe that food *has* meaning beyond the purely physical surely paves the way for the creation of a food system that is healthier, more ecologically sound, and ultimately more humane.

Besides, in the end, the food you grow in your backyard tastes really, really good! As well, it is undeniably very good for you and your community. Last, it is truly some of the most satisfying, most enjoyable hard work you will ever do. Taking meals together—breaking bread—represents the best of what humanity has to offer. Bon appetít!

CONCLUSION

From the backyard to the table, organic vegetable gardening from your home is one of the most satisfying and enduring efforts you can undertake. Planning a garden, preparing the soil, nurturing plants, outsmarting pests, harvesting, preserving, and preparing meals are many of the numerous benefits to both body and soul that come out of such an endeavor. Not only are you contributing to the health and well-being of yourself, your friends, and your family, but you are also actively participating in creating a healthier environment and a better world.

I hope you have appreciated this journey through the seasons and now have the confidence and knowledge to begin your own backyard garden. Advice on how to set up a garden; how to prepare the soil; how—and when and what—to plant; how to combat pests and diseases; how to harvest and preserve; how to succession plant to ensure continuous garden growth: these tips, techniques, recipes, and more are all here. In addition, the many positive reasons—from avoiding petrochemicals and their detrimental effects to the fostering of tastier and more nutritious food—for undertaking an organic garden are outlined throughout.

If you have enjoyed this book and learned from its contents, I urge you to take the time to rate this on Amazon. This will lead others to embark upon their own backyard projects, spreading health and happiness, just as your own organic vegetable garden exists as a beacon throughout your wider community.

DESCRIPTION

If you are ready for a fun-filled and deliciously satisfying project to dig into—literally!—then now is the time to embark upon the joyful challenge of growing your own vegetables—organically, healthfully—at home. This book will guide you through the process, from the basics of why and how to the fruitful activities of harvesting and preserving.

Organic Vegetable Gardening gets you started on this journey through the seasons, where you will learn everything from how to tackle the most practical basics to how to cultivate the most enjoyable results. The reasons to grow your own vegetables organically are many and important, from providing personal nourishment to contributing to an ethically sustainable environment.

Some of the tips, techniques, and knowledge you will find in this book includes:

- The Basics of Why and How: not only a compelling list of reasons to propel you into breaking ground for your garden, but also a basic step by step on how to get started
- Soil and Seeds: not only how to coax the best out of your soil, but also specific advice on how to make your own compost bin out of easily acquired materials, as well as tips on how to get the best seeds
- Vegetable Victory: a list of some of the best plants for the organic garden through all the seasons, as well as some information on companion planting and maximizing space
- Preparing for Pests: how to control pests and combat diseases organically
- Healthy Harvest: the basics on weeding and pruning, as well as lots of ideas on how to use all the beautiful produce you grow, including numerous easy recipe methods for each and every plant listed
- Preserving Your Produce: never waste a thing! Canning, freezing, dehydrating, smoking, and fermenting are all ways to extend the life of your harvest, with more recipes to guide you
- Sustaining the Seasons: how to make the most of winter, spring, summer, AND fall
- Imagining Your Impact: taking stock of your accomplishments and appreciating your efforts

The time has never been riper to get your hands dirty with organic vegetable gardening. In the end, you will reap the rewards of these efforts in ways both local and global. To feed your family and friends food that you grow is an immeasurable pleasure, the ultimate act of love, and to do this in a way that supports environmental sustainability is quite literally groundbreaking. Sustenance is more than mere fuel for the body; it is an active fare for the spirit.

HYDROPONICS

Beginner's Guide to Quickly Start Growing Your Own Vegetables, Fruits, & Herbs and Learn How to Build Your Own Hydroponics Home Gardening System

**By
Rachel Martin**

© Copyright 2019 by Rachel Martin - All rights reserved.

This content is provided with the sole purpose of providing relevant information on a specific topic for which every reasonable effort has been made to ensure that it is both accurate and reasonable. Nevertheless, by purchasing this content, you consent to the fact that the author, as well as the publisher, are in no way experts on the topics contained herein, regardless of any claims as such that may be made within. As such, any suggestions or recommendations that are made within are done so purely for entertainment value. It is recommended that you always consult a professional prior to undertaking any of the advice or techniques discussed within.

This is a legally binding declaration that is considered both valid and fair by both the Committee of Publishers Association and the American Bar Association and should be considered as legally binding within the United States.

The reproduction, transmission, and duplication of any of the content found herein, including any specific or extended information will be done as an illegal act regardless of the end form the information ultimately takes. This includes copied versions of the work both physical, digital and audio unless express consent of the Publisher is provided beforehand. Any additional rights reserved.

Furthermore, the information that can be found within the pages described forthwith shall be considered both accurate and truthful when it comes to the recounting of facts. As such, any use, correct or incorrect, of the provided information will render the Publisher free of responsibility as to the actions taken outside of their direct purview. Regardless, there are zero scenarios where the original author or the Publisher can be deemed liable in any fashion for any damages or hardships that may result from any of the information discussed herein.

Additionally, the information in the following pages is intended only for informational purposes and should thus be thought of as universal. As befitting its nature, it is presented without assurance regarding its prolonged validity or interim quality. Trademarks that are mentioned are done without written consent and can in no way be considered an endorsement from the trademark holder.

INTRODUCTION

Congratulations on purchasing *Hydroponics: Beginner's Guide to Quickly Start Growing Your Own Vegetables, Fruits, & Herbs, And Learn How to Build Your Own Hydroponics Home Gardening System*, and thank you for doing so. Hydroponics is increasingly being taken up the choice farming method, and by purchasing this book, you will get to know why hydroponics is becoming so popular, and what you need to do to get a piece of the action too.

Hydroponics is thought to be the bedrock of food security in the future. Crops are not planted in the soil, and instead, inert growing mediums are used to provide support. Since the plants are grown indoors, the farmer is in control of all growing conditions including the nutrients available to the plant. The result is an increased growth rate, increased yields, continuous production, and other benefits, as compared to conventional farming.

Seeing these benefits, big farms and individual farmers are moving in to cash in on these perks. Restaurants and grocery stores are also taking up hydroponics as a way to provide consumers with fresh food or produce, and in the process, beating the competition. The good thing about hydroponics is that it does not restrict in terms of scale; you could grow one plant or thousands of them; it all depends on you.

To that end, the following chapters will discuss hydroponics in detail, explaining to you what exactly hydroponics gardening is, how it works, what you need to have and the crops that can be grown this way. You will also get to know its various tools and equipment you need to assemble for your garden. Hydroponic plants are grown in systems, and this book will let you in on various kinds of hydroponic systems, including the advantages and disadvantages of each. There is so much more to learn from this book; it is hoped that it will be an interesting, yet informative read that will get you situated and ready to hitch the fun and rewarding hydroponics bandwagon.

There are plenty of books on this subject on the market, thanks again for choosing this one! Every effort was made to ensure it is full of as much useful information as possible. Please enjoy!

CHAPTER 1

What Is Hydroponics?

My experience growing flowers and vegetables added to the knowledge I derived from my science classes tells me that one of the most critical constituents for anyone who wants to plant something is soil. It is in the soil that you place the plant for support, apply fertilizer and pour the water that the plant needs. However, as science and technology would have it, soil is not a critical element; a plant just needs a place to anchor its roots and a supply of all the nutrients it would have absorbed from the soil. This is the bedrock of hydroponics.

Hydroponics

Hydroponics is the method of growing crops without soil but providing all the necessary mineral nutrients. A gardener who takes up hydroponics takes on the responsibility of regulating the nutrients composition in the liquid solution he or she prepares for watering the plants. The gardener must also regulate the frequency of this nutrients supply. In other words, the gardener takes the responsibility of regulating the growing environment of the crops. The good thing is that the entire growing process is highly automated, but it still requires a great deal of up-close management.

Although the hydroponics idea sounds like something drawn from a science-fiction movie, it is not new. The Aztecs had created floating farms around Tenochtitlan, their island city, and Marco Polo recorded having seen some floating gardens in some of his travels as he toured China during the 13th century. In addition, as early as the 1930s, Pan American Airways had built a hydroponic farm on a remote island in the Pacific, which would allow its flights to replenish their food supplies en route to Asia. Today, the use of hydroponics is becoming increasingly popular particularly as a way of handling the food demands of the future.

Hydroponics is preferred because it utilizes water and nutrients efficiently mainly because both are applied directly to the roots of the plant. The water and nutrients are primarily responsible for the plant's growth. However, their levels need to be controlled, not just managed, so that the nutrients and water levels can be provided at the required levels.

The availability of lighting is also an important component in crop production. Adequate lighting is achieved by planting the crops in vertical structures so that the crop's accessibility to light is maximized while the crowding, density, and shading are kept at a minimum. In the present day, hydroponic farming has now taken up 3D planting where the plants are grown vertically, and in multilevel beds.

So far, we have seen how hydroponics provides the ideal growing conditions for growing plants, in terms of water, nutrients, and light. These conditions are ideal for crops and will maximize the utility of the growing area, and use the space that could otherwise have been unused. Having a movable multilevel growing structure exposes plants to ideal lighting at all times, during the growing period.

Mainly, hydroponics is used as a controlled agriculture system for growing out of season crops, for producing crops in areas that are less suited for growing crops, and in areas where the water supply cannot support conventional farming. Research centers also take up hydroponics to grow crops they need to study plant nutrition, plant breeding, and plant diseases because the conditions under which the crops are grown can be regulated as desired. Almost all plants can be grown using hydroponics.

When crops are grown in this way, they use up 50% less land and 90% less water when contrasted with traditional crop growing methods. However, the yields from the crops are 4 times more, and the crop growth rate is twice as fast when using hydroponics. This is possible because the crops have everything they would need, at the right concentrations.

In place of the soil used in typical agriculture, the farmer or gardener roots the plants in compounds like vermiculite, clay pellets or rock wool. All substances used must be inert so that they do not introduce any new elements into the plant's environment. The solution of water and nutrients is then poured over the support material so that the plant can feed into it.

One primary advantage that hydroponics offer over traditional crop husbandry methods is that when the systems are carefully manipulated and the growing environment properly managed, in terms of the quantity of water provided, pH levels and the combination and concentration of the nutrients. When these conditions are looked into carefully, the crops grow faster. There is less waste in regards to the consumption of resources. There is also less reliance on fertilizers, pesticides and other potentially harmful products used in conventional agriculture.

Why Hydroponics?

As the world population has been expanding, there has been an increased need to produce more food, which led to the development of modern industrialized farming. Modern agriculture has lived up to its promise of increased production because there has been a greater supply of fresh, cheap and nutritious food compared to the past, and its effects have particularly been felt in the developed world. However, modern farming has also brought with it challenges such as the promotion of waste, pollution and increased strain on resources.

The development of hydroponics has not only been a response to the current food and resource problems. It is a solution for the future too. Experts say that by 2050, about 80% of all the food produced will be consumed in the cities, which makes it important for the cities to become producers of food. Currently, most cities are the good 'black holes' because all they do is suck in much of it, and at the same time, the cities are the biggest food wasters.

It is easy to see the wastefulness and excessive nature of normal food production in comparison to hydroponics. To supply food to the urban areas, producers need to produce it in large amounts and to transport it there, sometimes, across vast distances, before it is introduced into the market. From the initial step of production, harvesting, packaging, and shipping, the food takes up large amounts of resources that could be saved and re-used elsewhere. People are involved, pollution-causing fuels, buildings, and other resources, and this is wasteful, in comparison to what hydroponics entails.

As the world's population is getting close to 7.5 billion and the demand for more food increasing just as fast, with emphasis on resource-intensive foods, it is clear that farming needs to be done even in the cities, and even so, more productively.

Hydroponics Will Soon Take the Bulk of Agricultural Production

Although the vast majority of plants are grown using soil, the use of hydroponics has been rising. Thanet Earth, the largest greenhouse complex in the United Kingdom, took up controlled-environment agriculture to produce approximately 225 million tomato fruits, 16 million peppers and 13 million cucumbers in 2013. This production was 12, 11 and 8 percent of Britain's total annual production of these crops, respectively. Thanet Earth made this record-breaking production with only four greenhouses and was hoping to add to this number.

In 2015, it was estimated that hydroponic farming has grown, and was worth $21.4 billion, with an expected annual growth of 7%. It would seem that hydroponics farming is changing slowly, but steadily.

Besides the changing dynamics of farming itself, other outside forces are pushing for the change, advocating for more controlled-agriculture, to boost food production. The earth's population is one key factor. It is expected that by 2050, the global population will have risen by a staggering 3billion persons, and more than 80 percent of the total population will be dwelling in the urban centers. Since we are already using the available farming areas, the arid regions too will need to be converted to production centers, and the way to do this is by introducing hydroponic farming in these areas.

One of the more popular methods is vertical urban farming where hydroponic farms are stacked one over another, in buildings, even in tall skyscrapers. This would be an ideal solution, especially when much of the land is taken up to house the large urban population. It would also place the farms strategically, right where the fresh produce is needed. Singapore and Michigan are already constructing these vertical gardens, and south London is also placing the disused bomb shelters into good use.

Interestingly, as man ventures further and further away from the Earth, NASA is looking into creating hydroponic farms in space to feed the astronauts. The research has been taking place at the University of Arizona, where scientists are looking into the possibility of creating a closed-loop system that will feel carbon dioxide and human waste into a hydroponic farm, which will possibly lead to the creation of oxygen, food, and water.

You could look forward to seeing some space-grown tomatoes in the future, but good luck with the human waste growing material.

How Hydroponics Works

We have already established that in contrast to traditional agriculture where the soil provides support to the plant, allowing it to remain upright and providing a supply of nutrients, in hydroponics plants have artificial support and a solution containing all the required nutrients is provided. The idea behind the hydroponic setup is simple. It is thought that environmental factors often limit plant growth, and therefore, by providing a solution that contains nutrients to the plant's roots, the gardener provides a constant optimal supply of nutrients and water. The nutritional efficiency makes a plant live up to its potential by making it more productive.

The nutrient-rich solution is delivered in a number of ways:

- In the first, the plants are placed in an inert substance, as mentioned earlier, and its roots are occasionally flooded with the solution.

- Secondly, the plants could be placed on the inert substances and the solution rained on the plant using a solution dripper.

- The third option places the plants on a film that slightly slopes, and this allows the solution to trickle down to the roots of the plants
- The fourth way has the plant and its roots suspended in the air, and the roots are occasionally sprayed with the solution mist.

All the methods described above use machines to do one thing or another, either by the use of a mister, or using a pump to deliver the solution from its storage area. The solution must also be aerated so that the roots get the oxygen they require once the solution comes on. Plants need energy to absorb the minerals in the solution, and this absorption process requires energy, which is made possible by respiration.

Is It Hard?

Certainly, setting up and maintaining a hydroponics system can be quite a difficult task. This is because the plants need an assortment of nutrients, and each species' optimal amount of nutrients varies. In addition, each plant's nutritional requirements will change as it goes through various developmental stages. Local conditions such as the hardness of the water to be used also matters a lot.

It is also a fact that some nutrients are absorbed into the plant much faster than others which can cause a buildup of some ions in the solution, hence a change of the solution's pH. Once the pH is affected, the absorption of other nutrients by the plant is hindered because the uptake of some nutrients is pH-dependent, and because the excess availability of some nutrients prevents the uptake of others. For example, when the ammonia content is very high, the calcium uptake decreases, and on the other hand, too much calcium reduces the absorption of magnesium.

Another critical aspect to be careful about is that some elements react with one another, and form compounds that are difficult to absorb, which means that they have to be provided at different times.

With the above different variations, a hydroponic farmer must have a good grasp of the requirements of plants and the interaction of nutrients with each other, and with the plants themselves. They must carefully monitor the solutions they provide to the plants and check to see the changes in concentration that could come about. The alternative option is for the farmer to invest in an automated hydroponics system, which is quite expensive, to run the process on his or her behalf.

Farmers are also obliged to take great care of the solutions they are using to keep them from contamination by unwanted substances. Most choose to enclose the hydroponics project inside a greenhouse or a building to ensure that they alone have control of what is going on in the systems. This limitation also gives the farmers the liberty to optimize on the environmental influences of the plant, such as the light, carbon dioxide exposure and the temperatures, all to maximize the yields received.

This means that hydroponics is just not about growing crops without using soil; it also means that the farmer has absolute control of the plants and their growing process, at least.

Crops You Could Grow

If you are wondering what kind of crops you can grow using the hydroponic system, the simple answer is that you could grow any vegetable, fruit or houseplant you would want. The system, however, is best suited for crops that can grow well in hydroponic conditions.

The general rule is that the use of solution is best for plants that tend to have shallow roots. For example, you could grow some lettuce, radishes, herbs, or some spinach. The aggregate systems are best suited for crops that have a deep root system like beetroot, and those whose tops tend to be heavy like cucumbers, and squash. Other crops you could plant include tomatoes, strawberries, peppers, celery, and watercress.

Tomato varieties are particularly popular in this kind of farming because it is said that they bring forth larger fruits and that they grow indeterminately, which is to say that they will grow continually and repeatedly. You will always find fruit on their stems.

Farmers also tend to lean towards the disease-resistant crop varieties because the plants live longer and hence produce for a longer time.

Avoid growing plants that are not genetically suited to the hydroponic environment like wheat. Researchers found that for you to grow enough wheat to make a loaf of bread, you would need at least $23! That's too expensive.

The Growing Systems

Many innovative systems have been created to replace the traditional gravel bed that was taken up when people first started embracing hydroponics. When making a decision on which growing system you would wish to install, ensure that you take into account the economics of your agribusiness, space requirements of the plants, the type of crop that you would be growing, the support system and the growing time.

Once you have figured these details out, you can then decide on whether you wish to grow these plants in a greenhouse or growth room. Some farmers take both options and will use the growth room for germination purposes, after which the seedlings that come off the process are transferred to the greenhouse where they grow out as crops. The added advantage of this arrangement is that the heat emitted from the lights in the growth room redistributes into the greenhouse, heating and warming the air in there.

Some of the common growing material farmers use include:

Pipes and Troughs

Farmers use PVC pipes or open and closed plastic troughs to grow cucumbers, lettuce, and tomatoes. The troughs are either filled with just the nutrient solution, or they may be filled with vermiculite, perlite or peat moss. Some farmers mount these pipes or troughs on movable racks or rollers to enhance their spacing as they grow. In the case of PVC pipes, farmers prefer the 3-inch diameter kind that has 6-inch holes on the center to give enough room for the development of lettuce leaves. Majority of these troughs and pipes are 10 feet or 12 feet. The farmer then uses carts to move the pipes from the growing area to the packing room.

Stones or Sand Culture

This is the medium that is used for most of the plants that need a deep bed, that of about 18 to 23 inches. The bed is prepared by placing the pea stones, the trap rock, or the sand on a plastic-lined bed or trough that is sloping to one point to allow the excess nutrient solution to drain off. The minimum slope should be 2%. Once the farmer places the seedlings onto this medium, he then has to water with the nutrient solution several times during the day.

Beds

Hydroponics beds are plastic lined bed-like structures on whom the nutrient solution is pumped from one end, and flows to the other end. If you want to plant lettuce plants on beds like these, consider using foam polystyrene flats to help the plants float in the solution.

Trays

In this method, the trays are flooded with the nutrient solution periodically. The trays are suitable for growing crops that were started in 1 to 2-inch diameter growth blocks. Most farmers buy these plastic molded trays or those that are made from waterproof plywood.

Bags

Another option is to use polythene film bags, and filling them with a solution made with peat and vermiculite. The bags are then laid up in a trough, from one end to the other, and soaker hoses or drip tubes are inserted in them to deliver the nutrient solution. These bags can be reused several times before they are discarded.

Besides the plant support material mentioned above, there are other materials needed to complete various makes of the hydroponic systems used. Farmers will need controls, tanks, and pumps. The tanks should be made of inert material, such as plastic, concrete, or fiberglass because if the tanks were made of some reactive material, the reaction between the tank and the fertilizer solution would corrode the tank, pipes, and pumps.

The farmer can have manual switches and controls as simple as a time clock, or have a computer automated process where everything is adjusted automatically. The computer also adjusts the chemical content of the nutrient solution, in accordance with the nutrients that the plants are absorbing.

CHAPTER 2

Must Have Tools

As you venture into hydroponics farming, there are specific tools you need to get you started. Although there are several systems from which you shall choose, the kind of tools used in all of them is more or less the same.

The tools you will need include:

A Reservoir

From its name, the reservoir will be used for reserving the nutrient concentrate. The concentrate is typically a mixture of water and the required plant nutrients and depending on the kind of hydroponic system you choose to install; the liquid is pumped from it periodically into the growing chamber as set at the timers.

In some systems, the reservoir doubles as the growing chamber too, such that the plants grow suspending their roots in the nutrients concentrate 24 hours, every day.

You do not have to purchase a special reservoir; you can fashion it from almost any inert large container that you use to hold water, so long as it does not leak. The container should be able to hold enough of the solution to allow it to grow. In addition, the container should be opaque to prevent the rays of the sun from penetrating into the solution.

If the container available to you is not opaque, there are many ways to make it light proof. For example, you could wrap or cover it up with an opaque material, or you could paint over it. The idea behind the opaqueness is to prevent algae from growing on the inside of the container.

If the hustle of making your own reservoir seems a bit too much, you could also opt to purchase the commercial reservoirs, and they will serve you well.

A Growing Chamber

A growing chamber is one of the most critical parts of a hydroponic system because this is where the plant roots develop. The chamber is the container that holds the roots, provides support to the entire plant, and house the nutrient concentrate.

The chamber, just like the reservoir, should be kept from direct sunlight and extreme temperatures because these can introduce heat stress to the plants. In case of exposure to extreme temperatures, such as heat, the plants abort their fruits and flowers.

The size and shape of the growing chamber are dependent on the kind of hydroponic system you intend to run, and the plants you wish to grow. Plants that grow big roots will require a large growing chamber while those that develop small roots will be okay with just a small one. However, do not be stressed about sizes because any chamber size will make due so long as the plants you are growing get their deserved nutrients and space.

In your quest to find the best growing chamber, kindly keep off metallic containers because metals are subject to corrosion and they react with the nutrient concentrate. If you cannot purchase a commercial growing chamber, however, check around to see the non-metallic items you could transform into growing chambers. However, if you still need to maintain class and style while at it, you could opt for a commercial growing chamber; there are some fabulous makes available, and I am certain they will appeal to your pallet.

Delivery System

The delivery system is the system that delivers nutrients to the plant roots directly. The concept of this is quite simple, in fact, and can be customized to fit into any system you choose to take up and install. A typical delivery system must include connectors, PVC tubes, blue or black vinyl tubing, and tubing connectors, for garden irrigation.

Depending on the hydroponic system that you settle for, you can choose to use emitters and sprayers for the delivery system. Although the sprayers and emitters are quite useful, be prepared, however, for frequent clogs when the nutrients in the solution build up. Therefore, if you are looking forward to stress-free farming, avoid them as best as you can.

Submersible Pump

Most pumping systems have a submersible pump to regulate the pumping of the nutrient concentrate from the reservoir to the growing chamber. You can buy these pumps at home improvement stores or hydroponic shops in your area. The pumps come in varying sizes, and you just have to choose one that matches the size of your farm.

How do submersible pumps work, you ask? Well, the pumps are just impellers that take advantage of electromagnetic fields to spin then pump their water. It is easy to maintain them because the majority of the time, you are only required to clean the solution filter. If you bought your submersible pump without a filter, you could still make one by cutting some part of the furnace filter, ensuring that it fits the submersible pump.

Besides the filter, you also need to clean the pump occasionally to ensure that there are no clogs that would obstruct the nutrients as they flow to the plants.

Air Pump

Although it is not compulsory that you make an air pump part of your hydroponic system, you ought to give it a thought because it comes with so many benefits. An air pump is also widely available in stores, and inexpensive, particularly if you are able to buy yours at a store that sells aquarium supplies.

An air pump is primarily used to ensure that there is a steady supply of oxygen in the water so that the roots can absorb it for their respiration, in the growing chamber. The pump does this by pumping the air through the airlines, onto the air stones, which ten creates bubbles that bubble up into the nutrient solution.

In case you are using a water culture hydroponic system, for example, the air pump keeps the roots from drowning in the nutrient solution because they are kept suspended in it all day, every day. In other hydroponic systems, the air pumps are fitted into the reservoirs to keep pumping oxygen into the water, increasing the oxygen concentration in the water.

Since the air pumps pump all day, they cause constant movement, which keeps the water and nutrients in it in constant motion. The circulation that results from the process ensures that the nutrients dissolve into the water evenly, at all times. The presence of oxygen in the water is also good because it prevents the growth of pathogens and microbes.

Timer

Not all hydroponics farmers need to time their operations with a timer, based on their choice of hydroponics system and its location. If your system is to be situated indoors, for example, and you have installed artificial lighting, you need to install a timer that will turn the lights off or on.

Drip and aeroponics systems also need a timer to control their submersible pump that controls the process of draining and flooding. It is important to take note of the fact that some types of aeroponics would need some special kind of timer to work properly.

Although the light and standard pump timers work very well, it is better to opt for a timer that has a 15 amperes rating other than 10 amperes rating because the former is often heavy duty and will have a cover that effectively protects it from water. You only have to check at the back of the packaging of the timer you choose to ensure that you have made a good choice.

But for those who may have a battery backup, a digital timer is not preferred over an analog one because once you unplug it from the power source, it loses all the data previously stored in it. Analog timers are a better choice for the additional benefit of having on and off settings. Therefore, as you go out to purchase a timer, ensure that yours has pins all around the dial, so that you get the analog kind, and avoid future regrets.

Growing Medium

The growing medium is essentially the substance on which the plants grow. It provides physical support to the plants, just like soil does, only that it is inert, not containing any minerals or living organisms. Different systems demand different growing mediums. For example, while other systems use peat moss, Rockwool or lava stone as the growing medium, aeroponics system uses air as the growing medium.

Nevertheless, the right kind of medium is one that retains moisture in such a way that the water solution will not need to be pumped in continually, every single minute.

Growing Lights

Grow lights: you can have them you can stay without them. They are an optional part of the system because it all depends on where you intend to plant your garden. You may end up using natural light or having to take up artificial lighting for your plants. If possible, opt for natural lighting because it is free, and will not add to the cost of setup as you purchase the new equipment and its accompanying maintenance costs.

If, however, you cannot find any good lighting at the place you intend to plant your garden by having lots of exposure through the window or having a sunroom, or that the time of the year does not allow enough lighting through, you may need to include some supplemental artificial lighting in your set up budget.

Kindly realize that your ordinary bulbs cannot be used as grow lights: grow lights are specially made light bulbs that emit light containing special color spectrums that mimic natural light. Your plants will take in these color spectrums and use them to carry on the process of photosynthesis, hence the leaf growth, flower formation, and fruit growth. Realize also that the intensity and type of light that the plant has access to, by large, determines its photosynthetic abilities.

Most hydroponic kit systems will come with complimentary light fixtures, but if you are setting up a DIY (Do It Yourself) garden, piecing together the equipment you need, you will need to purchase lighting fixtures.

The most effective lighting for a hydroponics system is the High-Intensity Discharge (HID) light fixture made up of either Metal Halide (MH) bulbs or High-Pressure Sodium (HPS) bulbs. The HPS, in particular, emits a red or orange-looking light, which works well for plants, particularly in their vegetative growth stage.

Another type of lighting used is T5. It produces fluorescent light of a high output, and this lighting consumes low energy and only a little heat. The T5 is suitable for when growing plant cuttings, and for growing plants with short growth cycles.

Ensure that the light is kept on a time so that the lighting will go on and off at the same time, each day.

PH Testing Kit

If you don't test the pH of your nutrient solution from time to time, you will be running your farm purely by guesswork, subjecting your entire investment to a trial-and-error game. The reality is that for your plants to thrive in the hydroponic garden you have set up, there needs to be a balanced pH, and using a pH testing kit, you can regularly check on your garden to determine whether the pH of the nutrient solution is optimal. If the pH is too low, you can adjust by bringing it up, and if it's too high, you can lower it also.

On a related note, besides the pH meter, you will also need equipment to measure the temperature and the PPM of the water. You could also purchase the equipment you would need to measure the humidity and temperature of the grow room. If, for example, you find that you need to adjust the humidity in the room, use a dehumidifier or a humidifier, to ensure that the plants do not dry out and that they do not dampen.

A fan or any other equipment that can be used to improve the air circulation in the room would also be welcome. Although a small oscillating fan may work for a beginner, you will need a more sophisticated fan as your garden grows, one with an intake and an exhaust system.

The Nutrient Solution

While the nutrient solution is not a tool, you will need to set it aside as you set your tools aside, in readiness for the setup of your garden. As we have established many times so far, the nutrient solution will be the primary source of nutrients for your plants for them to thrive.

The nutrient solution provides three primary macronutrients that can be found in most fertilizers: potassium, phosphorus and nitrogen, and a host of 10 other micronutrients that may not be found in the fertilizers, yet the plants need them to survive, grow and reproduce. Some of these micronutrients include zinc, molybdenum, boron, copper, iron, chloride and manganese.

As a beginner, it may benefit you to purchase an already mixed solution offering a balance of all the nutrients mentioned above, but as you gain more experience, you will find it easier to mix create your own nutrient solution, one that will provide the plants with all the nutrients they require.

The fertilizers or nutrients used in the hydroponic system you can find in both dry and liquid forms, and there are both organic and synthetic kinds. Either type you choose will be dissolved in water to come up with the nutrient solution that we have associated with the hydroponic system severely.

As you look around the store, you will find that there are some specific fertilizers or nutrients specifically designed for hydroponic farming, and if you use them, you are bound to receive good results, provided you follow all instructions indicated on the packaging. Kindly avoid using standard soil fertilizers in a hydroponic system because their mixing formulas are specifically designed for garden soil, not for direct infusion into the roots as it happens in hydroponics.

While still on the point of hydroponic fertilizers, ensure that you choose the kind of hydroponic nutrient that is designed for your particular needs. For example, you will find that some fertilizers are designed for flowering plants, while others are good for promoting vegetative growth such as that used for lettuce. If you apply the latter to a flowering plant, you will promote the growth of the leaves rather than the formation, enlargement, and blossoming of flowers.

The Quality of the Water Used

The solubility of water and its ability to deliver the nutrients you dissolved into it is affected both by the salt level of the water, as can be seen from the PPM, and the water pH. Typically, hard water has a high mineral content, and this fact keeps it from dissolving the minerals as effectively as the water that has a low mineral content. Therefore, in the event that the water you have for your project is hard, you will need to filter it out to take out the high mineral content.

The ideal water pH for making the nutrient solution is between 5.8 and 6.2, which is somewhat acidic. If your water is not at this pH level, you can use some chemicals to adjust it so that the pH gets within this ideal range.

The Conditions of the Room

It is of utmost importance, and great value, that the hydroponic system be set in the right conditions. Some of the elements you ought to check to ensure that the conditions are right include the carbon dioxide levels, relative humidity, temperature, and air circulation.

The humidity level is ideal if it ranges between 40% to 60% relative humidity. If the humidity gets to higher levels, it may lead to the formation of powdery mildew and other kinds of fungi.

The ideal temperature should range from 68 to 70F. If the temperatures are higher, the plants will become stunted, and if it gets even higher, the roots may start to rot.

The level of carbon dioxide, CO_2, is of most importance in the grow room. The best way to ensure that there is an adequate supply of it is by ensuring that the room has a free flow of air. As your farm or garden becomes bigger, you could now begin to supplement the CO_2 levels in the room because the more the gas is available in the growth room, the faster the growth of crops.

A Greenhouse

Any serious hydroponics gardener should aim for the ultimate gardening tool, a greenhouse. A greenhouse offers a farmer lots of advantages including complete climatic control, a lot of growing room, and access to natural lighting. If you are serious about increasing the output from your hydroponics garden, then the greenhouse is the way to go. It may seem like an ambitious project at first, but the return is that you get to have a larger supply of nutritious, safe and high-quality food for your nutrition, and to supply to other people, in exchange for money.

Considerations to Make When Purchasing Hydroponic Tools and Equipment

Getting into the hydroponics world is a new exciting experience, and the results of your hard work can be very fulfilling, but only if you get into the trade the right way. If you make mistakes on your way in, hydroponics gardening may get quite challenging, intimidating and frustrating, especially if you get the wrong tools and equipment, the kind that does not match your needs. On the other side, you could end up purchasing equipment that is too expensive, so that it takes you very long to get a return on your investment.

Therefore, to avoid making mistakes, here are some important considerations you ought to make when deciding on the kind of tools and equipment you purchase:

1. The plants you intend to grow

It is likely that you already envision what would be in your farm once you set everything up. To ensure that your vision comes to life, your task now is to go ahead and look for hydroponics equipment that will help you bring your dream to life. You wouldn't want to buy shallow trays while you intend to plant plants that have large and thick roots. Likewise, you would not wish to spend your money in the purchase of some 8-inch deep buckets while you only intended to plant shallow-rooted plants.

For you to purchase the right kind of growing medium, fertilizer, and hydroponic system, the kind that would accommodate the plants you want to grow in terms of size and their growth rate, you need to consult a hydroponics expert. Many manufacturers of these things also give out some phone numbers from which you can contact hydroponic professionals about growing issues you may have.

2. The space available

Consider where you intend to be growing your crops. Do you want to set up a small greenhouse in your backyard, your basement, or do you intend to use some large closet? Prior to purchasing your equipment, ensure that you first calculate the size of the available space and determine just how much equipment can fit in the space you have determined. For example, if you intend to plant your crops in rows, ensure that the space available can allow at least a meter spacing between the plant rows to allow walking in between the rows as you tend to your garden.

3. Your budget

Before you walk into the shop and select the hydroponics equipment that best appeals to you, you need to take some time to determine the amount of money you can comfortably spend, and then try to make the best of that amount by creating a budget, and sticking to it. Keep in mind that the cost of buying tools and equipment is not the only cost you have to cover, factor in the cost of running the lights, the electricity bill, the labor costs, water bill, and the cost of replacing the equipment that could break down.

Sticking to a budget is not to mean that you should go cheap though because as you may have learned, cheap things are often the expensive ones. It will save you a lot of money in the long run if you choose to spend a little extra on the equipment when you purchase the best and highest quality ones on the market.

4. The time you have

Just like most people who engage in hydroponic farming as a hobby, you do not wish to spend your entire day at your garden. This is the reason you should consider just how well the hydroponics system you choose can function without your assistance before you purchase it. If you don't have time to wait it out or change systems manually, opt for a more mechanized automatic system that can run even when you are away.

Nevertheless, consider the risk of mechanizing the entire process. For example, if you chose the appealing aeroponics system, realize that if anything were to go wrong with your timer, there would be very quick drying out of the roots, which means that although the system can run by itself, it still requires as much attention as that in which everything is done manually.

Not everyone has the luxury of rushing home from work every now and then to check on their plants or to take countermeasures that could save the plants in the event there was a power outage. Therefore, if this is your life, opt for a system that gives you a large margin of error such as one whose medium can hold air and water very well.

Overall, besides the tools and equipment you need, the primary things to have include the hydroponic water concentrate where all the nutrients your plants would need are. In case you have chosen a system that recycles the nutrient solution, ensure that you change it at the end of every week or two, at most, so that the nutrients remain balanced.

If you are to grow your plants indoors, you will need supplemental lighting most of the time, and for a garden growing green vegetables, it would be nice if you installed a fluorescent cool-white shop light just a few inches above the plants for it to work very well. If you are planting crops that produce fruits and flowers, you also must provide a grow light or else they won't grow to maturity.

CHAPTER 3
Types Of Hydroponic Systems

One of the primary advantages of hydroponic farming is its versatility meaning that there is a large number of systems from which a farmer can choose from. The decision of which hydroponic system to choose is based on your needs, the plants you wish to grow, your budget, and the space you have set aside for the project.

Aeroponics

The aeroponics hydroponics system is the most high-tech of the possible setups, but this is not to mean that they are complex: once you understand how the system works, the rest is easy. In this method, the plants' roots hang loose in the air and are occasionally sprayed with the nutrient concentrate. There are two ways to do it: using a pond flogger and using a spray nozzle, to spray onto the roots. If you opt for a pond flogger, ensure that the flogger has been coated using Teflon because the coating makes it easier to maintain.

Some farmers time the misting cycles just like the ebb and flow hydroponics system, only that the aeroponics cycle is much shorter because the mistings are only minutes apart. If you have a very fine sprayer, however, it is possible to mist the roots continuously so that an even larger amount of oxygen is available to the roots.

The use of the aeroponics systems has shown that plants grow even quicker using this method in comparison to the simpler systems like the deep-water culture, although this is yet to be verified across the spectrum. In case you want to try this method out for yourself, ensure that you purchase finer sprayer nozzles than the typical ones, to help you atomize the solution.

The Advantages of Aeroponics

- Exposing the roots increases their access to oxygen, which is unlike other methods that submerge the plants' root systems in the nutrient solution
- This method saves on nutrients, water, and the growing medium

- It is cost effective and efficient, especially when you finish carrying out the initial setup

Disadvantages of Aeroponics

- At the very slightest interruption, suppose the high-pressure nozzles failed, the roots can dry out, and the effect can be even more severe than what would happen if you had the N.F.T. system setup.

- The timers and the pump need regular inspection, which causes the system to be quite demanding in terms of maintenance.

- The aeroponics system is not as easy or cheap to set up as other methods are.

What You Would Need to Start an Aeroponics System as A DIY

- A solution reservoir
- PH kit
- Mist nozzles, sprinklers or sprayers
- A fitted lid to keep the moisture in submersible pump that has tubing whose ends have mist sprayers.
- A timer that will activate the sprayers at regular intervals
- A nutrient kit

Nutrient Film Technique (N.F.T.)

In these systems, the farmer grows his or her crops in tubes called gullies. Alternatively, the farmer can also use grow tanks to increase the speed at which the roots are growing. The gully, or the growing tray, must be placed above the reservoir, at an angle, and ideally, a channel is created at the center of the grow tray so that it can be used to drain the solution with more efficiency.

The nutrient solution is pumped into the growing channels and it runs along the bottom of the channel. However, when the solution gets to the end of the channel, it falls back into the main reservoir and the pump sends the solution back again to the beginning of the system. This movement creates a recirculating system, like the one used in deep water culture.

This system does not need a timer because the pump effectively ensures a constant supply of nutrients to the plant roots. The plants only need to be situated in their net pots, and they do not require a growing medium; they are suspended in the air too, just as in the aeroponics setup. However, in the N.F.T system, the plants can only be harvested or replaced one after the other.

The nutrient solution must be kept aerated by use of an air pump and an air stone. The constant bubbling also helps to prevent the solution from settling while providing the roots with the oxygen they need to aid in the process of nutrient absorption, so that the plant will use less energy in sourcing for the nutrients it needs, and more energy in growing and producing fruit.

Having a submersible pump at the reservoir also helps to ensure that the nutrient solution is constantly supplied to the grow tray. Having a gap between the water and the plants also guarantees aeration before the water drains off back into the reservoir. The NFT is certainly an improvement of the drip system, as you shall see next.

Benefit of the N.F.T

- This technique is cost effective because it does not require a growing medium, and because the nutrient solution that is used is often recycled and recovered back to the reservoir.

Disadvantages of the N.F.T

- The cost of maintenance, in this case, is higher because the pumps need regular supervision to ensure that they are working well as it should be.

- In the event that there is an interruption of the power supply, the roots will dry out very quickly, particularly because the method does not use any growing medium.

- Some roots tend to overgrow and they clog the channels.

What You Would Need to Set Up an N.F.T System

- A nutrient kit

- A reservoir
- A pH kit
- Gullies or grow tanks, from which you grow the plants
- Tubes to direct the nutrient solution from the channel and into the reservoir tank
- Tubing and pump to direct the nutrient solution from the reservoir to the plants
- A spreader mat (this one is optional), to boost nutrient absorption
- A platform or a table to hold the gullies, together with a channel, that can be used to direct the nutrients back into the reservoir.

The Ebb and Flow Hydroponics System

The Ebb and Flow system, sometimes called the Flood and Drain system is more advanced and more complicated than any other. In it, the plants are placed in a grow tray in the growing medium and then placed at the top of the reservoir. There is also a scheduled timer, which causes the pump to switch on and flood the grow tray with the nutrient solution drawn from the reservoir, in regular intervals. Once the grow tray floods, the timer switches off, and the nutrient solution drains off.

The Ebb and Flow hydroponics system are either set as a recovery or as a non-recovery system to mean that the solution could be used only once and discarded, or that it could be collected and reused.

The frequency of flooding for this method depends on factors like the amount of water that the plants need, the size of the plants, where your plants stand in the growth cycle, and the temperature in the air.

The flooding cycle is easy. It starts with having a water pump, the reservoir placed underneath the grow tray and a timer to determine the frequency of flooding. Once you flood the tray, the law of gravity will order the excess solution back to the reservoir below, where it will be oxygenated by both the air stone and the air pump. The solution then sits in the reservoir, in readiness for the next flooding cycle.

Hydroponic farmers who choose the ebb and flow system do so for the flexibility of the system. The system allows the tray to fill with the growing medium of choice, and for the farmers to organize their plants in net pots. They also get better control of the plants' roots.

Advantages of the Ebb and Flow Hydroponics System

- The system allows the efficient use of energy and water

- It can be customized to match your needs

- It is easy to control the temperature of the project because it is set up indoors and because the reservoir is differently placed from the growing trays.

- The plants enjoy good aeration because they are not fully submerged in the nutrient solution, while at the same time, they get to enjoy absorption of nutrients at regular times.

- Since the plants do not have a direct connection to the reservoir, it is possible to grow a larger proportion of crops than the reservoir can hold.

Disadvantages of the Ebb and Flow Hydroponics System

- The system uses a great deal of the growing medium

- In case of a power supply disruption, the pumps and the timers will be affected, causing the roots to dry up. However, this problem can be resolved by simply choosing mediums that ideally take in and retain moisture in an efficient way.

- A farmer needs to have some level of experience maintaining the pH and nutrient levels and to ensure that the system, including the medium, does not clog with the salts contained in the nutrient solution.

Drip Irrigation System

The drip irrigation system is one of the more popular hydroponic systems. The system is set up to enable the transportation of nutrients from the reservoir using a tube down to an irrigation pipe that waters the plant's base.

Drip irrigation may recover the nutrient solution, or not. Home growers tend to lean towards recovery while commercial growers lean towards non-recovery.

Advantages of the Drip System

- A relatively cheap method
- The farmer has greater control of the watering and feeding schedule
- Less likely to break down
- It is possible to set the timers so precisely that the plants will be let until when more of the solution is needed

Disadvantages of the Drip System

- For a small garden, a drip system is slightly overkill
- The nutrients and pH levels tend to fluctuate, especially when using a recirculating system
- There is a high level of waste, especially if using a non-recovery method
- If the farmer takes the non-recovery option, the cost of purchasing nutrients may get so high

What You Need to Set Up the Drip Irrigation System

- A timer
- PH kit
- Growing medium
- Containers or growing trays for the plants
- Reservoir container to house the nutrient solution
- Air pump that contains air stones and tubing
- Drip lines and irrigation pipes with sets of joiners and adapters
- Nutrient kit
- Submersible pump and tubing to deliver the nutrients

The Wick System

The wick system is a naturally passive system. There are no moving parts that require automation, and hence no electricity is required to run activities and functions. This makes the wick system a perfect selection for persons that are just getting their feet wet, and those working with a tight budget.

The wick system is the simplest of them all. It works by causing the plant to receive nutrients using a wick that is attached to the reservoir on one end, and the plant on the other end. When the end in the reservoir soaks up, it transports the nutrient solution through the fiber of the wick, on to the plant.

One trick for succeeding in the use of a wick system is to use a growing media that is able to transport nutrients and water well. Some of the excellent options from which you may choose from include perlite, coconut coir, and vermiculite.

Advantages of the Wick System

- Easy to set up
- Excellent pick for beginners and children
- Affordable
- Once you have set it up correctly, this is a truly hands-off method
- The wick system is especially suited for small plants, those with lesser nutritional needs

Disadvantages of the Wick System

- Is not suited to larger plants that have higher nutrient requirements because they may need much more moisture and nutrient than the wick is able to deliver

- The wick system does not make the process of controlling the humidity of the growing room easy

- The system may cause uneven absorption of nutrients, and with time, there could be a buildup of nutrients in the growing medium

- If the wick is improperly placed, it could mean death for your crops

What You Would Need to Set Up a Wick System

- A nutrient kit
- A bucket, reservoir, or just a tub with a lid
- Some growing medium
- Basket or container
- A wick could be a rope, or any other absorbent material

The Deep-Water Culture System

Of all the active systems we have discussed, the deep-water culture system is the simplest of them all. It is a system in which many plants are placed on a tray, ideally made of polystyrene, which then floats at the top of the nutrient solution that has been held in a solution reservoir. In this setup, the plant's roots will be completely submerged in the water.

Instead of the polystyrene sheet, the plants can also be placed in net pots and the pots can be fitted into a lid that will fit the circumference of the reservoir, tank or tub in use.

An air stone connected to an air pump is used to keep the nutrient solution below oxygenated, which ensures that the plants' roots do not become waterlogged to the point that they would rot and be incapable of absorbing the nutrients below.

Plants that are best suited for this setup include Asian greens, lettuce, endives, and rocket, among others.

Advantages of the Deep-Water Culture System

- Affordable
- Easy to build
- Management is easy
- Requires only a small space
- Suited for beginners
- Suitable for commercial hydroponics farming
- Ideal for plants with short growing periods
- Less wastage because the system reuses the same nutrient solution

Disadvantages of Deep-Water Culture System

- Not suited for large plants
- Not suited to plants that have long growing periods

What You Need to Set Up the Deep-Water Culture System

- Air pump
- System-specific reservoirs
- PH kit
- Nutrient kit
- Air stone
- Air pump
- Growing medium

The above systems are the six major hydroponics systems types. You can clearly read how each works, and the advantages and disadvantages of each system.

Do not be anxious about which method you choose though because no matter the method you choose, provided you provide proper care. Your plants will grow very big, and very fast. With any of these systems, you will assuredly experience the ups that hydroponics offer, particularly the flexibility, so that whenever you are having trouble, you will have no reservations about correcting them and getting your farm back on the right track.

Advanced Hydroponic Systems

The above six hydroponics systems are best suited for beginners, and for your knowledge, we will discuss three more hydroponic systems in brief, so that you do not confuse between the beginners' and advanced kind.

The systems include:

The Kratky Method

The Kratky method is one that combines the deep-water culture system and the wick system. It brings in the constant adequate supply advantage of the deep-water culture system added to the passivity and low maintenance of the wick system.

In the Kratky method, the plants are held in a net pot, on top of anon-circulating solution reservoir that has a tight-fitting lid. The net pot is fitted into a hole that has been cut out of the lid. At first, the roots are submerged beneath the solution, and only a small air gap is left between the nutrient solution and the inside of the lid.

Once this is done, the farmer then leaves the system alone, and as the plant and the growing medium absorb the right nutrients, the roots of the plant grow, the water level falls and the space between the solution and the inside of the lid gets bigger. This space ensures that the plant receives the nutrition it needs from the solution while getting enough oxygen supply.

Advantages

- This method can be a good way for beginners to get into hydroponics farming
- It almost requires zero maintenance
- The method is affordable

Disadvantages

- Only suited for small foliage crops
- Not ideal for large scale farming

Fogponics

Fogponics is a great improvement of aeroponics, evidenced by the improved farming results. Fogponics has improved farming rapidly.

It works this way: rather than creating a mist at specified intervals, the farmer installs a fogger in the reservoir to create a humidified environment. The fogger, or the mist maker, as you can tell, changes the size of water droplets to the point that they become a mist or fog, which is then directed to the plants' root system.

The new gravity-defying nutrient solution droplets offer the plant a full nutrient coverage to the point that it stimulates the development of new root hairs as an adaptation, to increase the surface area of the root system, for greater absorption of the nutrients.

Advantages of the Fogponics System

- Reduces the water and nutrients usage by more than 40 percent
- Economical
- Easy to set up
- The nutrient solution does not reduce in concentration because the recirculation is not used up.

Disadvantages of Fogponics

- The cost of the initial setup is quite high
- The mist is very light, yet it must be contained
- In case there is a power outage, the havoc wreaked to the crops can be ridiculously big
- The setup requires regular cleaning of the equipment, and this increases the cost of maintenance

The Dutch Bucket System

The Dutch Bucket System is an adaptation of the Ebb and Flow system, only that it uses individual buckets placed in rows, and one irrigation line supplying nutrients from above, while a drainage pipe is located below the pipe, directing the liquid that drains back to the solution reservoir.

The Dutch Bucket System is suited for large operations because the individual rows can be joined to form one irrigation line that can easily accommodate large plants that bear fruit. Each plant is given its own bucket, and this makes it easy to move individual plants around. If you choose this system, you will want to have a growing medium that is capable of maintaining high moisture levels as well as be well aerated. Ensuring that the drainage is doing well is also essential because it prevents clogging so that the nutrients that are not absorbed into the plant can easily drain back into the nutrient solution reservoir.

The process of getting the excess solution back to the reservoir depends on gravity, but the process of getting the solution from the reservoir up onto the plant relies on a submersible pump placed at the bottom of the reservoir. An air pump and an air stone are also required to keep the solution in the reservoir oxygenated. In addition, salt and pH levels should be checked occasionally and maintained at a balance.

When it comes to choosing the ideal growing medium, you have a number of options. The seedlings, you can start off, using sphagnum peat, Rockwool or coco peat, and a water culture system. Once the seedlings have grown a bit and established themselves, you can then transfer them to a propagation area of the Dutch Bucket System.

You could also choose perlite. It is light, has excellent water and air retention, and drains excess fluid well. However, the farmer still needs to put measures in place to prevent blockage. It might help to cover the entrance of the drainage pipe with mesh. However, it is important to note that perlite works best when mixed with a medium like vermiculite

Another ideal medium for the Dutch Bucket System is Light Expanded Clay Aggregate (LECA). This medium is ideal due to its large pebbles because they cannot get stuck in the drain pipe, causing blockage of the circulation system.

In your search for a good growing medium, avoid coconut coir because it is highly absorbent, and its drainage is slow. The coir is suitable for a drain to waste system and not one that relies on flooding. If you wanted to use it, you would have to convert your system into a low volume or slow drip hydroponic system, and this would increase the running costs and beat the purpose of having a recovery system because the nutrient solution would not be recycled.

Advantages of the Dutch Bucket System

- Saves on water
- It is best if you are going large scale on your farming

- It boosts plant growth

Disadvantages of the Dutch Bucket System

- The cost of maintenance is high
- Expensive, because it requires high-quality machinery to succeed

CHAPTER 4

Advantages and Disadvantages of Hydroponics

Regardless of your crop production scale, hydroponics is for you. It would make an excellent choice for you because it accords you the freedom to vary and control the factors that determine the growth rate of your crops. Any day, any time, a fine-tuned hydroponic system will outdo soil-based agriculture in terms of the quality, quantity, yield, and the amount of space that the plants need to have to be productive.

Without politicking or appealing to your sentiments, take it that if you feel the need to grow some of the biggest, juiciest and the yummiest produce, you have to try hydroponics.

The process of getting the system on the ground might appear challenging at first, but the results you get make it all worth it. It is worth the time, money, and effort. The only thing you have to do is start small, and gradually watch as your dream comes to life.

Here are some of the Benefits you should expect to enjoy:

The Yields Are Higher

One of the most prominent benefits of hydroponics is the increased productivity of your farm and your crops. In a well-placed hydroponic system, expect the produce to be at least 30% higher than that of plants grown directly from the soil.

Plants Grow Quicker

What would happen if a child got the proper nutrition, did not fall ill and got enough rest? What would be the case if a business was situated in a place with a high demand for its products, the customer service was excellent, and the people could afford what is being sold? The result in the two scenarios is that growth would be quite high.

The plants are able to grow faster and bigger because they do not have to work harder to get the nutrients they need for growth. Even a small root system will be sufficient for delivering the required nutrients to the plants, so the plants do not have to advance their root systems to reach nutrients far below on the soil. Therefore, the only task the plant has is to develop upwards and produce its fruits. It is said that hydroponic plants grow at least 25% faster than those grown the traditional way.

Does Not Require a Yard

When people think about farming, the first thing that comes to mind are large tracts of land, or a yard, at the very least. However, even people without yards can grow their crops. Hydroponics allows you to plant your crops indoors. For example, you could transform the extra space you have in your house to a veggie or flower garden.

Saves Water

Since the hydroponics system, you will build is not exposed to weather elements, there is less water evaporation. This means that plants get to utilize less water than if you had planted them on the soil, outside. This makes hydroponics an environmentally friendly method for growing crops.

Production Can Be Done All-Year-Round

Using a hydroponics system puts the seasons in your hands, under your control. You do not have limitations in regards to when you can sow or harvest your produce because you will be using an internally controlled setup. However hard the winter hits or the summer burns itself, you are guaranteed that you will get what you have been working towards.

The ability to produce all-year-round allows the commercial farmer to eliminate risks involved in the business such as the effects of a poor crop season, and also ensures continuous production and accessibility of food to the farmers and others in the community.

Requires Less Labor

While hydroponics farming is capital intensive, less labor is needed. For example, you will not need to hire labor to weed your plants because this function is already automated.

In addition to reduced labor, hydroponics makes it easy to provide the little labor needed. This is because the systems can be constructed or placed on heights that are simpler to access. The farmer is not limited to growing his crops from the ground, because the plants can be placed on heights that are comfortable relative to the farmer's body. This way, the labor of weeding, planting or transporting becomes much easier.

Does Not Require Any Soil

This is a distinct advantage particularly in areas where the existing field soil is poor. It is also an advantage for people living in apartments because growing plants with soil can be quite inconveniencing.

The absence of soil also means that the plants and the produce are cleaner.

Requires Less Space

When using this system of agriculture, your plants will not develop an extensive root system that they would typically need to reach nutrients down below. Since plants are spaced out to give enough room to each plant's rooting system, the hydroponics plants can be planted close together. This is another advantage, in favor of indoor planting.

You also have the opportunity to move the plants as they grow, and this will guarantee an increase in the density of the crops. For example, let's say you are using growth room for germination and the production of seedlings. Now, if the density of some particular crops in the greenhouse decreases, the average area a plant will need in comparison to conventional crop production.

Less Wastage

Hydroponic crops are known to absorb all the mineral nutrients that are provided in the solution used, without any wastage, and hence this kind of farming produces less pollution.

Produces Higher Quality Yields

The produce collected from hydroponics is of higher quality in comparison to conventional farming because the plants have access to all the resources they would need to produce at maximum capacity.

When combined with greenhouse, it produces even better results. Hydroponics is all about control, and a greenhouse provides an excellent environment to allow it.

Hydroponics Farming Is Eco-Friendly

Water used in a hydroponic system can always be recycled, and because of this, a hydroponic system takes up only about 10% of the water that normal conventionally grown crops take up.

Another advantage is that since this is a closed system, nutrients applied do not leach away, which causes the hydroponics to use up only 25% of the fertilizers that regular farms apply

Farmers Do Not Have to Deal with Eutrophication When They Take Up Hydroponics

Eutrophication is the dense growth of aquatic plants such as algae that grow due to the run-off of fertilizers

Farmers Do Not Have to Deal with Soil Pests and Diseases

Even if there are natural predators, the use of a greenhouse makes it easier to control the pests. In the same way, a building with four walls and a roof creates a barrier that keeps off pests. Hence, there are artificial pesticides required. This is also the case for plant diseases.

Without soil acting as a medium, the likelihood of spreading and contracting diseases reduces significantly. As such, there is no need to fumigate the crops or to weed. There will also not be any microorganisms because there is not a soil stratum.

The failure to use herbicides and pesticides allows the farmer to grow cleaner food, promoting the health of the food consumers.

Hydroponics Makes Agriculture Feasible in Areas That Are Not Naturally Suited to Farming

The high-water efficiency of the hydroponics system makes it possible and easy to farm in arid environments. The farmer only has to stock the hydroponic trays on top of each other, and place the plants closer to each other, side by side, making the growing trays, and the entire system more space-efficient than regular farming.

Since it is possible to control, artificially, almost all environmental conditions, people who wish to get into farming can take up almost all kinds of spaces available such as disused railway tunnels, uninhabited buildings, and other unusual spaces.

In addition, now that commercial hydroponic farmers do not have any limitations, and plant their crops on rural agricultural land, food growers can now plant their crops closer to their markets, and the increased accessibility takes out the need for complex distribution that reduces the farmer's profit margin, and introduces third parties, the brokers.

Hydroponics Reduce the Need to Transport Food Items

Since anyone can become a farmer and can grow crops even far from their habitats, at a place that is in proximity to the consumers, the need for transportation is reduced, and so are the fuel emissions, hence allowing the people to enjoy both fresh produce and clean air.

Monoculture Is Allowed

Typically, growing the same crops all the time will exhaust the soil of particular elements, which either changes the soil pH or reduces the yields because the plants cannot access the nutrients they need. However, in hydroponics, farmers need not worry that they could exhaust the soil of a particular element when they plant one type of crop recurrently. Farmers need not rotate their crops, and they can instead focus wholly on the production of food items in demand, those that will fetch them some good money.

The quick succession of crops is also attributed to the fact that the system does not require a restoration period as land does. Therefore, immediately a farmer pulls out one plant, he can quickly plant another in its stead. This ensures that the farmer will have the maximum possible yields per square foot.

There Are No Weeds

One of the most back-breaking tasks associated with farming is the process of combating weeds. It consumes the farmer's time. When using hydroponics, the likelihood that your farm will grow weeds is quite low because the weeds seeds that are often found in the soil are not there. This is also an advantage to your crop because it grows unopposed, not having to fight for resources. Hence, it grows fast and produces higher than normal yields.

It Is Easy to Maintain Hydroponic Systems

Resources are used efficiently and effectively when using a hydroponics system. The water used to water the plants is recycled and the fertilizers used are the actual amounts, hence no wastage. It is easy to measure fertilizer and to determine the proportions of its constituent elements, which means that the farmer doesn't work out of guesswork. You will know when your plants have the right fertilizer concentration, and when there isn't a correct measure, you only have to adjust the amount that you have applied.

Easier to Control the Costs of Farming

Since only little, if any, nutrients are lost, the farmer only has to use a little of the fertilizer, among other resources. In addition, the plants have faster growth, which leads to higher yields.

Ph Control

Since the nutrients are administered through a water solution, it is easier to measure, monitor and adjust your solution's pH levels in comparison to when applying fertilizer to the soil directly in rural farming.

Hydroponics Is Fun and Makes for an Interesting Hobby

Dealing in hydroponics or any other nature activity puts you back in sync with nature. If you are tired from your daily activities, it is relieving to go back home and observe how your garden is progressing: weeding, watering the plants and harvesting the produce. Activities like these are great stress-relievers and can surely turn your day around. You could also set your pot on the stove and start preparing the tastiest and freshest vegetables and herbs or enjoy a bowl of fruit from your green space.

Disadvantages of Hydroponics

Requires Technical Knowledge and Experience

When running a hydroponics system, realize that you are running a system composed of many kinds of equipment, and this requires you to have specific expertise and knowledge of the devices you are to use, the plants you are to grow, and the mechanism of how these plants are to grow in the soilless environment. If you make mistakes in regard to setting up the systems or how you plan out your care of the crops, you may end up losing out on your investment.

There Are Risks Related to Electricity and Water

A hydroponics system primarily depends on water and electricity to operate. The combination of water and electricity, however, is a recipe for disaster, especially because they are used in such close proximity. Therefore, whenever you are working with electricity and the water systems equipment together, consider safety measures first.

The Initial Expenses Are Quite High

As you start out your hydroponics farm, you are sure to spend some considerable amount (the scale of your farming will also matter), to set up the space to be used for farming and to purchase the equipment needed. Whichever hydroponics system you take up, you will also need a pump, growing media, fertilizers, containers, lights, and seeds or seedlings.

Once your system is in place, you will only be paying for electricity, water, nutrients, and seedlings, as needed.

The Costs of Running Are Also Quite High

The control systems of the hydroponic garden, which would include the water purifiers, pumps, heaters, lights, and others, are electronically powered, and this costs money. In traditional farming, the water, the heat, and the light are naturally provided, and they are free, which makes them an added cost.

It Takes a While for You to Get a Return on Your Investment

Just recently, large scale hydroponic farms have been coming up, which shows that people now believe in the productivity of the soilless farms. That's a great development for agriculture and the development of hydroponics also. However, the issue is that the commercial growers setting up large-scale hydroponic farms will have to wait longer to receive a return on their investment.

The cost of setting up the large farms is particularly high, and the returns can be uncertain at times. As such, it would be difficult to come up with a profitable clear plan that would justify the investment while there are other attractive investment opportunities out there that would give a return on investment quicker, and more certainly than hydroponics farming.

Diseases and Pests Spread Quickly

Since you will be growing plants in a closed damp place, in the event that pests and infections come along, they can spread and escalate very fast among plants that are in the same nutrient reservoir.

In a small system, the pests or diseases would not cause so much havoc, which means that it is not quite a problem for beginners because you are advised to start small. For big farms, the issue could become problematic since the water is filtered and then recycled throughout the farm. Therefore, if a diseased plant is present in one section of the farm, it will infect the remaining area and could kill the entire crop in hours. Many large-scale farmers have lost their entire crop this way, which has made disease-control one of the critical factors to look out for when investing in hydroponics. All farmers, particularly those operating on a large scale, ought to have a proper disease and pest management plan early enough.

One of the best preventative measures is to ensure cleanliness in the farm. For one, only use clean pathogen-free water and growing materials, clean and check the hydroponic systems periodically. In case the diseases occur, you need to sterilize the infected nutrients, water, and the entire hydroponic system.

The downside of this cleanliness and sterilization exercise is that the water might also contain good microorganisms, and unfortunately, when the water is sterilized, it is impossible to eliminate the harmful streaks of bacteria and fungi and leave out the good ones; they all go out in the same swipe. In addition, the sterility of the water and the entire farm at large is only as good as the sterilization method that the farmer uses; the water could retain some harmful microorganisms.

Threats of System Failure

Farmers use electricity to manage the entire system and should take precautionary measures to prepare for a possible power outage. This is because were there to be a power outage or electrical failure, the entire system would stop working immediately, and the plants would dry out quickly, and die in a matter of hours. Therefore, farmers ought to have ready plans to prepare for power-related issues by having a backup power source, particularly those operating under large-scale systems. Most farmers opt to have several long-standing back-up generators that can run for a long time in case of an electrical emergency.

The Organic Question

There have been debates on whether crops grown under hydroponic systems can be labeled as organic or not. Some people raised questions as to whether plants grown as hydroponics get microbiomes as those that are grown in the soil.

Whatever the case, the fact remains that people have grown hydroponic crops all over the world including tomatoes, lettuce, strawberries, and others, for many years, and distributing them to the Netherlands, the United States, Australia, Tokyo, and other regions. This product has fed millions of people, and it poses fewer risks in regard to pesticides, pests, and diseases, compared to soil-grown crops.

Some suggestions into how hydroponics growers can turn their agriculture into an organic venture have been laid out, and some farmers have taken up this idea. Some have gone ahead to introduce microbiomes to the soil in the form of organic growing media such as coco coir, then adding worm casting into it. Others introduce natural nutrients instead of fertilizer in the form of alfalfas, neems, cotton seeds, fishes, and bones.

As for the organic debate though, there is yet to be a consensus on what qualifies to be organic and what does not, and as research continues to be carried out, we can hope to have a conclusive answer in the near future.

Requires a Heavy Investment of Time and Commitment

Just like any other worthwhile thing in life that requires hard work and a positive attitude to obtain any success, hydroponics requires your utmost dedication to attain the success that you anticipated. Plants that are planted on soil do not demand as much attention and dedication and can be left alone for many days and weeks, and they will continue to grow. The soil, together with Mother Nature, balance out whatever needs balancing.

The case of hydroponics is different. If the plants do not receive all the care and attention they need, they begin to die out. The plants are purely dependent on the farmer for survival, which means that the farmer must be equipped with the proper knowledge and expertise to care for them. Initially, farmers are advised to care for the plants themselves, and they can automate at a later time, once the system is up and running.

Hydroponics Limit Agricultural Production

Although growing your crops all year round increases the yield significantly, the space available remains an impediment to the amount you could possibly produce. In addition, the fact that you can plant more crops in a single space does not mean that the crops can be overcrowded; the plant still needs some space to enable it spread out, which means that there is still a limited number of crops you can plant at a time.

The Entire Hydroponic System Is Quite Vulnerable

As mentioned earlier, it only takes a few hours without power and the plants begin to dry out and die. In a system where the plants are exposed, if the plants are left unwatered for some hours, the drying out will be especially quick.

In addition, it is more likely to have pH and nutrient imbalances when using a solution as their source in comparison to when you use soil. If these imbalances happen, an entire crop could be wiped out very fast, and so is the situation in case of water contamination by either microorganisms or disease.

Requires Some Knowledge and Expertise

A farmer who wishes to venture into hydroponic farming needs to understand the entire process and the techniques used, and this can be quite complicated to grasp.

As you have seen, hydroponics farming stands to give you a number of advantages, but will still subject you to some disadvantages. If you still feel the need to press on and start your farm, go ahead and get started, there will always be a way around the challenges you face. Nothing should keep you from enjoying and selling to others the juicier, larger, tastier, and more nutritious foods you have been dying to try growing using the hydroponics method.

You also should ensure that you contact the local agricultural department to determine the requirements set for farm operations, as well as be informed of any existing risk of encountering fungi, bacteria, and other common diseases. Keep in mind that the most important lessons are learned by trial and error so that as you encounter challenges, you will keep learning and pushing yourself forward. In the end, your dream of successfully running a piece of this revolutionary method of agriculture will come to be.

CHAPTER 5

Getting Your Feet Wet

You know what hydroponic farming is, the tools you would need, and the systems from which you would choose, and this has aroused your interest in hydroponics farming, or that your heart did not sink, and you are still interested in following it through. Now, here is some more information to help you make your move into the business more graceful because it is by making the rights steps that you would succeed.

The right steps are:

1. **Select The Right Seeds And Plants For Your Venture**

You think that the hydroponics business is lucrative or you would want to venture into it to grow crops for you and your family's nutrition. However, what crops are you looking to grow? The answer you give to this question will determine what you do from now on, starting with the amount of money you set aside for the construction, the hydroponic system you choose, the amount of space you set aside, and the lighting. Different hydroponic systems work better than others for specific plant kinds.

For beginners, I recommend that they first try growing leafy veggies such as lettuce. Begin germinating your seeds in rapid rooter cubes because these cubes and once the seedlings are up, and after growing for several weeks, once you are sure that your plant has a healthy root system, now transfer the plants into your growth tray.

2. **Choose The Appropriate Hydroponic System For Your Garden**

You need to choose the hydroponic system early enough so that you may get some time to learn more about the setup and how it works. Read the alternatives too, and compare one to another, until you are able to choose the most appropriate of them.

The set up you pick will be determined by a few factors. The kind of plants you intend to grow, the amount of space that you have available, the number of plants you want to grow, and the budget you have. Even when your resources can allow you to start big, it is better to start small and then expand your craft in the future. As you start your garden, you will realize that there are many other new things to learn, and you might make some mistakes. It would be incredibly hurtful if anything bad happened while you had too many plants.

3. Choose the Light Source You Will Be Using

Lighting is a major factor and determinant of the success of your hydroponic garden. If you are not using natural light from the sun as your source of light, then you need to choose a hydroponic light from the market. There are some considerations to make though, because there are many kinds of lights in the market, and each has its unique advantages and disadvantages.

Kindly engage in some research to determine the light setup that will work best for the plants you intend to grow. Even then, you need to make some useful considerations such as light intensity, cost, coverage area, and the light spectrum. If you want fast growth and for the produce to be of high quality, it is best not to take the cheapest route in choosing the appropriate lighting.

If you cannot choose a light yourself, possibly from not knowing where to start, I suggest you get a full spectrum LED grow light. The light is cheap and suitable for leafy green plants and plants that produce fruit, and the lights are quite efficient. Don't forget to buy a timer, to go along with it too.

4. Choose The Hydroponic Medium

Once you have settled on your hydroponic setup, you now have to choose the growing medium you prefer, selecting from the options that would best work with the system you have chosen. The kinds that you should lean towards are those that are suitable for the plants you intend to be growing and the kind of system you have on.

There are different kinds of growing mediums, each with its own advantages. However, some of the factors to consider about the growing medium you choose include its water retention, pH stability, cost, and level of aeration. If you have problems choosing, then kindly take up hydroton expanded clay pebble because of their versatility. They work well with different kinds of hydroponic setups and different kinds of plants.

5. Purchase The Hydroponic Nutrients And Additives You Will Use In Your Garden

There are many nutrient concentrations and combinations, coming in 1, 2, and 3 part systems, and you make your choice based on the research you have conducted on what the plants would need. For beginners, you would be safe sticking with a 1-part nutrient solution, but if you feel that you have a good understanding of the nutrients the plants need, go ahead and take up even a 3 part nutrient solution. Most companies will have attached a feeding schedule on the product or their company websites, and you can follow up from there.

Additives are also very important because they assist in the process of sterilization of the system. They also affect your plants' growth rate, taste, and the size to which your plant grows. Think of additives as your plants' vitamins, and although they are not a critical part of your agriculture, they provide an extra boost to them.

6. Get A PH Meter And A PH Up/Down

As we have discussed prior, plants will only be able to take in the nutrients in the nutrient solution if it is at a specific pH range. To ensure this, purchase a pH meter that you shall regularly use to determine the pH of your nutrient solution.

When it comes to measuring pH levels, you will have different options. You can use test strips, a liquid kit, or an electronic meter. Electronic meters are preferred because they are inexpensive and convenient to use.

You should get a pH up and a pH down to help you in adjusting the pH of your nutrient solution. Start with a small amount of each because as you shall realize, plants tend to use nutrients that cause the solution to lean towards one direction, and you will find that you always use one and not the other. However, have both so that you can correct all the spikes and dips that could happen were there to be a nutrient lockout.

7. Add And Mix Your Nutrients to Get Your System Going

Once you have everything ready, it's time to get the system going. You must first get some water running in your setup, to test whether everything will work as smoothly. This step will allow you to catch any leaks that would come up. Wait it out for some minutes, at least, and if everything is still running as well as it could, mix your nutrients, let the solution rest for some 15 minutes, and then test its pH. Adjust your solution's pH if you deem it necessary.

Once that is done, set your plants on the system and set the timer of your grow light to the light duration that your plants need to grow properly.

As you can see, the process of getting your garden ready is very easy, but the key is to make preparations prior and to spend enough time planning upfront. This will save you both money and time, in the end.

Ensuring That Your Water Will Not Kill Your Plants

If you can, it is best to use Reverse Osmosis (RO) water to make your nutrient solution. Hydroponics produces the best when you invest the best. If you have already provided the best lighting, the best nutrients, the best hydroponic system, why would you skimp out and use poor water? You need great water to ensure that the plants get the most out of the solution you make. Great water simply comes from a great filtration process. Remember that water, particularly hard water contains minerals and other stuff that could knock over the balance you are seeking to achieve when it comes to your nutrients, even if you have followed the manufacturer's instructions to the letter.

There's one way to know whether your water is good enough or whether you will need reverse osmosis water. It is done by measuring the alkalinity of the water, by checking the presence of bicarbonates and carbonates. You just have to conduct a PPM test. If the results show that your water has a 10 or below PPM, you can go ahead and use your tap water. If the test shows over 10 PPM, you need to invest in a reverse osmosis system. It may surprise you to know that when such tests were conducted, some waters ended up with a 900PPM, completely choked by alkalinity. This water would be disastrous if used in hydroponics.

So, what is this reverse osmosis that is meant to reduce the nutrient concentration in alkaline water? Let's first understand what osmosis is. Osmosis is the process through which a solvent moves across a semipermeable membrane that separates two solutions of different concentration. Whenever osmosis is used to purify water, the same semipermeable membrane is used, but also a pressurized system is used to push the solvent across the membrane.

Reverse osmosis is a water purification technology that uses a semipermeable membrane to draw molecules, ions and large particles from drinking water. It can even draw out bacteria. This method is used in industries and the production of potable water. It results in the solute, in this case, dissolved nutrients, remaining on the pressurized side of the membrane while the pure water passes to the other side.

If you are using reverse osmosis to clean your water or if you are using your tap water for hydroponics farming, you need to realize that the recommended pH for most of the plants we have indicated above is somewhat low, between 5.5 and 6.3. Most tap water has a pH of between 7.0 and 8.0. Therefore, you need to purchase a testing kit to test your water, and if the pH is not within the recommended range, you will need to add, either the pH Up or the pH Down.

It is important that you be careful about the pH of your nutrient solution because if the pH gets out of the right range, which could happen very swiftly sometimes, your plants' ability to absorb secondary, macro and micronutrients, vitamins, and carbohydrates, among others, will be lowered.

The truth is that issues of pH in a hydroponics system can be a real source of headache. However, the good news is that if you take up the right products, you can eliminate all these issues and you would never have to worry about them.

Beginners Should Opt for Clones

If you are just getting into hydroponics farming, you want the process to be as seamless and as enjoyable as possible. The best way to do this is by taking out all kinds of factors that could go wrong. For this reason, it is recommended that beginners start growing their gardens from live plants, instead of using seeds. This is what is called 'cloning.'

Using the example of growing herbs, you just have to get an herb seedling, gently take it out of the soil and the potting container from which it had been growing, and wash the dirt from off the roots, so that it doesn't contaminate the water. If you leave any soil on the roots, it could lead to fungal or bacterial infestation, or even cause the roots to rot. Once you have cleaned off the roots, just add the plant into your net pot that is secured on the lid of the bucket holding the nutrient solution. Cover the roots with the growing media, and let the system take it up from there.

Preparing the Growing Media

With any of the growing media, you may choose, you will want to wash and disinfect it first before application. You need to do this before the initial application, and at each reuse. You could wash the material while it is in the grow pots, or take the easier option of washing it in a larger container so you can easily flush and drain it.

If the growing media has been used before, you need to even be more thorough in your cleaning exercise so that you get off all the previous nutrients and the old roots. Washing the material for initial application is not as tough because you only need to disinfect the growing material and to take out any dust that the media could have come with. You just need clean water for washing, don't try to use cleaners.

Disinfecting the growing medium is done using hydrogen peroxide or diluted bleach. Get the hydrogen peroxide to a 3% concentration or dilute the bleach to 10% concentration. Disinfecting the growing medium helps to protect the system from microscopic pests for which you cannot introduce a natural predator once they infect your hydroponic system. Therefore, ensure that you make an effort to ensure this for yourself, to avoid problems along the way.

Once you have prepared the disinfectant solution, dip the growing media in, and allow it to remain submerged for about an hour. When the hour lapses, now go ahead and vigorously rinse off all that disinfectant. If the media has developed mold, it would be very difficult to wash it off, and the best thing to do is to discard the growing media, and replacing it with a fresh bunch.

Coming Up with the Correct Watering Cycle for Your Plants

Make sure to test out your watering cycle before you get started with your plants. Most watering cycles have 15 minutes or more, between the cycles. Avoid having an off period of more than 30 minutes, and if you are using a slow drip system, set long watering times, like 5 or more hours, then take a 15 to 30-minute breaking interval.

Slow drip pumps take in very little power, and the long off cycles extend the pump's life. For example, a 250 gph pump can water up to 50 plants if the drip rate is at 1 gph per plant. This is not a usual rate, but still, the timer you buy will be the primary determinant and guide to your watering cycle.

Whatever timer or pump you go for, keep in mind the fact that it will serve you well to have a water application system that distributes water evenly over the surface of the growing media. Therefore, don't just buy one or two drips and call it a day; you want to install a drip every 16 square inches, or even less, to reduce the number of dry zones in your growing media.

Once the water gets to the growing media, it will redistribute itself outward through capillary action and from there, as the water begins to drain, the entire material will be adequately moist. Keep trying for different times on your timer until you establish a timing interval that gets you the best moisture level while avoiding the intermittent dry conditions. Don't be worried about the usage of the nutrient solution because the solution that drains from the growth medium into the reservoir below will be pumped back into the material again. Therefore, the entire affair will be about ensuring a moist environment for your plants.

If you take the drip system, ensure that you install an in-line screen to take out the debris from the water and to keep the emitters from plugging or the pipe from aging. If you are using clay pellets for a medium, know that the pellets will release some particles also, and these could clog the pipes too. Also, expect the growth of algae because it naturally occurs in water, and it grows very fast particularly where nutrients are involved. Once you install the inline filter, however, you can do away with the algae also. Therefore, you need to ensure that your filter remains clean by taking it out and washing it often.

You need to take note of the fact that since the solution reservoir has both water and nutrients, it makes an ideal breeding ground for algae. The algae will reduce the efficacy of the nutrients you place in the reservoir. However, to prevent this, ensure that your reservoir tank is opaque, to prevent light passing to the algae cells that need it for their growth.

The Right Nutrition for Hydroponics

When you have just transferred your clones from the germination room to the growth tray, application of a fertilizer that has a high nitrogen content is the wrong way to go. This is because nitrogen promotes foliar growth in plants, and the primary need for the plants at that young age is to develop their root system not to have large leaves. This is to show you that the nutrients you apply to the plant will change based on the plant's growth stage.

The soil already has a considerable amount of micro and macronutrients, but in the soilless hydroponic gardening style, there will be no nutrients in the solution, unless you add them. The good thing is that it is not difficult to determine what a plant needs at a particular stage; you just have to conduct research and seek advice from experienced farmers on the needs of the plants, and how to go about meeting those needs. Once you figure this out, you will be surprised at how healthy and vigorous the growth of your plants will be.

Why Your Attention Should Remain with the Roots

In a hydroponic setup, the main determinant of health, growth, and productivity of the plants are the roots. The roots are the point of contact between the rest of the plant and the essential nutrients the plant needs to survive and make food. It is also how the plant gets water, for cooling and transportation of nutrients produced in the leaves. Therefore, there is more than a sound reason why you should maintain healthy roots, and one of the key ways to ensure that the roots remain healthy is by ensuring that they have a sufficient amount of oxygen around them.

If the roots of a plant, whether planted in the soil or at a soilless environment, suffer from low oxygen, or lack of it, the roots shrivel up, and they die.

You also need to address water stagnation with immediacy. Although a hydroponic solution can be secured in a closed reservoir, the water therein needs to be in constant movement so that it can interact with the environment. This interaction allows the exchange of gas molecules, although this can also be achieved by installing an air pump at the bottom of the reservoir, as they do in aquariums.

Another fact to keep in mind in regards to the roots is the reality of transplant shock. It occurs when the roots of a seedling, transplanted from a smaller hydroponic germination setup, die upon arrival at the main system. To avoid this, ensure that you carry out the transplanting very slowly but surely. Avoid rushing the process, and ensure that your main agenda is to keep your fragile root hairs alive.

The roots need to be kept moist for as long as the plant needs to be kept alive. However, this is not to say that the roots should be submerged in some stagnant solution.

How Does A Good Hydroponics System Look Like?

A hydroponic system can be judged by its looks: not how colorful or beautiful it looks, but by how the setup has been placed. Want to know if the setup you have looks good, here are the factors you should consider:

- The overall system design should be simple, relatively inexpensive, and easy to implement

- The maintenance costs to the owner should be almost non-existence because the setup should take care of 99% of its issues.

- The system should be fully automated and the only role the farmer plays is to test the solution content, and add to them when the need arises

- The system should be ideal and ready to house and meet the needs of the plants it was meant to house. Simply, the system should serve the purpose for which it was set up.

- There should be no wastage of the nutrient solution.

- The setup should be able to deliver the right air, water and nutrient combination to the plants so that the crops do not just survive, but they thrive in the hydroponic setup.

The Best Low-Cost and Environmental-Friendly Way to Power Your Hydroponics System

So far, you have thought about everything you need for your garden, from the water, the nutrients, the solution, the growing medium, the physical setup, lighting, and it may look like you have covered everything. However, my goal here is to ensure that your plunge into the hydroponics world is as seamless as possible.

There is one more issue we need to think about: how best can we lower the running costs? One way to do this is to lower the cost of power. How would you like to tap solar power from the sun to your garden? Fantastic idea, right? Now let's see how you should do that.

A hydroponic system demands a continuous supply of a lot of power, especially if you are operating a recirculating system to provide your plants with the necessary nutrition, and to return the excess solution back to the reservoir.

As you would expect, the most reliable power source would be if you tapped into the alternating current provided through the national grid. However, some people are keen to ensure that while their farms are running smoothly, they do not contribute to the worsening of global warming scourge.

How would a hydroponics farmer achieve this objective? He or she would tap into solar power. If you do things the right way, you can run your entire greenhouse hydroponics operations relying on solar energy alone, powering it both day and night.

For this project, you would need a car or solar battery (you are not restricted to just one), a low voltage direct current breaker, some wires of an appropriate size, solar panels (Ideally, 100 watts or more. Your power needs will dictate this), a voltage regulator, an inverter to convert direct current to alternating current, and a solar charge controller.

Here are the steps you should take to bring the above items together:

1. Securely mount your solar panels at the top of a roof,
ensuring that the frames are angled appropriately, in a way that will set the panels up for maximum exposure to the sun's UV rays. Ensure that the panel is not positioned in the shade of a tree because the shade reduces the reach of the rays to your panel, thereby reducing the effectiveness of the solar setup. Do all you can to ensure maximum exposure.

2. Create the connection between the solar panels on the roof to low voltage breakers in the house. Ensure that you are connecting the right wire as you do this because setting up any electrical system, including the solar panel, can prove to be very dangerous. If you are doing this yourself, take some time to conduct thorough research before you join any wires. Otherwise, call an electrician.

Do not confuse the low voltage breakers with the normal circuit breakers though. A DC breaker is built to break short-circuits that come up when the voltages are very low while the normal AC circuit breaker breaks voltages that are very high, to restore normal functionality.

Therefore, the DC low voltage breakers you connect to the solar panels are meant to ensure that the line coming directly from the solar panel, were there to be an electrical catastrophe, will not burn the entire solar panel setup.

3. Connect the solar charge controller to the car battery or the solar battery. If you are running a hybrid solar setup, opt for a large capacity car or truck batteries. Normally, solar panels use 12-volt or 24-volt batteries, but getting a battery of a higher strength will cause it to last longer, and to provide more power in a day, compared to that given by the lower voltage batteries.

4. Now connect the batter to your DC-AC inverter. It inverts the direct current from the battery into alternating current that is used to run appliances and equipment in your garden, and even in your house.

5. The last connection of the solar setup is between the inverter and the regulator. A power regulator regulates the power going to your appliances or equipment, while also acting as a circuit breaker. In case of a short circuit, the fuse in the regulator blows, breaking the connection immediately, and protecting you and your appliances from fires that come when wires are shorted.

You can now connect the power regulator to your multi-tap power extension setup. The extension tap should be heavy-duty, and able to break the circuit in case of faults.

It is also of great importance that you get some lightning protect taps for the event your greenhouse is struck by lightning. The lightning cap should be able to turn itself on in the event there is an extreme power surge, and this will save your hydroponic equipment from electrical damage.

The setup you have created will function as follows: In the morning, your plants will be feeding off the light rays from the sun, and at the same time, your battery will be charging. When night reaches, the battery will be at a complete charge, powering the grow lights you purchases, the air pump, the submersible pump, and other systems, up until morning when your battery starts powering again.

Notice that although the pumps and timers will be running during the day, the energy they consume will be almost negligible because the battery will be continually charging.

The benefit of a solar system is that since you have installed numerous safety measures, the system can safely run on autopilot. Remember that one of the characteristics of a good hydroponic setup is that it should be able to take care of itself. Only ensure that each morning, you check the readings on different parts of the system to ensure that everything is working normally.

CHAPTER 6

Common Mistakes Hydroponics Beginners Make

Since you are just now getting into hydroponics gardening, you may want to take things as slowly and as carefully as you could. One mistake could send the entire project rolling down the hill, and no one wants that. What an investment you have made, and how sad it would be to see it all amount to nothing! What you do to prevent this is to get first, a clear understanding of what your intended plants expect of you and how to attend to each of their needs.

While knowing what to do is important, you should also beware of what not to do, because doing so would mess up your project. Below is a review of common mistakes beginner hydroponic gardeners can make:

#1: Going Cheap By Sourcing Ineffective or Not Buying Enough Lighting

Lighting can make or break your hydroponic garden. If you buy the wrong kind of bulb, your plants will suffer. The same will happen if you provide too little lighting. The growth of your plants will stunt. The cheapest bulbs too, may not perform as well as required.

One of the most critical investments you ought to make as a hydroponic farmer is to seek the best lighting for your crops. This requires you to conduct first, substantial research in the market, and among seasoned hydroponic farmers, on the right kind of lighting, bearing in mind that different bulbs will produce different kinds of energy and light spectrums.

Also, don't expect that placing your plants next to a window is enough substitution for grow lights because usually, the light that gets in through the window is not sufficient, or strong enough to support the vigorous growth common among hydroponic plants.

#2: Designing Unusable or Difficult-To-Use Hydroponic Farms

Some beginners make the mistake of designing an unusable farm because they lack experience or because they have not dealt with hydroponics before, at least not on a large scale.

Due to inexperience, they fail to think about factors like efficiency and workflow, which leads to farms that make regular maintenance operations difficult, make harvesting difficult and do not use the space available efficiently. These inefficient gardens may also demand lots of tending, transplanting due to death of the plants, and difficulties controlling pests. Farmers also have a difficult time accessing various parts of the systems.

Now that labor is the most expensive variable cost in a farm, it is of great importance that the farms have labor-efficient designs.

The solution to this mistake is to take some considerable time to plan out and think about how the system will work, and from there, you can now build individual components. Consider all the variables, including water, nutrients, light, pests, convenience, access, redundancy, and automation, right from the start, and only start planning out the design once you have figured out each of the variables mentioned.

It would help if you went benchmarking, by visiting and talking to seasoned growers to see the systems they are operating. Go ahead and ask questions, including seeking answers to the question of what they would do differently were they to turn back and begin afresh.

#3: Confusing Biological Viability with Economic Viability

One of the misconceptions flying around the agricultural product markets is that establishing a farm requires 90% growing while selling takes 10%. However, when it comes to reality, the opposite is true, and many farmers make mistakes on either of the systems.

The farmers fail to take into consideration the financial costs and the time it would take for them to get their produce to the market once it has matured, and because of this small omission, many do not budget either money or the time that they would need to get their produce to the consumers. This effectively disrupts the schedule they had previously set for the farm and can lead to frustration due to lack of a market.

The second batch are those that go-ahead to plan for the biological functions of their farms, including the crops to grow, the techniques to use, and the equipment to source for, but they do all this without testing the feasibility of what they are producing in the market. They are not careful to ensure that what they are producing matches the local demand. In the end, the farmers are frustrated at having a lot of produce and a facility, with no consumers to buy what they have grown.

The bottom line is that it will not matter how much effort you have dedicated to your farm, or how healthy and better tasting they are if no one wants them.

#4: Underestimating the Cost of Crop Production and Of Purchasing the Hydroponic System

It is typical of many motivated and determined hydroponic beginners to be so excited about getting into the hydroponic business that they underestimate just how they would have to spend to succeed at it. Beginners are often asked to start small and scale to bigger establishments with time, even if they feel like they have the resources they would need to go big. The problem is that some do not heed this instruction, and instead, they enter the industry and purchase large facilities, equipment, and expensive utilities.

Unfortunately, those who go ahead to start their gardens find that the costs of running hydroponic gardens are way too high, and some may quit in the middle of it due to the inadequacy of resources. Others do not even get to start the production process because by the time they finish purchasing the equipment and other resources, they no longer have any money to move ahead. The result is that in either case, the farmers do not get the chance to utilize their equipment fully due to unanticipated costs.

Therefore, as you make plans for your intended project, keep in mind costs like pest control, heat removal, replacement of equipment, labor, insurance, packaging, ongoing maintenance, and the cost of printing marketing materials. All these costs add up to a significant amount.

The most critical of the costs that are often underestimated is the cost of labor, whether the farmer is providing it himself or hiring someone to do it. If you are producing in rafts, for example, realize that it is a labor-intensive hydroponic production practice. The cost of labor for raft systems can go up to 45% or 60% of the total production costs. Many producers do not even take notice of this when calculating and making their estimates. Therefore, when they get to the harvesting and processing stages, they are left in shock, not believing what their returns have become.

#5: Choosing the Wrong Market

The market for which you are producing is another critical factor that you ought to consider, whether your project is producing food to be sold later, or to be consumed by your family. If you grow crops that your market does not want, you will be wasting resources and opportunity. The result is that you will be trying to push your products on unwilling consumers, leading to wastage, and a loss of resources because you will not get a return on your investment.

Some crops are easy to grow, and when they are grown under hydroponics, their production is especially high. However, the crops are just unwanted. Therefore, before you decide on the crop you want to grow, conduct a proper analysis of your market, and even so, look at what your competition is growing. From there, come up with something that will give you lots of customers.

If you are living in an area where field producers present fierce competition with their produce, choose to produce what the producers cannot grow in that period. In most cases, if a consumer, say a restaurant, wants to buy organic lettuce and the field producer offers it at 50 cents a pound, the field producer will have the attention of the consumer, at least for the summer period, when he is producing.

When the seasonal competition is too stiff, come up with ways to survive and not lose your spot in the market. If you prove to be reliable, you will win the loyalty of many consumers, and you can lock them into permanent purchasing contracts, such that they will not even consider other producers, cheaper or not.

The bottom line here is that you should choose a crop whose market is guaranteed.

#6: Choosing Hydroponic Systems That Have Poor Reputations, Then Expecting Different Results

When you are trying to choose the right system to implement, do not be so focused on the project's supposed profitability. Get some reliable information from system users on the experiences they had using the system. If you do not know any, ask your sellers to lead you to someone that has used the system for a while, and if the sellers cannot do this, walk away. If you get to see some referees, be careful to find out whether their systems are profitable or not.

#7: Choosing the Wrong Crop for Your Setup and Climate

The marketing language being used in most seed catalogs is filled with beautiful descriptions, and it is easy for a producer to be seduced into growing some exotic crops that are not suited to his hydroponic system or to his climate. In addition, the crops might not even be in demand in his local market.

Before you settle on a particular streak of crop for your project, consider some important factors. Consider the constraints that your environment could have placed on you, the growing technique you will take up, and whether the crop is suited to the production technique you have settled for.

Kindly note that different crops will have different needs, and some can only be grown in a particular, specified way. For example, those that are using rafts should not consider growing tomatoes. In the same way, growers who use granite as the growing medium should not expect to reap worthwhile root crops.

You need to put a lot of thought into your production decisions. If you live in the southern hemisphere and are constantly battling heat, your attempts to grow cool weather crops like rhubarb will be a poor decision. If you live in the Northern hemisphere and you want to grow crops with a long day length, the eight-hour day will not work well for you there.

#8: Becoming Too Big, Too Fast

Surprisingly, this is a common mistake among hydroponic growers. Some growers will go and look for funding to establish some big expensive facilities even before they understand the market they are trying to get into, and the cost structure of the entire production process. Growers that take this road tend to have more catastrophic failures, and they have them more often than not.

When a big project sinks, a lot of money and other resources go down too. Even more, failure leads to supply gaps for customers who need consistent product delivery. Whenever you do not deliver, the customers will go ahead and source for a different supplier, and by the time the food producer is back to the system, he will have lost many of his customers.

You need to be patient, and to understand the growth process. Once you are not in a hurry, you have time to look around the market, identify needs you can meet, and even source for the best production resources like seeds, and fertilizers. You are also likely to get good bargains, which would considerably reduce your production costs. Observe how large entrants flood the market with new products and see how they end up with mixed results. Learn from their experiences, and avoid getting losses like those yourself.

You can do three critical things to avoid the pain of growing very fast. First, develop a niche market. Secondly, become creative in what you do, and ensure that you are offering value to your consumers. Thirdly, do not submit to the desire of overwhelming your market. With that, you will move at a reasonable pace, acquiring all the lessons you need along the way, from your experience, and that of other growers.

#9: Pulling Leaves off Your Plants

Leaves are the plants' factories, where all the sugar production takes place. This sugar is critical for all plant processes including growth and flowering. Therefore, no matter what anyone says to you, refrain from getting the leaves off your plants. Although some say that taking some leaves off induces a growth stress response that helps to reduce stretching, the practice can be detrimental to growth, and it would just be better if you left it for when you are more advanced.

#10: Getting Into the Grow Room When the Lights Are Off

When you have just started your hydroponics gardening project, you will feel like a new parent, with the urge of wanting to check on your 'baby' every so often. Some check on their plants for up to 50 times a day, and this is not good. Save your inspection for when the lights come back on.

#11: Failure to Double Check That Your Equipment Is Running Correctly

If you forget to check whether your meters are calibrated and working correctly, fail to plug in your pumps and fail to check whether your timers have been set and are working correctly, you could fall into a whole lot of problems. Therefore, you need to check, and keep rechecking your equipment, and its settings.

#12: Using Unreliable Equipment to Conduct Very Important Tasks

We already mentioned that you should avoid cheap, inefficient lighting, but the same rule applies to other equipment like fans, and timers. Although you may be working on a budget now and may need to shop on price, ensure that once you have saved up some money, you get better quality equipment. If the quality of your equipment is good, you can rely on it, you will experience fewer equipment failures, and you will have safer gear that does not tear and wear easily.

#13: Adding Nutrients and Water Every Time You Top Up Your Nutrient Solution

This is mostly done by gardeners who are using tap water for their farms. Tap water already has some salt in it, and when you add some salt to it, in the form of the fertilizer you introduce, the nutrients will be taken up in varying ratios. Whenever you want to increase your solution, you add some water, and when you do this, you introduce some new salts into the solution, which could introduce a nutrient imbalance because the plant food may become so concentrated. An imbalance can harm or even burn the plants.

If you insist on tap water, you would be better off just adding water to your solution, without having to add any nutrients, until the nutrient salts reach desirable levels as indicated by the EC meter. In a number of days, when the liquid level in your tank will get lower, you may dump the current solution and refill your tank with a new batch. Ensure that the solution level is high because as experienced gardeners will tell you, particularly those that use recycling systems, the higher the solution level, the better. In addition, the more frequently you dump out your used solution, the better it is for your crops.

The bottom line is that when you add water, just add it up to the point where the salt ratios in the solution are maintained, at the most desirable levels.

#14: Failing to Take In Important Lessons As You Go

Parents talk of each of their children as different, despite having the same gene pool. Identical twins, despite being similar in appearance, will have unique characteristics. This is the case for all crops you will be rearing in your hydroponic system. You may plant the same crops you did the previous round and be surprised that there are problems with the current one, or the yields are different.

It is likely that you missed a step, did not mix the nutrient solution as you did previously, and other changes you may have effected. Take some time to compare and analyze the two growing periods, and see how you can adjust your practices for the next crops.

The best way to keep tabs on what you did in a particular crop cycle is to photograph, document and take note of all the bad and the good aspects of the system you have and the crops you planted. Whenever you have mapped out the problem, it is easier to keep thinking, and eventually finding a solution to your problems. Conduct research from websites, books, and the all-friendly YouTube, and you will find all kinds of solutions lined up.

#15: Failing To Take Note of the PH

One of the most critical yet often overlooked factors in hydroponic farming, particularly among beginners, is the pH issue. Plants are only able to take in particular minerals at specified pH levels. As stated earlier, hydroponics gardens tend to maintain a pH of between 5.5 and 6, because it is at this slightly acidic environment that plants are able to take in the right nutrients.

You need to have a pH meter with you so that you can measure the content of your nutrient solution more often, and when it doesn't fall in the recommended range, make adjustments accordingly. Monitor the pH at least once every day, as this is one of the most common reasons plants die, and since they are using the same solution if one is affected, they all are, and they all die.

#16: Failing To Learn

The hydroponics idea has been in existence since early on in the 20th century, and in that time, much research and learning has taken place, both formal and informal. Most people then transfer the lessons they have learned into information that they place in books while others offer training seminars. All this information is helpful and you can get it either by taking up courses or reading books. It would be wise if you did both: learning from experienced farmers and reading books. There are also regular updates on the internet, and these too will inform you of new developments in the practice, technology advancements and of changes in the market.

Whatever you do, don't get into hydroponics gardening alone. Even if you feel like you already know everything, there is always something you ought to learn. Share ideas with other hydroponic gardeners and get to know what they have been up to. The more knowledge you gather before making your first move, the more prepared you will be, the smoother the journey will be, and the more fulfilling your harvest will be.

#17: Giving Your Plants the Wrong Food

Sometimes, it will feel like it would not hurt too much if you just picked a sack of fertilizer from your local store and feed your plants before you accessed the right one. After all, the regular fertilizer contains the nutrients that your plants need too, right? Wrong.

Regular fertilizer may fail to dilute all the way and may clog the tubes and drains of your system. Instead, opt for the kind of fertilizer specially designed for hydroponic systems. The right kind will be in liquid form or granules. It is in the right concentration and will meet the needs of your plants have in their soilless environment. It will provide all the nutrients your plants need.

#18: Failing To Keep Your Garden Clean

If you are used to throwing stuff in your soil garden with the assurance that it will decompose, don't try that with a hydroponic garden. Your garden area is not a garbage bin, and the critical issue is that the level of hygiene you uphold will affect the flow of your hydroponic system and on your plants' health.

To ensure that your garden is in proper hygiene conditions, keep your floor dry and clean, sterilize your cleaning tools, and dispose of all plant waste. Sterilize and clean the entire system when you can, and don't forget to clean the containers holding the nutrient solution.

If you do not ensure proper sanitation, you could provide breeding and hiding spaces for pests, and encourage the spread of crop diseases.

#19: Failing To Ensure Proper Oxygen Flow

Most beginners assume that plants only need carbon dioxide to survive and therefore do not attend to the oxygen needs of their plants. The truth is that plant roots need access to oxygen to aid respiration. If the roots are not healthy, they become susceptible to disease and pathogens that cause rotting of the roots. However, the more the plant is able to access oxygen, the better it is for the plant and the farmer.

Some hydroponic systems do not require you to pump in oxygen into the nutrient solution because oxygen infuses into them just by how they operate. A good example would be an ebb and flow system that drains its excess nutrient solution down the grow bed, and in the process, allows the roots to be exposed to air. Other systems like the deep-water culture system require an air pump and an air stone to help oxygenate the nutrient solution. In the deep-water culture system particularly, ensure that you use at least more than one air stone.

#20: Failing To Regulate Temperature

Most often, beginners do not remember that the temperatures of the germination room and the grow room should be regulated. In addition, some will focus on the temperature of the room and forget to check the temperature of the nutrient solution.

Whenever the temperature of the solution rises, the air is continually bubbled out of the solution, which means that as temperature rises, the amount of dissolved oxygen keeps going down. A low oxygen volume affects the health of the roots and boosts the development and growth of pathogens. Therefore, ensure that the solution maintains a temperature of between 65 and 75 F. degrees.

The temperature of the air is also critical for different developmental stages of the plant. For seeds, if the temperature is too low or too high, the seeds can't germinate. This is the same case for fruit and flower production. General plant growth will also be affected. For example, if veggies like broccoli and lettuce are kept in a very hot environment, they begin to bolt. Therefore, for a maximum harvest, ensure that you stick to the recommended plant temperatures.

#21: A Lack of Understanding of Hydroponic Nutrients

Hydroponic solutions are not just about parts and mixing ratios; care must be taken to ensure that the plants are getting the right nutrients for their growth stage, plant type, and the contents of the fertilizers. To begin with, realize that plants need varying ratios of N-P-K nutrients depending on their growth stage. For example, at the vegetative stage, plants will require a high amount of nitrogen while flowering plants need more potassium and phosphorus.

The market is flooded with different fertilizers with varying nutrients ratios, but before you make a purchase, you ought to conduct first, a study of what your plant needs to ensure that you are providing proper nutrients, at the right stage, so that it can reach its full potential.

#22: Inadequate Circulation for Your Garden

When a growing space is warm and humid, there arises the potential for mold growth in your hydroponic garden. To reduce this risk, you need to ensure proper air circulation by including a fan or installing a proper air conditioning system that lets out the hot air and brings in some cool air. In the event your garden is fully enclosed, consider adding some vents to allow fresh air in. This air exchange keeps the temperatures of the place down. Therefore, as a hydroponics beginner, ensure that you do not overlook the issue of circulation through increased ventilation.

CHAPTER 7

Useful Tips for Hydroponic Farming

If you review any of the hydroponic farming tips, given in this topic, you may see that the tips center on three primary issues, which are: lack of knowledge, lack of discipline and inability. People lack an understanding of what should be and the things they need to do to see it through. Others know what is expected of them but do not care enough to put in the time and effort to see it through. The third category is of people who do not have the proper hydroponic equipment or lack proper knowledge of how to run activities on a hydroponic farm.

However, the tips that this chapter provides will give you the necessary knowledge to help you identify and avoid having any of the three issues mentioned, in your garden. While you may make some mistakes here and there, having foreknowledge of what to expect and the tricks to take up to reach your goal sooner and help you achieve greater success in what you do.

The tips you should keep in mind include:

1) Always have a plan

It is impossible to run a hydroponics garden and be successful at it without a plan. What to include in your plan is the nutritional needs of your plants, the light or photoperiod, the equipment you need to operate, how to meet the labor needs at the garden, and how to access the nutrients that your plants need.

You should actually have a week-by-week plan of what to do, and you should incorporate information about the nutrient changes to have and other important information. Some nutrient kits come with this information, but some packages will require you to consult a professional or an experienced farmer.

2) Prioritize the health of the roots

Damaged roots will paralyze the entire plant because they are unable to take up the required nutrients to the plant. Therefore, in case there is damage at the bottom, expect the same damage at the top, in the form of sick plants, wilting plants, and damaged leaves.

The way to protect your roots is by ensuring that your solution is at the right concentration, uncontaminated and aerated. You need two solution reservoirs, one to contain the water you will be using when you discard the current solution when 14 days lapse. The second precaution is putting in measures to reduce your solution's exposure to light. This is helpful because it prevents algae growth, which in turn prevent the formation of fungus gnats that cause most of the plant root problems.

3) Temperature control

One of the most critical tips in hydroponic farming is temperature control. Since hydroponic farming takes place in an enclosed humid location, a greenhouse or a house, the temperature can rise quickly, and when it gets to 85 degrees, plant growth stops, unless you install a pump that raises the CO_2 concentration in the room.

When using artificial lighting to grow the crops, especially the lights themselves will emit substantial heat that can become a problem for your in house garden. It could help if you found a way to place your light's ballast outside the grow room unless of course, you have the digital kind of ballast that does not emit heat. Since you need these lights, invest in something that will bring in some cold air, and note that fans are not an adequate measure.

4) You need to provide proper, adequate lighting

When it comes to bringing light to an indoor garden, you have a few options. At a minimum, you need to provide 40 to 60 watts lighting per square foot. The best choices in the market to help you bring this to life include the metal halide lights or the high-pressure sodium lights. The two are the most popular choices among farmers.

You need to know that when it comes to fluorescent lighting, regular fluorescent lights do not provide enough lighting to support healthy growth. This kind of lighting is only good for seedlings, clones, and plants that are very young, and in their vegetative stage like the spinach, kitchen herbs, and lettuce.

For your grow room, opt for T5 lights, also called Tek lights because they emit less heat in comparison to HID lights, and they use less energy. Ensure that your plants are only a few inches away from the lights. The lights should be overhead the plants.

5) Feeding or nutrition tips

Before you make any steps, such as deciding on the setup, the location and other details, conduct research to determine the nutritional needs of your intended crops. Take note of the expected strength of the concentration for each week of the plant's life, take note of the names of the fertilizers you will need and from where you will source them.

For example, most plants need a high amount of nitrogen in their infancy (not as young as clones) and then switch to needing high phosphorus amounts once they begin to flower and produce fruits. To ensure that you are kept abreast about the strength of your nutrient solution, ensure that you get yourself an EC meter or a TDS meter, and adjust the solution as the plants develop, moving from one stage to the next.

As a beginner, do not attempt to mix up your own plant solution, opt for the professionally made hydroponics nutrients concentrate. It is a three-part fertilizer, and it is easy to use. Once you have gotten used to the system and have had success producing crops, perhaps after you have recovered your cost of setup (for business persons), then you can try making your own nutrient solution, and observing how the plants respond to every change you make. If things are not working out, at least you will know exactly what the issue is, and you can make adjustments.

The same is the case for any additives. As a beginner, stay away from solutions said to improve your farm results. This issue is an especially common problem among beginner farmers who are anxious for the big results. Instead, farmers should work with the three-part nutrients first, because they are good enough and adequate for the plants, and they should postpone any plans to boost production until when their systems begin to work smoothly and to produce good results. Then you can add liquid seaweed, vitamin B1, Silica, or a combination of the three.

Another critical thing is on your need to check the nutrient solution reservoir every single day. We have already established that the nutrient solution ought to be changed every 14 days.

6) Your choice of growing medium is of absolute importance

The growing media is the core of your farming, and you need to realize that it is expensive, requires labor, and needs space. It provides support to your crops. With these considerations, you need to realize that it is only by choosing the right medium that your work will be made easier while choosing the wrong one will bring setbacks and speed bumps to your development.

Therefore, you need to arm yourself with some tips that have to do with the specific growing medium. They include:

a. You need to appreciate the process and the technique of using your specific medium

Each medium is different, and just because it worked out great for one person, it doesn't have to work out the same for another farmer. However, you need to have studied all there is to know about the medium you have chosen so that you know how, when and where to use it.

For example, coconut coir is good for systems for which you do not have to be concerned about the medium disintegrating or being washed through the system. It does not work well in systems where it will be handled heavily. Rockwool is not suited for systems where it would also be compressed. However, polymer-bound plugs are suitable for systems in which they would be compressed.

b. Be sure to ask the right questions

You need to know all there is about your hydroponic system and process, but some questions are more critical than others. You need to know how much you and your laborers will be handling the growing material, find out if the material is suited for automation and whether the medium will compress during the handling process or in the equipment. See also, whether you will be required to dispose of the medium, or whether you can re-use it.

c. Make an estimate of the external costs

Choosing a cheap medium ignores the cost of maintaining the product, especially in regard to the labor, germination requirements, and the issues of disposal. Know the external costs that come with your medium, and find out whether it may require any kind of special treatment from the germination, planting, growing and harvesting process.

d. Take into consideration the unique needs that come with particular growing material such as the structure of the hydroponic system, aeration, or the shear strength of the material.

e. Consider all factors present before making your decision.

Once you have known all there is to know about your growing media, learn how it will interact with the rest of the farm. Bring all the knowledge you have been collecting in regards to the hydroponic garden, and with careful consideration, go ahead and make your decision. Consider the certification objectives, conditions for germination, irrigation strategies, crop size, price, and automation goals.

7) The Process of Germinating Your Seed

There are many ways you could employ to germinate your seeds. They include:

a. Pre-soaking
In this method, the farmer puts some moist tissues on a plate, then places his seeds on top of the tissues. He then places another layer of wet tissues on the seeds and covers the plate with another upturned plate. The seeds remain in the dark space that has been created, and their environment remains moist due to lack of exposure to the air and the elements of the environment. Ensure that the place in which the seeds remain is warm, about 21 degrees Celsius.

Ensure that you check on your seeds every day and wet the tissues when the moisture in them begins to dry out. Once the seeds are germinated, carefully transplant them. The skin should have broken, and the tip of the root should be visible. Now, place the germinated seed on the growing medium, ensuring that it is approximately 5 mm from the surface.

b. Using the growing medium to germinate seeds

You could still germinate your seeds in the growing medium. You only have to place the seeds about 5mm under the surface, then regularly sprinkle the growth medium with some water, ensuring that it does not get too wet. The seed germinates and uses the food stored in its cotyledons to germinate and grow. At this point, the air is a critical component because it provides the oxygen needed for metabolism. Therefore, ensure that the medium remains somewhat airy by ensuring that it is not standing in the water and that it is able to drain properly when excess liquid is sprinkled on it.

c. Growing the plants outside
Although hydroponics is about growing your crops in a soilless environment, sometimes it helps to ask for help from the soil (pun intended). Since germinating seeds indoors takes a much shorter time than when you do it outdoors, farmers can take up hydroponics for the germination of their seeds before they transfer them to the fields. This method is also ideal because usually, the ground temperature is not ideal between the months of April and May. Only put out the emerged

seedlings outside, at a place where they can start to learn how to get used to the outdoor environment.

8) Caring for the young seedlings

Since the newly emerged plants from the seedlings are still quite delicate, ensure that you do not place them under a 400-watt lamp, and if using natural light, do not place them directly in the sun because they could burn. Only work on providing your plants with water containing nutrients to help them build and strengthen their roots system.

9) Get Proper Tools and Equipment

Unless you have figured out all details in regards to the tools and equipment you need, and how to properly use each of them, do not take any step towards starting your garden. For this, you will need a high-powered fan, a thermometer, an air conditioner, an oscillating fan, a digital timer, an extremely dark area, hydroponic gardening system, adequate lighting and other tools mentioned in a previous chapter. Each of the tools and equipment should be used with diligence and knowledge so that each serves its purpose, and to avoid any accidents or injuries.

10) Manipulate the light period

Most crops require a short daylight period to be able to get to the fruiting or flowering stage. However, consistency is key. You need to ensure a consistent on and off time for the lights, each day.

In addition, you also ought to ensure that when plants are in their dark period, they are left in complete, utter darkness for that period, without even a streak of light interrupting it. For this reason, consider getting yourself a blacked-out grow room or tent. Plants are extremely sensitive to the schedule you set, so avoid skirting around the lighting issue.

11) Clean the hydroponic system regularly

While all the steps and tips can be implemented to the letter, if the hydroponic system itself is contaminated and dirty, the effort you put into it will be reduced to naught. The system needs to be cleaned regularly to ensure its successful operation, and to keep off pests and disease.

Once you have finished sterilizing the grow room, move over to the solution reservoir. Do this by emptying the reservoir, filling it halfway, then using diluted bleach, clean it, and ensure there are no solid materials built up in the system's tubing. You could also reduce clogging by opening the system valves a few seconds each week. Once you have done that, now clean the grow buckets or trays to avoid the buildup of pathogens. The cleaning process is quite simple, and you only need the liquid containing dilute bleach and a scrubber. Do the scrub some several times, to ensure that the items are spotless, and then rinse them out with distilled water to carry away all nutrients or bleach deposits. Do this at the end of every harvest, or before the start of another growing season.

12) Take note of nutrient deficiencies in your plants

i. If a plant is lacking phosphorus, the entire plant turns bluish-green and may develop a purplish or red cast. You may also notice the lower leaves turn yellow, and the plant could start drying and adopting a greenish-brown color before it finally becomes black. A plant like this will often have stunted growth.

ii. If a plant has a potassium deficiency, its leaves will have a papery appearance and the edges of its leaves will have some dead areas. The plant's growth will also be stunted.

iii. An entire plant taking up a light green color and its lower leaves becoming yellow provides evidence of a nitrogen deficiency. Its growth also becomes stunted.

iv. When you notice that your plant's young stems and young leaves are falling off and dying, it is a sign that the plant itself is calcium deficient.

v. If the leaf tissue of your plants takes up a yellow appearance, but the veins on the leaves remain green, the plant lacks iron.

vi. If you notice that the lower leaves of your plant have turned yellow along the margin, the tips, and between the veins and that the lower leaves have wilted, know that your plant is suffering from magnesium deficiency.

vii. If the led tissue between the veins takes up a lighter color, yellow, and takes a papery appearance, know that the plant as a zinc deficiency.

viii. If you notice that the leaves of your plant have stunted, take a pale green color and they are malformed, it is likely that they lack Molybdenum.

ix. Scorched leaf tips and margins of young plants indicate boron deficiency.

x. If your young plants' leaves turn pale green but the older leaves are still green, and you notice that the plant is spindly and stunted, know that the plant is sulfur deficient.

xi. If the plant's growth has stunted, and the lower leaves have taken up a checkered pattern of green and yellow, know that they lack manganese.

xii. If the edges of your leaves appear blue or dark green, and the edges of the leaves curl upward, with the young leaves wilting permanently, know that your crops are lacking copper.

13) Taking note of powdery mildew

One of the most common fungal diseases affecting many plants is powdery mildew, also called mycelium. The fungus appears as a powder or a fuzzy white that coats the stems, leaves, and flowers. If the fungus is left unchecked, it could cause serious damage. Therefore, ensure that you take preventative steps to prevent the mildew onset, knowing that it thrives in damp, cool and poorly ventilated grow room. Therefore, opt to take preventative steps, first by ensuring that there is a clean flow of air in the growth room.

Natural cures and preventative measures for powdery mildew

a. *Using Epsom salt and baking soda*

This is both a cure and a preventative approach. You need to add three-quarters of a teaspoon of Epsom salt to a quarter teaspoon baking soda, and then add the mixture to a liter of water to come up with a solution. Once the solutions are mixed well, foliar spray on your plants generously, and then wash the solution off after a day or two, with misting water.

Please take note of the fact that because the solution you spray will contain salts, it will leave a powdery haze on your leaves, just as the mildew did. However, this will come off with time.

b. *The organic whole milk remedy*

This is a preventative method. The solution you need for it is prepared by diluting 10 parts water with one part organic whole milk. Spray this solution generously on your plants, and after a day or two, wash it off thoroughly to prevent the milk from going bad and causing an awful sour smell. Avoid spraying this solution when plants are in their flowering stage.

The dilute organic milk method is so effective that just a single treatment is enough. Kindly note that you should only use organic unpasteurized whole milk.

Here is a compilation of some quick facts and everyday practice tips to ensure that your plants grow just as anticipated:

- Ensure that you have all the equipment you would need for your hydroponic garden at home before you begin setting it up.

- Once you pick a location and leave your hydroponic system there, do not move the plants to a different location once they have adapted to their current environment

- Everything about your project must be done in a routine, from the feeding, exposure to light, dark times, and others. Plants tend to be very sensitive to their conditions, and if you allow them to work on a schedule, they will make the best of the time they have.

- Avoid walking into your garden after visiting another person's garden or having been outdoors. Only enter the garden once you have had a shower and changed your clothes.

- Ensure that anyone who intends to visit your garden follows the same protocol

- Ensure that you change your nutrients and your water every two weeks

- Clean and disinfect the entire system between crops. In addition, if your plants look discolored, stunt and unhealthy, get your pH kit and check the pH of your solution. If the pH level is just right, flush the entire hydroponic system with a detoxifying solution, such as Clearex.

- Quarantine all the new plants for 14 days before you take them to the growing room

- Keep your pets away from the garden

- Ensure that you install a filter or screen over the exhaust and the air intake

- Take note of all the equipment you will need, and realize the use of each

- Take note of all the nutritional needs of your plant

- Always use a three-part hydroponic nutrients fertilizer
- For your first attempt, avoid additional nutrient additives

- Take note of the light period your plants need

- Put down on paper, the feeding schedule of your plants even before you start your hydroponics project

- Ensure that the ballast of your lights is stored in a different room.

- Maximize the amount of exposure your plants get to the nutrient solution

- Check and regulate the nutrient concentration in your reservoir every day

- Minimize the light exposure of your fluid in the pipes and in the reservoir

- Control the dark periods using a digital timer

- Always have a reservoir of clean plain water in readiness for the next time you change nutrients

- The temperature of your solution in the reservoir should remain between 65 and 75 degrees. Use a water heater or a chiller to adjust temperature changes.

CHAPTER 8

New Developments in Hydroponics Gardening

Just like other high-tech fields, the hydroponic industry evolves constantly. We are continuously becoming aware of different plant physiology concepts, and in turn, scientists and farmers alike, are continually coming up with advanced techniques and technological developments for hydroponics. Serious farmers do not just wait for technology to advance, they are constantly thinking about how they can make their gardens more reproductive and efficient. Although it would be impossible to know where hydroponics gardening will be in the future, we can look at some of the recent gardening practices and scientific advancements to see where hydroponics gardening is headed.

In the next 50 to 60 years, hydroponics farming is likely to be the top agricultural method in use due to the increasing rate of soil degradation. In addition, as the population rises, hydroponics is likely to be the only means to grow food that can keep up with the food demands of the day. Some of the changes happening include:

New Developments in Lighting

The lighting system is at the heart of hydroponic gardening, and over the last 10 years, the advancements that have been made in regards to lighting have been astounding. For example, High-Intensity Discharge (HID) lighting is continuously being improved to increase its efficiency. Even more, double-ended lighting is increasingly becoming popular because of the advantages it offers, over and above that of standard HID lighting, such as longevity and high efficiency.

Sulphur primary lighting is also becoming increasingly popular for indoor gardens because of its unique spectral output. This is an excellent source of lighting, but what puts off gardeners is its high price. However, as manufacturing technology advances, it is expected that sulphur primary lighting will become cheaper, and more farmers will be able to afford it.

Although LED lighting has been here a while, its ability to give off customized, specific light spectrums that directly meet the needs of certain kinds of plants puts these lights ahead of other lighting technologies in terms of their potential. LED lights have been useful to the horticulture and hydroponics industries because they consume very little energy, have a long life, and are efficient.

Improvements Made on the Hydroponic Nutrients

There have been great advancements when it comes to hydroponic nutrients. For example, we can already see the rise of new specialty nutrients that 'self-buffer' to get to the desired pH. It is likely that there will be more of the self-buffering kind, some fully soluble ones that are able to maintain constant pH and ppm levels, and some time-release nutrients. The manufacturers are getting better at mixing various compounds and elements, to come up with a stable one-part formula. It is likely that the variety of one-part nutrients in the market will rise, even as we see an increase in the number of beginner gardeners dipping their feet into the pool of hydroponics.

The Rise of Micro Growing of Microgreens

As hydroponic technology continues to advance, we expect to see changes also, in the development and advancement of automated hydroponic systems used for growing microgreens like sprouts, and they will become more popular. We will still see much of the systems being used for growing grasses and microgreens because an increasing number of farmers are building hydroponic systems to grow fodder for their livestock. The systems they are using are not only affordable; they are also a source of superior food for livestock.

Increased Vertical Growing

Essentially, a hydroponic system serves the purpose of delivering nutrients. However, the vertical growing style is revolutionizing hydroponic gardens immensely by increasing the production capacity of every available space. This is due to the development of vertical gardening, which appears to be the perfect solution for dense urban area gardens because the space available there is limited. In fact, there are even vertical gardens being developed on the sides of buildings or other structures, and this trend is likely to increase in popularity.

We are also likely to see an increase in the establishment of hybrid systems, those that seek to combine the benefits of different hydroponic systems. There are likely to be more systems increasing or maximizing the delivery of oxygen to the roots and those delivering nutrients to the roots, both of which are expected to continue to shape up the future of hydroponics.

Good news to the gardeners is that in the future, they will not have to move from one store to another looking for the tools they need in their farms, because we expect an emergence of more kits that will contain everything that a gardener would need to start working on his project, including the proper nutrients and lighting. Already, these setups are quite popular, but they will become even more popular as more people begin to pick up hydroponics farming and practice it for the first time.

We also look forward to the establishment of more self-contained hydroponics gardens built into the kitchens. These gardens will be plumbed in, hard-wired, and made to look just like a dishwasher. More people now realize that it is beneficial to grow their own food, which means that the demand for the self-contained hydroponics gardens is likely to go up.

Combination of Aeroponics and Hydroponics

In 2016, a hydroponics farm, Preferred Produce, in Deming, New Mexico patented a new technology that would bring together aeroponics and hydroponics. In the new setup, tubes would be run through the hydroponic growing containers, and they would take the role of ferrying oxygen directly to the roots of the plants. The project's founder, Matthew Stong, said that the idea came from understanding that submerging the plants in water restricts their oxygen supply.

The growing of tomatoes, strawberries and bell peppers was used to test the new system, and the agriculturalists reported that the harvests were quicker and heavier than when other techniques were used. The new system proved to be a sure bet for cutting your plants' harvest time. For example, Stong was able to grow evergreen strawberries, that would usually take four months before the first harvest, and he was able to get pounds of the fruit in only two months.

Combination of Hydroponics and Soil Gardening

The Mittleider Grow Box is a relatively new concept invented by Jacob Mittleider. It combines hydroponics and soil gardening, as a way to grow the vegetable you wish to grow, even when your soil is of poor quality.

Mittleider felt that although hydroponics can be used to provide the plants with all the necessary nutrients, there still will be some nutrients or elements that the soil especially contains, but we have not been able to identify it.

The method Mittleider suggests involves anchoring plants in a growing medium while they are yet held in the grow box, which helps roots to penetrate down to the soil so that they are able to access 'the best of both' media. The grow box should be at least 8 inches high and can be of any length and width, without a bottom. Identify your desired gardening spot, fill the box with sand, perlite, peat moss, and sawdust. It does not matter what you will use as your medium; you only have to ensure that it is well aerated and that it drains properly. Now did down into the soil, about an inch deep.

Now, plant your seedlings in the growing medium and cover the top of the box with material like wood chips, which are meant to keep the medium from drying too quickly, now that it is exposed to the elements of weather. Work towards watering your plants with the hydroponic nutrient solution and occasionally, apply some bit of commercial garden fertilizer at the base of the plants.

When carrying this out, as a general concept, you might want to place your plants at half the recommended distance apart that which is suggested for soil gardening. Also, be careful to ensure that the garden fertilizer you apply to the base of the plants is an exact measure of the recommended amount, to avoid burning the roots of the plants, and killing them.

The Advantages

- The Mittleider method is of benefit in the following ways:
- It is a combination of soil gardening and hydroponic principles, and this increases the yields collected from the crops.
- It is inexpensive
- The method is ideal for areas where the soil is too poor to support soil gardening by itself
- Farmers can grow their crops using growing medium made from local material like smashed rocks

- You could place a Mittleider Box anywhere, on the driveway, at a flowerbed, and other areas that would be unsuitable for conventional gardening.

Changes in the Sphere of Commercial Hydroponics

In the last decade or more, strawberries, lettuce, tomatoes, peppers, cucumbers, and cut flowers have made the bulk of commercial hydroponic crops in parts of the world where they are grown. However, of late, farmers have taken to growing rate herbs, plants that produce essential oils, Chinese vegetables and medicinal plants. Others are also growing wasabi and gourmet potatoes. There is also a growing movement that craze of growing plants for nutraceutical and pharmaceutical use. It would seem that it is now possible to grow any crop for commercial purposes via hydroponics.

There is an increasing interest in the production of salad crops and cut herbs, driven by the demand for the proximity to healthy food. The primary benefit of hydroponics is that it produces the best quality results, increasing its competitiveness in the market, over cheaper quality crops. For example, it produces the most superbly favored tomatoes, and potatoes. In time, we expect to see an increase in the demand for edible flowers, those that particularly used in hotel complexes and restaurants. In truth, there are now very few crops that cannot be grown hydroponically, and the only factor that keeps farmers from operating commercially is the economic aspect.

Advances through Aquaponics and Other Systems

Aquaponics is the combination of hydroponic gardening and aquaculture, fish farming. Aquaponics is an efficient and sustainable food production approach because there is no wastage: fish waste is fed into the hydroponics farm to feed the plants while the plants filter the water for the fish. Therefore, the water goes from the fish to the plants, and back in a perfect circle.

As the future dictates, taking up sustainable methods of food production is going to be critical, and aquaponics is a great way to go about it, for both small-scale and large-scale food production.

Interestingly though, other animals are being integrated into the sustainable methods of farming such as rabbits, worms, chicken and crickets, among others. As more people launch creative ideas into their farms, we expect more animals to become part of this unique biological hydroponic system.

Hydroponics in Grocery Stores and Restaurants

Other latest trends like this one, are not related to hydroponic growing, or the system, but on the application of the system. You must have seen that grocery stores and restaurants are now making hydroponic systems part of their business structures, as a way to provide their customers with the freshest produce.

For example, restaurants are running living salad bars that set apart their food from restaurants that store their produce in freezers and fridges. Customers can now enjoy a fresh meal right from the garden. This development has not only helped to boost interest in the customers, but it is also a financially sound idea because the cost of growing produce is lesser than that of purchasing it. There has also been an upcoming trend of growing plants on the rooftop and vertically, on the walls. All these developments are meant to increase food production in the urban setup.

Transitioning to the Organic Side

Majority of the nutrients and fertilizers used in hydroponics systems, both in small scale and large scale farms, are synthetically manufactured chemical compounds. Although these nutrients have been behind the success and popularity of hydroponics farming, they are not organic. This is contrary to the growing trend where people only want to eat organic foods. In addition, the runoff you get into the environment when you empty your nutrient reservoir can be quite damaging to the environment. Therefore, farmers are opting for organic fertilizers and shunning the chemical compounds. The nutrient-filled organic produce is quickly replacing the manufactured substances.

Increased Conservation and Sustainability Measures

The concept of conservation and sustainability of processes has been ongoing for a while now, across the world. Sectors are looking for ways to get into the bandwagon from the construction industry and its green buildings, and now to hydroponics farming, among other sectors. Since hydroponics requires significantly less water and fewer fertilizers, the wastage is not as dire as in other methods of agriculture.

Therefore, hydroponics reduces pollution to the environment, reducing the need to conduct expensive studies, and the need for containment and catchment, which happens with other forms of agriculture. This advantage allows hydroponics farmers to tell a good story about their trade, which is appealing to the environmentally conscious consumer.

Hydroponics as Part of the Home Décor

The fact that there are now green plants in places where they never were, such as in wall hangings, on countertops, on window panes, on the roofs, and in other areas, is placing plants in new territories enhancing the beauty of where they are placed.

People who only saw hydroponics gardening as belonging to a secret room somewhere, the backyard or in a greenhouse, are now seeing its use in new elegant living spaces as a piece of art. As you will see around the spaces you visit, artificial and cut flowers are quickly losing their place to live flowers, as people increasingly realize the benefits of hydroponics in the home décor craft or industry.

Hydroponics as The Means to Enhance Breathing Air

Many people introduce container plants in a room to help clean up the air. This is the traditional way of doing it, and it has a few drawbacks. One of them is that it would take you many plants to make any significant difference because soil-grown plants are limited in their growth, which in turn limits their rate of carbon dioxide for oxygen exchange. Also, the plants can only have an effect on the little air that is around them.

However, once you install hydroponic plants into a building, you also introduce an air filter that combines the natural ability of many plants to cleanse the air, and the benefits of a fan, which overcome the limitations of soil-grown plants.

The fan gets in the air through the hydroponic system much faster than natural processes would, and once it is incorporated into the nutrient solution, it speeds up the plant's respiration, which in turn speeds up the plant's intake of carbon dioxide, and its growth rate. The growing medium also acts as an extra air filter. The result of this process is that the particulate and formaldehyde removal rate is faster, at least 1000% better than if you were to depend on the plants alone.

The Hydroponics Carnival Ride

For a serious gardener working with a small indoor space, making the most of the available space would mean growing your crops in several layers, providing each with its own grow lights, and a watering system. This requires a lot of money, causing many growers to give up and pull out of the business.

A garden in America, however, found the solution to working with small spaces. The owners found a way to save on the lighting and the nutrients solution too. They came up with a device that resembles a Ferris wheel, one large enough to hold about 80 plants, with its trays arrayed around an axis placed at the center. Rockwool or some similar medium is used to hold the plants in place, and only one light is placed along the axis, and it provides all the light the plants need for their development.

In comparison to the regular hydroponics setup, this new arrangement causes three times as much plant growth for every watt. The plants also get to pass through the trough containing the hydroponics nutrient solution to pick the nutrients they need for each 45 minutes cycle.

Growing Marijuana

Different parts of the United States are increasingly legalizing adult use of marijuana, and in the process, creating a standardized regulated market for the product. Marijuana is used for both recreational and medicinal use, and its market is quite huge across the world. Regardless of the individual reservations, some people have regarding the industry; we have to admit that big business and many opportunities are lying in this industry, that farmers can take up.

As you would expect, the infant marijuana industries have established some stringent regulations, similar to those we see in the production of food items. In addition, the consumption trends you see in food preferences among consumers are similar to those expressed by marijuana consumers: they want to ensure that what they are putting in their bodies is clean, does not contain any pesticides, and ideally, it was grown in an environmentally conservent environment.

Hydroponic systems make it easier to grow clean, chemical free, and quality marijuana. Farmers are able to respond to the plants' nutritional needs, and the result is that the produce is more, and its quality is superior to regularly grown marijuana. The farmers are able to stick to the standards set by the regulatory board, and they even meet the needs of the end user.

For farmers who think that the establishment of a regulatory board would make their farming much more difficult, hydroponics gardening would make their work easier. You will stay on the right side of the law without even knowing it. This is because hydroponics gardening only allows you to provide your plants with only that which is necessary, and stay away from chemicals that would have contaminants. You also do not have to apply pest and disease control chemicals because the hydroponics environment is clean and free of disease-causing pathogens. Pests do not get in there either.

Into the Future

As time goes by, we can expect to see many other radical technologies come up in hydroponic farming. For example, the solar panels we covered earlier is quickly being taken up, particularly in the aquaponic setup that seeks to capitalize on the self-sufficiency of the system. We are bound to see more homes taking up this technology because it will not only offset electricity costs related to hydroponics; households can also rely on it for various functions.

The idea of fiber optic solar connection systems is still in its infancy, but once it advances and turns into a practical power solution, it promises to be another development that will revolutionize hydroponics gardening and other forms of indoor production.

In summary

In this information age, people are increasingly aware that they are what they eat. Their health, their outward looks, and other functions of the body are all related to the diet. This knowledge has increased the demand for clean, fresh food in the markets and eateries, which has made hydroponics the perfect solution for feeding the fresh food demand in the dense urban areas.

In the next few years, we are sure to see hydroponic gardens popping up on the walls of buildings, on the rooftops, in people's kitchens, backyards, and other spaces. In addition, commercial farmers are taking up the hydroponic gardening idea to increase their production potential. Therefore, as we step into the future, we can be sure that food will not be an issue of concern, even as the world population increases, because hydroponics farming has proven to be an excellent antidote to issues of food and its availability.

You too could take matters into your hands and begin to produce healthy foods for your family, friends, or even as a way to make some extra money. You could set up some form of a home garden, even when living in an apartment. Place your plants on a countertop, or at the kitchen window, and you will be surprised that you can actually grow something good out of your small unused spaces. As you and others around you adopt this practice, hydroponics gardening is sure to become a major part of producing food, across the world.

As of 2018, the global hydroponics market was worth $23.94 billion, and in the period between 2019 and 2024, there's expected to be a 6.8% increase. Governments and non-governmental organizations are championing it due to the benefit of ensuring food security. While the costs of setup are currently high, the farmers continue to reap big profits. We expect that advancing technology will resolve the issues of costs, and when this happens, farmers will benefit greatly. Big companies are moving in to take advantage of the new big business, and you too deserve a piece of the action.

CONCLUSION

Thanks for making it through to the end of *Hydroponics: Beginner's Guide to Quickly Start Growing Your Own Vegetables, Fruits, & Herbs, and Learn How to Build Your Own Hydroponics Home Gardening System*. Let's hope it was informative and able to provide you with all of the tools you need to achieve your goals whatever it is that they may be. It would be impossible to exhaust all there is to hydroponics farming, but the author sampled the most important bits of information to help you understand, possibly rouse your interest, and get you moving into the world of hydroponics.

Our world is changing in all kinds of aspects. The population is increasing steadily, the land that we have been farming for centuries is becoming poorer, and the farming spaces are becoming smaller as people build houses and infrastructure. While the resources continue to shrink, our population is demanding more cleaner food, and science has come up with one of the most genius ideas: hydroponics. Without requiring any soil to grow plants, anyone can now take up farming, wherever he or she is, whatever space is available. Everyone can now get in on the move that seeks to ensure that we will be able to produce enough food for ourselves in the coming days.

Now that you have gathered all these important facts, the next step is to go ahead and put into practice. Teach others around you the basics of hydroponics farming, and possibly, the move towards self-sustainability will ensure that there are enough affordable, clean and healthy people for the people in our societies, in and out of season.

Finally, if you found this book useful in any way, a review on Amazon is always appreciated!

DESCRIPTION

It is always a good thing to get in on the action and participate in what has been tested and proven good for the society, such as hydroponics gardening, but it is even more profitable when you go into it with your eyes open. Some people will want to try out hydroponics just because they saw someone doing it, and they perceive it to be an easy thing to do. However, as fun and interesting as hydroponics may seem, it is challenging and needs to be taken up only by informed minds.

To that end, the author has arranged all relevant information on hydroponics into chapters that will let you in on all there is with hydroponics. You will get the proper definition of hydroponics, how it works, the tools you need to work it, and various hydroponics systems from which you can choose. You will also be informed of the benefits you stand to enjoy and the disadvantages you have to endure when you choose hydroponics. Nevertheless, this is one of the most profitable and practical ways to grow crops as we step into the future with a large health-conscious population who are all about the quality and not the quantity of food.

Going by popularity, you can already tell that hydroponics farming brings many benefits. It shortens the growth span of crops, increases the quality of produce and heightens the quantity of food produced. Hydroponics is also being taken up for its aesthetic value, to clean up the air indoors, and as a way to reduce environmental pollution due to the use of less water and fertilizers.

What's more, manufacturers are now starting to produce organic hydroponic fertilizers, which means that farmers will not only be enjoying the returns from selling their vegetables, they will also have a great story to tell about environmental conservation.

Every piece of information you would need as you get into this increasingly popular method of farming you will see in this book. Kindly take note of the common mistakes beginners make in hydroponics gardening, and take measures to avoid falling into those pitfalls. This way, you will avoid making the mistakes others have made, and therefore avoid suffering the devastating losses that they suffered.

Inside this book you will find:

- The most explicit description of hydroponics

- The most vivid explanation about how hydroponics work
- The most exhaustive list of crops for which hydroponics farming is best suited
- An extensive list of tools and equipment you will need for your hydroponics garden
- The most useful tips to get you through the business seamlessly
- A list of common mistakes hydroponics beginners make, and how to avoid them
- The most precise directions to guide you as you start your first hydroponics garden
- The most accurate prediction of the future of hydroponics farming, and how you need to position yourself to receive all the benefits there will be.

AQUAPONICS

Beginner's Guide to Building Your Own Aquaponics Garden System That Will Grow Organic Vegetables, Fruits, Herbs and Raising Fish with Your Own Aquaponics Home Gardening System

**By
Rachel Martin**

© **Copyright 2019 by Rachel Martin - All rights reserved.**

The information provided within this book is offered with the intent of giving pertinent information concerning the topic of Aquaponics and all efforts have been attempted to make sure that the information is correct, makes sense, and will aid in accomplishing the intended purpose of this book. In any case, your acquisition of this book, in any format, specifically denotes your understanding that any information provided to you here to forth within the pages of this book are solely the expressed thoughts of the author and/or the publisher and is not meant to be construed as expertise in any given subject discussed. That being said, all information expressed on the subject matter within this book, is specifically done so with the intent of your enjoyment. There are many experts in the Aquaponics industry, some of which is discussed in the book and it is suggested that prior to moving forth with implementing any of the setups and or purchases discussed within the pages of this book, you take the time to review some of the advice those professionals offer.

According to the American Bar Association and the Committee of Publishers Association, everything detailed here is considered legal and binding throughout the United States.

It is illegal and punishable by the constraints of the law to copy, transfer, reproduce any part of the contents within this book. This is inclusive of duplicated renditions of this book in physical, digital and/ or audio versions barring direct authorization from the publisher to do so.

It is important to note that all information provided within this book is to be taken as words put forth with honesty and accuracy in terms of interpreting or portraying facts. Due to this fact, the publisher is free and clear of any liability when it comes to its use, whether used properly or not, especially when taken out of its direct intended purpose. To reiterate, there are absolutely no circumstances for which neither the author nor the publisher can be held responsible for outcomes resulting from the information provided within regardless of the gravity of said outcome.

Any and all information provided within this book has been provided with the sole intent of being informational material and held as universal consensus. Though informational and instructional in nature, any and all within this book is held as opinion, practice, and research of the author. Trademarks potentially discussed without consent in writing are not and cannot be construed as permission from the person in possession of said trademark.

INTRODUCTION

Congratulations on purchasing *Aquaponics: Beginner's Guide To Building Your Own Aquaponic Garden System That Will Grow Organic Vegetables, Fruits, Herbs and Raising Fish with Your Own Aquaponics Home Gardening System* and we appreciate you doing so.

The subsequent chapters will discuss in detail everything you need to know about Aquaponics so that you can determine if Aquaponics is right for you. This guide will help you to get on the path to healthier, cost-effective living by giving you the knowledge and basics needed to easily develop your Aquaponics garden.

With the creation of "Farm to Table" restaurants being a new craze, it is no wonder that farming has taken on a whole new meaning. Not only are more and more people concerned with the environment and/or healthier lifestyles, but people are becoming increasingly concerned with the economy, how they can improve their financial well-being, or simply save money. The use of Aquaponics gardens at home addresses all of these concerns. Everyone knows how expensive fruits, vegetables, and fish can be. The negative effects of fast food craze caused major detriments to health, but its popularity continues due to time constraints and cost benefits. Aquaponics helps us get back to healthy eating while saving time and money!

Through Aquaponic gardening, you can produce plants faster and larger without watering, weeding, and worrying about unhealthy chemical additives. In addition to plants, you have the option to eat fresh fish, right from your own tank.

Aquaponics has taken what Mother Nature has done for centuries to keep plants and animals coexisting and thriving and has allowed us to mimic that process at our own homes, whether indoors or out!

With numerous books available to purchase on this topic, we want to thank you for selecting this particular one. We have put forth a diligent effort to ensure that it is packed with a plethora of information that we believe will prove very useful to you, so it is our hope that you enjoy it!

CHAPTER 1

What Is Aquaponics?

Aquaponics is essentially a system in which fish and plants work together so that both can thrive. The two are cultivated together by way of a system built that utilizes recirculation of its natural biological processes. This ecological system involves waste production from the fish to be processed by bacteria and repurposed into necessary plant food that will then clean the water for the fish. Each plays a helping hand in the Aquaponics system that allows people to have an abundance of environmentally friendly, healthy, fresh food sources of both vegetation and fish. This system was born from the combination of the best parts of Hydroponics and Aquaculture, while removing the negatives associated with both, such as chemical additives for fertilization, the need for discarding water, and filtration.

HISTORY AND CURRENT USES

Aquaponics may be on the rise in familiarity and use amongst both commercial farmers and home growers, but it is certainly not a new concept. We simply get the privilege of using the new and improved, and much easier versions of Aquaponics. As they say, history repeats itself, and those that are wise will learn from those before us. It will never cease to amaze me how centuries ago, before technology, before machinery, before mass communication and social networks, our ancestors were able to create such great inventions that allowed their people to not just survive but thrive, in many areas where the environment seemed to be a major impediment.

In some form or another, Aquaponics was used throughout the continent in places like China's rice paddy fields, in Africa, in Italy, throughout the islands, by Native Americans, and the Aztecs in Mexico, to name a few. The Aztecs migrated to an area that is known today as Mexico City. The land there did not have good soil for farming and the inner areas were all marshes. In order to adapt to this unproductive environment, they created numerous rafts on the lake out of substances found in the area, such as reeds and mud. On the rafts, they made gardens that utilized the nutrients from the aquatic species in the water to feed the plants.

Back in the day when people lived off the land, (in some places, they still do), it was vital to observe nature, take its natural processes, and use it in all aspects of life. Because of these observations, we have Aquaponics today! It is also important to note that in third world countries - just like the Aztecs so many centuries ago - faced obstacles in their environment such as bad soil, lack of water, and many people were starving. Many organizations are stepping in and introducing Aquaponics due to their fast-food growth without much water and soil-free gardening capabilities. In addition to a much-needed food source, it offers healthier, cleaner eating with much-needed vitamins and nutrients to aid in improving immune systems and fighting illness. The added bonus: Helping to prevent disease in one part of the world, stops the spread of disease to other parts of the world!

CHAPTER 2

Why Aquaponics?

The basic understanding of Organic is that the food was grown according to specific guidelines determined by the USDA that forbid the use of insecticides as well as requires strict adherence to the conservation of biodiversity and maintaining the welfare of animals. Essentially, this refers to the way Agriculture is raised and processed. The regulations differ greatly in every country. United States' crops labeled organic needs to be raised free of synthetic pesticides, bioengineered genes (GMO's), and petroleum-based and sewage-based fertilizers. For livestock raised for the purpose of meat, eggs, or dairy products to be labeled as organic, they must have access to the outdoors for the majority of the day, daily. They must also be fed organic feed and cannot be administered any antibiotics, growth hormones, or any by-products of animals.

Additionally, if you choose to get locally grown food versus shipped organic, you are aiding the local economy. More money goes to the local farmer instead of to the expense of marketing, packaging, and distribution. In the U.S. alone, food will likely travel approximately 1500 miles and in order to maintain freshness during the trip, the produce is picked before it is ripe and will ripen during travels or the food is processed with preservatives or other processes in an effort to keep it from going bad prior to sale. This means that food purchased from local farmers will be fresh and have much more flavor.

By choosing to grow your own food at home, you are getting the benefits you would from both organic and locally grown and having the added benefit of saving money.

In order to fully grasp how immensely beneficial Aquaponics is and why you should use it, it is important to also know about its roots, Hydroponics and Aquaculture. By comparing the three different systems, understanding their purpose, and noting their advantages and disadvantages, you will have a much better idea of which system is best for you. I believe, that like myself, you will gain a deeper appreciation for what Aquaponics can do for you as a new home garden and fish cultivator and through experiencing Aquaponics, you may expand further either into business endeavors or into larger home systems.

HYDROPONICS

Hydroponics is a soil-free system of cultivating plants. In this system, the plants sit directly in the nutrient-rich water or are placed in soil free media such as gravel where the water can easily flow through. Once the nutrients have been used by the plants, it is necessary to add more nutrients or recycle the water.

AQUACULTURE

Aquaculture means water life and is, therefore, is a system of cultivating fish. This system is basically tanks or aquariums where fish can be bred and grown and requires constant filtration in order to maintain clean water where fish could live and thrive.

AQUAPONICS

Aquaponics is a system that combines Hydroponics and Aquaculture to cultivate both fish and plants together in one harmonious ecosystem. In Hydroponics, it is vital to recycle the water and add much-needed nutrients for the plants and in Aquaculture, it is vital to have water filtration for your aquatic species. By combining the two, Aquaponics removes the need to waste water, filtrate, and fertilize. Additionally, time and energy are reduced in the process.

It may just be the perfect marriage, but as in any marriage, there is some work involved in keeping everyone happy and healthy. In the end, it is all worth it. This union has created so many positives that make the negatives insignificant. In addition, it is outweighed by the benefits.

The following chart will show the benefits and drawbacks to all three:

COMPARE AND CONTRAST

Based on the chart provided, it is clear that there are pros and cons to all three and it really is up to the individual as to which system they prefer, but in my opinion there is really no reason to look anywhere else but to Aquaponics for my cultivation needs.

For the purposes of this book, we will clarify what has been pointed out in this chart

SYSTEMS	BENEFITS	DRAWBACKS

HYDROPONICS		
	NO SOIL NEEDED	CHEMICAL FERTILIZERS
	FAST GROWTH	TIME INTENSIVE
	MAKE BETTER USE OF SPACE AND LOCATION	DAILY MONITORING
	CLIMATE CONTROL REMOVING SEASONAL BARRIERS	SYSTEM FAILURE THREATS
	CONTROL OVER WHAT PLANTS EAT	EXPENSES
	CONTROL OVER pH	LONG RETURN PER INVESTMENT
	NO WEEDS OR PESTS	DISEASES AND PESTS MAY SPREAD QUICKLY

Hydroponics Pros and Cons
There is no soil needed in a hydroponics system. It produces fast growth of plants while making better use of space and location. Hydroponics is climate controlled so it, therefore, removes any seasonal barriers that one would experience in a regular garden or farm. You have complete control over what your plants eat because you have to feed them nutrient concoctions or chemical fertilizers daily. You have control over pH levels. There are no weeds because of the lack of soil and the use of insecticides removes the potential for pests.

On the flip side, chemical fertilizers may be great for your plant growth but they may not necessarily be safe for human ingestion and therefore a vigorous washing process must be undertaken. Hydroponics is time-intensive and requires daily monitoring. It is important to conduct system checks throughout the day because a system failure can be catastrophic to your production. Hydroponics is not easy on the wallet. It can get quite expensive to maintain and the return on your investment may take quite a long while to occur. As mentioned before, pesticides may be used but would defeat the purpose of healthy produce so other measures would need to be taken to ensure pest control. If pests or diseases do show up, the spread in this type of environment can be extremely fast.

| SYSTEMS | BENEFITS | DRAWBACKS |

AQUACULTURE	SOURCE OF FOOD FOR PEOPLE AND MARINE SPECIES	WATER IS DISPOSED OF
	SOURCE OF INCOME	WASTE OF NATURAL RESOURCE
	FLEXIBILITY TO BUILD FISH FARMS, TANKS, AND CAGES ANYWHERE	WASTE OF INVALUABLE PLANT NUTRIENT SOURCE
	RECIRCULATING SYSTEMS HELP REDUCE, REUSE, AND RECYCLE WASTE	PROPAGATION OF INVASIVE SPECIES
	REDUCE STRAIN ON NATURAL POPULATIONS	THREATS TO COASTAL ECOSYSTEMS DUE TO WASTE DISPOSAL/ POLLUTION
		CONTAMINATES WATER AND THREATENS HEALTH
		AFFECTS WILD FISH POPULATION

Aquaculture Pros and Cons

Aquaculture can be used as a source of food for both people and marine species. It is a source of income for many who provide fresh fish to fish markets and
restaurants locally. It gives great flexibility to build fish farms, tanks, and cages anywhere. Systems created around the idea of recirculation help reduce, reuse, and recycle waste. Aquaculture has greatly reduced the strain on natural populations as fewer people are fishing and more people are breeding and raising the fish.

A major problem has occurred with the waste of water because many still have not incorporated recirculation into their Aquaculture setups. In addition to water waste, lack of recirculation would then waste valuable natural resources found in the water that is made by fish waste and waste of invaluable plant nutrient

source. Of course, there is also the argument about the propagation of invasive species and the threat to coastal ecosystems due to waste disposal and pollution. CDC states that this contaminates the water and threatens health.

An Aquaponics Garden using Deep Water Culture

SYSTEMS	BENEFITS	DRAWBACKS
AQUAPONICS	SOIL FREE	MUST GAIN KNOWLEDGE OF FISH, PLANTS, AND MICROBES
	ABUNDANT CHEMICAL FREE CROP	INITIAL EXPENSES CAN BE HIGH UNLESS YOU ARE WELL EQUIPPED TO DO IT YOURSELF
	ABUNDANT FRESH FISH	ELECTRICAL OUTPUT IS HIGH UNLESS USING SOLAR POWER OR ANOTHER FORM OF
	NO WASTE	NOT ALL CROPS CAN BE GROWN IN AQUAPONICS

DENSER PLANTATION/HIGHER PRODUCTION	SALTWATER FISH CANNOT BE BRED IN AQUAPONICS
STAGED PRODUCTION ALLOWS FOR YEAR ROUND HARVEST	MUST MONITOR NITRATE AND pH LEVELS REGULARLY
BACTERIA PRESENT MAKES THESE GARDENS IMMUNE TO DISEASE AND ARE SELF HEALING	
PRODUCE FISH AND PLANTS FROM SAME WATER SOURCE	
CAN BE CREATED ON ANY SCALE AND ANYWHERE	

Aquaponics Pros and Cons

By combining the positive attributes of Hydroponics and Aquaculture and removing the negative aspects of the two, Aquaponics was born. It was not simply a merger but a major advancement into what could be possible not just for a few but globally! It is a soil and weed free environment that produces an abundant fresh fish harvest and an abundant lush rapidly growing crop. There is absolutely no waste because everything is re-circulated and utilized with never any need to discard the water. Instead of getting rid of water, you would occasionally add a bit of water due to evaporation. Denser plantation equates to higher production. Because you have the ability to stage your production, you can reap a bountiful harvest year round. The bacteria found in an Aquaponics system fight disease and help to heal in an effort to keep a healthy ecosystem. Fish and plants are produced from the same water source. Aquaponics systems can be created in a tiny little one or two fish tank with one plant to an enormous prosperous business farming fish and vegetation. Because of the fact that they can be created on any scale, and because of the simplicity in the requirements of the system, it can be located pretty much anywhere. Aquaponics gardens do not adversely affect the wildlife population. It will not be long before you are able to see a return on your investment.

To be successful in Aquaponics, it is very important to educate yourself about fish, plants, and microbes. Initial expenses can be high unless you are very well equipped and knowledgeable in doing it yourself. The electrical output is very high unless you are able to incorporate solar power or other forms of sustainable energy sources. Though the variety and list are long and getting longer every day with new advances, not all crops can be grown in an Aquaponics system. Additionally, though technically you can cultivate any fish, it is not recommended to do saltwater as that would require a lot more work and system additions as well as very selective plants (minimal options) in order to make that function effectively. Though the maintenance is not as laborious as the other two systems that make up the core of Aquaponics, there is maintenance involved that requires regular monitoring of pH and nitrates.

CHAPTER 3

The Master Plan Basics

It is important to determine what exactly you want to achieve with your Aquaponics system, how you want it to look, and where you want it to be located. Coming up with a plan is necessary to ensure that all pieces of the puzzle not only fit together but that there aren't any pieces missing. No one likes working on a puzzle for hours only to find that they can't finish what they started. This project has many stages: planning stage, supply stage, building stage, and testing stage, plant and fish stages (don't occur at the same time), maintenance stage, and for some, the expansion stage. I personally enjoy the sit back and enjoy or feast stage and yet others are more concerned with reaping the reward. Whatever the desired outcome, a plan is vital.

DIY OR KIT

It is a matter of preference whether you choose to purchase a ready-made kit or do it yourself. Unless you happen to have a background in engineering or plumbing, I would strongly suggest that first time Aquaponics gardeners start with kits that are purchased from a very reputable company with knowledge and experience in Aquaponics. I stress this point because there are many kits on the market that can be bought pretty much anywhere and if you purchase it online from say a company like Walmart or Amazon, you would not have the ability to talk to anyone with expertise in Aquaponics that can help you choose the right system for you and answer any questions you might have. Further, after you have the system set up, it is good to be able to contact the company for any advice or assistance you may need. Your first kit is your opportunity to learn a great deal about Aquaponics as you are getting your feet wet. Purchasing a kit will remove much of the stress and allow you to enjoy what Aquaponics has to offer. If you choose to jump right in with a DO IT YOURSELF project, there will be a lot of trial and error, research, shopping around for supplies, and no direct contact person to aid you as you venture on this Aquaponics mission.

If you are able to find a kit that suits your needs and your wallet, go for it! It will allow you to get started on the road to a bountiful harvest much quicker, without the worry of troubleshooting the do it yourself project. DO IT YOURSELF can delay production by several months. The initial cost of purchasing a kit is worth it when you save time and money in the long run. DO IT YOURSELF can get expensive with the trial and error process one must endure plus you may not have all of the tools needed which is another purchase and of course the knowledge that is only gained over time to know exactly what supplies you need and which places are good to go (who you can trust) to get them from. Sometimes the simple task of purchasing supplies can be daunting because the Aquaponics supplies needed may not be easy to find. Kits come with everything you need to get started and are available for all sizes and levels of Aquaponics.

After you are used to Aquaponics and have a better understanding on how the system works and what it takes to be successful in Aquaponics, then you may choose to try your hand at a do it yourself project. Remember, Aquaponics is not for everyone and investing a lot of time and money in a do it yourself project initially doesn't make sense unless you are certain that Aquaponics is for you.

If you are an Aquaponics newbie and still choose to try your hand at a do it yourself project, you can buy excellent plans from reputable companies online and build it yourself. This would be the best option for DO IT YOURSELF Aquaponics first timers. If you have the time and skills, and choose the DO IT YOURSELF path, it can be significant savings for you. I pose the alternate point... If you attempt to DO IT YOURSELF and don't have the time and skills, you could end up spending considerably more as mentioned before.

Assuming that you chose to DO IT YOURSELF because you do have the time and skills, you have the distinct potential to customize the Aquaponics system to suit your needs and tastes. You will additionally benefit by gaining education about each part that you use to make your Aquaponics garden as you find out the intricacies of how they work and what they are needed for. Basically, DO IT YOURSELF leaves room for your inner creative soul to flourish and for those who enjoy the challenge of recycling and reusing, this could be very rewarding.

For the purpose of introducing readers to the basics of Aquaponics and how to create your very own Aquaponics garden, chapter 6 will delve into what DIY supplies are recommended and the best ways in which to connect the two worlds of fish and plants.

INSIDE OR OUT?

A matter of preference really, as Aquaponics can be done basically anywhere. It is for you to decide what is best for you and the Aquaponics goals you would like to achieve.

For those that desire an inside garden:
- You have the freedom to maintain the temperature in accordance with the needs of your plants and fish
- You must have grow lights
- Size and appearance are dependent on location
- You need to make sure that the location you select can withstand the weight of your system when the tank/aquarium is filled with water

For those that desire an outside garden:
- No soil is needed but an excellent lighted area is important
- Must have close proximity to a water source
- Must have connectivity to an outlet for electrical source
- Will your system be in a greenhouse or will it need protection such as a fence or netting to ward off pests?
- Dependent on the climate where you live, a heating system may be needed to maintain proper temperatures

SIZE AND APPEARANCE

For me, appearance is important, so the setup of my system is very important in that regard. I do not want it to resemble an industrial zone. This is my home, so I want to find a compromise between décor and function. Others may be more concerned with function and output and maybe with ease for productivity. Whatever your taste, putting the appearance aside, in Aquaponics, size does matter. It does not matter in barbaric terms of ah-hah mine is bigger than yours, but it does matter in regards to:

- What your ecosystem needs, in terms of ratios (example: plants to fish capacity)
- What your fish growth may be (remember, some fish like catfish get long and require much bigger tanks)
- Where your system is located (indoor area may not support large tanks)
- What you can afford overall (keep ongoing maintenance and utilities in mind)
- What your goals are (is this just a hobby? Is it just for ornamental purposes for both plants and fish? Or do you plan on expanding in the future?)

PLANTS AND FISH LIVING TOGETHER

It is highly recommended to use freshwater fish since saltwater fish will restrict which plants you can grow in your garden.

In addition to determining whether you want to eventually eat your fish you simply want fish for ornamental purposes, you will need to determine what plants you want to grow because this ecosystem needs good matchmaking in order for the marriage to last. It is important to know:

- Does your fish require warm water or cool water?
- Can your fish survive in both temperatures? A few can acclimate to both.
- How big will your fish get?
- How many plant beds do you plan on having?
- Do you want cool weather plants or warm weather plants? Or do you want seasonal plants?
- What size fish will you get? (Fish fry, Fingerlings, or Adult fish)
- What are your local laws? There are restrictions on the types of plants and fish you can grow in each area.

Fish like Catfish, Bluegill, (Food fish) Koi and Goldfish (Ornamental fish) are pretty resilient and adapts easily to different temperatures making them the most popular fish for both the fish for food and fish for ornamental categories. Other fish like Trout and Tilapia which are also very popular Aquaponics breeds have very specific temperature needs. Tilapia require warm water (above 70 degrees) while Trout require cooler waters falling below that temperature.

Likewise, Leafy Greens, peas, cabbage, carrots, beets and spinach require cooler temperatures. Beans, squash, and sweet corn require warmer temperatures while tomatoes, peppers, eggplant, and melon are all seasonal (summer vegetation).

In order for your ecosystem to align harmoniously, choosing which plant or fish that goes well together is of vital importance.

WHAT KINDS OF FISH-WORK IN AQUAPONICS?

The following fish have had the best results in Aquaponics systems:

- Tilapia
- Bluegill/ Brim
- Sunfish
- Crappie
- Koi
- Fancy Goldfish
- Pacu
- Ornamental Fish: Tetras, Angelfish, Mollies, Guppies, and Swordfish

These fishes are also popular Aquaponics fish that do well but may require more work:

- Carp
- Barramundi
- Silver Perch
- Yellow Perch
- Catfish
- Large Mouth Bass

- Cod (Murray, Sleepy)
- Salmon
- Rainbow Trout
- Minnows

It is important to note that nearly all freshwater fish are edible. The difference in each would be how easy it is to prepare, the taste, and health. Koi and Goldfish are not suggested as edible simply because they are known to carry cancer-causing factors that affect humans.

Another important determination is the size and age of the fish. Though the cost may be a big determining factor, it is important to note:
- Fish fry is cheaper, but it will take much longer to mature and thus will affect the nitrate production levels, taking longer to reach adequate supply needed for the plants to absorb.
- Fingerlings are expensive, but for good reason. They are ideal for waste production in early stages which results in expedited vegetable growth.
- Mature fish are the most expensive to purchase and cannot be mixed with fish fry as they will be eaten by the larger of the species. Additionally, larger fish require more plant beds and larger tanks.

Important to note: For a 100-gallon fish tank with a 100 gallon grow bed, the proper amount of fish would be about 12 to 15 pounds. The correct ratio would be one pound of fish for every square foot of grow bed volume, which amounts to approximately seven and a half gallons, if and only if you properly circulate the entire volume of water in the tank every hour on the hour.

When you harvest your own fish for the purpose of eating it as opposed to purchasing your fish from the store, aside from the convenience, of course, you have the added reassurance that your fish is fresh and safe. By raising the fish yourself, you have the distinct knowledge of what they eat and when it was harvested. You are the only one controlling every aspect of the environment, health, and growth of the fish which you consume. Additionally, the fact that they are cold blooded means that they are not susceptible to carrying harmful bacteria like E. Coli and Salmonella. The Center for Disease Control (CDC) is always monitoring and stressing that people need to be aware of potential risks of fish consumption because contaminants (such as mercury or polychlorinated biphenyls) from pollution (coming from industry, houses, or simply people) in the lakes, oceans, and rivers, work their way into the fish that reside there. This brings new meaning to "you are what you eat". By raising your own fish for consumption, you are removing any cause for concern because you know your fish are healthy.

Why is Fish consumption good for you? Fish that have white meat, more so than others, will have a lower fat content in comparison to other proteins sourced from animals. Fish that fall in the category of "oily fish", such as salmon, sardines, trout, mackerel, and bluefin tuna, are one of the best sources for good fats known as omega-3 fatty acids. Our bodies do not naturally create these vital nutrients in the quantities we need so it is very important to incorporate these into our diet through other sources and fish are not only a perfect source but a delicious one too!

- One of the healthiest foods out there
- Great source of abundant nutrients, protein, and vitamins (many people are highly deficient in vitamin D and this is a great source for improving that deficiency)
- Omega-3 fatty acids are essential for body and brain and scientifically proven to reduce the risk of numerous diseases. (They say an apple a day, keeps the doctor away, well a fatty fish or two a week, will give you all the omega-3 that your body requires).
- The fattier the fish, the better it is for us... super healthy!
- Whether you are pre-genetically disposed to heart attacks and/or strokes or you just want to do everything you can to avoid them (that would be all of us!), you can lower your risk of heart disease and other ailments simply by eating fish!

- Highly beneficial to children, fish contains DHA which helps development and growth.
- Researchers now state that eating fish regularly aids in the battle against deterioration in brain functions which tend to occur as people age. There is also evidence that grey matter of the brain is increased by consuming fish on a regular basis which would result in improved recollection and emotional status.
- Fish can not only make you healthier but studies have linked regular consumption to happiness and improvement in mental well-being.
- Source containing the highest level of vitamin D
- Fish is known to combat autoimmune diseases
- Studies show that when children consume fish regularly, it will help them combat asthma which will make it less likely to progress into adulthood
- Carrots are not the only thing recommended for eyesight. Fish has been studied in the battle against macular degeneration.
- Aside from the numerous health advantages linked to eating fish regularly, fish actually tastes amazing and comes in so many varieties. Fish is easy to prepare (for the most part) and there are so many recipes out there that you could literally not eat the same meal twice within the same year if you wanted the variety.
- Fish does not take long to cook and therefore those people who don't have a lot of time to spend on cooking their meals, fish is a great option.

WHAT KINDS OF PLANTS WORK IN AQUAPONICS?
The most common plants for Aquaponics gardens are:

- Leafy lettuce
- Bok Choy
- Kale
- Spinach
- Swiss Chard
- Arugula
- Herbs such as Basil, Coriander, Sage, Lemongrass, Parsley, and Mint

- Watercress
- Chives
- Common Houseplants

Other plants that do well but are dependent on a well-stocked fish tank are:

- Tomatoes
- Peppers
- Cucumbers
- Beans
- Peas
- Squash
- Broccoli
- Cauliflower
- Cabbage
- Eggplant
- Melon
- Fruiting plants such as Strawberries

Others have noted success with:

- Bananas
- Citrus trees like limes, lemons, and oranges
- Pomegranate
- Sweet Corn
- Microgreens
- Beets
- Radishes

- Carrots
- Onions
- Shallots
- Chili peppers
- Capsicum
- Celery
- Ginger
- Edible Flowers like Orchids and Violas

Why are vegetables good for you? Aside from being naturally lower in fat and calories and a major source of vitamins, minerals, and nutrients, there are many health benefits associated with the consumption of vegetables (and fruit too!)

- Vital for health and maintenance of the human body
- Reduces the risk of many chronic diseases
- An important source of potassium, fiber, folic acid, vitamin a, vitamin d
- Reduces blood pressure due to potassium
- Reduces cholesterol due to dietary fiber
- Reduces the risk of fetal defects in pregnant women due to the folic acid content
- Improves immune system
- Improves skin and eyes due to vitamin a
- Numerous benefits associated with vitamin c including oral health, iron absorption, and healing
- Reduces the risk of heart disease and illness associated with it
- Studies have shown that vegetables can combat specific cancers
- Healthy diets combat obesity and diabetes
- Combats Osteoporosis and some renal issues
- When eating more vegetables (and/or fruits) their high water levels aid in making you get the full feeling faster, and thus, help those that are trying to lose weight. It is low in calories, in conjunction with this, helps us to stay well below the daily required caloric intake.

Whatever you choose to grow, always keep in mind the harmony of the ecosystem, the rate, and extent to which your fish or plants will grow. As mentioned earlier in this chapter, temperature and location are also very important factors in your selection process. It is vital to the success of the Aquaponics garden, that you take the time to learn about the fish and plants for your developing ecosystem.

Some important things you should consider when selecting your plants and fish:
Let's start with plants:

First, in considering which plants to purchase, especially if they are going to be used specifically for consumption, it is important to note that because you are utilizing water-based methods versus soil-based methods, your production rate at its bare minimum will be 20-25% higher. Therefore, due to the fact that you are yielding such high quantities, determine which vegetation you will use for farming and which vegetation you would be willing to incorporate preservation methods such as canning or dehydrating, like some like to do with herbs and fruit.

Second, the suitable range for most vegetables is 18 to 30 degrees Celsius which converts to a temperature range of 64.4 to 89.6 degrees Fahrenheit. Winter vegetables do best in temperature ranges of 8 to 20 degrees Celsius (46.4 to 68 degrees Fahrenheit). Summer vegetables will do best in temperature ranges between 17 to 30 degrees Celsius (62.6 to 86 degrees Fahrenheit). Within these ranges, different vegetables and plants have different requirements, though they may do fine within the range assigned to their seasonal type, the specific required range will yield the best results. Leafy greens, for example, fall in the winter vegetable category, however, they prefer even cooler temperatures than most, requiring temperature ranges between 14 to 20 degrees Celsius (57.2 to 68 degrees Fahrenheit), mostly after sundown. Following the winter vegetable guidelines of range, if they were exposed to increased temperatures near the higher portion of the range, the flavor of these vegetables would be negatively impacted and inedible to most. More important than air temperature is water temperature, which has a far greater effect on the plants, however, both are equally important to monitor.

Third, when growing flowering plants or plants that yield fruit, light is an important factor. Each requires different amounts of daylight and/or darkness to cause the flowering or fruiting process to occur. Medicinal plants and some peppers fall into the category of short-day plants. This means they need more darkness and others such as many ornamentals fall into the category of long day plants because they require much more light than others to yield their beautiful blooms. All plants generally come with care guidelines when you purchase them but it is important in your planning process to do this research ahead of time to ensure that you are prepared and have an action plan for your production goals. There are plants, like most vegetables, that are light neutral, which makes things a bit easier to maintain and control.

Fourth, I have listed quite a few plants used in Aquaponics but the list of plant growth success with herbs, small trees, vegetables, and flowers is up around 150 and growing. Knowing the needs of your plants and matching those needs to your fish properly will help you to expand your selection of plants and the success you have in Aquaponics. In saying this, always remember, the goal is to keep everyone healthy and fed—people, fish, and plants—so, to achieve this goal, we must understand nutrient requirements. Different species have different nutrient requirements—some need more, some need less. For example, if you are planning on growing fruiting vegetable plants like tomatoes, peppers, cucumbers, eggplants, avocados, or fruits like strawberries and winter melon, they require higher nutrient-rich diets so they are better matched with a well established Aquaponics system in which the fish are able to yield the amounts of nutrients they need. Additionally, amongst these various species are root crops. These plants are better suited for a system in which deep media beds are utilized and they are very high maintenance so it may not be a good choice for you to attempt in an Aquaponics system. Leafy greens, legumes, and herbs are the most popular choices for Aquaponics because they have a low nutrient requirement. In the center of the nutrient, demand spectrum would be things like cabbage, cauliflower or broccoli. Radish falls on the very low end of the spectrum while beets, onions, and carrots fall somewhere between the center of the spectrum and the higher side of the demand spectrum.

Fifth, some plants grow much larger than others. This is the case with fruiting plants. If space is an issue, keep this in mind when selecting your plants. Also, depending on the type of system set up you choose, this could influence greatly which plants you will be able to grow. For example, bulbous or root based plants are better suited for media based beds versus a nutrient film technique system or a deep water culture system due to the support system and growing environment needed for these plants to flourish.

Lastly, because of the variations in needs of the different plants, and likewise the varying needs of the fish needed to coexist with these plants for a balanced ecosystem, it is important to ensure balance in all areas to maintain balance overall! Mixing plants with different nutrient needs or harvesting timeframes, for example, could result in great imbalance for all of the creatures in the ecosystem as an attempt to compensate for differing needs. Any unbalance that cannot be easily corrected can cause the entire ecosystem to fail.

Notes: If you are planting something that requires a long term grow period, it would be a good idea to plant some short term grow period plants with them. This way you not only reap the benefit of farm to table on a regular basis but the plants work together. For example, eggplants take a long time to mature so adding in herbs, tomatoes, and leafy greens around them yields quickly for your main salad ingredients, and will offer shading to the eggplant that it needs while also working with the other plants to clean the water for the fish. This maintains a balanced nutrient level, thus creating a healthy environment. Smart planning in your planting design can not only be beneficial in maximizing space but it can also aid in attracting beneficial insects and greatly improve your plant production.

Obviously, there is a lot to consider when selecting your plants, whether you want them for food consumption or simply want a houseplant or flowering plant. Always keep in mind the harmony of all species in your ecosystem, when making your decisions. Obviously, the fish and the plants need to be a match made in heaven but the other important thing here, especially when it comes to foods we plan on consuming, is what you personally enjoy. I mean, let's be honest here, what is the point of all this work (except maybe satisfaction of achievement) if you aren't able to enjoy what you have produced? Why grow tomatoes if you don't plan on eating them? Why grow a flower you have allergies too? You wouldn't obviously. That being said, if you know that you eat certain vegetables very often such as the common salad ingredients or herbs that you need for seasoning your foods, you would be more inclined to select these options to grow and the amount that you grow would be higher than say an artichoke, which you may eat when you are in the mood for it. There is no rule of thumb here. Everyone has different tastes so I will not tell you what to put in the garden but simply offer knowledge about the different options and things to consider. To support this sentiment, I have put together some information that should prove useful in your Aquaponics vegetable planning below, but first I want to address the non-edible variety of plants. Edible varieties of plants are not the only plants well suited for Aquaponics, in fact, some of the best options for Aquaponics gardening are ornamental varieties of plants and Aquaponics is exceptionally successful in growing many kinds of houseplants. Roses are one of the most popular and successful of flowering plants, though there are many others that you can grow. House plants are a great way to keep the air clean and the house looking beautiful. Many varieties thrive in Aquaponics such as ferns and philodendrons, to name just two. You can pretty much grow just about anything from vegetables to plants to flowers, with proper environment set up, except blueberries and azaleas (due to their high acid needs) and of course the root crops like potatoes are really difficult to grow because of their need for a deep media bed, but even these, like carrots, for instance, have been grown successfully. The most effective and proven process for planting root based vegetables is that these should be planted in wicking beds which are attached to the media beds.

Ornamental plants have seen great success in Aquaponics gardens due to the constant flow of water and nutrients it receives. In addition to the roses, some great outdoor options are asters, lilies, daisies, forget-me-nots, hollies, and lavender.

Here is a list of some of the best options for indoor plants with information on whether you can use seeds or cuttings for best results:

- Spider Plants can be grown from either a seed or from cuttings.
- Female Dragon can be grown from either a seed or from cuttings.
- Chinese Money Plants can be grown from either a seed or from cuttings.
- Philodendrons can be grown from either a seed or from cuttings.
- Peace Lilies can be grown from seeds or from cuttings.
- Chinese evergreen can be grown from either a seed or from a cutting but it is suggested that you start with cutting because growing these from seeds is very difficult in Aquaponics systems.
- Devil's Ivy cannot be grown from seed but can be grown from cutting. Leopard Lilies, also known as Dumb Cane, cannot be grown from seeds but can be grown from cuttings. Arrowhead Vines cannot be grown from seeds but can be grown from cuttings.

The smell and taste of fresh herbs is absolutely amazing. My mouth is watering just thinking about it. Lucky for us, herbs are one of the easiest things to grow in an Aquaponics garden. Tarragon, Peppermint, Green Mint, Oregano, Basil, Sage, Stevia, Lemon Balm, Rosemary, and Cilantro are just some of the herbs you can grow and yes, you can grow from both seeds and cuttings, with the exception of Tarragon and Peppermint, but I strongly suggest always using cuttings because it gets your plants to grow stronger and faster. Lettuce, spinach, bok choy, tomatoes, peppers, cucumbers, and celery are some of the most popular Aquaponics choices and all can be grown from either seeds or cuttings, however, as I said earlier, I am going to go into further detail on vegctables and expand past this list so that you can have more information to help you make decisions when planning your garden selections:

Let's start with the leafy greens because they are the basis to almost any salad and there are so many varieties to choose from. This, of course, is why it is number one on the Aquaponics selection list. It grows fast and it is easy to maintain. Aside from this, instead of having to harvest the entire head of lettuce, leaving the unused portion in your refrigerator with the potential to wilt, you can simply go to your garden and pull the leaves off that you need at that moment. You not only get a freshly picked salad ingredient, but you allow the lettuce to continue to grow and remain healthy. So many perks to Aquaponics, trust me you will be hooked too. The leafy varieties are preferred over iceberg for two reasons other than taste preference. One, they pack more nutrients in them for our health and two, because they grow in only 30 days, whereas Iceberg takes 90 days. Remember what I said about making everyone happy in your ecosystem harmony? Well, we can't talk about our vegetables without at least giving a brief mention to our fish (I will get into them in greater detail later in this chapter). The majority of leafy green varieties prefer air temperature ranges between 60 and 80 degrees Fahrenheit. This is just the exposed part of our favorite lettuce. We cannot forget about the needs of the root system which is exposed to the water. As I said before, though both are important, the water is even more important and leafy greens prefer their water to be in the temperature range of 70 to 74 degrees Fahrenheit. (Here is where our fish friends get their brief mention) Tilapia happens to be one of the fish that is a perfect match for our lettuce to thrive because they too prefer their water to be in the temperature ranges of 70 to 74 degrees Fahrenheit. This covers all your leafy greens like spinach, watercress, and arugula as well as all your herbs such as chives, basil, and rosemary.

Let's break this down further:

- LETTUCE (MIXED SALAD LEAVES)
    - pH level ranges are 6.0 to 7.0
    - Plant spacing requirements are 18 to 30 cm (20 to 25 heads/m^2)
    - Germination time and temperature will be 3 to 7 days at 13 to 21 degrees Celsius
    - Growth time is about 30 days (longer for some varieties like Iceberg)
    - Temperature range is 15 to 22 degrees Celsius (flowering over 24 degrees Celsius)
    - Light exposure needed is full sun
    - Plant height is 20 to 30 cm tall and plant width is 25 to 35 cm wide
    - Recommended Aquaponic method can be either media bed, NFT or DWC

The lettuce grows really well in an Aquaponics environment when nutrient concentrations in the water are more than sufficient. A number of them can be grown such as crisphead lettuce (iceberg), which has crispy leaves and a tight head, and is ideally suited for cool temps; butterhead lettuce has leaves that are loosely layered on another and tastes a bit sweet with no bitterness; Romaine lettuce has upright and tightly layered dark green leaves that are slow to seed and are sweet in taste; and loose leaf lettuce comes in a variety of colors and shapes with no head and can be directly planted on media beds and harvested by picking single leaves without collecting the whole plant. This allows for the plant to continue growth and for the grower to avoid having unused, harvested lettuce wilt. Lettuce is a winter vegetable, so it requires night temperatures to range between 3 and 12 degrees Celsius for head growth, and day temperatures to range between 17 and 28 degrees Celsius. Lettuce is highly dependent on light and temperature for proper growth conditions. It requires extended daylight and warm conditions that are more than 18 degrees Celsius at night can cause seeding. Water temperatures more than 26 degrees Celsius may also cause seeding and bitter leaves. Lettuce does not have a high nutrient demand, but it is advised that you increase calcium concentrations in your water in order to prevent the tips of the leaves from burning during summer months. The preferred pH is 5.8 to 6.2, but lettuce will still grow well with a pH level as high as 7, however, the lettuce could suffer from iron deficiencies at the higher pH levels. I would suggest that seedlings be transplanted to your Aquaponic set up around the three-week mark or when they are showing about 2 to 3 leaves. Adding phosphorus to the seedlings in the second and third weeks will aid in favorable root growth and help you to avoid stressing the plant when it is transplanted. Seedlings have an improved survival rate if they are exposed to colder temperatures direct sunlight for approximately 3 to 5 days prior to transplantation. On the contrary, when replanting in warm weather, light shade should be placed over the plants for two to three days beforehand to avoid water stress. If you maintain high nitrate levels, you should see faster growth rates as well as crisp, sweeter lettuce results.

- SWISS CHARD, also known as MANGOLD
    - pH levels are 6 to 7.5
    - Plant spacing requirements are 30 to 30 cm (15 to 20 plants/m^2)
    - Germination time and temperature will be 3 to 7 days at 25 to 30 degrees Celsius
    - Growth time is about 25 to 35 days
    - Temperature range is 16 to 24 degrees Celsius

- Light exposure needed is full sun (partial shade for temperatures greater than 26 degrees Celsius)
- Plant height and width will be 30 to 60 cm tall and 30 to 40 cm wide
- Recommended Aquaponic method can be either media beds, NFT pipes or DWC

It is a very popular leafy green vegetable to grow using Aquaponics, because it does not require high levels of nitrate and requires very little potassium and phosphorous, it is ideally suited for Aquaponics growth. Swiss chard has a fast growth rate and high nutritional value. Though it is known as a leafy "green", it has amazing hints of yellow, purple and/or red throughout its stem. Swiss chard is generally a late winter to spring vegetable however it prefers temperatures ranging between 16 and 24 degrees Celsius. Since it is a cool weather vegetable, it has the ability to survive temperatures as low as 5 degrees Celsius, yet it has also been known to fare well during mild summers. Swiss chard actually has a reasonable acceptance of salinity, which makes it an ideal plant for salt water. (This means it would be a great match for your Barramundi fish.) Swiss Chard is one of those leafy greens that allows us to remove larger leaves for use and leave the plant behind for the continued growth of new leaves.

Herbs: (We will highlight Basil and Parsley, to use for your guidelines to herbs)

- BASIL
  - pH levels are 5.5 to 6.5
  - Plant spacing requirements are 15 to 25 cm (8 to 40 plants/m^2)
  - Germination time and temperatures are 6 to 7 days with temperatures at 20 to 25 degrees Celsius
  - Growth time is about 5 to 6 weeks (harvest begins when the plant is about 15 cm)
  - Temperature ranges are 18 to 30 degrees Celsius but are best at 20 to 25 degrees Celsius
  - Light exposure needed is Sunny or lightly shaded
  - Plant height and width will be 30 to 70 cm tall and 30 cm wide
  - Recommended Aquaponic method can be either media beds, NFT or DWC uptake, however, it is important to avoid too much nutrient depletion in the water.

Basil seeds need a very high and constant temperature in order for germination to begin (20 to 25 degrees Celsius). After they have been transplanted to the media bed or desired set up, the basil will grow best in warm to very warm conditions and lots of sun with minimal shading for optimal leaves. If temperatures throughout the day exceed 27 degrees

Celsius, the plants will need to be in a ventilated and or shaded area to prevent the tips of the leaves from burning. It is best to transplant new seedlings once they have 4 or 5 leaves. To avoid disease, stress, or mold, air ventilation is vital and water temperatures should be maintained above 21 degrees Celsius at all times. Once the plant is about 15 cm tall, you can harvest the leaves and continue to do so for 30 to 50 days. Make sure to leave a few flowering plants behind because they will attract beneficial insects that can improve the entire garden and help to keep a constant supply of basil seeds in production.

- PARSLEY
    - pH levels are 6 to 7
    - Plant spacing requirements are 15 to 30 cm (10 to 15 plants/m^2)
    - Germination time and temperature ranges are 8 to 10 days and 20 to 25 degrees Celsius
    - Growth time will be about 20 to 30 days after transplantation
    - Temperatures are 15 to 25 degrees Celsius
    - Light exposure is full sun and partial shade when greater than 25 degrees Celsius
    - Plant height and width are 30 to 60 cm tall and 30 to 40 cm wide
    - Recommended aquaponic method can be either media beds, NFT or DWC

Parsley is a very common herb to grow due to its high levels of vitamins A and C, calcium and iron). Parsley is an easy herb to grow and has a low nutrient requirement. Parsley is a biennial herb, but it is traditionally grown as an annual. Highly resistant to temperatures as low as zero degrees Celsius but should not be exposed to temperatures lower than 8 degrees Celsius for optimal growth. Parsley needs full sunlight for up to eight hours a day. It should have partial shading if temperatures are greater than 25 degrees Celsius. Initial germination can take 2 to 5 weeks, depending on seeds freshness. Emerging seedlings will have the appearance of grass, with two narrow seed leaves opposite each other. After approximately 5 to 6 weeks you will be able to transplant the seedlings into your aquaponic setup. You can begin to harvest once the individual stalks of Parsley are at least 15 cm. If you harvest from the outside in, you will encourage growth production throughout the season. Many people remove the tops, but this will simply slow production.

Next, we will discuss tomatoes. Tomatoes have a complicated growth cycle and go through many changes during this time. There are two types of tomato plants amongst the variety of tomatoes. One type yields tomatoes all at one time and the other will yield tomato production periodically and continuously. This is important because if you choose the one that yields all at once, this species is a much smaller plant that

doesn't need a support structure and can easily be grown indoors. The other species will vary in size dependent on the variety. Tomato plants require high humidity and prefer a temperature of 78 degrees Fahrenheit in order to yield fruit. Though this is their preference, tomatoes can yield fruit in temperatures ranging from 68 to 88 degrees Fahrenheit. It is important to maintain pH levels between 5.8 and 6.8 but can handle pH levels up 7.2. They require up to 12 hours of light per day and no less than 8 hours per day. The
more light they get, the more fruit they will yield and the faster the plant will yield it. It is best to start from a cutting. If you start from seeds, you must have a separate seedling tray with a temperature at 77 degrees Fahrenheit and humidity at 100 percent. They will need to grow 2 to 6 weeks before transplanting them to the grow bed.

- TOMATO
    - pH levels are 5.5 to 6.5
    - Plant spacing requirements are 40 to 60 cm (3 to 5 plants/m^2)
    - Germination time and temperature are: 4 to 6 days in 20 to 30 degrees Celsius
    - Growth time will be 50 to 70 days till first harvest and fruiting 90 to 120 days upwards of 8 to 10 months (dependent on variety)
    - Optimal temperatures are 13 to 16 degrees Celsius at night, 22 to 26 degrees Celsius during daytime
    - Light exposure is full sun
    - Plant height and width will be 60 to 180 cm tall and 60 to 80 cm wide
    - Recommended Aquaponic method can be either media beds or DWC

Tomatoes are an excellent summer fruiting vegetable but they require structural support systems. It is important to consider the plant to fish ratios due to the high nutrient requirement of tomatoes. For proper growth, a high nitrogen concentration is needed during the early stages and potassium is needed during the flowering stage as well. Tomatoes enjoy warm temperatures with full sun exposure. If temperatures drop below 8 to 10 degrees Celsius, the plants will cease growth. Likewise, anything above 40 degrees Celsius can cause flowers to stop growing and the fruit to turn. Tomatoes have a moderate tolerance to salinity, which makes them suitable for areas where pure freshwater is not available. Higher saline levels during the fruiting stage can improve the quality of the tomato. Set stakes or plant support structures before transplanting to prevent root damage. You can transplant the seedlings at the 3 to 6-week mark, when the seedling is about 10 to 15 cm and when nighttime temperatures are consistently above 10 degrees Celsius. Once the plants reach a height of 60 cm, you need to determine whether you will continue the growth process as a bush or single stem, and you do so by pruning the unnecessary upper branches. Remove the leaves from the bottom 30 cm of the main stem for better air circulation and reduction of potential disease. Remove the leaves that are covering each fruit branch prior to ripening to aid in the proper flow of nutrition to the fruits and to accelerate growth.

Vegetables like cabbage, broccoli, cauliflower, radishes and kale all have similar preferences in the environment.

- CAULIFLOWER
  - pH levels are 6.0 to 6.5
  - Plant spacing requirements are 45 to 60 cm (3 to 5 plants/m^2)
  - Germination time and temperature are 4 to 7 days with temperature 8 to 20 degrees Celsius
  - Growth time is 2 to 3 months during spring and 3 to 4 months during autumn
  - Temperatures are 20 to 25 degrees Celsius for initial growth and 10 to 15 degrees Celsius for head setting in autumn
  - Light exposure is full sun
  - Plant height and width is 40 to 60 cm tall and 60 to 70 cm wide
  - Recommended Aquaponic method is media beds.

Cauliflower requires calcium for the production of heads. It is a very climate sensitive plant, therefore, selecting a suitable variety for your environment and ensuring proper timing for transplant is paramount for this plant to flourish. Preferred air temperature for the initial growth period of the plant is 15 to 25 degrees Celsius. Head formation requires colder temperatures of 10 to 15 degrees Celsius in autumn or 15 to 20 degrees Celsius in spring, as long as there is a good amount of humidity and full sun conditions. Cold temperatures are tolerated but there is a danger of frost damage. Also, light shade is good in warmer temperatures greater than 23 degrees Celsius. When plants are 3 to 5 weeks old and have 4 to 5 leaves, you can begin transplantation. Make sure they are placed about 50 cm apart. To keep the heads white, use string or rubber bands to keep the leaves covering it. When they reach about 6 to 10 cm in diameter, the harvest may take less than a week in ideal temperatures or as long as a month in cooler conditions. Harvest when the heads are compact, white and firm. Cauliflower is susceptible to pests, so it is important to incorporate some sort of pest control.

- HEAD CABBAGE
  - pH level is 6 to 7.2
  - Plant spacing requirements are 60 to 80 cm (4 to 8 plants/m^2)
  - Germination time and the temperature is 4 to 7 days with 8 to 29 degrees Celsius

- Growth time will be 45 to 70 days from transplanting (dependent on variety and climate)
- The preferred temperature is 15 to 20 degrees Celsius (growth ceases greater than 25 degrees Celsius)
- Light exposure is full sun
- Plant height and width is 30 to 60 cm high and 30 to 60 cm wide
- Recommended Aquaponic method is media beds

Cabbage is a winter crop with preferred growing temperatures of about 15 to 20 degrees Celsius. It is important to harvest the cabbage prior to daytime temperatures reaching 23 to 25 degrees Celsius. When the heads begin to grow, it is vital that they have high concentrations of phosphorus and potassium. You will want to transplant seedlings when there are about 4 to 6 leaves and are at a height of 15 cm. Start harvesting when cabbage heads are firm and about 10 to 15 cm in diameter depending on the variety grown.

- BROCCOLI
  - pH levels are 6 to 7
  - Plant spacing requirements are 40 to 70 cm (3 to 5 plants/m^2)
  - Germination time and the temperature is 4 to 6 days with 25 degrees Celsius
  - Growth time will be 60 to 100 days from transplantation
  - Average daily temperature preferred is 13 to 18 degrees Celsius
  - Light exposure is full sun. It can tolerate partial shade but will mature slowly.
  - Plant height and width is 30 to 60 cm tall and 30 to 60 cm wide
  - Recommended Aquaponic method is media beds

Broccoli growth is optimal when daytime temperatures are 14 to 17 degrees Celsius. Winter varieties require temperatures of 10 to 15 degrees Celsius for head formation. Broccoli can withstand higher temperatures if a higher humidity is present. Hot temperatures cause premature seeding. You can transplant seedlings into media beds once 4 to 5 leaves are visible and the plants are 15 to 20 cm tall. Seedlings need to be placed 40 to 50 cm apart. Broccoli is susceptible to pests so it is very important to maintain pest control methods. You can begin harvesting broccoli when the buds of the head are firm and tight.

Cucumbers, squash, and melons are vine crops and they have pretty much the same requirements for growth. These types of vegetables prefer temperatures ranging from 75 to 78 degrees Fahrenheit during the day and around 68 degrees Fahrenheit at night. Humidity levels must be no greater than 75 percent. They can take anywhere from 1 ½ to 2 months for full growth from seeds. There are many squash varieties such as summer squash like zucchini and yellow squash and the numerous winter squash like butternut, spaghetti, and acorn. Assorted melons include watermelon, cantaloupe, and honeydew.

- CUCUMBERS
    - pH levels are 5.5 to 6.5
    - Plant spacing requirements are 30 to 60 cm (depending on variety; 2 to 5 plants/m^2)
    - Germination time and the temperature is 3 to7 days with 20 to 30 degrees Celsius
    - Growth time is 55 to 65 days
    - Temperature is 22 to 28 degrees Celsius during the daytime, 18 to 20 degrees Celsius nightly; highly susceptible to frost.
    - Light exposure is full sun
    - Plant height and width is 20 to 200 cm tall and 20 to 80 cm wide
    - Recommended Aquaponic methods are media beds and DWC

Cucumbers, as well as squash, zucchini, and melons, are great summer vegetables. They are ideally suited to grow in media beds because they have a large root structure. Cucumbers can also be grown on floating rafts, but if you choose this method it is important to constantly check to grow pipes because there could be the risk of clogging from excessive root growth. Cucumbers require large quantities of nitrogen and potassium, so it is important to ensure proper plant to fish ratios. Cucumbers grow best with high humidity, lots of sunshine, and warm nights. They enjoy growth temperatures of 24 to 27 degrees Celsius during the daytime with 70 to 90 percent humidity. Plants cease growth and production at 10 to 13 degrees Celsius. Higher potassium concentration is preferred for higher fruit settings and yields. Cucumber seedlings can be transplanted at 2 to 3 weeks when there are 4 to 5 leaves showing. They grow very quickly. For optimal health of the fruit, you should cut their apical tips when the stem is two meters long, allowing more nutrient flow to the fruit. Remove the lateral branches to allow for enhanced ventilation. It is important to have beneficial insects around your cucumbers. It is also important to provide a support system for their growth and prevention of diseases and/ or molds. Once transplanted, cucumbers can start production in about 2 to 3 weeks. The plants can be harvested in ideal conditions 10 to 15 times. Make sure to harvest every few days to prevent the fruits from excessive growth and to promote new growth.

- EGGPLANT
    - pH level is 5.5 to 7.0
    - Plant spacing requirements are 40 to 60 cm (3 to 5 plants/m^2)
    - Germination time and the temperature is 8 to 10 days with 25 to 30 degrees Celsius

- Growth time will be 90 to 120 days
- Temperatures preferred are 15 to 18 degrees Celsius at night and 22 to 26 degrees Celsius during the day; highly susceptible to frost
- Light exposure is full sun
- Plant height and width is 60 to 120 cm tall and 60 to 80 cm wide
- Recommended Aquaponic method is media beds

Eggplant is a summer fruiting vegetable that grows well in media beds because of their deep root system growth. These plants can produce 10 to 15 fruits for a total yield of 3 to 7 kg. Eggplants have high nitrogen and potassium requirements. Because of this, it is important to ensure a proper balance throughout the ecosystem. Eggplants enjoy warm temperatures with full exposure to sunlight. They grow best with daily temperatures in the range of 22 to 26 degrees Celsius and humidity of 60 to 70 percent. Temperatures less than 9 to 10 degrees Celsius and more than 30 to 32 degrees Celsius can cause growth and production cessation. Seeds germinate in 8 to 10 days in warm temperatures ranging between 26 to 30 degrees Celsius. Seedlings can be transplanted when 4 to 5 leaves are showing. Near the end of the summer, start pinching off new blooms to promote the ripening of any existing fruit. Towards the end of the season, plants can be pruned at 20–30 cm, leaving just three branches for the following season. This will stop any further growth until favorable seasons return. Start harvesting when the eggplants are 10–15 cm long. The skin should be shiny and deep purple.

- BEANS AND PEAS
  - pH level is 5.5 to 7.0
  - Plant spacing requirements are 10 to 30 cm dependent on variety (bush varieties 20 to40 plants/m^2, climbing varieties 10 to 12 plants/m^2)
  - Germination time and the temperature is 8 to 10 days with 21 to 26 degrees Celsius
  - Growth time is 50 to 110 days to reach maturity depending on the variety
  - Temperature is 16 to 18 degrees Celsius nightly, 22 to 26 degrees Celsius daytime
  - Light exposure is full sun
  - Plant height and width is 60 to 250 cm (climbing) and 60 to 80 cm (bush)
  - Recommended Aquaponic method is media bed

Beans have low nitrate needs but have a moderate demand in terms of phosphorus and potassium. Beans are recommended for newly established units as they may fix atmospheric nitrogen for you. Climbing varieties prefer full sunlight but will tolerate partial shade in warm conditions. Bean plants do not grow in temperatures lower than 12 to 14 degrees Celsius. Temperatures greater than 35 degrees Celsius can cause flower and fruit growth cessation. They enjoy humidity of 70 to 80 percent. It is important to choose the right varieties according to the location and season. In general, climbing varieties are cultivated in summer while others are better suited for spring and autumn conditions. Beans are susceptible to aphids and spider mites. It is a good idea to employ regular pest control procedures and attention needs to be paid as to which companion plants are placed in the garden in an effort to avoid cross-contamination in case any treatment has to be carried out. Snap bean varieties such as green or yellow wax beans have pods that need to be firm and crisp at harvest. Try to avoid pulling off branches that can offer future pods when pulling off the pods you are harvesting currently. Make sure to pick all pods off in order to keep plants productive. Shell beans such as black, broad or fava beans should be picked when the pods change color and the beans inside are fully formed but not dried out. Pods should be plump and firm. Dried beans such as kidney beans and soybeans need to become as dry as possible before cooler weather sets in or when plants have turned brown and lost most of their leaves. These pods will easily open when very dry, making seed removal a simple procedure.

- PEPPERS
    - pH level is 5.5 to 6.5
    - Plant spacing requirements are 30 to 60 cm (3 to 4 plants/m^2, or more for small-sized plant varieties)
    - Germination time and the temperature is 8 to 12 days with 22 to 30 degrees Celsius (seeds will not germinate at a temperature lower than 13 degrees Celsius)
    - Growth time is 60 to 95 days
    - Temperature is 14 to 16 degrees Celsius at night time, 22 to 30 degrees Celsius during the daytime
    - Light exposure is full sun
    - Plant height and width is 30 to 90 cm tall and 30 to 80 cm wide
    - Recommended Aquaponics method is media beds

There are numerous varieties of peppers with numerous assortments of color and varying degrees of Scoville levels (heat index). Regardless whether they are sweet bell pepper, hot chili peppers (jalapeño or cayenne peppers), or anything in between, they can all be grown in your Aquaponics garden. Peppers are best grown with the media bed system though they can also grow in 11 cm diameter NFT pipes if they have a good structural support system. Peppers are a summer fruiting vegetable that prefers warm conditions and full exposure to sunlight. Seeds germinate in temperatures at about 22 to 34 degrees Celsius. They cannot germinate well in temperatures below 15 degrees Celsius. Best conditions

for fruiting are daytime temperatures of 22 to 28 degrees Celsius and night-time temperatures of 14 to 16 degrees Celsius. They also enjoy humidity of 60 to 65 percent. The best temperatures for the root levels are 15 to 20 degrees Celsius. Air temperatures below 10 to 12 degrees Celsius will cause plant growth cessation and additionally cause abnormally formed fruits. Temperatures that are higher than 30 to 35 degrees Celsius can lead to problems with the flowers and even cause them to fall off. Basically, peppers that are spicier can be grown at higher temperatures. The top leaves of the plant protect the fruit that is hanging below from getting sun exposure. As with other fruiting plants, nitrate is vital for the initial growth process. The best range of nitrate levels needed is 20–120 mg/liter but higher concentrations of potassium and phosphorus are needed for flowering and fruiting. Seeds should be transplanted when the plant shows 6 to 8 leaves and the night temperatures remain constant above 10 degrees Celsius. A strong structural support system is needed for bushy, heavy-yielding plants. Stakes or vertical strings hanging from iron wires pulled horizontally above the units should anchor them properly. If growing red sweet peppers, you need to leave the green fruits on the plants until they ripen and turn red. In order to encourage future plant growth, you should pick the first couple of flowers that make their appearance on the plant. Should excessive fruit setting occur, you will need to reduce the number of flowers on the plant. This will aid in promoting the growth of fruit to adequate sizes. You should begin harvesting when peppers reach appropriate sizes. Peppers need to be left on the plants until they ripen fully. You will recognize this by the change in color. Harvesting them at their optimal ripeness will improve their levels of vitamin C. If you harvest regularly throughout the season, your plants will continue to blossom fruit and promote growth. Peppers can be easily stored fresh for 10 days at 10 degrees Celsius with
90 to 95 percent humidity or they can be dehydrated or pickled for long-term storage.

Ornamental fish for Aquaponics Fish Tanks:

Some people simply want to reap the benefits of the Aquaponics system for Vegan consumption and enjoy the beauty of the fish that aid in the growth of their vegetables and herbs. Others too, want a purely ornamental set up for their home and are not concerned with food production at all. In either case, there are many fish to choose from. It is important to keep in mind the needs of the ecosystem as a whole to determine the size of the fish and/ or the amount of fish that you need in order to maintain proper balance throughout. Here are some suggestions for ornamental fish for the indoor tank:

- Angelfish are also known as the Koi Angel and come in many types and colors. Generally, they will be approximately six inches in size, therefore, a 20-gallon tank would be the minimum suggested and of course, is dependent on the amount of fish you desire.
- Goldfish tends to be the staple for home aquariums. These fish also come in many varieties differing in color, size, and shape. They are very durable fish so they can handle any size tank and do not require heat. They pretty much eat anything as they are not very picky eaters so the variety of foods and plants to choose from for their consumption are countless. Goldfish produce a large amount of waste for such a small fish, which actually makes them great for Aquaponics garden to grow. Because they tend to be shy, it is important to have plants in the tank itself for some type of retreat for the fish. The ideal water temperatures for Goldfish would be between 68 and 75 degrees Fahrenheit.
- Bloodfin Tetras are also very hardy fish that can withstand almost any environment. They are very beautiful with silver and red hues and therefore make for an attractive setup.
- The White Cloud Mountain Minnow is a small pretty fish well suited for the indoor aquarium as well as the outdoor pond! They do well with cold water conditions.
- Danios are also a small fish that are very durable fish that do well in almost any environment. They have beautiful striped features and bright colors that look amazing as they race around your tank, traveling in schools. These fish will come to greet you at the top of the water when you feed them their flakes so you may enjoy a setup that has the plants placed on one side while the water is exposed for feeding on the other.

Note: In colder areas, heaters may be warranted to ensure that the water does not get too cold. The same would be the case for extremely hot areas where
the temperatures can reach into the three digits. It is important to maintain regular temperature ranges and not have the fish experience drastic fluctuations to stress them out, no matter how durable the species may be. Temperatures should never fluctuate more than three degrees!

For those of you who would like to enjoy outdoor ponds using Aquaponics, Koi are no doubt the most popular choice. These fish are not just beautiful and come in assorted colors, but they are omnivorous, parasite-resistant and thus live very long life spans upwards of 60 years. They produce an abundant amount of waste so they are great at helping the plants in and around your pond grow large and fast. One thing to keep in mind about Koi, they are easy to find for purchasing however they are very expensive fish to buy. Due to their durability, unbelievable beauty, and long life, the cost may very well be worth it! How many fish can you honestly say with certainty (in the ornamental category) will live a good amount of time or even survive when you make your purchase. Aside from making my pond area bear proof where I live, I am fairly certain that my investment in Koi is a good one that I will enjoy for years to come! (They may very well be there for the next generation after me to enjoy!)

Edible varieties of fish for your Aquaponics system
Obviously, there are many freshwater fish to choose from so I am just going to cover a select few that tend to be the top choices for Aquaponics. You can use this guide to deviate from this list as many fish are related in one way or another (like the Carp, Goldfish, and Koi, for example).

- Tilapia seems to be the number one choice amongst Aquaponics growers. This is understandable because Tilapia are easy to breed and are fast growing fish that are basically ready to be on your plate within 6 to 9 months. They are a warm water breed that enjoys temperature ranges between 72 and 86 degrees Fahrenheit. Aside from their ease of breeding and fast growth, they are delicious with a mild flavor that is used in many cuisines in various culinary styles. These fish are durable and can adapt to many less desirable environments though they, like everyone else, have their preference, and it is very important to maintain constant warm water temperatures if you want to keep your fish healthy, breeding, and growing at a consistent pace. These fish are omnivorous and can be placed in tanks with other species without concern of them eating the other fish. It is important to note that Tilapia breed rapidly (about every four to six weeks) so you must have a tank large enough to contain all the new schools.

- Trout is another option however it is important to recognize that they must be closely monitored due to their high Dissolved Oxygen levels and pH balance. Anything that throws their environment out of whack can be detrimental. They are cold water fish that enjoy temperature ranges between 56 and 68 degrees Fahrenheit. Trout can be ready for eating in 12 to 16 months though it is a more delicate fish than the warm water Tilapia, Trout is a great source of protein and Omega fatty acids and it is a delicious fish option. In reference to the marriage in this ecosystem, the options for your plants are reduced because of the colder water requirements, therefore it is important if choosing this fish that you also choose plants that are very hardy and can withstand cooler water temperatures.

- Perch is a highly adaptable fish that comes in a variety of silver, yellow and jade. Because of their adaptability, they have been a good option for the beginner Aquaponics growers. They can handle cooler water temperatures but their ideal temperature range would be between 70 and 82 degrees Fahrenheit. Depending on which variety of Perch you choose, you can be eating your Perch as early as 9 months or in the case of the silver Perch, up to 16 months. Perch are carnivorous fish so you need to feed them smaller fish, bugs, and shrimp. This may be a more expensive diet for your fish but the taste of Perch is worth it for those who can afford the additional expense.

- Catfish have become very popular options for Aquaponics because they grow extremely fast allowing the breeder to enjoy the taste of this delectable fish in only 5 to 10 months. Catfish are sensitive to water temperature, water quality, and pH like the Trout, so there is a need to be diligent with maintaining a pristine environment. They require temperature ranges between 78 and 86 degrees Fahrenheit. Catfish are bottom dwellers that come in many sizes. This fish offers great flavor and are high in vitamin D, which most people tend to be deficient in. One thing to note about catfish is that they do not have scales, so it is important to skin the fish before you prepare it for consumption.

- Barramundi is a special option, in that this fish, unlike the others, can be kept in both freshwater systems and saltwater systems. (Pleases note: Saltwater is not recommended for Aquaponics simply because of the lack of plant options available for your system.) Barramundi must not be kept with small fish because they will get very aggressive and can injure or even eat the younger smaller fish. This is a white fish that is very flaky and tasty, thus the reason for its popularity. They grow rather quickly and can be on your plate within 12 months time. These fish do require perfect water conditions and therefore need to be monitored regularly. Dissolved Oxygen levels need to be regulated. That being said, they are great fish to watch in your tank and they have a high waste output for a thriving garden.

- Largemouth, smallmouth, and striped Bass are very popular Aquaponics fish as well. They prefer a temperature range between

75 and 85 degrees Fahrenheit. Dependent on the type you choose, it will be fully matured for serving in 12 to 18 months, with Striped Bass growing quicker. They require pristine water conditions, dark areas (they do not like bright lights), they need proper oxygen and pH levels and must follow a strict feeding schedule. Bass is a very delicious source of food and like Tilapia, has been used in many culinary forms and cuisines, so the recipes are numerous.

- It's funny but most people don't think about Crustaceans when deciding to do Aquaponics, however they are gaining in popularity the more Aquaponics becomes known around the world. Thinking outside the "fish" box (or tank, I should say, lol), Crustaceans offer great variety for your meals and are definitely a viable choice in Aquaponics systems. The best part is that many fish can cohabitate with your crustaceans! Setting the carnivores aside, you can place Mussels, Oysters, Crayfish, freshwater prawns, shrimp, crabs, and even lobster, in your tank. Aside from a food source for us humans, they are great at keeping the tank clean because they tend to eat dead organic plant matter. Many people tend to keep a separate tank for their crustaceans if they are planning on using them for human food as opposed to fish food. Even if your fish won't eat them, many may decide to attack them, and just like fish, we want to keep them healthy and stress-free. Mussels are a bit different than the others in this category because they can grow in the tank as well as in the grow beds! For your prawns, they prefer temperature ranges between 82 and 88 degrees Fahrenheit and can be served within 6 to 12 months. Your lobster prefers 71 to 76 degrees Fahrenheit and can be served in 24 months. The oysters enjoy temperatures of 75 to 79 degrees Fahrenheit and can be on your plate in 24 months.

Special Mention: The past few years, we hear about cannabis in the news either about the medical breakthroughs they are reporting in terms of benefits in the fight against cancer, Alzheimer's, PTSD, seizures and other ailments or about how state after state is approving the legalization of cannabis. With that being said, I thought I would briefly mention that Aquaponics is also an area in which Cannabis growth has seen great success. Since we are discussing plants, there may be a few of you interested in attempting this. Though it is not new to Hydroponics, it is newer to Aquaponics but there are plenty of articles online and books on this subject if you should be interested in doing so and they discuss legal allowances for different regions as well as proper set up conducive to growth for these particular plants.

CHAPTER 4

How to Create A Proper Aquaponics Environment

You now have a good idea of what you would like your Aquaponics garden to look like and where it will be located. You know what kind of plants you want in your garden and what kind of fish you would like in your tank. The next step is to choose the system you feel would work best for you and work on all of the factors that are required to ensure that your Aquaponics ecosystem will function properly and allow your plants and fish to thrive.

TYPES OF SYSTEMS
Sun Pond
The basic set up is reminiscent of that used by the Aztecs. It simply consists of the plants floating directly on the pond or tank water with its roots submerged in the water. The biggest issue with this design arises with the inability to stop fish from eating and damaging the plants.

Flood and Drain
This is the most common of the Aquaponics systems, due to its simplicity. An even ratio of fish tank volume to plant bed volume makes for an easy calculation. The system utilizes three components: the fish tank, the pump, and the grow bed. Water is pumped directly from the fish tank to the media bed. The media bed then drains back into the fish tank. It's the circle of life! This works best with a single bed area. Having two or more can lead to low water levels and stress on the fish.

CHOP
The acronym CHOP stands for constant height, one pump. This system is like the flood and drain except that there is the addition of the sump pump in order to maintain the water levels at a consistent height. The pump is located in a separate sump tank. The water from the fish tank overflows into the grow beds. The grow beds then drain into the sump tank which then pumps the water back to the fish tank.

This system is less stressful on the fish because of the water level maintenance but does require a lot more space and can present difficulties with supply needs. The set up for this system requires that the sump tank area is lower than the grow bed area which also needs to be lower than the fish tank.

CHOP 2

This system obviously is very much like the CHOP except the way that it is set up is very different. The CHOP has a more vertical relation to each part where the CHOP2 is horizontal in relation to where its life producing tanks are located. This system requires that the fish tank and the media beds sit level with each other with the only part sitting below them being the sump tank area. The sump tank pumps water to the media beds and the fish tank. The grow beds utilize an auto siphon to receive their much-needed water and the fish tank utilizes a gravity feed overflow mechanism. With this system, you can have two or more grow bed areas feeding off of the one fish tank. Doing so would require a larger setup and stronger pumping mechanisms. Because the sump tank doubles its duty, clean and dirty water mixes and filtration is not efficient. Additional filtration would be recommended in order to reach an optimal ecosystem environment.

AUTOMATION

There are so many things that go on in our day to day lives. If we could make one part of it that much easier and not have to think about it constantly, why wouldn't you?

An Aquaponics system can be run seamlessly on an automated system. Our ancestors did not have this luxury and had to maintain a rigorous schedule to ensure that they fed the fish, the water quality was tested, the temperature was as it should be, the filter was clear of any solid waste obstructions, and pumping mechanisms were doing their job.

These days, everything can be done by machines and computers and can even be monitored on smart devices from remote locations far away from the Aquaponics site. Sensors that are computer monitored don't have to be astronomically priced as they come in a range of prices and capacities. They are made to alert you when something in your system is not quite right and depends on what the problem is, they can automatically correct the problem. Not everyone is up to this technology. It does require some programming/setting. I still need help using my I-phone. Thank God for my kids. It's amazing what they know about technology even before they are teenagers.

For me, more simple systems of automation like timers work just fine, especially when you are using a flood and drain system. A timer must be set up to control the system as they use settings to cause the flood and drain to occur. The time is usually set for every hour on the hour for 15 minutes in duration, in an effort to fill the media beds. During the remaining 45 minutes of the hour, the media beds are draining into the fish tank.

For others, an auto siphon, also known as a bell siphon, is preferred. This method remains active at all times because it works through the use of an overflow spout. Once the water level rises causing overflow, the siphon automatically opens and releases the water from the media beds into the fish tank. Once the media bed is drained, the siphon closes again and waits to refill. The process will continue automatically unless a solid is caught in the siphon, causing a blockage.

If you are still interested in some type of automation at a budget but want something a bit more sophisticated, you might want to look into APDuino. APDuino is a firmware that is specifically designed for both Aquaponic and Hydroponic systems and can be set through wi-fi or hard-wired. There are others out there, so it is recommended that you do your research to see what best meets your needs and your budget.

Even for those who have been enjoying the relaxation of owning an aquarium, automatic feeders have become popular, especially for those with an assortment of fish with differing feeding needs. This is a great option for Aquaponics.

Aside from monitoring and repairing, automated systems have been beneficial in mimicking day and night. Shading and venting can be incorporated to ensure that the system is temperature regulated. The shade will minimize the heat produced from the sun and the vent will cool the garden by releasing the hot air that has accumulated. This, of course, is not a necessity since it is not difficult to open and close curtains and windows, however, if you are not near your Aquaponics garden for long periods of time (most people spend more time at work then they do at home) then this luxury doesn't sound so ridiculous, does it? Finding the right location for your garden that will allow for a good balance, may help to avoid the added expenditure.

Automatic lighting is another feature to consider indoors or out. It is important to have sunlight, but we don't always have sunny days and of course, when we do, it doesn't stay as day must go and night must come. Lighting doesn't just affect how much "sunlight" a plant gets but also the temperature the garden experiences. We will discuss lighting and temperatures in more detail later on in the chapter.

BIOFILTRATION
Biofilters are made to duplicate the processes naturally occurring in nature. Aquaponics incorporates biofilters to ensure that it mimics mother nature's work as closely as humanly possible. Aquaponics systems make sure that no waste occurs as everything is vitally important

just as it is in nature. Saying that, recycle and reuse is not just something we say but something we must do. Aquaponics does just that since the excreta from the fish is used as a source of food for the garden and, just like any natural ecosystem, one hand washes the other, so the plants will clean the water for the fish. In the next chapter, we will discuss in detail the nutrient cycle, but biofilters are a part of that necessary cycle. The medium which facilitates the nutrient cycle is called a biofilter. Regular aquariums require extensive filtration systems to achieve a healthy environment but with planted aquariums like in Aquaponics, the plants act as a natural biofilter, so the filtration needed is much less extensive and more inexpensive. In fact, in using the flood and drain method with media beds, added filtration is not needed. The plants in the Aquaponic garden remove all the nitrites and nitrates that are harmful to fish but stimulate growth in plants. If fish to plant bed ratios are properly calculated, biofiltration can simply be done by the plants. For the most part, in Aquaponics, this is the case. Sometimes the plants need a bit of help so additional filtration can be incorporated. This may occur in a DWC configured grow bed, but it is not likely needed with media beds.

TANKS
Depending on the type of system you choose, you may not only need a tank for your fish but a tank for your sump pump as well. Some people will additionally purchase a tank to grow fingerlings until they are big enough to survive in a tank with adult fish who might like to make a meal out of them. Generally, I like to keep one or the other so one tank would suffice.

It is important to keep in mind that aquariums are made for fish. Aquaponics gardens are made for plants and fish, edible fish mostly, and for that reason, the two don't automatically go together. Aquariums are chemically treated and require filtration systems to ensure that the water is not toxic to the fish who inhabit it. The biofiltration of plants in such an environment without an additional filtration system will cause algae to build up. Algae are detrimental to both plants and fish because it sucks the oxygen from the water for their own needs.

Additionally, ornamental fish versus fish breeds used for consumption have different environmental needs. A well-lit aquarium setting for Guppies, Mollies, or other ornamental fish, even Koi in a pond, works great but fish like Tilapia and Bluegill tend to prefer darker areas with places to hide, especially when they feel danger looming (and that could simply be someone looking in the tank).

Purchasing a kit, as previously discussed. It will ensure that you have the proper set up for your plants and fish. If you choose the DO IT

YOURSELF path and want an aquarium as part of your set up, the size must be considered to determine if biofiltration by the plants will be suitable or if an additional filtration system is needed. Aquariums are safe and watertight for marine inhabitants so if the worst thing you need to add to your DO IT YOURSELF project budget is a filtration system, it's worth it.

Other containment systems can be used like barrels, tanks, bathtubs, etc. but again, this would be covered extensively in a DO IT YOURSELF manual specific to Aquaponics. These alternate containment systems do require many more steps to ensure that there is no toxic residue and that the parts you choose for your system are food grade and/or drinking water safe. It is better to be safe than sorry, not just for the living organisms, plants, and fish in your Aquaponics ecosystem, but also for the people who intend to consume the plants and/or fish cultivated in the garden. So, therefore, DO IT YOURSELF people, when in doubt, don't use it, count it as out!!!

GROW BEDS
The general depth for Aquaponics' grow beds is 12 inches as that is optimal for growth, biofiltration, and temperatures. If you intend to utilize Aquaponics systems for large plants and/or trees, then doubling the depth to 24 inches is advised. For most grow beds, 12 inches is perfect to allow room for the root system and its natural processes. Whether your garden utilizes media (which allows, at this depth, biofiltration, conversion of ammonia to nitrate, to occur) or is directly submerging the roots in water (having the roots this deep allows for stability in temperature), 12 inches in depth has proven to deliver conditions conducive to a flourishing Aquaponics ecosystem.

TYPES OF GROW BEDS

Media Based
The most commonly used grow beds are those that use items like rocks or gravel for biofiltration. Media based refers to anything that is used to give a support system to the plants since they don't have the soil to do that function.

Media can include:

- Rocks
- Gravel
- Sand
- Perlite

- Styrofoam
- Mineral wood
- Clay beads

Mostly commonly used media:

- Gravel
- Expanded Shale
- Clay beads

The ideal size of the medium should be ¾ inches in diameter to allow for proper drainage from plant bed to fish tank.

Previously discussed in this book, it is important to consider weight when setting up your Aquaponics garden because it is not only the fish tank that has considerable weight (example: a 100 gallon fish tank weighs about 1150 pounds when filled with water) but the grow beds have a great amount of weight also, especially in those using media based beds.

The use of media in your beds allows for a broader selection of plants, trees, bushes, or root vegetables to be grown. Heavier, taller plants can be cultivated because of the support system that media-based beds offer.

Media based beds create ideal surfaces for mineralization to occur whereas water-based beds tend to be too diluted to allow the plants to gain the nourishment that they need. As the oxygenated water and excretions from the fish collect on the rocks (or whatever medium is chosen) in the bed, the natural cycle will begin to transform the chemical compounds into the nutrients plants so desperately need.

Another benefit of using media based beds is algae prevention. The media used like rocks block the light from hitting the roots of the plants whereas water-based systems do not have any natural shields. If the roots get attacked by algae, it impairs their ability to breathe, drink, and filter. Likewise, if the roots are exposed to direct light, they can get burnt and impair their ability to absorb water.

Also, an important function of media based beds, as mentioned earlier, is the filtration. Removing the media from the equation opens the doors for several issues. If waste is not removed from the fish tank, it is not only deadly to the fish but it can also cause blockage in the roots of the plants which will prevent them from eating and drinking. They need water and nutrients to survive. For both the fish and plants, water-based systems require added filtration systems whereas media based beds eliminate the need because of their natural biofiltration process.

As I've said earlier, I aim to find a happy balance between form and function. Media beds allow for creativity, beauty, and a harmoniously functioning ecosystem to happen all in the same place. Koi ponds are great examples of this. Koi ponds have been designed with Aquaponics systems and amazing elements of design using media beds. They have beautiful plants and trees surrounding the pond and some even have plants on the pond, which make for a hybrid design of sorts. Incorporating Lily pads or other floating plants are elements of water-based systems. Additionally, waterfalls aid in biofiltration and water movement throughout the system and rock placement creates a beautiful environment.

The design you choose can be a real statement piece indoors or out and media based systems make it easier to do so, whereas, the need for filtration in water-based systems can be a real eyesore.

Obviously, media-based beds have many positive attributes but there are a few negatives that need to be mentioned for the sake of allowing you to make fully informed decisions as to which system you prefer for your personal Aquaponics garden.
As noted before, weight is certainly a factor to consider. Water alone is heavy but the addition of media such as rocks will increase the weight requirements of the area you choose, significantly.

Secondly, just like any filter, media beds can get clogged, which will cause a lack of oxygen to travel to the plants and ultimately to the fish. There are several indicators that will let you know that there is a potential threat from clogging:

- Rapid increase in pH
- Reduction in water flow through the bed
- Dense balls of roots have formed

Third, if the media used in the beds are not pH neutral or hasn't been rinsed first, a simple item like dirt or sand on the media might throw the pH levels out of balance.

Fourth, media doesn't just vary in assorted options, but it also varies in weight and cost.

It is very common for Aquaponics enthusiasts to select media such as:
- Gravel

- River rock
- Clay pellets
- Expanded shale

As far as price and availability, gravel is the least expensive, easy to obtain, and is beautiful for the garden, however, it is the heaviest option. Additionally, edges can be jagged and sharp, making it difficult to clean and arrange in beds without the use of thick protective gloves. River rocks are a good alternative since they have smooth edges but they are just as heavy. They are ideal for the support of heavier, taller plants.

The clay pellets are extremely lightweight but are much more difficult to find which results in a much more expensive purchase. Shale is very lightweight, weighing in slightly more than clay, and looks just like gravel. Shale is also in high demand and therefore carries a much higher price tag.

It is important to note, regardless of whether you purchase lightweight or heavier medium, media based grow beds will still be considerably weighty.

It is also important to stick to the dimensions advised. Anything smaller than ¾ inches will clog your system. It defeats the intention of the media bed altogether.

Water Based Grow Beds
There are two major ways of growing in water using Aquaponics:

- **DWC** (Deep Water Culture)
- **NFT** (Nutrient Film Technique)

We have discussed the benefits and drawbacks of media based beds and now we are going to explore the water-based grow beds and their pros and cons of use in Aquaponics. Before we discuss the two major ways to grow in water (DWC and NFT), we will look at the basics of water-based gardens.

Water-based gardening can be placed in locations that the heavier media based gardens simply could not go due to their weight restrictions. Because the roots of your plants are submerged, or partially submerged in water, there is no need for flooding and draining, and aside from occasional evaporation, water levels should remain consistent.

Water-based systems will require that filtration systems be put in place to remove fish solids and maintain proper levels for fish and plants. Plants will need to be in specialized containers for proper support. Because a filter is incorporated into the process to remove fish solids from clogging the plant roots which will prevent oxygen and nutrient absorption, it is absolutely imperative that proper nutrient rich mixtures be added to the environment. Also, filters require cleaning to ensure that they continue to work properly. In addition to the filter, it is important to add an aeration system to ensure adequate oxygen levels are achieved.

NFT
In Nutrient Film Technique, the plants will be handing over a water-filled container that the roots of the plant drop into in order to drink and eat. The water in these containers is shallow, as it is just enough for the roots to get what they need.

In an NFT system, it is important to maintain the same temperature for the water as you do for the growing area. Because of this, it is difficult to maintain these systems outdoors regardless of the season.

DWC
In the Deep Water Culture system, the grow beds are flooded at all times. This system is much more productive than the NFT system. This system most closely resembles that of our ancestors, centuries ago, as it is a raft-like system of floating the plant holders in deep water.

PLUMBING
Utilizing a kit versus DO IT YOURSELF does not require any plumbing knowledge and techniques, however, DO IT YOURSELF plumbing requires much more skill and knowledge. Some things to keep in mind in DO IT YOURSELF and of course to be covered in an extensive DO IT YOURSELF manual, would be:

- Always be mindful of using products that are drinking water safe. If it says "non-potable", you cannot use it for the Aquaponics system. Did you know that garden hoses are not drinking water safe?
- Plumbing used to take water to the grow beds is often exposed to sunlight which can erode piping like PVC, which is the common piping choice due to its inexpensive cost.
- 90-degree angled piping will cause flow reduction and can have blockages occur due to water pressure and direction of flow.
- Be mindful of plumbing near electrical outlets. A leak could be extremely dangerous.

- Always keep in mind your plant and fish needs when developing your plumbing structures. Air and water are vital components and therefore the set up you choose for aeration, filtration, and water movement is of utmost importance to the life of the ecosystem you build.
- The entire amount of water in your system must be circulated hourly.
- An inexpensive way to ensure adequate oxygen supply is to have an air pump with a diffuser.

WATER

Water makes the Aquaponics system go round. Literally, without water, the plants and fish could not survive. We cover some form of Biology in most of what we do in learning how to be successful in Aquaponics, but now it's time to discuss another area of science. Hold on and get onboard our time machine, we are going back to chemistry 101 class to get a brief review. I loved science, but Chemistry was not my favorite. However, now that we are delving into the world of Aquaponics and creating our own ecosystem, the knowledge of basic chemistry becomes very important, especially when discussing water.

Without getting too heavy into chemical breakdowns and equations, this section will discuss the difference between acids, neutrals, and alkalis, so that we have a better understanding of pH balance.

Water (H_2O) is a compound made up of two Hydrogen atoms and one Oxygen atom. In water, Hydrogen ions and Hydroxide ions are of equal counts in Water and were formed when molecules divided up. Those molecules that lost a hydrogen become known as Hydroxide ions and that little hydrogen that left the molecule, connected with water molecules to make Hydrogen ions. Because there is an equal balance of the two types of ions, water is neutral.

Once this balance is thrown off in either direction, we get an acid or a base, also known as an alkaline. When a substance is dissolved in water, it will either become acidic or basic (alkaline). An acid will demonstrate a higher amount of Hydrogen ions than Hydroxide ions when dissolved in water. The opposite is true of alkalis. A base is a solution with more Hydroxide ions than Hydrogen ions when it is dissolved in water.

We measure acidity and alkalinity with a pH scale. What does this mean? A one unit value on the pH scale corresponds to a change in Hydrogen ions multiplied by 10 for each value change. Water sits on the center of the pH scale at a value of 7. Basically, anything registering a value lower than water on the pH scale is considered Acids and anything registering values higher than water on the pH scale are considered bases or alkaline.

So that you can get an idea of what might register a pH value of an acid or a base in comparison to water, I have listed some acids and alkaline you might be familiar with below:

Acids
- Battery Acid (pH= 0)
- Vinegar (pH= 2)
- Orange Juice (pH= 3)
- Black Coffee; Bananas (pH= 5)
- Milk (pH= 6)

Alkalines
- Eggs (pH= 8)
- Baking Soda (pH= 9)
- Milk of Magnesia (pH= 10)
- Soapy Water (pH= 12)
- Liquid Drano (pH= 14)

So why is this chemistry lesson so important? Both acids and bases can cause a lot of damage. Plants thrive in an environment that has a pH levels registering anywhere between a value of 6 or 7. Most people automatically think of acids as harmful substances, but bases contain a lot of salts and metals in them which can be highly corrosive. Distilled water is completely safe for your ecosystem as it is a neutral, pH value of 7. Due to the damaging effects that acids and bases can have on both your plants and your fish, and yes, even the plumbing and tank, it is extremely important that pH levels are tested regularly.

Water Weight
I use this excuse every time I get on the scale, but it is true, water weighs a lot! I mentioned this fact several times throughout the book so I will just touch upon this briefly here. Sometimes math can throw us for a loop, and like chemistry, math was not my favorite subject but it comes in handy in Aquaponics. Most people will automatically know how many gallons of water they may be able to fit in their tank or container but being aware of what each of those gallons weighs is very important. Did you know that one gallon of water is equivalent to eight pounds? Let's put those numbers in perspective. If you buy a 100-gallon tank to house your fish, this means that yes; it will hold 100 gallons of water. The tank full of water will then weigh approximately 1150 pounds! That is a major amount of weight and not every location can support this kind of weight and in Aquaponics gardens, water is not the only factor causing the scales

to tip. Additionally, it is important to consider square footage in regards to weight. The dirt outside can actually withstand up to 200 pounds per square foot and a basement made of concrete flooring could withstand half that weight.

Water Temperature
The climate that your fish prefer plays an important role in their survival and growth. There are not many plants or fish that can adapt to varying habitats. Temperature is a key factor in ensuring an ideal environment for your ecosystem. Water, important to both fish and plants, is very sensitive to temperatures and can easily heat up or cool down due to intervention from an external source that comes in direct contact with it. Additionally, the plants and fish in your Aquaponic ecosystem need oxygen to thrive, and in fact, without it would perish. They get their oxygen from water. Did you know that temperature can affect the amount of oxygen that is dissolved in water and therefore how much oxygen the pants and fish are getting?

During warm days, as the sun beats down on your garden, everything is feeling the effects of the heat. You may not think about it, but the rocks hold a lot of heat, the plumbing holds in heat, and of course, the tank itself. When the water comes in contact with hot surfaces, it will absorb their heat, which will increase the temperature of the water. Maintaining specific temperature ranges for your plants and fish in the ecosystem you created, is vital for it to thrive. In order to do so, use a thermometer specifically designed to measure water temperatures. It is important to check this on a daily basis, and if possible, several times per day. For those that choose to automate, this is one of those areas that I would recommend having an automated monitor because it will alert you the moment the temperatures rise or drop out of proper range. Temperature fluctuations happen constantly throughout the course of a day, whether your garden is inside or out, it will feel those changes. Not all fluctuations will be enough to make a difference that will knock temperatures out of range, however, keeping an eye on this is very important. If you live in an area where you don't experience a change in seasons, it's a bit easier avoiding drastic temperature changes, but for those of us that do experience the four seasons, extra measures, pardon the pun, need to be taken. Here are some suggestions:

- Whether you are heading into the hot summer months or the freezing winter months, insulation is a great way to moderate temperatures. Keep in mind that there are different types of insulation. In order to keep the pipes from getting too much heat exposure, an insulation that has a reflective outer shield is recommended. Other types of insulation (without reflective shield) would work well to maintain normal temperatures and

keep pipes from freezing. It is also suggested that tanks and/or containers have insulation if outdoors during the colder months and adding extra rocks (or other media) to your grow beds will help give them additional insulation.
- If your garden is outdoors and exposed to the elements of seasonal changes, it would help to put a temporary covering over the area, giving it a greenhouse effect.
- When water is moving, the energy produced is converted to heat and therefore will be less likely to freeze. To keep water movement constant, make sure to run your air pump at all times.
    - Maintaining a constant flow of water through the use of an air pump will additionally ensure that oxygen is circulating throughout your system.

Evaporation and Condensation

Warm, dry air attracts moisture and cold air repels it. When your tank water is exposed to the thirsty warm air, the air will start to drink from the tank. When the water disappears from the tank into the air it is called evaporation. Differences in temperatures can react in other ways. If the air is colder than your garden, it will cause moisture from the air to be released and build upon area surfaces outside of your garden like perhaps a window. If your garden is cooler than the air, this effect known as condensation will occur right in your garden. Remember, it is important to maintain balance in the ecosystem you create, so both conditions should be avoided as they can affect temperature fluctuations as well as dissolved oxygen levels. I will discuss dissolved oxygen shortly but first, let's discuss ways in which you can deal with evaporation and condensation.

- Having a thermometer that measures the humidity is a good start.
- Try to reduce how much water is exposed to the air. Placing a cover over the tank or container would help minimize exposure.
- You can cover areas of water in the grow beds as well by simply adding an additional couple of inches of media.

The amount of natural evaporation that occurs in the Aquaponics garden will only be about 1/10 of the amount that would occur in a soil grown garden so top off your tank water to maintain optimal water levels. Remember, you never have to replace the water in Aquaponics because doing so would waste all the natural nutrients produced in that water.

Dissolved Oxygen
The water temperature has a profound effect on the activity and behavior of fish. It also affects their feeding habits, growth rates, and reproduction.

As I mentioned earlier, water temperatures affect oxygen levels, which are not just important to fish but are also important to the plants and bacteria in your Aquaponic ecosystem. In order for aquatic creatures to get the oxygen they need, it must be dissolved in water. When those dissolved oxygen levels are lower than a reading of 5, fish in your garden will become stressed. The closer that reading comes to 2 and the longer it remains in that vicinity, stress is increased and the death of the fish will be imminent.

How do temperatures affect the dissolved oxygen levels? Warmer temperatures of water are saturated by oxygen and as a result, can hold less oxygen; therefore, the dissolved oxygen levels are lower. Colder temperatures of water are the opposite; therefore, the dissolved oxygen levels are higher. This conversation always reminds me of the three little bears and Goldilocks. One is too hot. One is too cold. Well, the fish want it "just right" also. Let's look at dissolved oxygen and temperature another way. In warmer water environments, fish metabolism speeds up, so the fish require more oxygen, but warmer water has low dissolved oxygen levels. As you can imagine, if the fish are desperately in need of oxygen, they begin to get erratic, kind of like someone who is drowning, they act panicked. In colder water environments, the metabolism of the fish slows down, so they need less oxygen, however, cold water has a higher level of dissolved oxygen. The high levels cause the fish to be tired and sleepy, which affects feeding habits and reproduction.

If your levels are low, in addition to monitoring and controlling temperatures to avoid issues with oxygen levels, using an aeration system will help to add oxygen to both the fish tank and the grow beds. When levels are high, it may be time to add more grow beds since the plants share the oxygenated water with the fish.

Adding plants mean more life using the oxygen and thus dissolved oxygen levels should decrease. Aside from your oxygen monitors reflecting a change in oxygen levels, you should see a change in behavior of your aquatic species.

Light

Light is essential to the well being of plants and for that reason, just as it is important to know about water, temperature, nutrients, and oxygen (vital knowledge to have in order to maintain a thriving ecosystem), it is equally important to understand the many facets of light, the difference in light sources, and how these variables affect life in your Aquaponics garden.

There is obviously a big difference between growing indoors and outdoors when it comes to light, and though there are natural advantages of the sun's light outdoors, there are still things that need to be taken into consideration when growing outside. This section will discuss proper lighting for both indoor Aquaponics and outdoor Aquaponics gardening.

Plants have a molecule called Chlorophyll which takes light and changes it into energy that the plants can absorb. Because the plants feed off the energy produced by light to grow, having the proper lighting is a must for them to thrive. Different plants require different amounts of light (called lumens) and different plants respond to different colors of light (called wavelengths).

Amount
First, it is important to recognize that the light people process with their eyes to see, is very different from the light plants need to process for their energy requirements. The wavelengths plants use are red and/or blue and are known as photosynthetically active radiation referred to by its acronym PAR. To figure out the optimal PAR quantity for your indoor garden plants, you must consider four things:

- Distance of light to plants
- Type of bulb
- Type of light fixture
- Amount of natural light present

If your garden is outside in direct sunlight, it is receiving 100,000 lux (lumens per square meter). Not all plants thrive in direct sun exposure like a cactus. Most plants require 20,000 lux which is what they would get on a day with normal clear conditions. Regular indoor lights found in a kitchen or office, may produce 400 lux. These differences alone explain why proper lighting conditions are so important. In an Aquaponics garden, a variety of plants can be grown at the same time and though you may have all warm weather plants or all cold climate plants, requiring the same temperatures and lighting, the height of the plants can also make a difference. A tall plant in the wrong location may block light from getting to some of the shorter plants. Because Aquaponics uses grow beds versus soil, you can easily rearrange the plants in your garden to ensure they all get the light they need.
Artificial lighting known as grow lights are a serious blessing but there are so many options out there and the price is not the only factor to consider. Dependent on the amount of area you need to light and which bulbs that you use, you will need to figure out how many of that particular bulb it will take to release the sufficient amount of energy the plants in your garden require. For example, if you have a 16 sq ft area garden, you would need only one high-intensity discharge HPS bulb of 400 watts. But if you chose to use fluorescent light bulbs, you would need five of the 125 watt compact to grow lights, ten of the high output 54 watt lights, or forty-two of the 40 watt standard fluorescent lights. You would need twice as many standard white 60 watt light bulbs than standard fluorescent.

Obviously, you would probably vote for buying and using fewer bulbs but you also need to consider price and how often you would need to replace them. Though fluorescent lighting requires more bulbs, the lighting fixture and the bulbs are relatively inexpensive, energy efficient, and take up a smaller amount of space. The issue is that they need to be replaced after only six months in order to get proper PAR for your garden. Also, fluorescents are not a highly effective PAR for denser gardens.

High-intensity discharge bulbs work the best and most closely resemble the light given off by the sun, however, it is expensive and so are the fixtures. Additionally, they are energy intensive and emit a lot of heat.

CHAPTER 5

Nutrient Cycle & Bacteria

Well, if you thought your science lesson was over, you were definitely mistaken. Chemistry 101 continues as we delve deeper into Aquaponics. It is time to learn about a major part of the circle of life in our Aquaponics system. Many seem to forget about this process and how it works when they attempt to simply define how exactly Aquaponics works. I imagine the same is true for how cow manure fertilizes the crops. How many people have actually thought about how and why manure actually helps the crops grow? I know I never gave it a second thought. I just knew it worked. Well, in Aquaponics it is extremely important to know how to fish poop feeds your plants. Because we are essentially creating an ecosystem, for the ecosystem to function like a natural ecosystem, we have to help it out and play "mother nature" in our garden. How can we help our fish to help our plants to help our fish? Well, Mother Nature does her job so efficiently that we don't think a lot about the inner workings and intricacies behind nature and how it is able to thrive. Hopefully, by the time you are done with not just this chapter, but this book, you will have a much better grasp and ability to help nature take its course in the Aquaponics ecosystem you create.

Ammonia, Nitrites, and Nitrates

Nitrogen is extremely important to the life of plants and through nitrogen is found in the air we breathe, it is not in a form that is usable to plants, so plants need to get their necessary nitrogen from an alternate source. Through the use of an Aquaponics system, plants can get nitrogen in the form that's suitable to them. This form of nitrogen is called Nitrate and it is made by bacteria that process Ammonia in order to grow. These bacteria are known as beneficial bacteria because they help achieve a positive outcome. Penicillin falls in this category. The more beneficial bacteria there is, the better it will be for your ecosystem because the fish release ammonia constantly through their waste and through their gills. The bacteria eat the fish waste and process it, turning ammonia into nitrates for the plants to get fertilized.

When you first start your Aquaponics system, there are specific stages you take in which plants and fish are introduced. Before both, you will simply have water that will not only be used to test and make sure the system flows properly, but also to test for temperatures, oxygen, pH, and other balances. One of these tests which you will run periodically is to test for ammonia, nitrites, and nitrates. Obviously, we can't see bacteria because they are microscopic, so this test is very important. You might be thinking at this point:

- How can we be testing for something that comes out of fish when there are no fish?
- How can we introduce plants before fish, when fish feed the plants?

Both are good questions. Water in the tank right now will show no ammonia, no nitrites, and no nitrates, which as the question above pointed out, is a problem for the plants. It is not only a problem for the plants but also for the good bacteria we want to grow in our tank. If there is no ammonia, there will be no bacteria. As I said, this is a circle of life and we play Mother Nature so we must intervene and add ammonia so that there is a food source for bacteria. We essentially step in as substitutes for the fish until they can assume the role on a regular basis. We must monitor the process regularly and once we get to a level that works for our plants, then we can introduce them to the system. In the meantime, as we add ammonia, bacteria appear and start to do their job of converting it to nitrate. Our measurements will gradually show a decline in ammonia and a rise in nitrites. This is the level between ammonia and nitrates. Bacteria are doing its thing, but we are not quite there yet. Next, measurements will show a decrease further in ammonia, a decrease in nitrate, and now an increase in nitrate. Soon our measurements will reflect the necessary nitrate levels to effectively fertilize our plants and this means that bacteria levels are growing. This is good news and should only take about two weeks to achieve. This bacterial process is known as cycling. You know that your garden is fully cycled when there is a continual process of transforming ammonia into nitrite into nitrate. The addition of fish should maintain a fully cycled system.

Let us go back to the question about fish being introduced after plants. You could technically add plants and fish simultaneously as long as the ammonia levels have officially dropped to zero. Ammonia is poisonous to fish and though they are the ones producing it, they cannot live in it. Fish in an aquarium would have a filter to remove waste products to keep levels safe but in Aquaponics, we need to rely on the bacteria and the plants to keep the water safe for the fish.

Ammonia kits will advise proper levels and amount to add to your tank to ignite bacteria production and eventually nitrate. As each level is achieved through the cycle, less ammonia should be added. Generally, liquid ammonia is used and administered with a dropper. Another way to increase ammonia levels is to drop a few dead fish in the water since decomposing organisms release ammonia.

The intermediary level of the cycle, nitrite, usually occurs in the second week of the process. Though it is not quite as lethal as ammonia, it is important to continue measuring these levels until you reach the third level, nitrate, where it is beneficial to plants and safe for fish. During this nitrite cycle, do not add fish because nitrites stop blood from oxygen absorption and can cause gastrointestinal, renal, and nervous system failures. Because oxygen absorption is prevented, fish can stop breathing regardless of the oxygen supply available in their water.

Plants and fish will both benefit from the nitrate level of the cycle. Once your plants are consuming the nitrates, and you are in full cycle, your measurements may reflect zero on all three levels of the cycle once again: ammonia, nitrite, and nitrate.

Mineralization

The process by which chemical compounds are broken down in organic matter for plants to utilize is known as mineralization. The media surfaces of your garden are highly conducive to this process since the water and waste from the tank flows through their regularly, allowing for the transformation into minerals and nutrients to occur naturally.

Other Additives

Ammonia is added to achieve cycling but there are other things you could add to help your plants flourish. Adding chelated iron powder will help the plants convert light to energy and look vibrant and full. Another additive would be kelp or seaweed because they have a host of vitamins and minerals needed by plants.

CHAPTER 6

How to Do It Yourself

Though it can be time-consuming and a bit daunting at times, it is extremely rewarding to be able to say you did it yourself and yes, it works! Believe me, it will be so worth it, in the end, knowing that you did your part for the environment and have the ability to successfully sustain your family through the food cultivated in an Aquaponics garden that you created with your bare hands!

Okay, so let's get started creating the environment for your own Aquaponic ecosystem. The main components of this ecosystem structure are the fish tank or tanks, the grow bed(s), and plumbing. Having the correct pieces for the puzzle and putting them together properly is vital for the living elements of your garden to flourish.

As you have read in the previous chapters, there are several options to choose from for your set up and functionality. This chapter will cover all of those options and functions so that you have the details needed to create your Aquaponic ecosystem as you wish to. The first thing to consider is the fish tank. It is important to determine whether you want to start big or small. If you want a small system, then a regular aquarium of about 10 or 20 gallons would suffice. If you want to go for the gold and go big, you need something with the capacity to contain a few hundred gallons of water, at least. This is not determined by what you wish to do with the fish (whether you are eating them or not), but how large a production of vegetables, herbs, and/or fruits you wish to have. Remember that no matter the size, any piece used in this puzzle must meet the standards of food/drinking water safety. If you do happen to find an aquarium that meets your capacity and cost requirements, you will need to take added measures to protect its inhabitants. First, it is wise to have a tank cover and secondly, additional filtration and aeration must be used to assist the plants in keeping the fish happy and healthy. These added items will protect them from algae, reduced oxygen levels, and overexposure (to light sources and peering eyes).

Some people choose to avoid the added expenses of the aquarium set up and enjoy taking on do it yourself to the level of building everything from scratch, increasing the amount of work and time involved for sure, but also the level of creative freedom. This avenue will allow for more control over your piggy bank as well as how much recycling and reusing actually gets incorporated into this process. There are numerous items you can use to build your tank and grow beds such as plastic barrels, IBC's, stock tanks, bathtubs, fish pond containers, and more. The list is long but what you choose depends on needs, size, whether you are indoors or out, appearance, cost, ability to locate specific supplies and ability to transport those supplies. So many variables!

Some Options:
One popular money-saving option is to use plastic barrels, otherwise known as 55-gallon drums. Though there are several color options for these however blue is the ideal option for the Aquaponics gardener due to its ability to block sun exposure and because blue barrels are specifically made to carry food products which makes it safe to use for your system. These barrels can be used for both the fish tank and the garden grow beds so they will need to be cut accordingly which means you will need to break out the jigsaw. As an option, these items are easy to find and easy to transport due to size and weight. Though they are not pretty to look at, they can be used inside or out. Some people choose to decorate the exterior when using indoors.

Another option is the IBC (Intermediate Bulk Container).

- Holds 275 gallons or more
- Wrapped in a metal cage
- Much more difficult to transform to a fish tank, sump tank, or grow bed—heavy duty tools needed!
- 48 inches tall on average
- Takes up a lot of yard space
- Need a truck to transport
- IBC tote kits are available at Aquaponics store
- To make building easier, you can visit backyardaquaponics.com to learn how

Stock tanks are made from sturdy plastic and can be found at agriculture or hardware chain stores.

- Considerably less expensive than an aquarium of the equivalent size which would cost about ten times more
- Fit in an SUV or van versus needing a truck
- Only 25 inches tall, making it ideal for the multilevel capability of grow beds over tanks and ease of access
- Can be purchased in assorted sizes
- A 50-gallon stock tank is usually about 12 inches high, which is an ideal height requirement for your garden grow beds
- The rounded shape of the stock tank is ideal for water circulation removing the ability to have dead zones that would likely occur in a rectangular aquarium set up

Specialty tanks like pond shells are made specifically for fish to thrive and can have over 1000 gallons in capacity. Additionally, they can be specially made with viewing areas so that you can see your fish. This can be a great option however it is important to consider that retailers in the United States are scarce still when it comes to Aquaponic specific items and therefore prices and shipping can be high.

As I stated earlier, the options are many and after you read this book or physically build your first system, you may come up with your own ingenious, creative ideas on how to set up your Aquaponics garden. You will have the knowledge to do so with confidence.

I will discuss how to create your system using stock tanks and also show you how to do so with plastic barrels in two formats: with sump pump and without. One format is a vertical, more compact set up that doesn't require a stand, and saves space, and the other format is a side by side setup that takes up more area. Keep in mind, when setting any Aquaponics system indoors, you must add proper lighting and maintain proper temperatures. Weight also needs to be taken into consideration. For your outdoor setups, you may want to consider some type of coverage like a greenhouse for added protection from the elements and pests. Another note if you want to cultivate plants which need to grow high and/or wide, you need to provide additional support and structures. Considering a pergola may be a good idea and they are not difficult to build if you prefer not to purchase one.

Here are some specifics on the various parts you would use:

Bulkhead Fittings & Standpipes
Bulkhead fittings are used in plumbing done specifically in liquid storage. They are made so that a connection can pass through a watertight wall. These items have three main components: The threaded male part that projects through the watertight wall, also known as a bulkhead; The threaded female part that screws onto the male part; and a gasket to form enough pressure to prevent leakage. A bulkhead fitting is purposely made to allow pipes to connect from to another for water passage. The standpipe is a pipe that is vertical and extends from a supply of water. This pipe is placed inside the bulkhead fitting. As the water rises in the grow bed, where your standpipe is placed and reaches the top of the standpipe, the water will flow over it and out of the grow bed.

Uniseal
Uniseal is a rubber O shaped gasket that fits right into a hole and can be used as an alternative to the bulkhead fitting accomplishing the same task of passing piping through a watertight seal.

PVC
PVC is the most commonly used piping for plumbing because it is inexpensive, easy to work with, and easy to find.

Irrigation Poly Tubing
Irrigation Poly Tubing is a very durable tubing used in irrigation however most cases not used in plumbing and therefore not safe for drinking water. Finding an exception in this category could prove very difficult.

Garden Hose
Garden hoses can be a great use for Aquaponics however you must be mindful of which hoses are non potable, like the green ones which are very toxic. If you purchase the hose in 5/8" diameter, it will coincide with most of the fittings you have in your system and it is flexible so allows you to run it easily from one place to another.

Vinyl Tubing
Black vinyl tubing is another great option for plumbing, however it is important to note that it needs to be securely attached to something, due to its tendency to move around when water pressure flows through it.

Corrugated Tubing
Corrugated tubing is the fancy looking black vinyl tubing that has coils in it to prevent kinking. This tubing is very common and easy to find.

Air Pumps
Air pumps come in many capacities however your Aquaponics system will need a specific air volume so purchasing one should be based on this criterion as opposed to water volume. These pumps are vital components to your system as they add much-needed oxygen to the water in your tank while circulating the water, which is also very important for the fish. I suggest purchasing one that has numerous outlets for more air flow.

Diffusers
Diffusers are made to divide the air that flows from the air pump producing smaller bubbles and a wider area of air coverage. Air stones and line diffusers are popular types of diffusers used in Aquaponics systems.

Water Pumps
Generally speaking, submersible water pumps are used in home Aquaponics systems. When purchasing a water pump, you need o make sure that the pump has the ability to circulate the entire volume of water in your Aquaponics system, every hour on the hour. The more powerful the better and though pumps are made for aquariums, it is more likely

that you will get the proper pump if you purchase from a store that specializes in hydroponics or aquaponics. One last note would be that you should always remove the mesh filter from the pump to allow adequate flow.

SLO
A solids lifting overflow is a type of standpipe that will remove the debris from the bottom of the fish tank while maintaining consistent water levels.

Timers
This a device to turn things on and off and can be set for automatic time frames and apply to flood and drain, lighting, and more. Specialty stores will carry ones that can be programmed to repeat cycles.

Indexing Valve
Used in conjunction with a timer that has repeat cycles, the indexing valve will move the flow of water from one inlet to many outlets and is commonly used when there are multiple grow beds. These valves based on settings will allow flow to one bed at a time and as one is done, it will close that outlet and open another.

Auto Siphon
An auto siphon is made to automatically drain a container when the fluid level rises above the rim of the siphon and requires no electricity. The most popular siphons used are loop configuration and bell configuration. When using a loop siphon configuration, tubing is looped from the bottom of the media bed to the point at which you want the flood and drain to occur. When using the bell siphon configuration, the bell is placed over the standpipe itself and drains once the water reaches the top. Basically, a siphon occurs when the water overflows the standpipe and drains until air enters the bottom of the bell breaking the cycle of the siphon. The Affnan bell siphon has a funnel shape at the top to increase the amount of water flowing through the siphon. Coanda drains are also used in the siphon process since it connects the lower section with the drain section using a 45-degree connector causing the water flow to remain high and reduce obstruction.

Here are some options for system design:

Aquaponics Design #1: 100-Gallon Stock Tank System
Supplies Needed:
- (2) 10-foot kiln dried 2x6 planks
- (2) 50-gallon stock tanks
- (1) 100-gallon stock tank

- (1) 1 x 3 board
- (1) 2 x 3 board
- (12) 8 x 8 x 16 concrete blocks
- (2) bulkhead fittings
- (2) Coanda drains with 2-inch lengths of PVC
- (2) Affnan-style standpipes
- (2) bell assemblies (2" PVC pipe and 2" PVC cap)
- (2) media guards
- (1) 25-foot 5/8" hose that is drinking water safe
- (2) female hose fittings
- (1) 400 gph (gallon per hour) water pump
- (1) plastic hose splitter
- (1) roll synthetic twine
- (1) air stone
- (1) ¼" vinyl air tubing
- (1) air check valve
- (1) small air pump
- 13 cubic feet of rocks from quarry

Tools Needed:
- Permanent Marker
- 1" spade drill bit, ¼" bit, and drill
- Miter saw
- Scissors

Start by preparing the frame. Place the two 2x6 planks on the ground about 4" apart. Place one of the 50-gallon grows beds on the planks, bottom side down. Mark, where the bottom of the grow bed, hits the planks to determine where to cut. Move the grow bed over about 4 feet and mark the planks again. Cut the planks with the miter saw and set aside. Trim the 2x6 scraps pieces so that they are 16 inches in length. Trim the 1x3 board and the 2x3 board into as many 16 inch pieces as you can. Next, position the fish tank and grow bed support system. Place the 100-gallon tank in the center of your space where it will be permanently positioned. Create two stacks of three concrete block stacks. Shim the planks with the 16 inch long boards you have cut. Next cut the holes in the grow beds to insert fittings. You will do this by turning the 50-gallon stock tanks upside down. Make a hole for the standpipe in the middle near one end using the 1" spade bit in the drill. The hole should be drilled in the bottom of each 50-gallon stock tank.

Assemble the bulkheads, Coanda drains, and standpipes in the beds. Assemble the bulkhead fittings in the hole through the bin. Put the male conduit connector through the whole first then slide the O-ring over the male pipe threads and then screw on the female conduit fitting. Stick the Coanda drain into the bottom of the bulkhead fittings. Stick the Affnan-style standpipe into the top of the bulkhead fitting. A 5 1/2" PVC pipe is a good length for connecting the fittings to the bulkhead. Position the 50-gallon stock tanks on the planks so the water will drain into the fish tank. These will be your grow beds. Place the PVC bell assemblies over the standpipes and slide the media guards over the bell portion of the standpipe drain.

Assemble the water pump and tubing. Cut the hose about 2 feet away from the male fitting. Cut two more lengths of hose about 7 feet long. Attach the cut end of the short hose to the pump. If the pump has a mesh or foam filter pad inside, remove it. Attach the hose splitter to the male end of the hose connected to the pump. Connect the female hose fittings to each of the 7-foot hose sections. Connect the 7-foot hose sections to the hose splitter. Make sure the splitter levers are turned in a direction that allows water to flow out.

Connect the hose to the fish tank and grow beds. Use the twine to connect the splitter to the fish tank. Use the twine to fasten the hoses so they will add water to the far end of each grows bed. You want the water coming in at the opposite side of the grow beds from where it will drain out. The length of twine should be sufficient enough to tie the hose along the side of the grow bed.

Assemble the air pump, tubing, and air stone by pushing the air stone onto the ¼" tubing. Clip a small portion of the tubing to use later on. Push the other end of the short length of tubing onto the opposite end of the check valve. Next, push the free portion of short tubing onto the air pump and place the air stone into the fish tank.

It's time to add media and water and turn the system on to conduct testing. First, rinse the stones one bucket at a time and add the rinsed stones to the grow beds. Add water to the system and turn the pumps on, adjusting the levers on the hose splitters to reduce the flow rate if necessary. If the flow rate is too high, your siphon cycle won't break. Once you see that everything is working properly and water tests are reading properly, you can move forward with plants and fish. This system should hold up to 15 fish at around a pound each when matured.

Aquaponics Design #2: Plastic Barrel
Supplies Needed:
- (1) 55-gallon BLUE barrel
- (1) 200 gph water pump
- Grow Medium
- (1) T fitting
- ½" PVC piping
- (2) #18 O-rings for grow bed connections

- (2) #14 O-rings for intake connections
- (1) ¾" PVC pipe 6" long for bell siphon
- (2) ¾" 90-degree elbow for the drain pipe
- (2) ¾" PVC pipe 4" long
- (1) ¾" male adapter threaded to slip for grow bed connections
- (1) ¾" female adapter threaded to slip for grow bed connections
- (1) ½" male adapter threaded to slip for intake connections
- (1) ½" female adapter threaded to slip for intake connections
- (1) ¾" to 1 ½" Bell Adapter
- (1) 2" PVC pipe 10" long for bell dome
- (1) 2" PVC pipe cap for bell dome
- (1) 3" PVC pipe 12" long for gravel guard

Tools Needed:
- Anything you prefer to use to cut holes into plastic PVC and slice barrels, like a Drill, Dremel or jigsaw
- 1/8" Drill bit
- 100% silicone and caulk gun
- Sandpaper (or rotary filing tool like a Bur)
- Sharpie

The barrel needs to be cut into two parts. Lay the barrel on its side and measure 12 inches from the top to cut around the barrel and remove one-third of it for the grow beds. The bottom two-thirds remaining will be used for the fish tank. After cutting, you want to smooth the edges with either sandpaper or a Bur, if you have one. Once you have smoothed the cut areas, wash out the barrels for added safety measures.

On the grow bed portion of your set up, you will need to make holes for the bell siphon and intake hose. Flip the bottom of the grow bed portion upside down and make your diameter measurements to match the actual parts being used. Once you have determined the size that the holes need to be to ensure a snug fit around pipes and hoses, use the Dremel to drill out your desired holes. Make sure you set the two holes on opposite sides of the grow bed container. Once holes are made, smooth out the cut surface.

Next, you will need to measure two holes to be cut in the fish tank portion of the barrel. One hole will be for fish viewing and access and the other hole will be for the power cord of the water pump. Some barrels have markings on them that tell you where the 30-gallon mark would be. If the barrel that you have purchased does not have this marking, simply measure about 16 ¾" from the bottom of the fish tank. This will be where you mark your water line. The next step will be to determine what shape you want for your viewing window. Some people have used fish or whale shapes, but an oval or circle will work just fine. Use a pre-made template or plastic plate to ensure that you outline the cutting line with a sharpie exactly the size and shape you wish. Remember to make sure that you set this area above the water level and leave a bit of space from the top as well (maybe two inches for both). Once you have done this, use your jigsaw, Dremel or whatever tool works for you, and cut out the viewing area. The next hole will be smaller since it is simply for cord passage, maybe the size of a plastic soup bowl. This hole will also need to be placed above the water zone. This should be followed by smoothing out the rough areas of your cut outs.

In order to attach the grow bed portion to the fish tank portion, you will need to make eight small holes that are equally spaced out around the very top of the fish tank. This will be attached to the grow bed with zip ties so that gives you an idea of diameter of the holes, but also means that you must place eight small holes on the lip at the bottom of the grow bed that line up exactly to the fish tank holes. Once you have done this, run the zip ties through each hole and tighten the grow bed to the fish tank. Cut the excess zip tie section off after you have secured everything together.

Now that the frame is built, you need to install the plumbing mechanisms. In order to do so, you will start by building your bell siphon. Take the male adapter and slip a #18 o-ring over the threads. Insert the adapter through the access hole that you have made in your grow bed. Slip another #18 o-ring over the top of the male threads. Screw the female and male adapters together ensuring that there is a tight connection. Slip a four to a six-inch piece of ¾" PVC pipe into the female adapter. The length will be determined by the water height so start at six and cut down to four if necessary. Slip the ¾" to 1 ½" bell adapter on top of the ¾" PVC pipe. To create an effective drain flow, it is important that the opening of the Bell is double the size of the pipe. Slide the PVC bell dome, 10" (can be adjusted to a shorter length if need be), over the drain pipe and the PVC gravel guard over this. For the side of the grow bed facing the fish, slide a piece of ¾" pipe into the bottom of the male adapter. Slide a ¾" PVC pipe and 90-degree elbow into the bottom of this pipe and then repeat with another ¾" PVC pipe and another 90-degree elbow. The next step is to build the intake mechanism. Just as you did for the bell siphon, you will make a watertight seal in the hole you created using the male and female adapters, ½" this time, and the #14 O-rings. Place the water pump in the bottom of the fish tank (run the electrical cord out of the rear hole you created) and connect it to the bottom of the ½" adapter with a piece of ½" PVC pipe. The pump line will run about ten inches into the top of the intake adapter in the grow bed. Attach this to a T fitting and cap any openings. It is important to drill a tiny hole into the horizontal section of the pipe to let some water out. Check the flow rate when testing and add another tiny hole or two, if necessary.

Now that your plumbing is in place, you will run the system with the water in the tank and check the intake flow rate, drain rate, and potential leaks. If the bungee holes have leaks, seal the leaks with the silicon. Once you are satisfied that your system is working correctly, you can add your medium to the grow bed and test for blockages.

Once all of this is complete, you may then move on to cycling the system for the proper introduction of your plants and fish.

Aquaponics Garden #3 Plastic Barrel with Stand, Sump, and Lighting

Supplies needed:
- 10 feet of one inch PVC
- 3 feet of three inch PVC cut into two eighteen inch lengths
- (4) slip elbows for one inch PVC
- (1) T fitting for one inch PVC
- (2) end caps for one inch PVC
- (2) eight foot 2x6 pressure treated wood that should be cut into (6) thirty-inch lengths
- (2) eight foot 2x8 pressure treated wood that should be cut into (6) thirty-inch lengths
- (4) ten foot 2x4 pressure treated wood that should be cut into (4) 64-inch lengths and (4) 33-inch lengths
- (2) ten foot 2x4 pressure treated wood that should be cut into (4) 54 ½" inch lengths
- (2) eight foot 1x2 pressure treated wood that should be cut into (4) 48-inch lengths
- (4) sixty-inch lengths of metal chain
- (2) twelve-inch lengths of metal chain
- (4) S-hooks
- 300 gph water pump
- 20 feet of ½" flexible non-toxic tubing (drinking water safe)
- Metal Clamps
- Metal C-clamp
- (2) forty-eight-inch fluorescent shop lights with plugs
- (2) cool forty-eight-inch bulbs
- (2) warm forty-eight-inch bulbs
- (8) cinder blocks
- Twine

- Box of 2" deck screws
- Power Strip
- Timer
- Aquarium aerator with four nozzles
- (4) air stones
- 20 feet of airline tubing
- (2) ¾" to ½" tubing barb bulkhead fittings
- (1) Uniseal for 1" PVC
- Aquarium heater for 100-gallon tank
- (4) BLUE plastic barrels
- A ¼ cubic yard of Kenlite (or another medium)

Tools Needed:
- Power Drill
- Drill bit ¼"
- Drill hole saw bit 1.75" and 1.375"
- Jig Saw

The first step in the building process is to prepare the blue barrels. Each barrel has a different purpose and therefore needs to be prepared differently. The first barrel will be prepared for use as a fish tank. To start, lay the barrel on its side and cut a rectangular hole in the center measuring 13" x 23". Next, you will need to drill a hole on the circular side of the barrel using a 1.75" hole saw. The hole should be located approximately 4" from the lip of the barrel and lined up with the hole that you cut on the side. Make sure any rough edges are smoothed. Make sure to wash the barrels. Place the 1" Uniseal through the hole. Next, you will need to cut the rectangular window in the side of the barrel for the sump tank as well. It is important that both the fish tank barrel and the sump tank barrel have securely plugged bungholes, due to the fact that they will be containing water and you want to avoid leaks. The third barrel is going to be used for the grow beds so you just need to cut the barrel in half, lengthwise. Measure 1 inch from the lip of the barrel and drill a hole, with the 1.375 holes saw bit, on the bottom of each of these halves. Thread the barbed bulkhead fitting through the hole in each. Attach it so that the ½" barbed fitting is on the outside of the half tank and make sure that the bulkhead is flush on the inside. The last tank will be used as a water reserve for topping off evaporated water in your system. For this, simply remove the top. It will remain standing upright. The water will be aerated and transferred as needed over time.

The next thing you will need to prepare is the frame that will hold the tanks and grow beds. Two of each length of 2x4 boards need to be combined. Use the deck screws to secure two 2x4's together to achieve

4x4's in length of 33, 54.5, and 64 inches. Create a V shape by attaching the 30-inch 2x6 boards and 30-inch 2x8 boards using deck screws. The mouth of the V created should be about ten inches in width. You will need to build 6 altogether. Position three of the V's face down (one on each end and one in the center) onto the 54.5 inches long 4x4, about 12 inches apart, to create the grow bed stand. Next, lay out the two 30 inch pieces of lumber so that they are parallel to each other, about 30 inches apart. With the V facing down, position one on each end and attach them to the 54.5-inch boards using the deck screws. Drill the screws through the outer edge of the V into the board on both sides. This will be used as the fish tank stand. Cinder blocks need to be set up at the corners of an area measuring 36 x 56 inches. Place the second set of cinder blocks on top of these. Take the 64 inch 4x4's and place them the 56-inch length of the area on the cinder blocks. The grow bed stand will sit atop of the 64 inch 4x4 with Vs facing forward. This should be flush at the edge of the 64 inch 4x4 putting the grow bed stands towards the front portion of the 64 inch 4x4. The fish tank stand will be placed at the back end of the 64 inch 4x4 with the V's perpendicular to the grow beds, flush to the back edge of 64 inch 4x4. Position a 48-inch length of 1x2 to the corner of the grow bed stand, keeping the bottom of the board flush with the bottom of the 54.5 inch 4x4. The 2-inch width of the board should be along the 30-inch side of the grow bed stand. Use deck screws to attach the board in place. Do this to all four corners. Attach a single screw to the top of each of this 1x2's with a small portion of the screw sticking out for light fixtures to attach to later on.

Now that the frame has been built, you can place the grow beds and the fish tank on their respective stands with the V's as support structures. The sump tank will be placed on the floor in front of the grow bed stand and supported by the remaining V facing down.

Now, it's time to work on the plumbing. Cut a short section of 1 inch PVC pipe, approximately 3 inches in length. Push this section through the Uniseal in the fish tank so that only 1-inch sticks into the tank with the remainder sticking out. Add an L connector to the end of this piece so that the next PVC pipe will go straight down along the side of the tank. Cut another piece of PVC approximately 4 inches in length and attach it to the L connector, ending about midway down the height of the fish tank. Add another L connector to the end of this piece to change the direction to head towards the Grow Beds. Cut a 4-inch section of PVC to slip into the L connector and travel beyond the edge of the fish tank. Add another L connector to the end of this piece to change the direction to wrap around the midsection of the tank. This will make the next piece of PVC travel along the length of the fish tank. Cut a 16-inch length of PVC and fit it into the L connector. This piece should end roughly near the midpoint of the long dimension of the fish tank. Add a final L connector to the end of the PVC to change the direction to point away from the fish tank and towards the grow beds. Cut a final 4-inch section of PVC and slip it into the L. It should end over the Grow Beds, running between the two halves. Add a T connector to the end of the pipe to split the flow between the two grow beds. If necessary, add a short section of PVC to each side of the T so that water flows into the grow beds rather than into the space between the two beds.

Using a ¼" drill bit, drill a hole into the end wall of each grow bed half barrel tank near the upper edge. This should be on the same side near the bulkhead fitting sticking out of the bottom. Attach a 24-inch section of ½" black vinyl tubing onto the barbed end of the bulkhead fitting in the grow bed half barrel tank. If needed, you can use a metal clamp, to secure this tubing on so that it doesn't leak from the barbed fitting. Thread a 12-inch section of twine through the ¼" hole at the top of the half tank. Twist the vinyl tube into a loop so that the other end of the tube end hangs above the sump tank below. Hold it in place by looping the string through the highest point of the tube and tying it in a knot. The highest part of the tube should be approximately 2 inches from the top lip of the half tank and this will be the high water mark of the grow beds. Do the same process to the other half tank. Using a metal clamp, attach the end of the remaining black vinyl tubing to the outflow of the water pump. Place the pump in the bottom of the Sump tank. Snake the tubing along the outside of the sump tank and grow beds and up the side of the fish tank so that it ends up at the opening of the fish tank. This will return the water from the sump tank back to the fish tank. You can attach the tubing to the fish tank using a metal C clamp.

Using one of the 18-inch lengths of 3-inch diameter PVC, center it on the hole in the grow bed that leads to the bulkhead fitting and the loop siphon. Holding this pipe in place, fill the bed with either of the suggested mediums discussed in this book until it is 1 inch below the rim of the half tank. Do the same for the second grow bed? Install the heater so that it rests in the fish tank. This can be dangled into the fish tank through the opening on the top. Run two lengths of airline tubing with air stones from the air pump to the fish tank. This will provide the necessary oxygen to your fish. Run two more lengths of airline tubing with air stones from the air pump to the extra water tank that will be used for topping off. This aeration will help dissipate the chlorine from the tap water.

From this point, you begin testing systemic functions, and then cycling. Once everything is all set, you may add your fish and plants. Once plants are added, make sure to turn on the lights and if you wish, set them to a timer to ensure proper amounts of day and night. The lights will be attached to the posts you set up on the four corners of your frame.

An Alternate Option to Media Bed Systems:

Aside from the various ways to create a media bed system, there are numerous ways to get creative with the Nutrient Film Technique also. This may be an option you are considering and many utilize PVC piping to create rows or even levels of grow beds in varying sizes. Depending on your set up, plumbing for these systems would differ greatly and would need to be adapted accordingly. In my opinion, these systems tend to be better suited for herbs and smaller vegetation. If used for vegetation that will become sizable, the plants will need to be transplanted at a certain point in their growth process. I prefer to maintain a system in which the plants can grow through their entire cycle.

Maintenance
Now that you have the basics down and your Aquaponics garden seems to be running smoothly, you will want to keep it that way so there are general maintenance steps to perform daily, weekly, monthly and seasonally. This chapter will cover these steps as well as advise on how to perform certain maintenance tests. I highly recommend keeping an agenda book where you maintain logs, to do list, supply lists, vendor contacts, and calendar. This will make life so much easier. Staying organized will remove stress factors like remembering what to do and when, allowing you to enjoy the benefits of a healthy, productive garden with an abundance of healthy fish.

Daily
- Feed fish
- Check water
    - Temperature
    - Level
- Check plants
    - Growth
    - Pests

These are important to check regularly because if the temperatures are off, it can greatly affect your fish including feeding habits. If food is put in the tank and fish don't eat it, it will accumulate and can raise the ammonia levels that are toxic to fish. A proper environment will have healthy fish eating all food within a five-minute time span. Checking the water levels is also important due to the potential evaporation. Distilled water is pH neutral, so it is the best option to top off the tank. Since everything in an Aquaponics system affects the other, you want to check on your plants too. Make sure there aren't any pests nibbling on your plants and check to see if any plants are ready to be harvested.

Weekly
- Check pH, oxygen, ammonia, nitrite, and nitrate levels.

- Check plumbing for any clogs and make sure everything is running smoothly.
- Prune plants.

Monthly
- Purchase supplies
- Purchase seeds
- Check pump and make sure everything is clear and running as it should be.

Seasonal/ Annual
- Change plants to correspond with the correct season
- Renew any licenses you may need (most expire annually, and each state has its own requirements)
- Work on budget planning for following season/ year
- Determine if you are going to expand or if you need to make more fish purchases
- Make any repairs to Aquaponics area such as greenhouse
- Harvest fish to eat or freeze for a later date

Pest Control
Your garden can be your answer to fresh healthy eating, "farm to table". You grow your garden to feed your family, not to feed pests. Even if your garden is ornamental, that beauty and all that work should not be wasted on pests. Here are some solutions:

- Fight fire with fire. Some bugs are indeed good bugs for your garden.
    - Ladybugs eat a long list of the most common garden pests
    - Lacewings are also known to eat most common garden pests
    - Praying Mantises love to eat and are great bug hunters.
- There are some plants that are insect repellants
    - Marigolds: bugs hate the smell and taste (especially mosquitoes and aphids)
    - Garlic and chives keep slugs away
    - Peppermint is a great ant repellant
    - Lavender deters flying and crawling insects and it smells great.

- Of course, you can always go with the traditional bug zappers, sticky strips, and/or a safe bacteria known as BT or Bacillus thuringiensis

Maintenance Tests

It is extremely important to take care of the ecosystem that you have created. If you care for your system, the system will return the favor to you in abundance. One of the best purchases you can make and ironically one of the less expensive items will be a freshwater master test kit. This kit will have everything included that is necessary to conduct enough tests, throughout the year, for pH, ammonia, nitrites, and nitrates and will take only five minutes of your time. Each kit will advise the proper way to conduct the test and the results desired. This section covers all of the tests that you will need to conduct and how to conduct them.

pH

Changes can happen very quickly in the system and therefore testing the pH balance is important each month. If the pH test demonstrates that the water is not neutral, meaning it is higher in either acid or alkaline, you will need to create balance again. In order to reduce the alkalinity levels because they are registering over 7.0 (neutral), you would need to add some acid to the water until the levels go down to neutral readings. The suggested acid additive would be hydrochloric acid which can be easily purchased at any home and garden improvement store. Instead of adding the HCL directly to the water in the fish tank, it is advised that you add it to grow beds so that they can do their necessary biofiltration process which will be much safer for your fish. It is also important to remember not to use products specifically made for Aquariums because of their tendency to have high levels of sodium which could be highly detrimental to your plants. The opposite can also occur and you may find that you need to increase your pH levels (lower than 7.0 neutral reading) because there is too much acid present in the fish tank water. Bicarbonate or Hydroxide compounds of potassium and calcium will aid in increasing your bases and reducing the acid readings. While they neutralize your levels, they work to improve the health of your plants because they are necessary nutrients for your garden. Again, the compound you choose should be administered through the grow beds and not directly into the fish tank water.

Dissolved Oxygen

As discussed earlier, there are definite signs that there is an issue with the oxygen levels in your fish tank water. Your fish may not speak with words, but they can tell you volumes if you pay attention to them and one clear sign that there is an oxygen deficiency is when the fish seem to be gasping for air and spending most of their time at the top of the water.

Either way, if the fish are acting funky, something is wrong in the water so you will need to run tests. If it is the oxygen versus one of the other levels being out of whack, simply run an air pump to increase air flow. Additionally, your plant to fish ratios may need to be adjusted by increasing your grow beds. A popular and efficient kit for testing the dissolved oxygen levels is made by Salifert.

You will also need to monitor your temperature, humidity, light and the water levels, as these can impact the readings of other things you are testing for.

Ammonia, Nitrite, and Nitrate

As discussed earlier, vital to the health of your plants and fish, maintaining a proper Nitrogen Cycle is so important. The same kit that advised to purchase for pH testing, will give you enough tests to conduct throughout the course of a year for each of these categories as well. If you find that the levels are not at zero which would be evident in a full cycle, then you will need to add minimal amounts of ammonia until the cycle completes and your readings reflect zero ammonia, zero nitrites, and either have nitrate or are in full cycle again reading nitrate at zero.

CONCLUSION

Thank you for making it through to the end of Aquaponics: Beginner's Guide To Building Your Own Aquaponic Garden System That Will Grow Organic Vegetables, Fruits, Herbs and Raising Fish With Your Own Aquaponics Home Gardening System. Let's hope it was informative and able to provide you with all of the tools you need to achieve your goals, whatever they may be.

The next step is to either purchase your Aquaponics kit or if you choose to go down the DO IT YOURSELF path, purchase a blueprint or design your own structure. Whatever path you choose, in order to embark on your first Aquaponics journey, you are now equipped with the basics to be successful growing your own Aquaponics garden and reaping the rewards of a bountiful harvest and healthy fresh fish to eat.

As you now know, Aquaponics is not simply about the food you eat but it is also about your contribution to the environment, how much money you can save, and how much pleasure and satisfaction Aquaponics gardening gives you when you accomplish your first harvest. I am hoping this book will continue to guide you along your journey as it can be referenced every step of the way. Always be mindful of the ecosystem you have created and all of the living organisms that inhabit it. Remember that you are stepping in as Mother Nature and the plants, fish, and bacteria are your responsibility to nurture and protect. As long as you do, they will be good to you in return and continue to feed you for years to come!

Finally, if you found this book useful in any way, a review on Amazon is always appreciated!

DESCRIPTION

In a world where we must be concerned with so many potentially negative occurrences environmentally, politically, or otherwise, and are surrounded by many potentially harmful things or vices that may or may not be out of our control, it is reassuring to know that there is one way that we can take back some degree of power over the outcome. It may seem insignificant in the overall scheme of things at first, but making the choice to read this book Aquaponics: Beginner's Guide To Building Your Own Aquaponic Garden System That Will Grow Organic Vegetables, Fruits, Herbs and Raising Fish With Your Own Aquaponics Home Gardening System and learn what you can about Aquaponics, will create the stepping stones you need to start the change you desire in your life and in your family's life.

Every little bit that we do can count and it can impact not only ourselves but the world around us in both a positive or negative way. The choice you make today can be a very powerful one. This book does not just offer a wealth of knowledge but invites you to begin a wonderful journey to a new lifestyle. This new lifestyle will give you the ability to control the freshness of the foods you eat and the choice of which foods you have readily available to prepare for your meals, without leaving your home. Choosing this path will give you the peace of mind in knowing that what you are preparing has not been contaminated and offers you and your family a healthy option. This journey will also pave the way for you to take control of your physical and mental health due to your dietary choices.

Aquaponics is a great way to produce your own fish and plants not just simply for the benefit of a meal or saving the expense you would have if bought at a grocery store, but it is also an excellent way for you to wage battle against major illnesses.

The benefits of choosing Aquaponics are numerous but most are not aware of how it helps on a global level. There are many companies out there helping to improve the sustainability of the world as a whole, especially in areas where the soil is not conducive to farming and there is a lack of water and food but what many people may not realize is that by doing Aquaponics at home, you are also helping the environment and can even help to improve the economy if you choose to expand this process into a business. Start your journey now by buying this book and you will reap the benefits easily, shortly thereafter!

In this book, you will find

- All the answers to your questions about what exactly Aquaponics is, how does it work and how does it differ from Hydroponics and Aquaculture. Is it really better?
- Everything you need to know to get started, whether you start with a kit or do it yourself
- This guide will explain in detail how to create the most ideal Aquaponics environment and the differences in using assorted types of grow beds, filtration, containment systems, plumbing, water, light, temperatures, etc.
- You will learn what types of fish and plants work best and gain a better understanding of their requirements and differences amongst the varying seasons. In addition to this, you will gain a good understanding of how to maintain your system so that you have a thriving ecosystem that is productive in providing sustenance for you and your family
- And much more!

GREENHOUSE GARDENING

Beginner's Guide to Growing Your Own Vegetables, Fruits and Herbs All Year-Round and Learn How to Quickly Build Your Own Greenhouse Garden

**by
Rachel Martin**

© Copyright 2019 by Rachel Martin - All rights reserved.

This book is provided with the sole purpose of giving relevant information on a specific topic for which every reasonable effort has been made to ensure that it is both accurate and reasonable. Nevertheless, by purchasing this book, you consent to the fact that the author and the publisher are in no way experts on the topics contained herein, regardless of any claims as such that may be made within. As such, any suggestions or recommendations that are made within are done so purely for entertainment value. It is recommended that you always consult a professional prior to undertaking any of the advice or techniques discussed within.

This is a legally binding declaration that is considered valid and fair by both the Committee of Publishers Association and the American Bar Association and should be considered as legally binding within the United States.

The reproduction, transmission, and duplication of any of the content found herein, including any specific or extended information, will be done as an illegal act regardless of the end form that the information ultimately takes. This includes copied versions of the work—whether physical, digital, or audio—unless express consent of the Publisher is provided beforehand. Any additional rights reserved.

Furthermore, the information that can be found within the pages described forthwith shall be considered both accurate and truthful when it comes to the recounting of facts. As such, any use, correct or incorrect, of the provided information will render the Publisher free of responsibility as to the actions taken outside of their direct purview. Regardless, there are zero scenarios where the original author or the Publisher can be deemed liable in any fashion for any damages or hardships that may result from any of the information discussed herein. Additionally, the information in the following pages is intended only for informational purposes and should thus be thought of as universal. As befitting its nature, it is presented without assurance regarding its prolonged validity or interim quality. Trademarks that are mentioned are done without written consent and can in no way be considered an endorsement from the trademark holder.

INTRODUCTION

Are you looking for a new way to garden? Do you want to create your own space where you can grow plants and collect produce year round? If so, you have come to the right place!

In this book, we are going to learn all about greenhouse gardening. As you probably know, greenhouses are special outdoor buildings made specifically for growing plants. They allow you to create the perfect environment for growth in any season. They are good for any climate but are especially helpful in areas where the weather takes away the possibility of year-round, outdoor gardening. They can be used to grow any type of plant—from vegetables and herbs to tropical plant variations.

We will start by explaining the benefits of greenhouses. We will learn about the different types of greenhouses and what they are best used for. We will then look into how you can build yourself your very own greenhouse. We will talk about DIY options, greenhouse construction kits, and more. We will go through a planning checklist that will help you to decide exactly how you want your greenhouse to be designed. This checklist will touch on things like location, size, flooring, framing, and much more.

After we cover everything there is to know about greenhouses, we will look into how you can garden inside them. We will start by discussing what you can plant in a greenhouse. In this chapter, we will provide you with a wide variety of ideas to help you figure out what you would most enjoy growing in your new year-round plant home.

We will then move into the topic of planting seeds. We will go through the best places to buy your seeds, the best soil to use, and the best containers to plant them in. After covering seeds, we will talk through how to care for the plants in your greenhouse after they sprout from the ground. This chapter will contain a large amount of useful and necessary information—from lighting and temperature to pollination of plants in a place without bees. We will talk about how to time your plants so that they are able to provide a year-round supply of crops.

After we have covered everything that you need to know in order to create your greenhouse and grow healthy plants inside of it, we will go through a list of common problems that can happen in a greenhouse. We will look into how you can solve these problems, as well as ways to prevent them from happening in the first place.

When you finish reading this book, you will be a greenhouse expert—even if you have never stepped foot inside of one of these buildings before. You will know why greenhouses are talked about so often, as well as all of the benefits that can come from growing your plants inside of them. You'll be able to build a greenhouse from the ground up and create a harvest from simple seeds. You will know how to solve any problems that may arise so that your plants always remain healthy and strong. If you are ready to open your mind and discover a new way to enjoy gardening, turn the page and begin your greenhouse gardening journey now!

PART ONE
BUILDING YOUR OWN GREENHOUSE

CHAPTER ONE
Why Should I Build A Greenhouse?

Before we dive too deep into building your own greenhouse and doing all of your plantings inside of it, let's look at why greenhouses are so great. In this chapter, we will look into the top ten advantages to greenhouse gardening. We are sure that by the time that you reach the end of these ten reasons, you will be daydreaming about the moment you get to start on your own greenhouse adventure.

1. The main and most obvious benefit of greenhouses is that they give you a longer growing season. Depending on how you design and construct your greenhouse and depending on what type of climate you live in, this extension could add a couple of months onto your typical summer-growing season, or it could extend your time to the point that you could garden all year long. Greenhouses extend your growing season because they provide the perfect growing atmosphere inside of them. This makes you as the greenhouse owner and designer in charge of how long your gardening season lasts—when typically, that would be left up to the weather.

2. If we're playing off of this first reason, greenhouses also give you the ability to keep your plants safe during inclement weather. Normally, if there were a thunderstorm and flash flooding, you would have to sit inside just hoping that your plants would survive the night. If there were strong winds coming through, you would have to worry that they would break the stems of your plants and prevent them from being able to produce a crop for the season. With a greenhouse, your entire garden is protected by a roof and sturdy walls. No weather will be able to affect your plants when you keep them safe.

3. While speaking of keeping your plants safe, greenhouses also help to protect your garden from critters that live in the wild. Most people who grow gardens have sad stories about rabbits eating their tomatoes before they could get to them to harvest or birds flying down to steal their strawberries before they are ripe enough

for humans to eat. With a greenhouse, no animals or critters are able to get inside. This means that your produce will be safe up until the moment that you are able to harvest from your plants.
4. Outdoor gardens are not only affected by furry critters like rabbits and birds. They also are often discovered by bugs. Some types of insects, like bees and ants, should be welcomed in the outdoor garden since bees help to pollinate plants and ants help to turn the soil, allowing extra nutrients to reach the roots of the plants. Other bugs, however, can be pests to a garden. Some bugs may eat your crop or even cause your plants to become diseased and die. Because a greenhouse is a closed-off space, it helps to keep your garden safe from these unwanted bugs as well.
5. With those pest-like bugs in mind, we will move into our next greenhouse advantage. When you grow a greenhouse, you do not have to worry about unwanted bugs in your garden. Because of this, you have no need for pesticides and other dangerous bug-related chemicals in your garden. This helps you to avoid the use of chemicals in your garden and helps to keep your produce safer.
6. Without pesticides, you are one step closer to growing an organic garden. If you are interested in going organic and growing a garden that is completely chemical free, a greenhouse makes this a much easier task to handle. Typically, in a greenhouse, you will be doing some sort of variety of container gardening. Because of this, you can choose high-quality soils and growing media that eliminate your need for chemical fertilizers. With no need for pesticides or chemical fertilizers, having an organic garden inside a greenhouse is easy to do.
7. A greenhouse also allows you to grow any type of plant that you would like to grow. Normally if you live in a climate where you can only garden during a few specific months out of the year, you would have a hard time growing something like tropical plants. You would have to keep them inside your home most of the time, and if you wanted to have an entire tropical garden, this would not work out well. With a greenhouse, you have a dedicated space for your plants that do not have to follow along with the climate you live in, so you can grow anything.
8. Greenhouses really live up to having "green" in their name. With a greenhouse, you have the ability to be more environmentally friendly than you can be with a regular, outdoor garden. This is not only because the design of the greenhouse reduces the need for heat and extra lights, but you have more control over your space, so you are able to be more conservative with water as well. It also gives you a chance to add a larger amount of plants to the Earth, which is a great environmentally friendly effort as well as the things that we have already mentioned.

9. Because greenhouses are able to have their environments perfected and they do not have to rely on unreliable factors like the sun or air temperature in order to survive, plants in greenhouses are able to thrive. This means that if you are growing fruits, vegetables, or herbs, your plants will be able to provide you with healthier food than they would be able to if your garden was outside.
10. Scientists have found that if you are surrounded by living things like plants, your rate of depression and anxiety drops dramatically. Being surrounded by greenery is great for stress relief and helping with mental illnesses. It is such a powerful force that many therapists include greenery in their offices and some psychologists even hold group therapy courses inside of greenhouses. With a greenhouse, you can feel these stress relieving feelings whenever you need to. This is a great tool for fighting any type of stress or mental illness, especially seasonal depression since you have a warm, living green place to go to all year round.

Overall, it is clear that greenhouses have many benefits. Just in case it is not clear yet, let's look into why you should grow a greenhouse and how these benefits can affect your life. We believe that every single person on Earth would benefit from growing plants in a greenhouse, but it would especially help you if you happen to find yourself in any of the following situations or scenarios.

If you love to grow plants but do not have space, build a greenhouse. It will provide you with all of the space you need to be dedicated solely to your plants. If you love to garden but find yourself only able to grow plants a few months out of the year, build a greenhouse. It will give you the ability to extend your growing season as long as you want to, even if you want your garden to keep growing on a year-round basis. If you have sad experiences of losing garden crops to summer storms, build a greenhouse. You will never have to experience this loss of your hard work ever again. If you are looking to grow an organic garden, but you seem to struggle with insect infestations or poor soil, build a greenhouse. These factors will be able to be controlled with ease with no need to bring chemicals into the mix—if you are looking for a cheap way to feed your family, build a greenhouse. It will allow you to grow enough food to provide for a large amount of what your family consumes. The cost of the greenhouse will soon be outweighed by all of the money that you save from not having to buy as many groceries. The fewer trips to the grocery store are a great positive note as well. If you are looking to be more environmentally friendly, build a greenhouse. It will allow you to put more plants on the Earth as well as to conserve energy and water in your gardening practice. If you want to grow a type of plant that your specific climate does not support well, build a greenhouse. You will be able to grow anything inside of it that you would like to grow. If you struggle with stress or mental illness, build a greenhouse. Being surrounded by living greenery that you work hard to support will be a great tool in helping you cope and thrive in life.

Overall, we believe that building a greenhouse and growing a garden inside of it truly could benefit the life of any person. Throughout the rest of the book, we will look into the details of how to do this, and these benefits will continue to be weaved throughout the pages. If you are not convinced that growing a greenhouse is right for you yet, we are sure that you will be by the time you reach the last page of this book.

CHAPTER TWO

Types Of Greenhouses

In this chapter, we are going to look into the different types of greenhouses. It is important to know about the different types of greenhouses and what they are best used for so that you are able to choose the best type of greenhouse for you. We are going to start by looking into the different structures that greenhouses can be made in. We will then look at some specific details that you may want to consider when deciding how exactly to build your greenhouse for the biggest personalized benefit. Lastly, we will look into different building techniques that you can use to build the greenhouse of your dreams.

In order to start creating that greenhouse dream, let's look at the big picture. There are seven different structures that greenhouses are usually made in. They include post and rafter, a-frame, gothic arch, hoop house, lean-to, window, and cold frame. We will explain each of these greenhouse types in detail below.

A post and rafter greenhouse takes the structure that you may consider as a typical house structure. It has a pointed roof like you would imagine seeing in a child's drawing of a house. This is a very common structure for greenhouse building. It is typically made with wooden posts and has strong support in its roof with rafters as well, which is where it gets its name of course. One of the best things about it is that it is very strong. If you live in an area with strong winds that happen fairly often, this greenhouse structure may be a good choice for you. It is also a good structure space if you have a large, open area to build it in since it does take up more space than other types of structures. Because it takes up more space though, it also provides you with more space for planting.

Next, let's look into a-frame greenhouses. These are simple to build because they have fewer materials than other types of greenhouses. It is a triangular structure, so its two side walls lean together to make a point at its top. This makes its walls and roof basically the same pieces. This can make it harder to fit as many plants inside since the walls are so slanted, but you can overcome this obstacle pretty easily with some creative shelving ideas. It is nice because it is easy to put together. It is still a good structure for if you have a large open space for it to go in, similar to the post and rafter models. The main difference between these two models is that an A-frame greenhouse is lighter and easier to build.

A gothic arch greenhouse is a common option as well. The frame of this greenhouse is built in a semicircle shape. This frame can easily be covered with plastic sheeting, which helps the building process to be pretty simple. It again requires a large open space for it to be built in. The rounded shape makes this type of greenhouse a particularly good choice for people who live in snowy or rainy climates because the snow and rain have nowhere to get caught on the rounded surfaces.

The hoop house structure for greenhouses is pretty similar to the gothic arch structure. It is again easy to build, and it is again good for areas that have a lot of rain or a lot of snow. The qualities that are unique to the hoop house are that it is the cheapest structure of greenhouse to build, so it is a good choice if you find yourself to be on a tight budget, and it is a little bit easier to squeeze into small yard spaces if you do not have enough room to build one of the previous structures. It is, however, less sturdy than the options that we have looked into before it.

Next, let's look into a structure called a lean-to greenhouse. A lean-to greenhouse can be built to be leaning up to another structure on your property. This allows for one of the walls of the greenhouse to simply be the wall of the structure that it is built up against. This is both an affordable way to build a greenhouse as well as a great option for small spaces. It is even better protected from strong winds since it is built up against such a stable base. One thing that is not so great about this structure of greenhouse is that it is harder to heat. This is because some of the heat may be lost on the wall of the home. It also has to be built on the south side of a home because that is the place where it will get the best sunlight.

Our next two greenhouse options are for people who do not have space in their yards to build a new greenhouse structure. They are much smaller and do not provide all of the same great benefits as larger, walk-in greenhouses do, but they are still better than not being able to grow in a greenhouse at all.

The first small greenhouse option is window greenhouses. This works best if you have greenhouse windows, or bay windows, that stick out from the walls of your house. If you have these types of windows, they are great for plants because the sun can hit the plants from more than just one angle. These windows do a pretty good job at providing a greenhouse effect for your indoor plants. If you do not have these types of windows, you can use something called a window farm. Window farms can be used in almost any window. It is basically a hydroponic system that grows plants in water in a structure that is made to sit in your window sill. These are small, and you cannot have a large garden in them, but they still provide the greenhouse effect for people who do not have big yards or even bay windows to grow their plants in.

The second small greenhouse option we will look into is something that still sits outside like a normal greenhouse instead of sitting in your home's windows. These greenhouses are called cold frames. Cold frames are greenhouse boxes that you can plant in. They provide the same effects that a larger, walk-in greenhouse would provide but instead of being able to walk inside of them to garden, you lift up the top and garden from them like a typical garden box. They are a cheap option for outdoor gardening that can still greatly extend the growing season that your area's natural climate provides you with.

Now that we have looked into the different types of greenhouses, it is time for you to decide which structure is right for you. If you have no backyard but have beautiful bay windows inside of your home, you may want to consider a window greenhouse. If you have a large outdoor space with an open field on the south side of your home, you may want to consider a Post-and-Rafter greenhouse. To decide what type of greenhouse you would like to build, start by looking at your space. What do you have room for? Where could your greenhouse go? Then, consider what you want from your greenhouse. Do you want to grow enough food to feed your family? Do you just want to try out some new herb growing techniques? Lastly, consider your skill level. What can you manage to build by yourself or with the help of your friends and family? After taking these factors into consideration, go back and look into the details of each of the greenhouses we talked about. Which one best suits your needs?

Picking the type of structure is not the last step in deciding what type of greenhouse to build, however. Next, you need to decide which route you would like to take in order to build the greenhouse of your dreams. You could go the completely DIY route, you could get a greenhouse building kit, or you could get a used greenhouse and turn it into exactly what you want it to be.

First, let's look at what to consider before deciding to go the completely DIY route when building your greenhouse. If you choose this option, you need to be prepared to do a lot of work. Building a greenhouse from scratch will require a lot of knowledge as well. It will help if you or someone you know has a background in construction. If you know how to go to Home Depot and get the type of wood you need, and if you know how to measure and cut wood, you will be off to a good start. You will need tools for this route as well. If you do not own the correct tools you could borrow them from a friend or see if your city has a tool library that they could be borrowed from; just make sure that you know how to use the tools that you need in a safe manner.

If building a greenhouse from scratch seems like it might be a little bit too difficult, but you still want to do some of the work in putting things together and using tools, you could consider buying a greenhouse kit. These kits come with everything you need to build the greenhouse structure from the boards to the nails and screws. To build these, you just need to know how to read an instruction guide, and you need to have access to tools. Again, you could reach out to a friend or family member or a nearby tool library for this necessity. Greenhouse kits are going to be a little bit more expensive than if you chose to build your greenhouse completely on your own, but if this is a building level that you are more comfortable with then the added price may be worth the extra benefits.

Lastly, let's look into what to do if you are really not comfortable building a greenhouse from scratch or from a kit with just the pieces and an instruction guide, but you still really want to make your own customized growing space. In this scenario, you could buy a used greenhouse and simply turn it into exactly what you want. In this case, the structure is already put together for you but you are still able to do a little work, and you are able to make you very own greenhouse space. This option may cost more than the previous two options, but if you are unable to put a structure together on your own, then this may be the best way to go about building your own greenhouse.

When you are considering what type of greenhouse to build and exactly how to do it, you need to look at the structure shape and the way that you are going to make it, but there are some other factors to consider as well. First, you will want to decide if you want to build your greenhouse out of wood or out of aluminum. Aluminum can be easier to put together, but wood posts are typically sturdier and will last longer, especially if you live in areas that can have strong winds fairly often.

You will also need to decide if you want glass or polycarbonate panes. In the past, glass was the most popular option. Recently, however, more people have been choosing to build with polycarbonate panels. These panes hold up better, and they are able to insulate your greenhouse better than glass. Glass lets in more light, but the light that polycarbonate panes let in is diffused, so it is actually a better light when looking into the growth of plants. The only advantages that glass possesses are that it lasts longer if it is not broken and that it does not need any specialized treatments, while polycarbonate panels do. When looking into this decision, decide if you will be able to handle the upkeep that comes with polycarbonate panels. If you can, they are the best choice with your plant's health and ability to thrive in mind.

Another option is to consider if you would like to build your structure as a half-brick greenhouse. These greenhouses are built with brick on the bottom where light does not really need to come in, and glass or polycarbonate panes on the rest of the structure. This allows for a sturdier base. It helps the greenhouse to last longer and also provides a nice aesthetic look to the structure.

With all of these options in mind, you should be able to pick out the type of greenhouse that is best for you. You can choose the size and shape that will work best for your area as well as the building plan that you are the most comfortable with. You can decide between aluminum and wood as well as between glass and polycarbonate. You can consider half-brick or typical greenhouse structures. With all of these choices made, you will be able to imagine the greenhouse that is absolutely perfect for your space and for your needs as a gardener.

CHAPTER THREE

Planning Your Greenhouse

Now that we have looked into how to plan the outside of your structure, we need to learn about how to plan the inside of your structure. This is the space that your plants will grow in and the space that you will see whenever you are out taking care of them. It needs to be beautiful and functional. In this chapter, we are going to look into some things that your greenhouse needs to be capable of, as well as what you need to plan in order to make these things work. We will look into location, size, air flow, humidity, light, heating, cooling, flooring, and glazing. We will also look into a few additional things you need to keep in mind when planning your greenhouse like safety and when to secure it from the wind.

First, when starting the process of planning your greenhouse, you need to make sure that you have chosen the type of greenhouse that you are going to build. This will make the rest of the decisions that you are about to make it much easier. Make sure you look back at the information that we covered in the last chapter to choose the type of greenhouse that is perfect for you.

Next, you will need to choose where your greenhouse will be located. Typically, the south side of your home is the best place to put a greenhouse. This is because it will get the best and most sunlight in this location. Be sure when choosing your location, though, that there will be nothing that blocks the sun from reaching your greenhouse. For example, if your yard is bordered by tall trees and the south side of your property never sees the sun, then your property is an exception from the fact that the south side is typically the best for greenhouses. If you do not have space on the south side, it is also okay to choose a different location. You want to ensure that you get to create a perfect greenhouse—no matter what its location is. The most important thing to consider is that the space receives a decent amount of direct sunlight throughout the day.

You also need to figure out how big you want your greenhouse to be. You will want to think about the big picture while you are making this choice. How many plants you would like to grow this year is one thing to consider, but you will also want to think about how many plants you could see yourself growing ten years down the road. You will probably want to build your greenhouse big enough to fit your dream garden so that later on you do not have to regret making it too small. You also need to consider the space that you have available when you are making this decision. Do you have enough space in your designated location for a large greenhouse or do you need to build a structure that is on the smaller side? Do you want to take up your entire designated space with the greenhouse or would you like to leave some outdoor area to enjoy as well? When you look into answering these questions for yourself, you should be able to decide how big you would like the greenhouse that you are building to be.

Now that we know the basics of the greenhouse structure and its location, it is time for us to move our planning inside. The inside of your greenhouse needs to create the perfect environment for the plants that you are most wanting to grow. Because of this, when you are planning the interior of your greenhouse, you will be looking mostly into its functionality. You certainly can plan the looks of the inside of your structure, but this is nowhere near as important as how well it performs. Let's start looking into how to design the inside of your greenhouse in a practical and functional way by looking at air flow. Airflow is needed to ensure that the plants get what they need. Plants breathe in a way that is the opposite of humans. Humans breathe in oxygen and out carbon dioxide. Humans need fresh air to supply oxygen where they are breathing, because breathing back in the carbon dioxide that they breathed out will do no good for sustaining life. This same principle is true with plants. Plants need carbon dioxide in the air so that they can breathe it in. When they breathe out, they release oxygen. Oxygen is not good for sustaining the life of the plants. Because of this, the air in greenhouses needs to be circulated just like it is naturally outside so that plants are breathing in the things that they actually need in order for them to survive.

Airflow in greenhouses is achieved mainly through the use of fans. There are quite a few options based on types of fans and the location of fans that you will need to plant out, however. Each of these options comes with its own specific set of benefits. You will need to decide what will work best in your structure and for the plants that you are most wanting to grow.

You can arrange your fans in something called a parallel layout, which means that all of the fans are on the same side of the greenhouse and lined up parallel to each other. When they are turned on, they blow the air in the same direction which causes the air to circulate around the whole greenhouse. This method for fans is best in areas that are on flat land as it does not work well with hills.

If your greenhouse is on hilly land, you may benefit more from a fan arrangement called the series method. This is an arrangement of fans that starts at the outside of the greenhouse and moves toward the middle. It again helps to move the air in a circular motion around the greenhouse structure.

Next, let's look into the different types of fans that you can choose from. The first type of fan that is commonly found in greenhouses is called a basket fan. Basket fans are very powerful and have wide slots. They are strong fans, so they are able to circulate air well, but when they are used in sequences, they do not always provide a uniform stream of air. This can cause some plants to get a lot of airflow and others to get none at all. Shrouded fans are an option as well. They are able to provide more consistent air flow to all plants. They are also great for conserving energy, so if you are looking to "go green" with your greenhouse, shrouded fans could be a great choice.

After you choose a fan type, you will have to decide if you want your air flow to be vertical or horizontal. Both methods have their good points and not so good points. Vertical air flow, for example, helps to ensure that the temperature of the greenhouse stays even throughout the entire structure from top to bottom. Horizontal airflow is better at making sure that the humidity levels are consistent among every area of plants in the greenhouse.

Next, let's look into cooling and heating. We know that these are two of the most important factors to look into when designing a new greenhouse. The purpose of a greenhouse is actually to extend the growing season of your plants and your garden, and one of the biggest ways that they can do this is through temperature control. When you can control the temperature of your greenhouse, you do not need to rely on the natural climate in your area for the health and success of your plants. Let's look into some things that you can do to your greenhouse so that you are able to control the temperature well.

First, let's look into greenhouse heating techniques. One of the simplest ways to make sure that your greenhouse stays warm is to make sure that it is built well. Make sure that it is in a location that gets a lot of sunlight and that it is made from a material that allows heat to enter inside. You can also make sure that your greenhouse has no cracks that could let breezes of cold air come in.

If you live in an extremely cold climate, you may need to consider some more heating techniques. You could use a greenhouse heater to apply heat inside your structure. You could also consider using solar panels on top of your greenhouse to collect energy for heat so that you could continue along the environmentally friendly path that your greenhouse idea started.

When you live in a cold area, you will need to plant for these things during the design process. Consider installing a heater or solar panels right away so that your plants are never hurt by painfully cold temperatures.

If you live in a climate that gets extremely hot during certain seasons, you may actually need to find ways to cool it down. The first thing to try when your greenhouse begins to get too warm is to cool it down with the fans that you use for air circulation. If this does not work, you could consider some sort of ventilation in your walls. If this also does not work, you can buy a cover for your greenhouse to give your plants a break from the heat that the sun provides them with.

When designing your greenhouse, you will want to make sure that you have the option to use these methods if you live in a very warm climate. You can consider walls that can be rolled up partially to allow for ventilation. You'll want to make sure that your design includes fans. You may even want to consider having a cover ready for the days that you know your greenhouse will get too much sun and therefore too much heat.

Next, let's look at the humidity in your greenhouse. If your greenhouse is too humid, you will want to make sure that you are using the horizontal fan method. This helps to circulate the air directly around the plants so that the humidity does not sit in them for too long. Another way to design your greenhouse so that humidity is never an issue is to have flooring that drains well. This will make sure that there is never excess water in your greenhouse that could lead to too much humidity in the air.

The flooring of your greenhouse is also important. As we mentioned earlier, it is important to have floor drains if you think that humidity is going to be a problem because of the climate that you live in. Besides this, though, there are many things to keep in mind when choosing a greenhouse flooring material. Let's look into the different types of materials that are commonly used in greenhouse flooring as well as what each different choice is good for.

Next, let's look into the different types of greenhouse floors as well as what each different type is good for. One popular flooring type for a greenhouse is concrete. Concrete is easy to walk on and easy to keep clean. It is also easy to slope so that you can get good drainage in your building. To have a concrete floor, you will probably have to have a concrete slab made before you build your greenhouse.

You can also have gravel for the inside of your greenhouse. This is typically done with weed cloth so that weeds do not grow through the bottom of your flooring. The gravel is then dumped on top of that and is a few inches thick. This is a good choice if you want a more natural look. It is also a good choice if you want the option of adding extra humidity because you can spray the flooring with water and the extra water will not be slippery, but it will also stick around so that it is able to add to the humidity in your greenhouse.

Similar to the gravel flooring, some people also have landscape rock as flooring inside of their greenhouse. This has all of the same benefits that the gravel flooring has, it is just a little fancier and a little better looking. You could also choose to make your floor out of brick. This again makes a really sturdy base similar to the concrete flooring, but it also allows for added humidity similar to the rock and gravel flooring. Brick floors are also very sturdy and lasts a long time.

If you are on a tight budget, you could choose to make a floor out of mulch in your greenhouse. Mulch is not the best greenhouse floor because you cannot clean it. It works well and is fine to walk on, but you will need to replace it as soon as it gets dirty or too wet. You do not want the mulch floor in your greenhouse to introduce near your plants.

There are also some companies who sell greenhouse flooring. These words can be made of materials like rubber. These floors are often really nice to have because they are made specifically for greenhouses. They are typically easy to walk on and drain well. The downside of them as they may be expensive as they are made specifically for greenhouses and nothing else.

Will also want to look into the glazing that you use for your greenhouse. Glazing is the material that covers the outside of your greenhouse. It is the plastic, or glass, or polycarbonate material that keeps your plants safe, keeps the temperature warm and humidity in, and overall makes your structure the greenhouse that it is. Choosing the right type of glazing is an important choice, so let's look into the different options and what their biggest benefits are.

First, let's look into the glass as a glazing material. Glass is a nice material because it is strong and lasts a long time. It only ever breaks down or needs replacing if it breaks. It also does a good job of letting light in. However, it has some downsides as well. It is really expensive to replace as if the glass on your greenhouse brakes you basically have to just pay for it all to be replaced again. It also allows direct light to go straight into your plants and does not diffuse the light as it enters, so it's not as good for your plans as other types of glazing that allow for diffusion of light.

Next, let's look into polycarbonate. Polycarbonate glazing is strong, and it allows for light to be diffused as it enters into the greenhouse. This is really good for the plants that you are growing. It is a durable material, and it lasts a long time. However, it has the downside of having to be treated with deliberately every once in a while so that it keeps its nice color and functionality.

The last type of glazing that we will look into is called the poly film. A poly film is a cheap option for glazing, which makes it a great option for many people who are on a tight budget. It works best in warm climates because it is not the best insulator. It does, however, work well if you do not need your greenhouse to the insulated extremely well. Sadly, it does not last as long as the other materials either. It is basically just a good choice if you need something cheap for the time being while you wait to get something nicer later on.

Next, let's look into the safety and security of your greenhouse. If you choose to have a greenhouse that is made of lightweight materials, you would need to make sure that it is safe in the wind. To do this, you will need to think about using greenhouse stakes. You can put these stakes through the corners of your lightweight material and into the ground. This will help to keep your greenhouse from blowing away in inclement weather.

Overall, it is clear that there are a lot of things to keep in mind when you are choosing how to build your greenhouse. There are even more things to keep in mind when you are looking into the inside of your greenhouse and the functionality that it will need to have. You will need to look into the temperature that your greenhouse will need to be as well as how to allow that to happen. You will need to figure out how to keep the humidity levels where you need them to be. You will need to look into heat and cooling. You will need to look into the floor that it drains well and that it is the material that you prefer. You will need to look into glazing and choose which material is best for what you can afford. You will also need to make sure that your greenhouses safe and secure and inclement weather. If you keep all of this in mind while you are designing a greenhouse, you will end up with a greenhouse that works well for you in any situation.

CHAPTER FOUR

Greenhouse Essentials

Congratulations! You have gotten through the hard part of planning your greenhouse. You have figured out the structure that you want to use. You know where you are going to put your greenhouse. You know what it's going to look like on the inside and what features you needed to have so that it can function well. Next, let's start looking at some of the fun stuff. Let's look into greenhouse essentials. These are added features that you can put into your greenhouse to allow it to do every purpose that you needed to do. These features can help you to optimize your plant growth and health.

One fun greenhouse essential is an irrigation system. An irrigation system is a device that water's your plans for you. It is typically a set of tubing or hoses that runs throughout your greenhouse near all of your plans. It has things that are almost like mini sprinklers on it. These little sprinklers go off at certain times of the day, scheduled by you, to water your plants. You can set them up to water your plants for a certain amount of time. For example, you could tell them to start spraying water for 5 minutes straight. You can also tell them when to turn on. For example, you could tell them to turn on five times a day. In some cases, you could even tell them which five times a day you would like this to be. For example, you could tell them that you want them to turn on at 5 a.m., 8 a.m., 11 a.m., 2 p.m., and 5 p.m. They are a customizable machine that can save you a lot of time when you would have been watering your plants for hours each day though.

Irrigation systems are cool because they allow you to set up how much water to give to your plants. It's not like a simple sprinkler that turns on, and you need to remember to turn it off when your plant has had too much. You can turn it on to only spray a little bit for your tropical plants, or you can turn it on to completely soak your vegetables. It's customizable and can fit your goals with any type of plant that you have.

Irrigation systems can also be very environmentally friendly. This is because they are very precise with their watering and they do not waste much water. They can add to your conservation efforts to help you to save water. They can help make your greenhouse even more "green."

Another essential that you may need to have in your greenhouses lighting. Typically, greenhouses provide all of the access that a plant needs through the sun. However, if your greenhouse is not in the location where it gets enough sun or if you have plans that need excess sun during a time of year where your area of the world does not get much done at all, you might need your own nights.

The type of lights that you will need to buy depends on the type of plants that you are boring. For example, there are certain types of plant lights that are made specifically for growing flowers. There are other types of plant lights that are made specifically for growing seedlings.

And that you know how to pick the right type of light for your plant. Not all lights are the same. You cannot just take out light bulbs from your kitchen lamp and put it in your greenhouse. This will not help your plants to grow. You need "grow lights" to help your plants to your best ability. Let's look into these lights, how they work, and what you should know before you buy them below.

Let's look into fluorescent lights. Fluorescent lights are the lights that you typically see in stores or schools, so they may look familiar to you. They are a good choice for people who own homes and have their greenhouses on their property because they are energy efficient and should not make the electric bill go up to high. They are made up with a blue light, which makes them good for growing seeds. They also do not get very hot, so they are able to be placed right next to the seeds, and they will not be able to burn them.

HID, or high-intensity discharge lights, are a common trait as well. These are very bright lights that can help a lot of plants grow at the same time. They work best in large greenhouses with high ceilings. This is because they can help a lot of plants at the same time and because they should be placed high above the plants because they get hot and you do not want them to burn your plants.

A lot of people use high-pressure sodium lights in their greenhouses as well. These are another type of HID lights. These lights have a positive note of lasting a long time, but they have the negative note of not being the best for your plants. This is because they are closer to the website of the light spectrum and not the blue side. This makes them not as good for growing plants as other lights that are closer to the blue side of the spectrum.

With all of these options, you should be able to choose what type of light to design your greenhouse with. This information shows you which lights are good for which causes, and how far away they should be placed from the plants. If you are greenhouse does not have adequate sunlight, or if you live in a climate that goes through times of the year that the sun is not out for long, you may want to consider some of these light choices.

The thing that is essential to your success in growing inside of your greenhouse is shelving. You also want to plan and design your shelving so that you are able to use it to its best ability. Later in the book, we will look into shelving and how to use the space in your greenhouse creatively, but for now, let's just look into it a little bit.

You will need to choose what type of shelving you would like to use in your greenhouse. You can use resin as shelving if you want something that is durable, plastic, and long-lasting. You can choose to use wood shelves if you want to build something yourself. You could also choose to use metal shelves for something that is sturdy. You want to make sure that your shelves are sturdy, durable and that they will not tip over. If they are tipping, you might want to secure them to the wall or to the ground. It would be really sad if a shelf tipped over and all of your plans were lost. Because of this, you need to take your shelving seriously and make sure that it is the best type of shelving for your space. You will want to have shelves that fit in your space and allow you to optimize the use of your space as well.

You may also want to have some sort of natural pest control as a greenhouse essential. This does not have to be chemicals, especially if you are looking to keep your greenhouse and your garden organic in nature. You could use a sheet of mash near the door to make sure that no bugs follow you in when you come into the greenhouse. This would be a good way to keep bugs outside so that you do not have to worry about chemicals later on down the road if your plants happened to be infested by bugs.

Another greenhouse essential that is small but something that you really need and that is something that you might forget about, is a thermometer. You will always want to know how warm your plants are. This will help you to be able to allow them to be successful. It will help you to know if they are too hot or too cold and if you need to add extra heating or cooling efforts to your greenhouse. Make sure that when you are designing your greenhouse, you have a thermometer right away. This will help you from avoiding many unnecessary struggles with temperature and plants along the road.

Are designing your greenhouse, you may also want to think about how you are going to clean it. Especially if your windows are made of glass, they will look dirty really fast. You also do not want your greenhouse to get dirty or moldy because you want your plants to say how the inside of it. You also do not want it to get dirty because you want it to last a long time and you want to treat your new creation for a while. Because of this, while you are designing your greenhouse, you might want to consider having an area for your cleaning supplies or creating a cleaning kit to have inside. This could include things that will help to clean your windows, your walls, or your floors. It could help to make sure your shelves are clean. These efforts will not only protect rain house, but they could help protect your plants from diseases, molds, and bacteria as well. Another really simple thing that you might forget about is containers. Containers are what you are going to be growing most of your plants in. When you are growing in a garden inside a greenhouse, you will need an assortment of different sized containers for your different size plants. You may want small containers for planting seeds. You may want larger containers for your larger plants. You may want trays for plants that are litter-related or can go near each other. You will want to make sure that your containers that you pick outfit on your shelves and that they look nice in your greenhouse so that your overall look can be aesthetically pleasing.

Another greenhouse essential may be a specific place to plant your plants. Potting plants can take up a lot of space. It can be a messy process when you start to involve soil and seeds. Because of this, you might want to have a special place to do it. This will keep you from having to plant plants inside of your house. It will avoid a lot of unnecessary messes. Because of this, you may want to have a bench or table where you can start your plants whenever you need to. This could even have a little storage space to keep extra containers, seeds, or soil if you have enough space to do so. It could really make your greenhouse into a perfect growing and gardening atmosphere. It could allow you to have everything you need to start plants and see them through all the way until harvest inside one small building.

We mentioned this earlier a little bit when we were talking about cooling your greenhouse, but another greenhouse essential could be shading covers. You need a shade cover when it is a hot summer day and when your plants are getting too much sun. Without this, your plants could actually die from getting too much direct sunlight or too much heat. You do not want to allow this to happen. To avoid this, you could have shade covers ready from the moment you design your greenhouse. You could have a special place to keep them, or you could have some sort of shade cover that is already attached and just needed to be stretched out to cover the top of your greenhouse. With this added essential, you will be protected from one of the easiest ways to lose plants in a greenhouse.

Another greenhouse essential that you will want to make sure you have a Spence. This kind of goes back to structure, but it is a little thing that you need to remember to have. It might be something that you forget when you are looking at the big picture, but it is very important—so let's look into it. You want to have vents so that your plants can get the air that they need to. Vents can help with both cooling and air circulation. Cooling and air circulation are both extremely important in the life of plants in a greenhouse. If plants get too hot, they will not make it. If plants do not get enough carbon dioxide to breathe in, they also will not make it. Because of this, but can be a huge tool and keeping your plants alive. Make sure that you have vents in the walls of a greenhouse that you can open and close. You do not want them to be open all the time because that may make them major greenhouse cold in the winter. You will want them to open and shut, and you will want them to be a part of your greenhouse right away in its first design.

Overall, you can see that greenhouses have many essential pieces. You have a lot to think about when you are designing a greenhouse. The things that you have to think about do not stop with the outer structure or even with the indoor design. They lead to you needing to think about the little things that you need to have ready inside of your greenhouse. These things can be a part of the structure like the vents that we just talked about, or they can be something as little as a cleaning kit. No matter what these essentials are, they are all equally important. You need to make sure that you were thinking about things like irrigation systems, lighting, and even space to do things like planting seeds. If you include all of these essentials into your greenhouse, you will have the perfect space where you can do everything you need to do and where your plants can survive and succeed. These essentials will create the perfect greenhouse atmosphere for you to design.

CHAPTER FIVE

Maximizing Your Greenhouse Space

Now that we have looked into everything that you will need to make your greenhouse the perfect environment based on your space and climate and for your favorite plants let's look into how you can maximize the space inside of it. This is especially important if you have a small greenhouse that you are planning to build in the small space that you have available. It is important for bug greenhouses as well, though. No matter how big your greenhouse is going to be, you more than likely want to fit as many plants as possible inside of it. There are a few different things that you can do to make sure that you are using every little bit of space that your greenhouse can give you.

One of the most important tips in making sure that you will be able to use every space that your greenhouse has to offer is to plan ahead. You need to know how you are planning on making this work before you start. That way, if there are certain benches that will work better to plant on, for example, you can get the correct ones from the start. It will also help because you will know that a space-saving greenhouse has been your goal all along, so you will not need to reframe your thinking on your interior greenhouse design.

One way to maximize the growing space in your greenhouse is by using movable benches or shelving units. If your benches or shelves are moveable, you can actually plant in up to ninety percent of the space inside of your greenhouse. This works by only leaving enough space for one aisle to walk through the inside of your greenhouse, and the rest of the space is completely filled with plants. You then move the shelves or benches in order to get to other areas of the greenhouse. This can make your plant care a little more time consuming, but the added growing space can be worth the extra effort.

You could also consider having two sets of different leveled benches to plant on. One set would be a typical height and would stay in place at all times. The other would be on wheels. It would be shorter, and it would be able to roll right under the other bench. In this system, you would roll the lower bench out into the aisle during the day so that it could get adequate sunlight. You would then roll it back underneath at night or whenever you needed to walk throughout the greenhouse.

You can also maximize the space in your greenhouse that you are able to use for planting by using the floor space that you have available. Typically, the floor space in greenhouses is just empty and almost wasted space. If you place plants all around the floor, you will be able to almost double your growing space while giving a function to that previously purposeless space.

Similar to using the floor space, you can use the space above your plants as well. To use this space, you could install hanging rods toward the top of your greenhouse. You could then use these rods to grow plants inside of hanging baskets. This would allow you to use the space in the air above your plants that were previously completely empty. It is another way to maximize the use of every space inside of your greenhouse.

It is not only hanging pots that can maximize the use of your vertical space, however. There are many tools available on today's market that allow you to partake in what is called vertical gardening. Vertical gardening maximizes vertical space. It is extremely popular for people who want to have large gardens but do not have much space. These same tools and ideas can be used inside of your greenhouse. You can use special shelving techniques, pot holders, and more to make sure that you are maximizing your vertical space as much as you possibly can.

When you are maximizing your vertical space, however, there is something that you need to look out for. You need to make sure that all of your plants are still getting adequate lighting. You do not want to place vertical gardening tools or potholders in places that will cause them to block the sun that the plants that you have growing on your benches will need. If you really need to use your vertical space but find yourself blocking a lot of much-needed sunlight, you could consider adding additional lighting inside of your greenhouse to make sure that all of your plants are getting all of the sunshine that they need to grow and thrive.

You could even consider something called under bench production. It is the process of growing plants under the benches that hold your other plants on top of them. This process is not like the moveable benches because these plants really never need to come out. To grow plants in this area, you would need to have extra lighting underneath your benches. The lighting would need to be a variety that can be close to growing plants because there would not be a lot of space available between the lights and the plants when they are already confined to a certain space underneath a bench.

Another way to make sure that you are maximizing your growing space inside of your greenhouse is to ensure that you have chosen the right type of container to grow in. If you choose containers that do not work well together on benches, you might be losing growing space. If you choose containers that have too much space for the plant that is inside of them, you could be losing growing space from this choice as well. When you choose what type of growing containers to use, you will want to make sure that they are both the right size for the plants that will be in them and that they sit nicely next to each other on the benches so that no unused space is left in between containers. Typically, square containers that are made for planting work well for this. Trays are also a good choice since they basically turn the whole bench into a planting space so that no space is lost to container edges at all.

Crop scheduling can be a good tool for not only your production but for your greenhouse space maximization as well. If you are scheduling your crops, you know when one plant will be ready to harvested and when it will need to be replaced by a new seedling. This is an extremely helpful tool in seeds that only produce one crop like celery. If you know when your celery will be ready, you can have a new seedling ready to replace it in its same spot. This will help you not to have to lose space to the new group of crops, and it will immediately help you know how to fill the hole that your harvest just created.

Greenhouse zoning can help you to maximize your space as well. Typically staging is used as a convenience to the gardener and an organization tool, but it'll definitely benefit the amount of growing space that you have available as well. When you are zoning plants, you will want to put them near other plants that have the same needs as them. For example, if you have five types of plants that need the same strong light on for many hours of the day, you will want to place them next to each other. This gives you extra space because it allows you to press all of those plants close to each other under the one lamp. If you have them spread out, you would probably end up having to give each separate plat their own light as well as some extra empty space so that the light would not shine on plants that would be hurt by it. By allowing you to place all of the plants close together and making sure the light touches them but no other plants that do not need it, you will save quite a bit of space from going unused.

Overall, it is clear that there are a lot of different ways to maximize the space inside of your greenhouse. As we mentioned earlier, it is important to maximize your space if you have a small greenhouse, but also if you have a large one as well. You do not want to have to miss out on any available growing space. When you are planning out how to use your growing space to its full potential, come back to this chapter for ideas and information. You can maximize your space through things like benches, organization plans, and zoning. You can use your vertical space by planting in hanging devices and by planting on the floor. You can ensure that you have great space saving containers and trays and you can be ready to plan your crops. All of these things will allow you to plant as much as your greenhouse can possibly hold. These things will help you to get the most out of the structure that you are planning to build.

CHAPTER SIX
Seasonal Preparation and Care

The main reason why you are building a greenhouse is probably that you want to extend your growing season. In order to do this, there are a few things that you will need to do. When a new season comes, you will need to prepare your greenhouse to help the plants inside of it succeed. In this chapter, we are going to look into everything that you have to do to prepare your greenhouse for the upcoming season. This information will allow you to use your greenhouse in the way that you plan to use it. If you can make sure your greenhouses ready for every season, you can ensure that your plans will have success no matter what the temperature is outside.

First, let's look into what you need to do to winterize your greenhouse. We are going to start in winter because it is the most common season that people use greenhouses for. This is because, in most areas of the world, winter is not the best time to grow plants outside in the garden. It is, however, a great time to grow inside of a greenhouse if you know how to winterize your structure.

The first thing that you will want to do is make sure your greenhouse is clean and ready for the winter. Winter is not a great time to be opening doors or taking a lot of trips in and out of your greenhouse. In the winter, you don't want the cold air to enter when you walk into your greenhouse, so you should make sure that you were going in and out as little as possible and as fast as possible. Because of this, you want to make sure that your greenhouses all ready for the winter before the winter comes. That way, you don't have to be moving shelves in and out, taking plants in and out, or anything else that will cost you to open the door more than you need to.

Cleaning your greenhouse may not be the first thing that you think of when you start the process of winterizing, but it is the most important thing to start with. Because, after you begin the other winterizing methods that you will need to do, you will already be done with the simple stuff. If you think that you will have to rearrange your greenhouse or take anything in and out of it, this is the most important place to start.

Next, you will want to make sure that there are no places in your greenhouse that could allow cold air to get inside. You will want to look at the walls and make sure that there are no holes. If there are holes in the wall, you will want to patch them. You will even need to look at your windows and doorways during this process. You will need to make sure that your door is lined up correctly so that it cannot allow cold air through cracks that may be around their edges. You will want to make sure that any of your windows are shut tight. You may want to check on the ground of your greenhouse to make sure there are no cracks or gaps as well. If you see cracks are gaps in any of these spaces, you will need to cover them.

If your greenhouse has vents that allow for additional air circulation in the summer, you will want to make sure that these are closed or covered as well. If your vents do not close tightly, you can cover them with a plastic window treatment to make sure no cold air will be able to seep through its holes.

If you live in a particularly cold area, you may need a heater inside of your greenhouse to keep your plants healthy in the winter. You will know if your greenhouse needs a heater if the sun is not enough to keep your plants warm during the colder months. If this is something that you will need, it is important that you get your heater set up and make sure that it is working well before the cold air hits your area. You do not want your plants to be affected by a freeze before you have the chance to protect them with the heater.

When you are thinking of how you are going to heat your greenhouse, make sure that you remember to keep in mind the size of your structure. If you have a large greenhouse, some heating systems may not be able to provide enough warmth to cover your entire large space. Make sure that you are able to check how much square footage the heater will cover and that it matches up to the square footage that your greenhouse has before you decide to purchase the device.

If you heat your greenhouse in the winter, it is also a good idea to think about having a backup heating option. If your power goes out one night, you do not want to have to lose all of your plants just because you were not completely prepared for the things that could go wrong. You could consider having a battery powered back up heating system in case struggles like this ever does appear.

Aside from heaters, you can also help to keep your greenhouse warm through the use of insulation. If your greenhouse is insulated well, not as much cold air will be able to get inside of it. How do you insulate a greenhouse that has to have walls thin enough to allow the sunlight through, though? You can use certain linings on your greenhouse walls that help to reflect light and heat. These will help to keep warm air in and cold air out.

One important thing to remember when you are winterizing your greenhouse is just because it is cold outside does not mean that your plants do not need fresh air. You still need to use fans to circulate the air in your greenhouse and ventilation is necessary to some level, even in the cold. This is because plants cannot survive solely on the oxygen that they breathe back out into the air. They need carbon dioxide as well. If they breathe up the carbon dioxide in the greenhouse and they are not given any fresh air, they will not have what they need in order to survive.

When the long, cold winter ends, you will need to start preparing your garden for spring. This may at first feel like you are just undoing everything that you did to winterize your greenhouse, but it is much more than that, and it is very important to the health of your plants and the success of your crops.

When spring comes, you may want to start your preparation in the same way that we started the winter preparation; cleaning. Typically, greenhouses are taken care of less during the winter mainly because the big focus of the gardeners is to keep the plants warm, not really to keep it looking nice. You can start by making sure that your greenhouse is clean, anything that you no longer wish to use is removed, and the setup is what you would like to see it stay as throughout the next growing season.

You will then want to make sure that your plants are getting lots of fresh air once again. Make sure that the fans are up and running well, uncover or open up all of the vents, and even open up the windows if you have them. A long winter with minimal fresh air is hard on plants, so giving them some clean air is an important step in the spring preparation process.

After getting your greenhouse ready for spring, you will need to start thinking about summer. Your spring greenhouse should work the same as your summer greenhouse unless you need to use certain types of cooling techniques. You could consider using a shade cover on your greenhouse. This would be a good thing to get ready before the sun gets too hot so that you are prepared when the time actually comes when you need to use it.

After summer, you will need to start preparing for fall. For fall preparation, you will basically just be starting to think about your winterization techniques. Make sure that you are ready early in case winter decides to show up sooner than it is expected.

Overall, there are different types of preparations that you will need to do for every season of the year. These preparations will allow you to keep your greenhouse as the perfect environment for your plants and their success throughout the entire year. There is a very large amount of work to do to prepare your greenhouse for winter, but preparations for the other three seasons requires minimal work. If you follow these guidelines while you are getting your greenhouse ready for each season, you should be able to keep your plants happy and healthy all year long.

PART TWO
Growing in Your Greenhouse

CHAPTER SEVEN

What to Plant in Your Greenhouse

We have talked about everything you need to know in order to build your greenhouse. We've talked about the structure as well as the interior. We've talked about everything that you need in order to allow your greenhouse to be the perfect environment for your plants. We've talked about how to maximize the space in your greenhouse, and we've even talked about how you can prepare your greenhouse for the different seasons of the year. Now, it's time to look at the reason why you are building a greenhouse. In this chapter, we are going to learn about the different types of plants that you can grow in a greenhouse. We will look at fruits, vegetables, herbs, tropical plants, and hydroponics.

First, let's look at fruits. You can grow fruits in a variety of ways in a greenhouse. You can grow them in containers or tray, and you can also grow entire trees inside of greenhouses. Growing fruit trees is not probably something that you think about when you think about greenhouses and what can be grown inside of them. However, greenhouses were actually created to grow orange trees inside them. They used to be called orangeries. Orangeries were made so that oranges could be found throughout the entire year in areas of the world that have cold weather such as England.

You can grow fruit trees in your greenhouse today just as well as people used to when they were still called or injuries. In order to grow fruit trees in your greenhouse, you want your greenhouse to be warm and humid. You will want to make sure that the temperature never goes below 50 degrees and that you are watering your plants often. You could even consider using a misting system as fruit trees like light watering in short intervals. Growing fruit trees inside of greenhouses is a fun option because a lot of areas in the world are areas that fruit trees cannot be grown at all if they are outside. Greenhouses make it possible for people who live in these areas to grow the trees of their own.

If you are not looking to grow an entire fruit tree and wants an easier and more commonly used option, you can grow fruit plants like strawberries as well. Growing fruit plants inside of greenhouses is an easy way to gain nutritious fruits for you and your family all year long. They can be grown in greenhouses just like they're growing outside. It's often even easier to grow food in greenhouses than it is from an outdoor garden because wild animals love them, and wild animals are not able to get your fruits when they are grown in a greenhouse.

From fruit trees and small plants, you can also grow fruit bushes. This allows you to grow plants like blueberries, raspberries, and blackberries. You can grow this in a greenhouse fairly easily. They do take up more space than a small plant like strawberry would, because they are tall and need large containers for their long roots. However, you are able to fit them in many different sized greenhouses pretty easily. To fit them best, you can consider not putting them on the shelf at all. Since bushes are tall, you can put them right on the ground, and they would still be had a good harvest level for you.

Overall, if you are looking to grow fruit in a greenhouse, you have many ways to do it, and most of the ways are pretty simple. You can grow fruit with trees, bushes, or plants. All you will need to be able to do this is a warm greenhouse with a good humidity level; this is really easy to achieve through sunshine and watering your plants often.

Oh, let's look into growing vegetables in a greenhouse. Vegetables are one of the most commonly found things pro greenhouses. They are easy to grow in small spaces. They are also easy to grow in containers. This makes them great for growing on bunches in a small space like a greenhouse. They're also commonly grown in greenhouses because they provide food for you and your family. A lot of people grow vegetables to cut back on their grocery bill or two just to introduce more natural and healthy foods into their lives and onto their dinner plates. Because of this, vegetables are a great option for plants to grow in your greenhouse. Let's look into some of the different vegetable types that you may want to grow inside of your house as well as some tips that will help you to do so.

First, you will want to know when choosing vegetables that there are cool season vegetables and warm season vegetables. You can either choose to have cool season vegetables and keep your greenhouse a little bit colder or warm season vegetables and keep your greenhouse a little bit warmer. You can also choose to have both and simply give the warm season vegetables a little bit more light than the cold seasoned vegetables need. You can do this through the use of light bulbs and artificial lighting. Vegetables like lettuce and broccoli are considered cool seasoned vegetables and vegetables like peppers and cucumbers are considered warm season vegetables.

However, pretty much any type of vegetable can be planted in a greenhouse. Vegetables that are easy to plant in small containers include tomatoes, peppers, broccoli, lettuce, spinach, kale, peas, carrots, radishes, and cucumbers. Vegetables are good for small spaces and are fine with staying in a container their entire lives. Vegetables that we need bigger containers to enclose them in are plants like potatoes because these grow underground and take up a lot of space.

You can also choose to grow a vegetable garden inside a greenhouse and later transplanted to be outside. If you do this, you will want to start your vegetables and smoke tanners in the greenhouse. You can start your vegetables when the weather is still too cold for outdoor gardening. The best time to start these vegetables is in early spring. This will allow your vegetables to be the right size to transfer once the ground is warm enough to plant them outside. You will not want to plant your seedlings outside until the ground does not freeze anymore. If there is still a chance of a hard frost happening in the future, you will not want to put them outside yet. This is because this hard frost could kill your plans. So, it is best to keep your seedlings in your greenhouse for as long as possible.

Once you move busy things outside, they will be able to grow just fine in the ground. However, not all seeds can be transmitted to be grown outside. See you like carrots should not be transplanted. This is because once the carrots start growing, they need to stay in the same place. If you want them or transplant them, they will come out of the ground in odd shapes. They can even sometimes not survive the transplant. Plants that are easy to transplant include tomatoes, peppers, cucumbers, celery, kale, onions, and eggplant.

What to transplant your seeds to an outdoor garden, you can grow vegetables in your greenhouse and keep them there until it is harvest time as well. To do this, you will want to make sure that your containers are big enough to hold the entire plant. For example, you do not want to grow a tomato plant in a 3in by 3in container, when you know that it will soon be too big for this. You want to make sure that the containers that you use are able to support the adult version of the plant. You will also want to make sure that there is adequate space in your greenhouse. Growing vegetables and harvesting them inside of your greenhouse will take up more space than going simply sweet thanks. It is still a great option to grow vegetables and be able to harvest them all year long, however—even if it does come with its difficulties.

Overall, vegetables are a great thing to grow in a greenhouse. You can grow them to transport them to the garden, or you can grow them to harvest inside of the greenhouse. You can grow many different types of vegetables, and you can use this hobby to add a lot of nutritious ingredients to the dinner table in your home. Growing vegetables is easy, and it is rewarding. With the information in this section, you should be able to figure out what temperature to keep your greenhouse app for certain vegetables, and you should be able to look through some ideas and find out if you want to grow any vegetables in your own greenhouse. Another thing that you can grow in a greenhouse is herbs. Herbs are a good thing to grow because they are something that you can use in a lot of meals. They are also fairly small and can be grown in small spaces. This means that they will not take up much space in your big greenhouse. It also means that they are a great thing to be grown in a smaller greenhouse such as a cold frame or a window greenhouse.

If you want to go something in a Cold Frame greenhouse, herbs are a great choice. They are a great choice because you do not need very many Arabs in order to have enough to cook for you and your family. You only need to use a little bit of time, so having one plant of each herb is plenty for most people. If you want to grow herbs on a bigger scale, you can grow them in your bigger greenhouse. Growing a lot of herbs in a large greenhouse would typically mean that you would want to sell them because there is not watch that people can do with large amounts of herbs.

Now that we know why you would want to grow herbs in your greenhouse, let's look into how to do it. The process of growing herbs in your greenhouse is very similar to growing vegetables in your greenhouse. Herbs are easy to grow, and they do well in greenhouses.

The most important thing to know when you are growing herbs in your greenhouse is to make sure that they are getting out of the water. The most common reason that Arabs do not survive when people try to grow them is that they are not watered often enough. Herbs are not plants that like to be drenched in water. They like to be constantly missed it with small amounts of water. Because of this, if you want to grow herbs in your greenhouse, it might be a good idea to install a misting system. If you do not have a misting system, you will have to be outside watering your herbs many times a day. You could also consider installing a dripping system, which can be much cheaper than a misting system. A dripping system is simply a container our machine that drips water down onto your plants. This allows the plants to get a small amount of water at a time and it helps the humidity in the greenhouse to rise.

Another thing to consider when you want to grow herbs in your greenhouses that herbs do not like all day sunshine. Herbs do best when they are grown in places that have adequate amounts of shade. Because of this, if you want to grow herbs in your greenhouse, you will probably need to install a shade on top of your structure. This shade will allow your herbs to get the amount of shade that they need well still getting the heat that they need from the sun.

Some great herbs to grow in a greenhouse include basil, cilantro, chives, parsley, and dill. These herbs are actually pretty sensitive and are hard to grow in an outdoor garden. Because of this, people love to grow them and greenhouses. Greenhouses are actually one of the main places that these types of herbs survive well.

You can also grow mint in a greenhouse. However, it is important to know that mint is an invasive plant. Because it is invasive, mint should be planted in a container and should not be planted near other plans. You do not want you to take over the other plants and kill them. However, if you grow mint correctly, it can be a great plant for you to have.

Overall, it is easy to see that a greenhouse is a great place to grow arms. It takes plants that are typically hard to grow and give a perfect atmosphere. It takes plants that also do not take up much space, and give some the perfect place to be grown. Herbs can be grown in greenhouses as small as windows or cold frames and in a bag of greenhouses as our bill today. They are very versatile, and their harvest can benefit many meals people enjoy eating today. Because of all these factors, herbs are a great thing to consider growing in your greenhouse.

If you are looking to grow something other than food, tropical plants can be a great thing to grow in greenhouses. Tropical plants are typically only able to be grown in warm climates. They are beautiful, however, so people in colder climates are often jealous of these majestic plants. Often times, people in colder climates actually even grow these plants in the summer months and then let them die in the winter because they cannot handle the cold, but they still want to be able to enjoy the beauty of them when they are able to survive. If you grow these tropical plants in greenhouses, however, you are able to keep them alive all year long no matter where you live in the world.

Let's listen to some of the different types of tropical plants that you can grow in a greenhouse. Typically, people grow plants in the greenhouse has to provide food for themselves or to sell the food that they grow. So, why would you want to have a greenhouse filled with plants that you cannot eat? One answer to this is that tropical plants are relaxing and refreshing. When you are able to walk out and surround yourself in a humid, warm environment that is filled with green and beautiful leaves, you may find yourself with less stress and in an overall happier mood. It is also fun to grow tropical plants in greenhouses because they are beautiful. There's something that people want to be able to enjoy all over the world but they cannot when the climate is too cold for them.

Typically, if you want to have a tropical greenhouse, you might want to have a large space. This is because a lot of the beautiful tropical plants are fairly large. If you have a larger space, you will be able to fit these big plants—if you could even grow a tropical plant that grows food that is large, like a banana tree. Banana trees are fun because they produce large amounts of bananas all the same time and because they are beautiful to look at. Even when they do not have food on them, and they are a majestic plant.

There are many types of tropical plants. You can grow fruit trees, flowering plants, or things like palm trees. You can grow all sorts of things depending on what you want to look at or what you want to benefit from. You can design your tropical greenhouse to have plants that remind you of a certain area of the world or do you have plants that are useful to you in ways of giving you food or in ways of helping you with medicine like that aloe vera plant. There are many different ways that you can use tropical plants. Even if they do not seem to have a use, they may just help you to feel happy, and they may make a great space for you to spend time in.

When you have a tropical greenhouse, you will have to pay special attention to the lighting and heating. Tropical greenhouses obviously need more light and more heat. They need to be extra humid, so you may want to have a missing or dripping system to allow this to work.

Even though tropical greenhouses may require a lot of work for a lot of extra equipment, they are still a good choice if you love the warm areas of the world. You can create this face right in your backyard. They are fun, and they're useful. They have many benefits. If you would like to grow a tropical greenhouse, we encourage you to give it a try. We do not think that you will be disappointed.

A different type of greenhouse growing that we are going to look into is called hydroponics. It is not necessarily a type of thing that you can plant in your greenhouse, but it is a way of planting. It is a way of planting that when many people start, they stick with it. Typically, people either plant normally or they plant hydroponically. Let's look into what hydroponics is.

Hydroponics is a way of growing plants without dirt or soil. Typically, hydroponics is grown in water or material like perlite. This unique writing system gives many benefits to the plants that are grown in this way. It allows the ribs of the plants to soak water in well and it allows the roots of the plants to gain all of the nutrients that are available for them as well.

A lot of people who use hydroponics are big-time gardeners. Because of this, they may also have greenhouses as well. If you would like to use hydroponics in your friend's house, it is definitely something that you can work out. To use hydroponics near the greenhouse, you simply need to set hydroponic systems up instead of using dirt and containers. It is just like having a normal greenhouse, but you use your hydroponic system instead.

Through hydroponics, you can grow any type of plant. You can grow fruits or vegetables just like we were talking about earlier. The only difference is how you would plant them. They would still give you the same benefits if you planted them hydroponically.

One downside of planting your plants in your greenhouse through the hydroponic way is that it can be expensive. You need to buy a lot of material that is not as cheap as small plastic containers that hold dirt. If you do like hydroponics and you are willing to spend the money on it, however, it can still be a good choice.

Hydroponic greenhouses can look just like normal ones. They can still be designed to maximize space and can still be grown vertically in many circumstances. They can still girl any of the plants that can be grown in soil. They still need greenhouse essentials, and they still need to be prepped for every season. Basically, hydroponic greenhouses are just like normal greenhouses except for the growing media that is used to put the plants in. No matter how you choose to plant your plants in your greenhouse, almost everything you do will be the same. You will still get great results from your structure either way.

It is clear that there are many different things that you can plant in greenhouses. Greenhouses are made for just about any type of planting. There are no restrictions on what you can grow inside of them. All you need to ensure is that what you are growing fits inside of the greenhouse and that you are able to provide the plants with what they need in terms of heat, humidity, watering, etc. When you are choosing what to grow in your greenhouse, consider that you could grow fruits, vegetables, herbs, tropical plants, or you could grow these things through hydroponics. Also, consider that you could choose a mix of all of these things. Look into these ideas in detail, and decide which ones excite you. Figure out which ones will benefit your life the most. When you have found some answers to what you would like to plant, go ahead and start the process. We know that no matter what you choose, your greenhouse will be full of things that you enjoy and things that will benefit your life greatly.

CHAPTER EIGHT

Starting Seeds

One of the best ways to get the plants to grow in your greenhouses by planting seeds. Seeds are available to buy at a very low price point when compared to buying entire plants. They are also rewarding. When you decide to plant a seed, and then it sprouts, you get the satisfaction of helping that tiny seed to turn into something great. Seeds are a great thing to plant inside of your greenhouse. In this chapter, we will look into how to start seeds in your greenhouse.

There are two different reasons why you would want to plant seeds in your greenhouse. The first of these reasons is that you are wanting to get a head start on growing plants that can be transplanted into your outdoor garden once the weather is nice enough.

If you want to start seeds to transplant into your outdoor garden, you will want to start them in your greenhouse so that they are able to grow when the weather is still too cold for them to grow outside. Typically, you are going to want to plant your seeds about six weeks before the last estimated frost date in your area. You cannot put your seeds outside before the last frost date as we mentioned earlier. However, if you start your seeds in the greenhouse, your plants will be mature and ready to go by the time that the last frost happens. This will make your harvest be able to happen earlier, and it will increase the odds of your plants surviving outside since they already got a good strong start in your perfect greenhouse environment.

The other way that you can start seeds in a greenhouse is if you want them to live in your greenhouse for their entire life span. In this method, you would start your seeds in your greenhouse in you would keep the plants in your greenhouse all the way through harvest time. If you choose this method, you can choose to plant your seeds that any time of year that you would like to.

Let's look into how you can grow seeds in your greenhouse. The most commonly used way of planting seeds in a greenhouse is through the soil. You will need a few different things for this process. You will need two containers, soil, and seeds. Each type of seed is different—but typically, all you will need to do is fill your container with soil, make a small hole for the seed, and cover it up. You will then need to water the seed often until it sprouts. Once it sprouts, you will need to continue to care for it by watering it often and making sure it has adequate light and fresh air. Growing seeds in a greenhouse is a fairly simple process, and it is basically just the same as if you were growing them inside of your house or in a garden.

You can also grow seeds in a greenhouse through hydroponics. If you choose this method, you will be planting your seeds in water or a different growing media like perlite. You will still need to make sure that your plant has what it needs before and after it sprouts.

There are a few different tools that can make growing seeds in a greenhouse much easier. The worst thing that can make growing seeds in a greenhouse easy is the type of tray that you choose to use. You can choose to use a tray that has individual pockets for each seed to grow in. These trays are nice because you know that you planted one seed in each pocket.

You can also grow your seeds in a plain, flat tray. If you choose to do this, you will just want to poke holes into the soil where you want your seeds to grow. You will not have specific pockets for each need to go in, so you can just pick a spot. You will want to make sure that your seeds are spaced appropriately from each other so that they have space to grow. Typically, this is the spacing that is close to 1 or 2 in part for each seed. However, the exact spacing that you need to follow will usually be listed on the back of the package of seeds. It depends on the type of seed in many circumstances.

Now that we have looked at the basics, let's talk through some tips and tricks that can help you to grow the best plants from seeds. This is one way to grow seeds. There are other ways that you can do so successfully, but we believe that this method is strong and that it works well. Because of this, we are going to explain this method and details so that you are able to use it in your own greenhouse seed sowing if you want to.

You will need to get your trays ready. We recommend the trays that have a pocket for each seed. This is because they are the easiest to use. They help each plant to stay separate, and they helped to make sure that you are giving each seed enough space to grow. The trays that have separate containers for each plant have more benefits as well. For example, these trays are better at providing warmth and moisture to each separate seat. This is because the moisture and warmth stay in a certain area to protect the seed and it does not spread out through the entire container. It is also better because it keeps the roots of each plant in their own space. If you use a tray that is flat and has many seeds in the same opening, their roots often become entwined with each other. When the roots of the plant become entwined with those of the plants around it, it hurts their survival rate greatly. This is because, in order to separate the plants, like you will have to do to move them into larger and deeper containers, you have to separate the roots. If you break the roots of the plant, it is much harder for the plant to survive. The roots are a very important part of the plant, and you do not want to break them or hurt them in any way.

After you get your trays, you will want to fill them with soil. We recommend starting with a seed starting mix. This is because seed-starting mixes have all of the nutrients that you will need in order to start your seeds successfully. If you use a different type of potting mix, your seeds may still come up, but the success rate is lower than if you choose a potting mix that is specifically made for seeds and nothing else.

You can buy the seed starting mix at a store, or if you feel like making your own, you can use that option as well. If you want to make your own seed starting mix, you can start with a typical potting mix that you would find at any store. You would then want to add a few things to it. You would want to add equal parts of perlite, peat moss, and organic compost. Adding these things to your regular soil will make the soil have just the right nutrients that your seedlings need to have a strong beginning of life. Making your own soil can be a good option, especially if you are on a budget or if you simply like to make things yourself. However, it is important to know that it is best to use new soil when you are planting seedlings. If you do happen to reuse soil that you have used in seedlings or in other plans in the past, you need to sterilize this soil. This is because some germs or diseases that plants can get could be in that soil. If you plant your seedlings into the soil, they either will not sprout, or they will grow diseased plants. This is not what you want, of course. You want healthy seeds so you will need to start with healthy soil.

Once you fill your tray with soil, it will be time to plant your seeds. You will want to push your finger into each seed pocket filled with soil to make a small indentation. Inside this hole, you will want to place two to three seeds. It made me feel silly to put 2 to 3 seeds inside each pocket when you only want one plant to grow. However, we believe that this is the best option. This is because not every seed is going to be successful and its mission to turn into a sea link. If you plant two to three seeds inside of each pocket, you have a much better chance that at least one of them will have enough luck in surviving. If you do happen to have two or even all three of the seeds make it and turn into seedlings, you will need to trim the seedlings that are the least strong. For example, if you have three seedlings come up in one container and one of them is tall, one of them is short, and one of them is tipping over—you will want to trim the one that is short in the one that is tipping over. This leaves the strongest and tallest seedling in your tray so that you are able to grow it into a mature plant. The strongest and tallest seedling is chosen because it has the best chance of surviving all the way through until it grows a crop and is able to be harvested from.

It is important to note that some seeds need extra care before they are planted. Larger seeds from plants like peas, pumpkins, and squash need to be soaked before they can be planted. This helps them to sprout easier and faster since they have such a hard shell. You do not want to soak all seeds, however, because small seeds like those of tomatoes and carrots can be really hard to handle after they are soaked and they don't need to be soaked anyway. Because of this, you will want to research what each type of seed needs before you decide to plant it.

After you plant your seeds, you will want to cover them with the soil. You can either use extra soil for this or simply push the soil over that you use to make the hole earlier in the process. Either way will work just as well, so this decision is just up to your own judgment and what you feel will be easiest for you.

Once your seeds are planted and covered up with soil, it is time to care for them. In regards to the temperature of your greenhouse, most seeds germinate best if they are kept at a temperature that is between 70 and 80 degrees Fahrenheit. At night, this temperature can dip down to between 50 and 60 degrees Fahrenheit. You will want to keep your greenhouse at this temperature with either the use of sunlight or the use of heaters. If you do not have these temperatures in your greenhouse, your seeds may not do as well as you are hoping that they will do. If you have a greenhouse that is not warm enough but can still grow seedlings, you can consider something called a seedling heat mat. These are heat mats that go on the benches in your greenhouse. You can then put your trays filled with seedlings on top of them. These heat mats help the soil to stay the right temperature for the seeds. Even if the air is the wrong temperature, if the soil is the right temperature, your seedlings can have a successful start to their life.

Another trick that you can try with growing seeds is to cover your plants up before they sprout. Sometimes, seeds do best when they are covered during their germination. Once they sprout, though, you need to uncover them right away—this is because that is the time when they will start to need light to grow healthily.

Tips for growing seeds in a greenhouse is to record the results of your crops. If you grow a batch of seedlings one day after soaking your seeds in water, write down what you did to them before planting them and then write down how they end up sprouting. Compare your results to a crop that you did not soak in water. Using this technique, you will be able to tell if you are tips and tricks that you are using for your seed starting are working or if they are not working at all. Using this technique, you will also be able to tell what works best for you and what really doesn't work. Once you have planted many batches of seeds and tried out many different tricks, you will be able to find the very best way for you to grow seedlings in your greenhouse.

Overall, growing seedlings in your greenhouse is a great thing to do. Starting plants from seeds not only saves money, but it is also a very rewarding process. You'll get to take something so small, and turn it into something large. You can take one tiny seed and turn it into a plant that can feed you multiple times throughout the year. When you are growing seeds, remember to start them in either a flat open tray or a tray that has multiple openings for the seeds. Remember to put money seeds in each hole so that at least one comes out, and then pick the strongest seedling to be the one that survives. Remember to use an appropriate soil mixture for seed starting whether that means making your own seed starting mix or buying a seed-starting potting mix from the store. Remember to keep the temperature of your greenhouse correct and make sure that your plants are getting adequate water and light. Water your plants off so that they are able to grow strong. Try out different growing techniques if you want to see if you can get your plants to grow faster than normal. Try covering your soil during the germination. Or try soaking your seeds in water before you plant them. Remember to write down your results so that you are able to compare what works and what doesn't work for you specifically in your greenhouse. Growing seeds in your greenhouse is a great adventure, and we know that with the tips and tricks in this chapter, you will be able to have great success.

CHAPTER NINE

Caring for Your Plants

Whether you choose to start your plants from seeds or buy plants from the store, the next step in the process of growing in your greenhouse will be to take care of your plants. This may be the step that you have envisioned yourself doing the most so far. You may have been picturing yourself walking out into your greenhouse to be surrounded by life. You may have seen yourself watering plant after plant—maybe even letting a little bit of the cool water touch your toes in the hot and humid greenhouse air. You may have been looking forward to creating the perfect feel for your favorite plants or harvesting your favorite fruits and vegetables. In this chapter, we are finally going to talk about all of these fun topics. In this chapter, we are going to discuss temperature, lighting, watering, pollination, and harvesting crops in detail.

First, let's begin to discuss temperature. Temperature is the biggest reason why greenhouses are such a useful tool in gardening. When you are using your greenhouse, you can control the temperature in three different ways. We will look into each of these two ways in detail below.

The first way that you can control the temperature of your greenhouse is through the use of the sun. The sun is the natural heating source that greenhouses really on for a majority of their heating needs. One of the first ways that you can ensure that you are able to use the sun as a heating source is by placing your greenhouse in a good location. Preferably, you want to place your greenhouse on the south side of your property. As we mentioned a little bit earlier, the south side of your home is usually the area on your property that gets the most sun. However, if the south side of your property has the sun blocked by other houses or is lined with tall, sun-blocking trees, you would want to choose a different part of your property and likely a different side of your home. The most important thing to do when choosing a location for your greenhouse with temperature in mind is to make sure that you are choosing the sunniest location possible.

It is true that greenhouses can get too hot. However, a hot greenhouse is much easier to cool down than a cold greenhouse is to warm up. Because of this, the sunniest location on your property is almost always the best choice for the location of your greenhouse in regards to temperature. If the sun does make your greenhouse too hot, you still have options to help you give your plants the environment that is absolutely perfect for them. You can use sun shades, which we also talked about a little bit earlier. Sun shades are a great temperature control product. They can be spread across the roof of your greenhouse if you are getting too much heat from the sun. They can cover your entire roof or just a portion of it. They can be used for any time span that you need to use them for. With this much versatility, sun shades are the perfect tool to use if you need to naturally bring the temperature of your greenhouse down due to it having too much sunlight.

Sometimes, however, sunshades may not be enough. This point brings us to our second tool that can be used to control the temperature of a greenhouse. If the sun shades are not enough, you may need to rely on air flow to help you cool the temperature of your greenhouse. You can gain air flow by the use of vents or opening windows if the air outside has a cool breeze. If your greenhouse is too hot and the outside air is too hot and humid as well, however, you will need to rely on fans for your air circulation instead. As we mentioned earlier in the book, almost all greenhouses need fans for air circulation anyway. This makes this temperature cooling technique easy and accessible to almost all greenhouse gardeners.

Next, let's look into our third and last temperature controlling technique. Sometimes your greenhouse will not be too hot. In fact, at times it will probably become much too cold. If the sun is not enough to warm the temperature of your greenhouse, you will need to use heaters. Heaters are a strong tool that you can use to create the perfect air temperature that your plants need. Heaters are often needed to control the temperature of your greenhouse during the winter and possibly even during early spring and late fall in the colder areas of the world.

So now that we know ways that you can make your greenhouse warmer or colder, why do you need to do this in order to care for your plants? You need to control the air temperature that surrounds your plants because plants cannot grow in any temperature. They need to have the correct climate feel and growing environment. This means they simply will not thrive and may not even survive if they are not grown at the right temperature. When you are growing your plants, it is important to read up on each specific plant type that you choose to grow. Check what their optimal temperature is or look at what the temperature typically is in the area of the world that they are native to. Then, work to match the temperature of your greenhouse to the number that you find.

It is also important to note when looking at caring for your plants in your greenhouse in regards to temperature, that every plant in your greenhouse does not need to be grown at the same temperature. You can successfully grow plants that need different climate feels inside of the same greenhouse. To do this, you simply need to use artificial lighting.

That brings us to our next way to care for your plants. Let's look into lighting, why your plants need it, and how you can use it inside of your own greenhouse to create the perfect environment for your plants to live in. Of course, the most important and most well-working light that plants need comes from the sun. The sun provides natural light that oftentimes is something that you do not even need to think about. However, sometimes, in greenhouse gardening, your plants will need more light than the sun is able to provide in your area at a specific time of year. Let's look into how you can use artificial light to your plants when these situations arise.

First, let's look into the most common time that greenhouse gardeners find they need to use artificial light. This time is during the majority of the winter season. This is because during winter, the sun is both farther away and it does not shine for as many hours in the day. This makes the plants that are located in greenhouses not get enough sunlight.

Even if plants are kept warm enough through the use of heaters, they still need adequate time in the sunshine. This is because plants need sunlight in order to survive. Sunlight is the power behind photosynthesis. Photosynthesis is the process that plants use to make their food. They take the carbon dioxide that they breathe in and combine it with the water they take in to create their own food. Without the sun shining on them, they would not be able to do photosynthesis in order to make food for themselves, and they would starve. This information shows us that if plants do not get adequate sunlight, they will not survive.

Luckily, artificial light can be the power behind the photosynthesis process as well. If you are growing plants in the greenhouse during the cold and dark winter, you will need to supplement the light that your plants get with artificial lighting. Typically, your plants will need at least six hours of direct light per day. You can pay attention to how many hours of direct sunlight your greenhouse gets during any given day. You will then need to make sure you provide artificial lighting for however many of the six hours that your plants did not receive. For example, if you look out at your greenhouse and learn that it is getting only four hours of direct sunlight per day, you will need to give you plants two hours of time under artificial lighting to keep them healthy.

You also need to look at how much daylight a plant is receiving, even when it is not sitting in direct sunlight. This type of light that a plant needs in a day is called a photoperiod. In the winter, our days are short and our nights are long. During this time, you will want to provide additional lighting to give your plants inside of your greenhouse the feel of longer days. These are called photoperiod control lights. If you want your plants to be successful, you should consider adding these lights to your greenhouse plant care routine as well.

Growing plants with artificial lights and without much sunlight at all can be an option as well. Of course, it is preferable to give your plant as much sunlight as possible. This is because sunlight is natural, it is free, and it is what plants are truly seeking. However, if for some reason you need to grow plants under artificial lights you should know that it can be done. This technique would be helpful if you are using one of the space-saving methods that we talked about earlier in the book. For example, if you are growing another crop underneath your normal growing benches, you will need to provide them completely with artificial lighting. This adds a little bit of extra work to your plant care, but it can be worth it for the added space and the extra crop at harvest time.

When you are caring for the plants in your greenhouse by means of lighting, it is important that you know your types of lighting as well. Fluorescent lights are one option that you can use as a grow light. They do a good job at imitating the sun's light, and they are cool to the touch so they can be placed close to your plants. Another type of lighting that works well in greenhouses is metal halide lighting. This is the best type of lighting to choose if your greenhouse gets no natural light or just a small amount of natural light. High-Pressure Sodium lighting can be used as well. This type of lighting works well in addition to a lot of sunlight and burns hot, so it should be placed far away from plants. Because of that, it is best for greenhouses that sit in sunny locations and that are large in size. The last type of lighting that is commonly used in greenhouses is LED lighting. The LED lighting is very environmentally friendly, and it works well for areas that need their lights to be on for long periods of time and also works well with greenhouses that grow plants in hydroponics.

It is pretty clear that greenhouse lighting is extremely important when looking into the care of plants inside a greenhouse. Remember to ensure that if your plants are not getting enough direct sunlight or daylight, that you are supplementing with artificial light. Remember that artificial light can grow plants without sunlight at all if it is necessary, though sunlight is always the most natural and overall best option. Remember to think about the benefits and downfalls to each of the four main types of greenhouse lighting before you choose one to use in your own space. With these tips, you should be able to grow your plants with the help of artificial lighting with great success.

Watering, of course, is a very important part of caring for your greenhouse plants as well. There are some homemade ways to water in your greenhouse. One of those ways is through an irrigation system, and another is by hand watering. We will look into both of these ways of watering below.

First, let's look into irrigation systems. Irrigation systems can be sprinklers, or they can be drip systems. The sprinklers can be large and on the ceilings, or they can be small and next to the plants. These systems turn on automatically in time intervals that you set them to use. Irrigation systems work best if all of the plants in your greenhouse need the same amount of water. This is because irrigation systems put the same amount of water out in every part of the greenhouse. They might not be a great choice if you have some plants that need to be watered once a week and other plants that need to be watered every day all mixed in with each other. However, you could use an irrigation system even with plants with separate needs if you separated your plants in two different sections according to how much they needed to be watered. It is also important to note that irrigation systems are fairly affordable, so they can be used in many greenhouses even if you do not have a very large budget. Next, let's look into hand watering. Hand watering can be difficult because it is time-consuming and it can be a lot of work. It definitely takes a lot longer than irrigation systems do because irrigation systems don't require any work. However, hand-watering is free, and it is very customizable. With hand-watering, you will always be able to tell if your plants need water or not. Typically plant should be watered when their top inch or two of soil is dry. Of course, irrigation systems will not be able to tell if your soil is dry or wet. However, if you are hand watering, you will be able to see this, and you will be able to adjust how much water you give to your plants based on how they are looking.

Now that we have looked into both ways of watering and what each way is good for as well as what is difficult about each method, let's look into the watering process, in general. Watering is one of the most important things that you can do for your plants and for their health. Plants need water so that they are able to complete photosynthesis. As we mentioned earlier, plants make their food through the photosynthesis process using carbon dioxide and water. If you do not put water into your plants, they cannot make food for themselves, and they will not survive.

Now that we know how important watering is—let's look into some tips and tricks that you can use while watering. One of the most important things to know while watering your plants is that it is important to water thoroughly. You want the soil of your plants to be watered evenly throughout their service. If they are not, some roots make it too much water, and some roots may not get enough water. If this happens, your plants will not thrive as they should. One trick to make sure that your plans are being watered early is to give your plants a quick rinse, let that water soak in, and then go back to water again. This will help your plants to be watered evenly throughout their entire soil base.

You should also know when watering plants that hand watering can often cause disease to spread among plants. This is because oftentimes when you are hand watering, you may let the hose, wand, or watering can touch the plant and then touch another plant. If you do this and the plan that your test originally had a disease, this disease can spread to the other plants. Because of this, it is really important to make sure that your watering tool is not touching the plants where you water them. A good trick to help with this is to get a watering tool that has a good and spread out water flow. A watering wand or attachment to your hose that allows the water to spread evenly across the plant is a good investment so that you do not have to touch your watering tool to your plants.

Watering is a simple task, but it is something that you need to know about in order to do well. In a greenhouse, watering is an extremely important thing to do. When you are watering your plants, remember to make sure that they are getting the amount of water that they need according to their specific plant type. Make sure that you are watering evenly and thoroughly and that you are not touching your watering tool to the plants. Whether you are using an irrigation system or are hand watering your plants, these tips and tricks should allow you to get the job done well.

Next, in regards to plant care, we are going to look at a topic that you probably never thought of while dreaming about your greenhouse—pollination. In the outdoor world, pollination is done without the help of humans, so it is something that we rarely think about when we think about gardens and growing plants. In the wild, pollination is simply not our job. Even if we create an entire garden on our own, we still leave pollination up to nature. In greenhouses, however, nature is not there to do its job. Because of that, pollination becomes our job and our responsibility.

Before we look into how to pollinate plants in your greenhouse, let's talk about what pollination is exactly and why it is so important. Since it is something that we really never even have to think about, these are the topics that we may need to freshen up on.

Pollination is the process of transferring pollen from one flower to the next. Pollination is necessary to allow a flower of a plant to turn into a fruit. These fruits contain the seeds of the plant so that more plants are able to be grown. Without pollination, plant species would die out. It is their own way of reproducing. It is an extremely important process to the keeping of plants in our world. Pollination is typically done by bees, butterflies, and other types of flying bugs. They fly from flower to flower to collect nectar, and while doing so, they pick up traces of pollen and drop it off onto the next flower they land on. This natural act pollinates the plants of the Earth and allows plants to continue to make seeds and be able to reproduce.

Now that we know what pollination is and why it is so important, let's look into how you can make pollination happen inside of your greenhouse. The simplest way to pollinate your plants inside of your greenhouse is through manual pollination. This is easiest if you have a small garden with a small number of plants, as it can be a time-consuming job. To do manual pollination, you will need to gently shake each flower on your plants to allow their pollens to be released.

You can also use a method called device pollination. This is done with a pollinating tool, which is simply a battery-powered wand that vibrates. An electric toothbrush is able to do the same job. To do this process, you simply touch the device to the pollen in each flower.

Lastly, if you have a large greenhouse or if you do not have time to pollinate your plants by yourself or by hand, you could consider introducing bees into your greenhouse. You can buy bees and let a colony of them live inside of your greenhouse. If you chose this method, your pollination would be taken care of naturally. This is by far the easiest way to pollinate, but before you choose this method make sure that you think through the responsibilities of it. If you introduce bees into your greenhouse, you will not only have plants to keep alive and healthy but bees as well. This can be a big responsibility for some, so only choose it if you are up to the task.

some people may worry about bee stings when choosing to get bees to help with pollination inside of your greenhouse. This should not be a huge concern, however—typically, the bees that are used for pollination are bumblebees, and bumblebees do not often sting at all. Most bumblebees die after they sting, so they use this tactic as a very last resort. If you are kind to bumblebees, they will almost always be kind to you. If you are a family member is allergic to bees, though, this chance may not be worth the risk.

Pollination can seem like a scary thing to deal with in a greenhouse, but this fear is just because it is not something that comes to mind quickly when you think of greenhouse gardening. However, pollination indoors can actually be a fairly simple process. If you choose one of these three pollination methods, we believe that pollination your plants will not be a very hard thing to do.

Lastly, in regards to caring for the plants in your greenhouse, we are going to look forward to one of the most fun topics. Let's talk about harvesting your crop. The whole reason that you plant fruits and vegetables in a greenhouse is that so you will be able to enjoy your crop. The most important part of harvesting is that you know when your plants are ready to be picked. Make sure you know when the things you are growing will be ready. You can read on the back of the seed package how long they take to grow to maturity. You can also research what your produce should look like when it is ready to be picked. For example, you know that your tomato should be picked when they are red and that they should not typically be picked when they are green. This is common sense, but you need to make sure that you are harvesting well in your greenhouse to make sure that you are getting the best crop possible.

Harvesting is one of the most fun parts of owning a greenhouse. With an outdoor garden, harvesting only happens once a year. Luckily, with indoor gardening and greenhouses, harvesting can happen as often as you want it to. In the next chapter, we are going to look into this in detail. Overall, there is quite a lot of work that you need to do to care for plants in a greenhouse. You need to make sure that they have the right environment and this includes making sure that their temperature is not too warm and not too cold. It includes making sure that they have enough sunlight and enough daylight to provide them with what they need for photosynthesis. It means making sure that they have enough water and that they are being watered well. It also means making sure that your plants have a way of being pollinated, whether that is through bees or through hand pollination or device pollination. If you have looked into all of these subjects and you know how to care for your plants in each of these ways, you will have a very successful greenhouse. When you give plants the things that they need and care for them in the ways that they need to be cared for, they will reward you with a healthy and bountiful crop. Make sure that you enjoy the process of caring for your plants along the way. It can be a lot of work while you are doing it, but being surrounded by life is beneficial for not only the life of the plants but your own life as well.

CHAPTER TEN

Year-Round Growing

As we mentioned briefly in the last chapter, plants in greenhouses do not only need to have one harvest time per year. When you plant your plants in a greenhouse, you can allow them to give you harvest as often as you want to. Obviously, plants will only give you a harvest when they are ready to. However, with the process of growing your plants on a schedule, you can make sure that you have some sort of harvest coming in all year long. In this chapter, we are going to look into how to do this. We will look into how this works and some tips and tricks to help you along the way.

First, let's look into why you would want to have a harvest all year long. If you have plants that can be harvested from all year long, you have fresh fruits and vegetables available to you every day of the year. If you grow enough plants, this could even replace your produce purchases at the grocery store. It will allow your family and yourself to be the healthiest versions of yourself that you can possibly be. It will give you something to look forward to each day, and it will allow you to continue to feel the success of growing in your greenhouse throughout every single season. Having a year-round harvest greenhouse can be a challenging process, and we will look into these struggles below along with the benefits—but it can be a great thing as well.

Next, let's look into how you can make this happen. How can you possibly have a greenhouse that has produce available to you every single day of the year? It sounds like something that would be fairly difficult. In reality, it is actually a simple process. It requires a lot of work and a lot of planning, but once you get that plan into action, I can be a simple thing to follow through with.

In order to learn about how you can make this happen, let us look into what we already know. We already know that you can plant in greenhouses all year long. We already know that you can keep your plants alive in your greenhouse all year long and that you do not need to keep planting new plants for each season. Your plants can stay alive. We know that this is possible through the use of heaters and adequate lighting through artificial sources when it is winter, and we know that this is possible through fans and vents when it's hot in the summer. When you have a greenhouse that is able to be used every season of the year, you can, of course, plant in every season of the year.

No, let's look into what we do not yet know. We do not yet know how you can have plants give you a crop all year long. Of course, you are not going to get a tomato plant to keep producing your tomatoes constantly day after day for years straight. Fruits and vegetables have growing seasons. They have seasons were they grow food and seasons were they prepare themselves to do so. You cannot make an apple tree have apples all year long. You cannot make an orange tree grow oranges all year long. The plants need to have their time to prepare themselves oh, they cannot have food on them every single day.

Because of this, there must be another way to allow you to gain a crop from your greenhouse every day of the year. This other way is by planting your plants on the schedule. When you plant a seed, you know when it will become mature by the number of days it provides you on the back of the packet. For example, if a tomato plant takes 120 days to reach maturity, this will be listed on the back of the seed packet. When you know how long it will take in order to produce fruit or vegetables, you will be able to count on that plant to produce a crop for you at that time. Because of this, you will then know if you plant a tomato plant that you will have tomatoes in 120 or so days. The same holds true for every type of plant. When you plant something, you should be able to tell how long it will take that seedling to turn into a plant that bears food.

Now, if you want to have every month of the year filled with these tomatoes, you will need to plan a harvest for each month of the year. In order to do this, you will need to pick out that month that you want the plan to be ready, and count back 120 days or however long it takes tomatoes to reach maturity. Once you count back these 120 days, you will find that the day that you need to plant your seed on. Columbus Day, you will probably want to plant many seeds. If you plant many seeds, you will have a better chance of getting at least some of them to survive. As we mentioned earlier in the book, not all seeds will turn into seedlings. Because of this, you will want to plant many seeds to ensure that you get some plants out of your effort.

After you have planted your seeds, go ahead and find the next date when you would like a new tomato harvest to happen and do the process all over again. If you want your hair was to happen once a month, you can simply plant the seeds on the first day of every month. Once you have gotten the pattern started, the math will always be 30 days later. Because of this, you can simply plant on one day of the month every month.

If you plant one day of the month every month for a year, you should then have a harvest coming in every single day of the year. As long as you care for your plants in a way that allows them to bear fruit and vegetables, will have your plants set up on a staggering schedule to give you a crop.

You can choose to do this year-round growing with one type of plant or with all of your plants. If you only want carrots year round, for example, you could simply just choose to keep planting carrot seeds when you want them to grow. If you want all of your plants to have a harvest every day of the year, you will do this with all of your plants. Obviously, to do this, you might need a bigger greenhouse. If you only have a small greenhouse, you can consider only doing year-round growing with your favorite plants. If you still do not have space, you could consider some of the space-maximizing techniques that we talked about earlier in the book in chapter five.

Another important factor to consider when growing plants all your robes is that your females need to be ready for every season. If you live in a cold area, you will want to make sure that your greenhouse is winterized and ready for the cold winter. To do this, you will want to use the techniques that we looked at in our Seasonal Preparations and Care chapter, in chapter 6 of this book. You will want to make sure that your heater is working and that it is running, as well as that all cracks and holes that could be in your greenhouse are covered and are not letting air in. He will also want to make sure that any big jobs are done before winter comes so that you do not have to open the doors or windows for long amounts of time as this can make the air in the greenhouse become very cold very quickly. If you are growing your round and you live in a place that has very hot summers, you may want to be prepared with things like some shades and vents on your greenhouse for air circulation. For the spring and fall, you need to be prepared as well. The preparation for these seasons varies based on where you live—but for the fall, you should basically be prepared for winter; and for the spring, you should be basically prepared for summer.

Why do you need to have your greenhouse ready for every season? You need to have your greenhouse ready for every season because you are growing in every season. If you have a harvest every day, that means you are growing every day. This means that your plants need to be alive and healthy every day. In order to make this happen, your greenhouse needs to be repaired and in the optimal environment for the health of your plants as well as their success every day of the year. This means that you need to take your seasonal preparation and care very seriously. If you need a refresher on the details of seasonal preparation and care of, look back to chapter 6 in this book. It has a much more detailed approach to this information.

Another thing to consider when you look into year-round growing is that you need to be ready to do a lot of work every single day of the year. When you do year-round growing, you do not have an off-season. You do not have a break in between crops where you do not need to go out into your greenhouse. You do not have a time where you are not doing multiple jobs at once, actually. You are actually growing seedlings, planting seeds, caring for plants, and harvesting all in the same day. This means that you are around growing can take a lot of your time and energy in ways that typical greenhouse gardening cannot. Of course, for this extra effort, it does provide a lot of added benefits with its increased amount of crop and harvest, but it needs to be a level of work that you are ready for if it is something that you want to consider. This extra work also takes up a lot of extra time. If you want to have a year-round growing garden inside of your greenhouse, you need to make sure that you have enough time to do so. Finding the time to prep for each season, plant seeds, care for your plants, and harvest all at the same time can be really challenging. Year-round growing inside of your friend house is a commitment that you really need to be all in for if you want even to consider it.

With extra harvests, year-round growing also comes with extra costs. If you want to grow plants year-round, you will be buying many more seeds. You will also be buying much more soil, and maybe even many more trays if you cannot reuse the old ones. You will be using more water well water in your extra plants, and he will be using more light to provide the heat and lighting that your extra plants need. Make sure that you are able to cover these extra costs if you are ready to have extra harvests year-round growing in your greenhouse.

Another thing that you should know about year-round gardening is it is great for people who want to sell their crops. If you are looking to sell fruits or vegetables, year-round gardening can be a great choice. If you do your own gardening and sell your crops, you will be one of the few farmers or gardeners who are able to sell fruits and vegetables during their offseason. If you can sell fruits and vegetables during their offseason, you will have a huge advantage over your competition. Typically, people really miss fresh fruits and vegetables in the winter time. If you are able to provide them with you is, you will have a lot of business. You will have a lot of happy customers, and the extra work that you put into your year-round gardening will pay off quickly.

Year-round growing can be hard. Because of this, we want to share with you some pieces of advice. Let's look into some tips and tricks that you can use to make year-round growing easier for you. Our first step is that you should start with a plant. Make sure that you know what you want to do. If you do not have a plan in place before you begin, you are around growing can seem really overwhelming. You need to know what types of plants you want to have and when you want to harvest them. You also want to have a plan for where you are going to grow your plants since they take up extra space as well as how you are going to get the extra resources. You may even want to plan out how you are going to have enough time to spend growing all of these plants at once.

Our next tip is that you should make sure you have a large greenhouse for a creative space plan before planning on having a year-round harvest. It is okay if you have a small greenhouse, but if you do have a small greenhouse, you need to be creative with the small space that you have. Look into different shelving units, or even considered growing one set the plants underneath the normal bench with artificial grow lights in order to maximize your space.

Also, if you are planning on participating in year-round growing, consider asking for help. Ask your friends and family to help you with watering once in a while. Ask your neighborhood children to help you with planting seeds. These are things that your family, friends, and neighbors would probably love to help you with if you asked him. The extra help would also give you the ability to care for plants in a way that you may not be able to do on your own.

Along with that last tip, if you offer some of the harvests to your helpers, they may be much more willing to help. Tell your neighbors that they can take some tomatoes whenever they like if they come over and help water them or help you plant some seeds. If you spread the word that you are helpers will get it back in produce that comes from your garden, you will probably have many more volunteers as well as much better luck getting them actually to come and help.

Our biggest tip for year-round growing is to be prepared. Look ahead at the challenges that you might face. Be ready for what you need to do if you have some sort of greenhouse emergency. Make sure that you understand you will be using many more lights and much more water. Understand that you will be spending a lot of time in the greenhouse. Make yourself comfortable with these facts and even happy with them. If you do these things, it will be much easier for you to grow your plants year-round in a greenhouse.

Even though growing plants year-round in a greenhouse is hard, we want you to find success. We believe that if you follow these tips and tricks and learn all the information that we have shared with you, you will be able to have success at year-round gardening. As long as you have the tools, knowledge, and passion necessary to do this large task, you will have great success.

Overall, it is easy to see that year-round growing inside of a greenhouse is a difficult but rewarding task. It is something that takes extra time, extra money, extra resources, extra effort, and extra dedication in order to keep up with. Along with all of these things, however, year-round growing in a greenhouse also provides you with added benefits. It gives you harvests year-round. It allows you to have healthy food to put on your table every day of the year. It allows you to plan for what you want to eat and when you want to have it ready. It is a rewarding and beneficial process in many ways. Year-round growing can be a great thing to do—you just need to make sure that you are up for the challenge before you begin.

CHAPTER ELEVEN

Common Greenhouse Problems

We have tackled so much information together in this book so far. We have now reached our last chapter together. We have already covered everything that you need to know about building a greenhouse, growing plants in your greenhouse, and finding success in doing so. We've talked about all the different ways of planting and all the different tips and tricks that we have for you. Now that we've reached the end, let's look back and talk about some common greenhouse problems that you might face. Problems can pop up in greenhouses no matter how well you treat your plants. Do you not feel bad if any of these problems pop up? Simply look back at this information and figure out how you can solve the issue quickly and effectively. In this chapter, we are going to go over every common greenhouse problem that you might come up against you in your journey of growing a garden inside of a greenhouse. We will look into the problem in detail, who learn why it occurs, and learn how to fix it. Let's get started.

First, let's look into what to do if you get bugs in your greenhouse. Is there something that you would think of dealing with outside? Obviously, you do not want to need to deal with them inside of your greenhouse. The first reason is that you are already in a structure—you should not have to deal with something like bugs. The second reason is if bugs are in your greenhouse, it is not like they're simply going to be like when they are outside. If bugs are in your greenhouse, they probably think that they are there to stay. You will need to do something to get them out of your greenhouse. They are not going to fly away like they were outside.

Let's start by looking into why bugs get into greenhouses. If there is any space that allows bugs to get into your greenhouse—like a crack or hole or even vent or door that was open for a few seconds—bugs can get in. Bugs go inside greenhouses because they know they're filled with plants and because they want to pollinate them. Bugs can also go to clean houses just to simply explore. Other bugs are looking for plants to eat. Obviously, you really do not want these latter bugs in your greenhouse. You definitely do not want your plants getting eaten by anyone except for you. Next, let's look into some ways that you can prevent bugs from getting into your greenhouse. One of the easiest ways to prevent getting bumped into your greenhouses is to look at the things that you are bringing inside. If you are bringing inside a plant, make sure there are no bugs in it. If you are bringing in new soil, make sure you do the same. Anything that you bring in should be checked to ensure that there are no bugs that could hurt your plants on them.

Another thing that you can do to avoid getting bugs in your greenhouses to make sure that they do not have a way in. Make sure that all cracks and holes are filled. Also, if you have a fence, you could consider putting a screen on them. You can put screens on the windows as well. You can also make sure that when you come in and out of the greenhouse, you do so quickly and you do not leave the door open.

It is also a good idea to not plant anything around the outside of your greenhouse. If you put plants around the outside of your greenhouse, these plants can attract bugs. If you attract bugs next to your greenhouse, they will likely know that there are plants inside and they will likely find a way in. You want to keep all of your outdoor plants far away from the greenhouse to avoid this happening.

Now, let's look into what to do if you already have bugs inside of your greenhouse. In an outdoor garden, you might reach for the pesticides. This is not a great idea inside of a greenhouse not only because they are toxic chemicals but because in such a small space they can be a hazard. One helpful way to catch bugs inside of your greenhouse is to use bug traps like tape. You can hang out tape all around in your greenhouse, and it will not affect your plants. It will, however, catch the bugs that you do not want to be there. You could also consider making sure to get rid of anything that will attract bugs. For example, make sure that there is no standing water available in your greenhouse. If your bugs are not attracted to anything inside of your greenhouse, they may leave. If you are really having a hard time with bugs in your greenhouse, you could always ask a professional exterminator for help.

Something that can be problematic is your greenhouses diseases. There are many different things that can cause diseases in your plants. These diseases can come from mold, bacteria, and viruses. Greenhouse diseases can be some things that are hard to beat. Let's look into some ways that you can prevent these diseases from occurring in your greenhouse.

What is the most important thing that you can do to prevent disease in your greenhouses? It is to sanitize. You want to make sure that you sanitize everything after you use it. You will need to sanitize 2, trays, and even shelves. If you do not sanitize your tools, it increases your risk of spreading disease inside of your greenhouse from plant to plant. This is because if one plant had a disease and you used a shovel to scoop it out and throw it away, and then use the same shovel in another plant, the new plant would probably get the disease as well just from being touched with the same shovel. The spread of disease in plants inside of greenhouses is really similar to the spread of disease in humans. If you stay clean, you will have a much better chance of not spreading diseases. You allow someone to watch your humidity and make sure that you are greenhouse does not get overly humid. If your greenhouse is too humid, mold and fungus are likely to grow on your soil. If these grow in your soil, your plants will get the disease because of them. Mold and fungus can also spread very quickly and easily. It is something that you really want to avoid having in your greenhouse.

When watering your plants, you will want to make sure that the tool does not touch your plant's insurgencies, and you will also want to make sure that the water does not splash while you are watering. If water splashes from one plant to another, it can spread disease. Because of this, you will want to use a tool for watering that does not allow water to splash. You will want to use the tool that has a light spray that soaks into the soil and does not splash at all.

Another thing that can help prevent disease is to make sure that plants have adequate space between them. If your plants are too close together, they will be touching each other, and this can cause them to spread diseases to each other. If your plans are spaced apart, when one plant becomes diseased, the ones around it will not be touching it and will likely not become diseased along with it. Sometimes, it can be a hassle to spread plants out in your greenhouse because it feels like a wasted space, but it is better to waste space than to allow all of your plants to become sick.

One last thing that you can do to protect your plants from disease is to look at them every day. Walk around your greenhouse and look for signs of disease. Look for things that look out of the ordinary. If you see a plant that does not look healthy, consider taking it out of the greenhouse and quarantining it for a while. This will allow you to tell if the plant is infected with the disease as well as keep it away from other healthy plants to make sure that they do not catch a disease if it has one. With this process, it is helpful to know what plants look like when they are diseased. If the plant has mold or fungus, you will probably be able to tell right away. If it has mold growing in the soil or mushrooms growing in the soil, it means that it has mold or fungus. This is one of the easiest diseases to tell if your plant has. Another sign that your plant has a disease is that it has large, raised brown lumps on its leaves. These lumps typically mean the plant is sick. Plants that seem to be dying even though you are taking great care of them can be diseased as well. Any plant that is showing signs that are not normal should be taken away from your healthy plants just in case a disease is present.

Next, let's look into what to do if a plant is serious. If you see that a plant is diseased, make sure you take it out for greenhouse right away. This will help to make it not infect other pants. Also, you should look at helping it right away—especially if you are able to save your plant when all signs of the disease are gone and bring it back to the greenhouse. If not, at least, you only lost one plant and not your entire greenhouse to a disease.

Diseases in greenhouses are not fun to deal with, but with the tips in this chapter, you should be able to handle them with success. If you take the necessary precautions to make sure that diseases do not enter your plants and take it seriously when a plant is looking unhealthy, you should have good success in keeping this problem away.

We are going to look into what to do if you look at some plants in your greenhouse and see that their leaves are turning yellow. Yellow leaves are a common occurrence and plants, but they are not a good sign. There's something that you want to deal with and help right away. If you do not help a plant that has yellow leaves, it is very likely that it will die from the cause of the discoloration. There are many different things that can cause yellow leaves in plants, so let's get started in figuring out what they are.

The first thing that can cause yellow leaves in plants is something called moisture stress. Moisture stress is when a plant gets either too little water or too much water. If a plant is not watered often enough, it will have both dry soil and yellow leaves. If a plant is watered too much, it will have wet soil as well as possible mold or fungus growing in it and yellow leaves. It should be pretty easy to tell the difference between these two problems. You will know if you have been watering your plant a lot or if you have forgotten many days in a row. Even if you do not know this information, you will be able to tell by the moisture level in the soil. If your plant has yellow leaves that have too much water or too little water, it is very easy to fix. Simply make sure that you give your plant the accurate amount of water starting at the moment that you notice the yellow leaves. If your plant is under-watered, you can consider giving it a water soak. To do this, you can soak the plant in water in assessing or in a tub for anywhere from a few minutes to a few hours. If your plant is overwatered, consider giving it some period without water. Once it is dry again, however, make sure you water it normally. Do not wait too long to water it again because then it could turn yellow from not being watered enough.

If you find yellow leaves on a plant and you know that you have been giving it the correct amount of water, think about how much light it is getting. If a plant does not get enough light, its leaves can turn yellow. If you have a plant with yellow leaves and you know that it has not gotten enough lately, considering moving it to a location that it will get more sun in. If you do not have a space in your greenhouse available where this plant and get more sun, you will need to give the plant adequate artificial lighting in order to help it survive. This again is an easy fix. If you find a plant with yellow leaves and it needs like, once you give it light its leaves should correct themselves, and it should go back to being a healthy plant. Another reason why a plant can have yellow leaves is that the temperature for the plant is wrong in the environment that it is in. If your greenhouse is too hot or too cold, the leaves of plants can turn yellow. Most likely, if this is the cause, many plants in your greenhouse will have yellow leaves and not just one. This is because all of the plants are experiencing the same temperature, not just one. That is one good way to tell if yellow leaves are caused by temperature. If a plant in your greenhouse is too hot or too cold, you simply need to fix the temperature in the greenhouse to allow it to go back to normal. Once the plant reaches the temperature that it wants to have, it should fix itself, and its leaves should start growing green instead of yellow. This again is an easy fix if you notice it while the plant is still able to be healthy.

If you believe that the environment for your plant is completely perfect and that you have been wondering it well, the yellow leaves may be caused by something else. The last cause for yellow leaves that we will look into is plant nutrition. If you have been treating your plant perfectly and it still has yellow leaves, this could be the cost. Typically, you will be able to tell when plants are turning yellow from a nutrition problem because the yellow will appear in strange patterns. It will not just be a yellow leaf for half of the yellow leaf. The yellow may come in lines, or it may appear only in the veins of the plant. Usually, when a plant has a nutrition problem, it is either caused by having too much fertilizer in the soil or by the plant having a disease. If you have been treating your plant and have not put too much fertilizer in it, consider separating the plant from the others to make sure that you are not allowing it to spread disease.

Overall, there are a lot of causes that can cause a plant to have yellow leaves. Luckily, most of them are very solvable and very easy to figure out. If you have a plant with yellow leaves, look back to the chapter or think of the information in this book. When you look at your plants and consider what it means and what it is not getting, you will be able to figure out why it is yellow, and you will be able to fix it quickly.

The last issue that we are going to look at is the occurrence of dying plants. Dying plants are typically caused by one of the greenhouse problems that we have already mentioned. They are typically caused by greenhouse problems that go on seeing, however. Because of this, if you keep a good eye on your plans and watch their symptoms, you should not have to deal with dying plants.

If you have plants that have bugs in them, for example, you should be able to notice the bugs right away. Every time you go into the greenhouse, you should see bugs flying around, or you should see bugs crawling on your plants when you inspect them closely. You may even notice that your plants are being eaten by these bugs. These signs are hard to miss. However, if you miss them, you will start to see dying plants in your greenhouse.

The same is true with diseases. If you have these plants in your greenhouse and you do not notice them, you will eventually have dying plants instead. If you do not catch the disease in time, the disease will spread. They will kill the plans that they have already gotten too, and they will spread to even more plants. If you do not notice diseases in time, they could wipe out your entire greenhouse. This would be a tragedy. It would take all of your work and bring it to a loss. If you do not notice diseases in your greenhouse, you will eventually have dying plants in your greenhouse instead.

Once again, the same holds true the yellow leaves. Yellow leaves usually have easy fixes as we read about just now. However, if you do not notice yellow leaves and you let the plants continue to suffer and not get what they need to survive, you will eventually have dying plants instead. You need to notice your yellow leaves when they are only on a few leaves of the plant. If you notice that your plant is covered in completely yellow leaves, it is probably too late to save.

To combat dying plants, consider simply keeping a closer eye on your place. Make sure that you go out to them and look at them often. Do not solely rely on automatic lights and irrigation systems. Make sure that you were going out into your garden inside of your greenhouse and looking at your plants with your own eyes. Automatic things to help us in our growing techniques are awesome, but they do not replace our human green thumb. You need to be close with your plants to make sure that they can survive.

If you start to have many dying plants in your greenhouse, make sure that you are spending enough time outside with them. Then, look at the common problems that we have already talked about such as bugs, diseases, and yellow leaves, and look at your plants with these in mind. Try to figure out if any of these issues are taking over your greenhouse. If they are, you will know exactly how to solve your dying plant problem. Most likely, the problem will be easy to solve. You just need to see what it is in order to bring it to an end.

Overall, we can see that there are a lot of problems that can go around your greenhouses. Luckily, common greenhouse problems are easy to solve. If you follow the information that you have learned in this chapter and if you spend enough time in your greenhouse with your plants, you should never have a problem with losing a lot of plants. You should be able to see a problem right away and know how to fix it using the right, appropriate, and efficient methods. We know that this information will help you and that you will be able to have success every time you come upon a problem if you use these tips and tricks.

CONCLUSION

We have discovered so much information so far, and we have finally come to the end of our time together. Just imagine—you started this book barely knowing how to garden in a greenhouse. Now, you know how to grow your own plants in a greenhouse that you have built all by yourself. We have covered all sorts of information—from building your own greenhouse and why greenhouses are so great, to the essential things that you need in a greenhouse and to be able to prepare your greenhouse for each separate season. We have looked into what you can plant in your greenhouse, how to start a few things from seeds, and how to care for your plants. We have learned about how to have year-round harvests, as well as how to handle problems that may occur in your greenhouse.

Now that you have learned about everything that you need to know before starting your own greenhouse journey, it is time for you to begin. It is time for you to choose what type of greenhouse you would like to build and where you would like to put it. It is time for you to choose what types of accessories you will put inside of your greenhouse, as well as how you will arrange your greenhouse to maximize whatever space you have available. It is time for you to consider what you would like to grow and what tools and techniques you will use to do so. It is time for you to choose seeds and plant them in soil. It is time for you to care for those seeds and watch them grow and then mature into plants that will give you a crop to harvest. It is time for you to harvest that crop and enjoy it with your family and friends. It is time for you to decide if you want a once-a-year problem or a year-long harvest. It is time that you see struggles in your greenhouse and for you to know how to face them.

Now that the time has come for you to go off on your own, we are so thankful that we were able to help you get to the point where you can be successful in your own greenhouse gardening journey. We know that with the information that you have learned so far in this book, you will grow healthy plants, and you will gain a large harvest.

We thank you for walking alongside us through all of this information and trusting us to teach you about greenhouse gardening. We hope that you enjoyed our book, and we know that you will benefit from the information that you have read. If you agree that our book was helpful, please rate with five stars on Amazon. We appreciate this act greatly, and we will be looking forward to hearing your feedback.

Again, thank you for joining us on this journey, and we wish you luck as you go off on your own!

DESCRIPTION

Are you a lover of plants? Are you looking for a new way to garden? Do you live in a cold climate and wish that you could pursue this passion all year long, even in the winter? If you answered yes to any of these questions, you have come to the right place!
In this book, you are going to learn all about greenhouse gardening. You will start by learning about what greenhouses are and why they are so beneficial. You will learn why they are beneficial to the environment, as well as to yourself and your own life. Once you know a little more about greenhouses, you will learn how to build your own greenhouse. You will learn all about the different structures and types of greenhouses, as well as what each type works well for. You will learn about the best locations for your greenhouse and the different techniques that are used for building them.
Once you have learned how to build your own greenhouse, you will learn all about the insides of these amazing structures. You will learn about the essentials that can help you with daily greenhouse routines. You will learn about how to arrange your greenhouse and how to maximize whatever space you have.
You will then learn about how to plant in your greenhouse. You will start by learning about how to plant seeds and how to actually get them to sprout. You will learn how to care for the plants once they have sprouted, as well as how to harvest them once that time comes. You will even learn some tips for year-round harvesting, which is a challenging but rewarding task.
You will learn about watering plants, keeping your greenhouse at the right temperature, and making sure your plans have adequate lighting. You will get to look into different problems that can go wrong and greenhouses including bugs, diseases, yellow leaves, and dying plants. You will even learn about pollination and how it can be done without bugs.
This book will not only teach you about how to care for the plants in your greenhouse, but it will also teach you about how plants live and why you need to perform each task. It will help you to build a passion for gardening and in anticipation to do each of these tasks on your own.
If you are looking to become a gardening expert in the greenhouse area, this book is perfect for you. It will teach you how to have a garden in a cold climate. It will show you how greenhouses work and how plants live. It can take you from a beginner in all of these areas to someone who knows everything about gardening and greenhouses combined. If you are ready to take the next step forward in this wonderful hobby, turn the page and walk alongside us on this journey. We are excited to have you, and we want to help you learn all there is to know about this subject!

www.ingramcontent.com/pod-product-compliance
Lightning Source LLC
Chambersburg PA
CBHW071426070526
44578CB00001B/16